Exploration on China's Economic System Reform under New Normal of Development

Xiaojing Zhang
Editor

# Exploration on China's Economic System Reform under New Normal of Development

中国社会科学出版社
CHINA SOCIAL SCIENCES PRESS

Springer

*Editor*
Xiaojing Zhang
Academic Division of Economics
Beijing, China

*Translated by*
Xu Yan
Beijing, China

ISBN 978-981-95-2460-0 ISBN 978-981-95-2461-7 (eBook)
https://doi.org/10.1007/978-981-95-2461-7

Jointly published with China Social Sciences Press
The print edition is not for sale in China (Mainland). Customers from China (Mainland) please order the print book from: China Social Sciences Press.



This Springer imprint is published by the registered company Springer Nature Singapore Pte Ltd.
The registered company address is: 152 Beach Road, #21-01/04 Gateway East, Singapore 189721, Singapore

# Contents

# Chapter 1
# Introduction

**Cai Fang**

**Abstract** Since Comrade Xi Jinping proposed in 2014 that China's economic development had entered the "new normal" and comprehensively and thoroughly outlined the characteristics of the "new normal" in terms of speed change, structural optimization and impetus changes, this insightful judgment has become a guiding light for understanding the economic situations, identifying main challenges and implementing targeted policies.

Since Comrade Xi Jinping proposed in 2014 that China's economic development had entered the "new normal" and comprehensively and thoroughly outlined the characteristics of the "new normal" in terms of speed change, structural optimization and impetus changes, this insightful judgment has become a guiding light for understanding the economic situations, identifying main challenges and implementing targeted policies. With the deepening of understanding and the advancement of practice, the "new normal" is not only just a buzzword, but, after the continuous improvement and enrichment of its theory, has gradually become a new epistemology of economic theories, which has marked a key milestone in socialist political economy with Chinese characteristics and will keep playing a vital role in providing guidance for the general direction of China's economic work in the decisive stage of building a moderately prosperous society in all aspects.

For more accurate understanding and knowledge of the "new normal" in theory and more conscious adaptation and leadership towards the "new normal" in practice, it is necessary to put the issues and challenges we face in the context of the world economic landscape, the current phased changes in China's economic development, and the ambitious vision that we are striving for, so as to form a more coherent analytical framework that clearly defines the relevant concepts and clarifies the ambiguous perceptions that exist before we can have a clear idea of how to work and advance the economic reforms and development. More specifically, a clear distinction is required to be made between the "new normal" that China's economic development has entered and the "new mediocre" that the world economy is witnessing,

C. Fang (✉)
Chinese Academy of Social Sciences, Beijing, China

 
X. Zhang (ed.), *Exploration on China's Economic System Reform under New Normal of Development*, https://doi.org/10.1007/978-981-95-2461-7_1

between the phased supply-side factors and the cyclical demand-side factors of the economic slowdown, and between the supply-side structural reforms and the demand-side aggregate stimulus policies. This preface is an attempt to provide a preliminary discussion on the relationship between the "new normal" and the reforms, which is followed by brief introductions to each chapter of this book in subsequent paragraphs.

## 1.1 Distinction Between the "New Normal" of China's Economic Development from the "New Mediocre" of the World Economy

In 2014, Christine Lagarde, Managing Director of the International Monetary Fund (IMF), described for the first time the trends of the world economy as a "new mediocre," and the IMF also repeatedly downgraded its global economic growth forecasts. In 2015, as the world economy remained sluggish, Lagarde re-emphasized the need to prevent the "new mediocre" from becoming the "new reality." However, the "new normal" of China's economy is quite different from the "new mediocre" of the world economy, both in terms of causes and actual performance.

After the world financial crisis triggered by the US subprime mortgage crisis in 2007, the global economy as a whole witnessed a weak recovery, with the world economy growing at an average rate of only 2.5% in 2014, which remained well below the pre-financial crisis level of 4.1% in 2006. Specifically, among the developed countries, the UK and the US recovered relatively strongly, and the US also announced its first interest rate increase in more than nine years in December 2015, but the foundations of economic growth remained shaky; the eurozone and Japan continued facing structural problems, with unsatisfactory productivity and economic growth performance. Among the emerging economies, Brazil and Russia showed stagflation characteristics as they suffered a severe economic downturn due to falling commodity prices, but India witnessed a gradual increase in growth rate as it started to benefit from its demographic dividend (see Fig. 1.1). It can be seen that, although countries were more or less swayed by the long cycle of the world economy and the global economy as a whole showed a "new mediocre" in the aftermath of the financial crisis, the specific constraints faced by each country were not the same.

However, despite the different levels of economic growth in different countries, some regularities can still be found from the perspective of long-term economic growth: as the per capita income level increased, the "low-hanging fruits" contributing to high-speed economic growth were gradually diminishing, so that only relatively low growth rates could be achieved at the subsequent stage of development. In 2014, for example, the average growth rates of low-income countries (with a GDP per capita below USD 1000), lower-middle-income countries (with a GDP per capita between USD 1000 and USD 4000), and upper-middle-income countries (with a GDP per capita between USD 4000 and USD 12,000), as defined by the World Bank, were 6.3%, 5.8%, and 4.5%, respectively, while the average growth

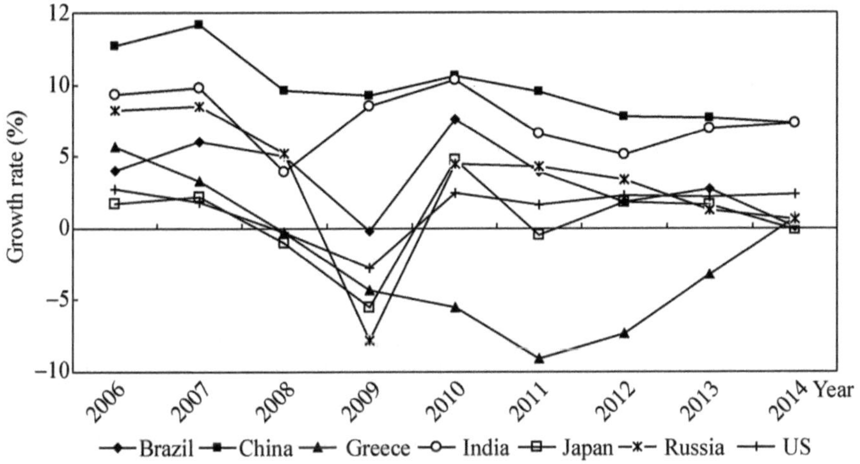


**Fig. 1.1** Countries' economic recovery in terms of growth rates. *Data Source* World Bank database: http://data.worldbank.org/indicator/NY.GDP.MKTP.KD.ZG

rate of high-income countries (with a GDP per capita above USD 12,000) was only 1.7%.

In other words, the high economic growth was essentially a phenomenon of catching-up. At the developmental stage of the typical dual economy, a demographic dividend meant the sufficient labor supply, the continuous improvement of human capital, the maintenance of the high-level returns on capital, and the rapid growth rate of TFP thanks to the efficiency of resource reallocation and the technological late-mover advantage. However, following the changes in the economic development stage, the economies were increasingly characterized by neoclassical growth as the per capita income level increased, which meant that the traditional sources of growth weakened and the economic growth mainly relied on innovation and productivity increase, so the economic slowdown was a phenomenon consistent with the regularities.

According to the World Bank's criteria and data for grouping, China went through a catching-up process from a low-income country to a lower-middle-income country and then to an upper-middle-income country during its entire reform and opening-up period. For example, after leaping from a low-income country to a lower-middle-income country with a GDP per capita of more than USD 1000 in 2001, China made another leap from a lower-middle-income country to an upper-middle-income country with a GDP per capita of more than USD 4000 in 2010 and USD 7590 in 2014. The process of the increase in GDP per capita was also a process in which the economic development stage changed. This was related to the aforementioned regularities. The year 2010 was an important turning point.

Just as China overtook Japan as the world's second-largest economy and reached the upper-middle-income threshold in terms of GDP per capita, the sixth national census showed that China's total working age population aged 15–59 peaked in 2010 and entered negative growth after that. The high economic growth during the reform and opening-up period was directly related to the rapid increase in the working age population and the significant decrease in the population dependency ratio before 2010, which meant that the characteristic of the unlimited supply of labor force increased the savings rate, delayed the diminishing returns on capital, maintained the sufficient supply of labor force and human capital, and improved resource reallocation efficiency through labor migration.

According to our previous econometric analysis, for the average GDP growth rate of 10% from 1982 to 2009, the contribution of capital accumulation was 7.1%, the contribution of labor supply was 0.8%, the contribution of workers' education level (i.e. human capital) was 0.4%, the contribution of declining population dependency ratio was 0.7%, and the contribution of TFP was 1.0% (Cai and Zhao 2012). As far as the increase in TFP was concerned, nearly half of the contribution came from the efficiency of resource reallocation due to the agricultural labor migration. Therefore, the change in the development stage, highlighted by the disappearance of demographic dividend, meant that the traditional driving force of high economic growth weakened, which led to a decrease in the potential growth rate.

## 1.2 Distinction Between Phased Supply-Side Factors and Cyclical Demand-Side Factors

According to the estimates, China's potential growth rate will decline from about 10% in 1978–2010 to an average of 7.6% in the 12th Five-Year Plan period (2011–2015), and will further decline to 6.2% in the 13th Five-Year Plan period (2016–2020), if the growth factors to be brought about by the economic system reforms are not taken into account. The potential growth rate is defined as the economic growth rate that can be achieved for a given period, with a given factor supply and TFP growth rate, under conditions free from cyclical unemployment and significant inflation; therefore, a decline in the potential growth rate is caused by the supply-side factors. Meanwhile, the supply-side factors that cause a decline in the potential growth rate and a slowdown in real growth are not the same as a shortage of supply, so the supply-side efforts will not simply increase the supply.

Some researchers argued that the factors that led to the downturn in China's economic growth were the lack of external demand caused by the global financial crisis, which was cyclical in nature (Lin 2011). Therefore, they believed that through demand-side efforts, a V-shaped recovery trajectory of economic growth could be expected. However, as mentioned above, the supply-side factors reflected as the disappearance of demographic dividends have prevented the economic growth from returning to its original base point. For example, by comparing China's exports of 11 representative labor-intensive products as a percentage of China's total exports with the same percentage of the world trade, we can find that China's comparative advantage index for labor-intensive products has been declining year by year since 2000, with a total decline of 36% by 2013.

The supply-side factors cause a decrease in the potential growth rate through the relative scarcity of production factors and the changes in the TFP growth rate, so they are inevitable and irreversible factors. Meanwhile, there are many institutional distortions that raise the institutional transaction costs and production costs of economic activities from the supply side, but these distortions can be corrected through reforms. Under the combined effect of these reversible and irreversible factors, China's economic growth will not suffer a "hard landing," but will experience an L-shaped trajectory in which "the potential growth rate first goes down with the change in the development stage, then remains stable by gaining new growth momentum through reforms, and finally rebounds due to the reform dividend."

From the supply side, we can identify several factors affecting economic growth, and find the reasons for the economic slowdown, so that the focuses and priorities of the reforms can be defined:

First, the labor shortages resulted in a continuous and rapid rise in wages. For example, from 2004 to 2014, the actual wages of migrant workers grew at an average rate of 11%, faster than the growth rate of labor productivity. Meanwhile, the significant decrease in the number of the emerging labor force (i.e. graduates from all levels and all types of schools) and the deceleration in the improvement of human capital also inhibited the productivity increase. According to estimates, the unit labor cost (i.e., the ratio of wages to labor productivity) in China's manufacturing sectors showed an increasing trend since 2004 and rose by 40% in 2012 (Du Yang 2014). Although the foreign media reports on China's unit labor costs exceeding those of some developed countries were not true, the comparative advantage and international competitiveness of China's labor-intensive manufacturing sectors have indeed weakened.

Second, the returns on capital diminished and the returns on investment decreased. The unlimited supply of labor force, which could delay the phenomenon of diminishing returns on capital, had supported the investment-driven high economic growth for a long period of time. However, as labor shortage occurred across the country, the returns on capital declined significantly, which became the main reason for the slowdown in economic growth. Studies showed that China's decline in the returns on capital was first observed in the early 1990s and accelerated significantly after 2008, and the total returns on capital often fell below the interest rates on loans paid by many enterprises (Bai Chongen and Zhang Qiong 2014).

Third, the labor migration slowed down, resulting in the deceleration of the TFP growth. The improvement of the TFP was largely attributable to the efficiency of resource reallocation due to the agricultural labor migration. As mentioned above, nearly half of the TFP came from the contribution of the reallocation of the labor force from agriculture to non-agricultural industries, while this contribution was predicated on a 4% annual increase in the number of migrant workers before 2010. Both in terms of resident population and household population, the population aged 16–19 in rural areas peaked in 2014 and then entered a stage of negative growth. The labor force aged 16–19 consisted mainly of rural migrant workers, so this trend of demographic change inevitably reduced the rate of agricultural labor migration.

Fourth, numerous institutional barriers raised enterprise transaction costs and reduced the efficiency of resource allocation. Under the "new normal," the decisive role of the market in resource allocation is more prominent. However, the role of the market is not abstract but needs to be brought into play through a variety of specific functions and mechanisms. In China's economic operations, there were such problems as excessive government regulation, cumbersome approval processes, high tax burdens and high social insurance premium rates, ineffective financing channels, local protection and market segmentation, distorted factor prices, and discriminatory treatment of enterprises, all of which seriously hindered the good functioning of the market, raised the institutional transaction costs borne by enterprises, and objectively inhibited innovation in the micro sphere.

## 1.3 Distinction Between Supply-Side Structural Reforms and Demand-Side Aggregate Stimulus

Under the "new normal," the traditional sources of growth are weakening rapidly, while a new growth impetus does not arise naturally and needs to be incubated over a certain period of time. For example, the demographic dividend, which directly affects the quantity and quality of labor force, the speed of labor migration and the returns on capital, is rapidly disappearing, but the TFP, which supports sustained economic growth, cannot be improved in the short term, and will even tend to decrease as the space for resource reallocation becomes narrower, the improvement of human capital slows down, and the early-stage stimulus policies are not absorbed in time.

For avoiding an excessively sharp decline in economic growth, the macroeconomic policy should remain moderately accommodative. However, if we adopt strong stimulus policies that go beyond this "moderate" scope to keep the real growth rate above the potential growth rate for a long time, it will lead to the opposite results. First, given the decline in comparative advantages, the effectiveness of policies to stimulate enterprise investment will also decrease. If we rely on measures such as subsidies to boost enterprise loans, it will often lead to excess capacity and even make enterprises become "zombies." Second, the demand for infrastructure construction is derived from the real economy, and if such investment is detached from the demand of the real economy and exceeds the limit for shoring up the weak links, it will also cause excess capacity and accumulate the government's debt risks. Third, the money supply released from stimulus policies is often absorbed by speculative needs, and flows into real estate, stock markets, overseas assets and other bubble-prone fields, thus piling up financial risks. Therefore, the stimulus policies cannot incubate a new growth impetus, and the efforts to keep growth sustainable must be made on the supply side, with a focus on reducing enterprise costs and improving the TFP through reforms.

First, we should focus on the institutional barriers causing the unbalanced, uncoordinated and unsustainable development in China and promote supply-side structural reforms. To this end, two things need to be done at the same time: (1) adjust the stock of excess capacity, high leverage and "zombie" enterprises that have been formed; and (2) accelerate the formation of new institutional mechanisms to eliminate and prevent the circularity in increments. The essence of innovation-driven development is "creative destruction," in which the use of resources is changed from an inefficient to a highly-efficient manner. As such, both creation and destruction can lead to an increase in TFP. Only by allowing destruction can we transform creative destruction into creative innovation. According to studies, it is possible to contribute as much as one-third to one-half of the TFP increase by exiting or even eliminating inefficient enterprises and allowing more innovative ones to enter and grow (Foster et al. 2008).

Second, we should focus on reducing transaction costs and improving the TFP, and push forward with reforms from the areas that yield the immediate reform dividend. The structural reforms are not in a "black-or-white" relationship with the mid- to high-speed growth but can increase the potential growth rate and bring about the real reform dividend. The reforms in such aspects as administrative approval, tax and financial systems, household registration system, state-owned enterprises, and competition policies will all deliver significant reform dividends.

Third, we should improve the role of social policies in supporting the people's livelihood and integrate the reform dividend into shared development. The supply-side structural reforms certainly need to resort to creative destruction mechanisms, but in the destruction of excess capacity and "zombie" enterprises, the ineffective allocation pattern of material factors of production, and even the jobs associated with them, we must not destruct labor, which is a factor of production based on people. Therefore, as the structural reforms go into depth, it is increasingly urgent to improve public employment services and social security. Increasing the coverage and strength of social protection for laborers is more of a righteousness that should be included under the theme of sharing the reform and development achievements.

## 1.4 This Book's Logic and Structure

The theoretical studies on China's economy should focus on discussing how to recognize and adapt to the "new normal" from the supply side and lead it with structural reforms. The following chapters in this book contain the research findings of a number of economists from the Chinese Academy of Social Sciences based on these two issues in their respective fields. In accordance with our understanding of the reform areas that urgently need to be advanced and broken through and their priorities, this book is divided into six parts, with the specific structure as follows:

The first part is about theoretical thinking on deepening the economic system reforms. Chapter 2 "Theoretical Thinking on Deepening the Economic System Reforms" written by Zhang Xiaojing, takes the "new normal" of economic development as the new context of China's economic reforms, makes the judgment that the reforms have entered the unchartered water and the tough period, and presents his thinking from the perspectives of rebuilding reform consensus, improving reform impetus mechanism, realizing reform interests balancing and incentive compatibility, highlighting reform mechanism design and combining top-level design and "crossing the river by feeling the stones." He underlined the importance of strengthening reform determination, maintaining reform tenacity and continuously promoting reforms, and introduced the idea that continuously pushing forward our own reforms is the most critical logic of China's reforms in the context of global institutional competition and reform competition.

The second part is about the structural slowdown and how to improve the TFP and obtain the reform dividend through reforms. This part includes Chapter 3 "Enhancing TFP Through Comprehensively Deepening Reforms" written by Zhang Ping and Yuan Fuhua, and Chapter 4 "Measurement of Reform Dividend and Priority Areas for Reforms" written by Lu Yang and Cai Fang. Zhang Ping and others measured the structural slowdown of China's economy based on the growth measurement method and found that the contribution of the TFP among the growth factors dropped from about 30% in the peak growth period to the current level of 17%. They proposed that the reforms in the tertiary sectors, such as "science, education, culture and health" public institutions, should be carried out to improve the development space and efficiency of the tertiary sectors, the reforms on the government's administrative systems and state-owned enterprises under the support of monopolistic, administrative or selective industrial policies should be carried out to correct the resource misallocation and improve efficiency, and the reforms on improving distribution and increasing consumption should be carried out to promote a shift of China's economy from a supply-oriented to a demand-oriented one. Using the disappearance of the demographic dividend as a baseline and by means of econometric simulations, Lu Yang et al. simulated and measured the reform dividend, namely the increase in the potential growth rate of China's economy that may result from the increase in the labor force participation rate, the TFP, the level of human capital stock and the total fertility rate, thus providing an empirical basis for firming up the confidence and determination to reforms.

The third part is about the discussion on how to achieve innovation-driven development, including Chapter 5 "Sci-Tech System Reforms under Innovation-driven Development Strategy" written by Li Ping, Wang Hongwei and Cai Yuezhou, and Chapter 6 "Demand for Human Capital and Education Reforms" written by Cai Fang. Li Ping et al. pointed out that the implementation of an innovation-driven development strategy is the inevitable choice of the times. In the context of the new round of technological revolution and industrial changes, a new technology-economy paradigm is taking shape, and the role of sci-tech innovation in supporting economic and social development has become more prominent. They put forward policy advice that we should follow the trend of the times, continue deepening the sci-tech system reforms, and reduce the constraints and obstacles to sci-tech innovation. Cai Fang described the emerging competition between human capital accumulation and robotics, pointed out that we can only win this competition by relying on a higher quality of labor, and further summarized the characteristics of the human capital demand and the returns on various levels and types of education as a result of "mass entrepreneurship and innovation initiative." He also provided policy advice on education development and reforms in terms of resource allocation as well as individual, social and governmental responsibilities in view of China's development stage and related challenges.

The fourth part is about the reform and opening-up of financial system and the reforms of fiscal and taxation system, including Chapter 7 "Financial Reforms: From the Third Plenary Session to the Fifth Plenary Session of the 18th CPC Central Committee" written by Yin Jianfeng, Chapter 8 "Reforms for External Financial Opening and Their Prioritization" written by Zhang Bin, and Chapter 9 "Comprehensively Building a New Pattern of China's Fiscal and Taxation System" written by Gao Peiyong. Yin Jianfeng pointed out three reform directions, including a shift from a government-led constrained financial system to a liberalized financial system in which the market plays a decisive role in the allocation of financial resources, a shift from a bank-oriented system to a (capital) market-oriented system in which the capital market plays a major role in the transformation of savings into investment and in which banks and the market are integrated with each other, and an open financial system that plays a supporting role in the international financial system and aims to make the RMB a key reserve currency.

Zhang Bin discussed the concrete methods and the sequence arrangement of reform and opening-up measures such as the reform of RMB exchange rate formation mechanism, the reform of foreign exchange reserve management system, the reform of capital account and the advancement of RMB internationalization. He argued that in terms of the reasonable order of reform, the reform of RMB exchange rate formation mechanism should be given priority, and a broadly fluctuating RMB exchange rate formation mechanism is advisable in the near future. The main content of the reform on foreign exchange reserve management system includes using part of the foreign exchange reserves to set up foreign exchange-based sovereign pension funds, so as to improve the investment returns of foreign exchange reserves and give foreign exchange reserves back to the people. The RMB internationalization and the further opening of the capital account should be placed in the second half of the reform process, the opening of the capital account should be promoted in a gradual and pilot manner, and the key to RMB internationalization lies in the construction of market infrastructure.

Gao Peiyong pointed out that the "new normal" has determined the new context for the next round of fiscal and taxation system reforms in China, that is, to promote fiscal and taxation reforms against the backdrop of the slowdown in labor productivity growth and overall economic growth, as well as the significant decline in fiscal revenue growth. He defined the goal of tax reforms as a modern taxation system, the goal of budget reforms as the establishment of a modern budget system, and the goal of adjusting the fiscal relationship between the central and local governments as facilitating two positive effects, and proposed reform tasks and methods for promoting reforms from the above aspects.

The fifth part is about reforms in three areas of special importance, including Chapter 10 "Strategic Adjustment of State-owned Economy" written by Huang

Qunhui, Chapter 11 "Urban–Rural Integration Pattern and Promotion Strategies" written by Wei Houkai, and Chapter 12 "Challenges and Solutions for Deepening Service Industry Reforms" written by Xia Jiechang. Huang Qunhui proposed to promote the strategic restructuring of the state-owned economy based on functional positioning and classification, to adjust the industrial layout of the state-owned economy based on the choices of national strategic criteria and public service criteria, and to collaboratively promote the merger and reorganization of state-owned enterprises based on the dual objectives of comprehensively deepening reforms and optimizing market structures. Wei Houkai revealed the new trend of urban–rural integration pattern that the urbanization rate increase, the willingness of citizenship decrease, the urban–rural gap will continue narrowing, the factors change from one-way flow to two-way interaction, and the policies shift from urban-biased to rural-biased, and proposed that it is necessary to adopt a systematic and integrated "package" of solutions, instead of a piecemeal approach, to promote the urban–rural integration. Xia Jiechang pointed out that the rigidity of the service industry systems and mechanisms has directly restricted the rapid, healthy and orderly development of China's service industry, and that the reforms of the service industry system should be carried out as a systematic project, so as to create the necessary supporting conditions and achieve both key breakthroughs and overall promotion.

The sixth part is about the reforms on the people's livelihood, including Chapter 13 "Promoting the Construction of Labor Market Systems" written by Wang Meiyan, Jia Peng and Cai Fang. Wang Meiyan et al. pointed out that China's current stage of development has provided an opportunity for the formation of a more complete social protection mechanism, i.e., the government and society as the main actors should develop an efficient labor market, reduce the employment risks faced by people, improve the residents' ability to protect their income and living standards, and further reduce the incidence of poverty and decrease vulnerability.

## References

Bai Chongen and Zhang Qiong (2014), Analysis of China's Returns on Capital and the Influencing Factors, The Journal of World Economy, Issue 10.

Cai, F. and Y Lu (2013), The End of China's Demographic Dividend: the Perspective of Potential GDP Growth, in R. Garnaut, F. Cai and L. Song (eds), China: A New Model for Growth and Development, ANU E. Press, Canberra, pp. 55–74.

Cai, F. and W. Zhao (2012), When Demographic Dividend Disappears: Growth Sustainability of China, in M. Aoki and J. Wu (eds), The Chinese Economy: A New Transition, Palgrave Macmillan, Basingstoke.

Du Yang (2014), Labor Market Changes and New Sources of Economic Growth, China Opening Journal, Issue 3.

Foster, Lucia, John Haltiwanger, and Chad Syverson (2008), Reallocation, Firm Turnover, and Efficiency: Selection on Productivity or Profitability? American Economic Review 98: 394–425.

Lin, Justin (2011), China and the global economy, China Economic Journal 4, No. 1: 1–14.

# Chapter 2
# Theoretical Thinking on Deepening the Economic System Reforms

**Zhang Xiaojing**

**Abstract** The basic logic of China's economic system reforms over the past 30 years or so is outlined at the beginning of this paper: reforms are cyclical in nature; economic reforms are inseparable from reforms in other fields; the relationship among reforms, development and stability is properly dealt with; and the theoretical logic of reforms is in line with the practical logic. The new context of China's current reform is then pointed out: the economy has entered the "new normal"; the reforms have stepped into the unchartered water and the tough period. The political economics of reforms in the new context are: rebuilding reform consensus; improving reform impetus mechanism; reform interests balancing and incentive compatibility; reform mechanism design; combination of top-level design and "crossing the river by feeling the stones"; and allowing the people to obtain a reform dividend. At the end of this paper, the importance of enhancing reform determination, maintaining reform tenacity and continuously promoting reform is emphasized. A state without the means of some change is without the means of its conservation. Without such means, it might even risk the loss of that part of the constitution that it wished the most religiously to preserve. It reveals what is the driving force of reforms at the deepest level, that is, we are continuously reforming exactly for the purpose of preserving the nature of the socialist system. In the context of global institutional competition and reform competition, China's continuous efforts in reforming itself can be said the most important logic of its reforms.

## 2.1 Basic Logic of China's Economic System Reforms

In 1978, China started its economic reforms. Over the past three decades, China created a world-renowned growth miracle through economic reforms. In 2013, the third plenary session of the 18th Central Committee of the Communist Party of China (CPC) adopted the *Decision of the CPC Central Committee on Some Major Issues*

Z. Xiaojing (✉)
Institute of Economics, Chinese Academy of Social Sciences, Beijing, China



X. Zhang (ed.), *Exploration on China's Economic System Reform under New Normal of Development*, https://doi.org/10.1007/978-981-95-2461-7_2

*Concerning Comprehensively Deepening Reforms*, a guideline of actions by which China announced to the world that it would start reforms again.

China's economic reforms were and are pushed forward amidst controversy. Although it is premature to comprehensively summarize China's economic reforms, we can gain a wealth of experience and data from the reforms over the past thirty years or so. This allows us to get a glimpse into the path of China's economic reforms and the general logic behind it.

First, reforms are cyclical in nature. Given the inertia of systems and institutions, reforms are often made without choice, which is true for both the world and China. China's reform in the late 1970s was the result of its proximity to economic and social collapse. At that time, the whole society was clamoring for changes, and the people's fervent desire for reforms, without any hint of fear, formed an unparalleled drive and impetus for reform. After more than 30 years, the reform impetus and reform dividend have basically been depleted. Now, we have reached a low-point period of reforms, and also a tough period for overcoming reform difficulties. For this reason, the reform needs to be started again and the reform consensus needs to be rebuilt.

Second, economic reforms are inseparable from reforms in other fields. As a systemic project, reforms should be pushed forward as a whole under mutual support and coordination. Promoting economic reforms alone often result in nothing but one-sided effects, and may even undo the previous efforts. In particular, partial and fragmented reforms often lead to imbalances and mutual constraints, and can even create institutional frictions. Institutional reforms should essentially be promoted as a whole; otherwise, they will incur huge costs for operating institutions. Therefore, China needs to promote economic reforms in parallel with political, cultural, social and ecological civilization reforms, thus forming a new stage of "five-in-one" all-round reforms.

Third, the relationship among reforms, development and stability is properly dealt with. The past course of China's transformation and development was essentially a process in which the three elements—reforms, development and stability—were unified. Despite some degree of efficiency loss (for example, the reform speed was constrained by the stability considerations), long-term continuous growth was ultimately achieved. Only when the society is stable, the reform and development can be continuously promoted; only when reform and development are continuously promoted, the social stability has a solid foundation. In the absence of social stability, not only is it impossible to smoothly advance reform and development, but also the gains that have been achieved may be lost. This is why China opted for incremental reforms, allowed the existence of a dual system, and tolerated the resulting arbitrage and efficiency losses. This kind of incomplete reforms is often criticized as the cause of many problems, and is especially considered as the reason for the solidification of some group interests. However, when compared to "shock therapy," it is clear that China's success in achieving long-term stable growth is directly related to the implementation of an effective reform path by upholding the unification of reforms, development and stability. This unification of the three elements is quite different from mainstream western economics, in which the single element of efficiency is emphasized.

Fourth, the theoretical logic of reforms is in line with the practical logic. China's reforms did not follow the mainstream western theories, but were guided by the principle that "practice is the sole criterion for testing the truth." China's reform practice was often ahead of theories and even rewrote the theories. Of course, it did not mean that China's reforms were devoid of theoretical logic. History proved that the success of China's reform was no coincidence. From rural reform, township enterprise development, state-owned enterprise reform, market system establishment, gradual and orderly opening, to the attempts to meet the high standards of the Trans-Pacific Partnership (TPP) through the Free Trade Area (FTA), all these practices contained China's reform wisdom, were in line with the theoretical logic, and could be explained by the theory. Generally speaking, this theoretical logic is that, on the one hand, China understands the peculiarities of the initial conditions of reform and stands on its national conditions; on the other hand, China actively participates in globalization and takes the initiative to adapt to and fit in with the world's development trends. By promoting reforms in various fields with such logic, China has gone beyond the debate about gradual reforms versus radical reforms.

## 2.2 New Context of Reforms

The current reforms are quite different from the past ones. The new context of reforms has two meanings: (1) China's economy has entered a "new normal"; and (2) China's reforms have stepped into uncharted waters and a tough period.

The general logic of reforms follows the general logic of economic development, and the "new normal" of the economy has set the basic context for China's next step of reforms. The "new normal" of the economy means a lot, with at least two points that are worth noting:

First, after entering the "new normal," China's economic growth rate has slowed down compared to the high growth over the past 30 years. It is an economic rule that conforms to both international experience and the stage of development that China now finds itself in. In terms of labor, capital, technological innovation, resource and energy constraints, as well as the international environment, China's weakened growth impetus and increased constraints are bound to cause a structural slowdown. As the economy slows down, many problems (such as excess capacity, structural distortions, lack of efficiency and even income disparity) that were masked or ignored during the high-growth period will surface and become truly serious challenges for the economy and society. If no reform is carried out at this time to act as a new impetus for economic growth and structural optimization, the "new normal" will bring a period of low-speed and inefficient economic growth, or even a development stage where problems and contradictions abound.

Second, the decline in economic growth is not the whole picture of the "new normal." It also implies a revolutionary transformation to a stage where the economy evolves towards a more advanced form, a more complex division of labor and a more rational structure. However, only by comprehensively deepening reforms can we lead the way to achieve this transformation. In other words, whether the "new normal" can be transformed into a new platform, a new mechanism and a new realm depends on whether the reforms can be really and effectively promoted. All hopes for the "new normal" rest on the "real reforms."

According to further analysis, the new stage and context of reforms have richer meanings, such as the entry into uncharted waters and a tough period.

The entry of reforms into uncharted waters is characterized by the fact that most of the issues facing China are major and sensitive. Among them, quite a number of issues relate to deep-rooted social contradictions and involve the adjustment of interest relations, so any one of them may cause a butterfly effect; some problems remain a hard nut to crack despite years of efforts for change. From the perspective of the long cycle of reforms, the emergence of such a situation means a low-point period of reforms. We need to restart the reforms because the original reform impetus has been dissipated but the new impetus has not yet been formed.

In terms of the causes, the current dilemma of reforms is related to the choice of the path of gradual reforms.

The strategy of gradual reforms often means starting from the issues outside the system that are easy to change and have little resistance, so that results can be achieved quickly and strength can be built up in order to continue the reforms. However, the gradual reforms also have some drawbacks: after the issues that are easy to change are changed, the remaining issues are hard nuts. The gradual reforms also tend to solidify some group interests. The experience over the years has proven that if reform is not thorough, new vested interest groups are usually formed at a particular stage. As we further break up the original pattern, these interest groups will become a major resistance to the advancement of reforms. Currently, the phenomenon of interest consolidation is almost everywhere, while government interests, industry monopolies and various vested interest groups will form a strong "fence." The "fence of solidified interests" refers to a defensive barrier set up to protect vested interests and has two characteristics: (1) the interests are gained from the use of public power; (2) those who gain interests are not the public class that the reform is intended to benefit. For the vested interest class, the fence is the umbrella and talisman of their interests, but for the general public, the fence is the barrier to their access to interests. As a chronic disease in systems and mechanisms, the "fence of solidified interests" has widely appeared among urban and rural areas, among regions, among industries, among state-owned and private economies, and among different social groups, becoming a huge obstacle to the further deepening of reforms. It inhibits the creativity of economy and society, reduces the efficiency of resource allocation, restricts the space for upward mobility of social members, and decreases the positive energy of reform. The past reforms were about adjusting others' interests by the departments that designed reforms, while the future reforms will be more about adjusting the departments' own vested interests within the system. In other words, by shifting from adjusting others to adjusting themselves, the future reforms will weaken their own power and interests.

At the early stage of reforms, the Pareto-improvement environment that harms no one excited all parties and the resistance to reforms was therefore relatively small. But now, when the reforms enter uncharted waters, we will find it difficult to see the phenomenon of "no one's interests being compromised" in the real reforms. In the face of deep-rooted conflicts and problems in social and economic development, we should not evade and bypass them; no adjustment is no way out, and slow adjustment will cause delays and greater costs. Therefore, we must promote reforms with a strong sense of historical mission and responsibility, and with firm determination and courage to win the tough battle of reform.

Over the past three decades, the reform and opening-up has resulted in achievements as well as challenges. Currently, the biggest challenge is that the reforms have entered uncharted waters and a tough period, the pace of reforms has slowed down, and the difficulty of advancement has increased, thus resulting in a stalemate, including the entanglement among different interest groups and the collision among different reform demands. From the past's rapid advancement to today's stalemate, the reforms also seem to be caught in a cycle similar to the economic operating cycle. How to deal with the problems such as the barriers of interest groups, the weak reform impetus, the need to rebuild reform consensus and the insufficiency of top-level design are the major challenges that we must face when the reforms enter uncharted waters.

## 2.3 Political Economics of Economic System Reforms Under the "New Normal"

Apart from the adjustment of interests, the reforms also involve many aspects such as reform consensus, reform impetus mechanism, reform path, and policy implementation. It is fair to call this series of theoretical thinking the political economics of reforms.

### *2.3.1 Rebuilding Reform Consensus*

The reform more than 30 years ago was started with the greatest consensus in society, as China would really be dead if no reform was made at that time, but today, it is not easy to reach a reform consensus when there are still some resources available for squandering, and when there are profound changes in the economic system, profound changes in the social structure, profound adjustments in the pattern of interests and profound changes in the ideology. The lack of reform consensus makes it difficult to create a reform impetus, thus making the efforts to promote reforms become empty words.

As the old saying goes, "The side with unity of purpose among its officers and men will win." The unity of "officers" and "men" in the war can minimize internal friction and pool forces. Advancing the reforms requires cognitive unity between the central and local governments, as well as between the authorities and the public, so that synergy in action can be achieved. The consensus—"unity of purpose among its officers and men"—can stimulate the greatest positive energy for reforms and provide a solid guarantee for overcoming reform difficulties.

The reform and opening-up has been going on for more than 30 years. Why do we need to continue the reforms today? It's the first question to face with the reforms. Theoretically, it is a dynamic process to adjust the production relations to adapt them to productivity development, so the adjustment of production relations through reforms has no end; practically, it is also a fundamental way to solve today's practical problems through reforms: the solution to each specific problem in the fields of economy, society, culture, finance, state-owned enterprises, rural areas, education, medical care, pensions, etc., is inseparable from the efforts of comprehensively deepening reforms.

There is no denying that China's current basic realities include the multi-layered social structure, the diversified interest pattern, and the changing social mentality, and the different expectations on reforms from different regions, sectors and social groups. Naturally, dealing with different reform demands and clarifying complex interests will become a new and greater challenge to be faced in further deepening reforms. In the current implementation of reform measures, special attention should be paid to avoiding the tendency of "change when agreed, but no change when disagreed" and to breaking the mindsets that hinder the reform progress.

It is unlikely that the reforms can be made to the unanimous satisfaction of all people and groups without any disagreement, but it does not mean that the reforms will lose consensus and fall into the simple division of interests. The unity of thoughts and ideas is about finding the greatest common divisor, and allowing the existence of differences in the process of seeking common ground. In fact, the universal demands, including "market economy," "democratic politics," "a country with a strong socialist culture," "harmonious society" and "beautiful China," are still continuously unleashing the dividends. There are plenty of reforms that are in the fundamental interests of the general public and in line with the long-term goals of overall development, which can remain our greatest consensus. Whether a reform reaches the greatest consensus and whether the people pay attention to and support the reform is not dependent on the emergence of dissenting voices, but on the extent to which the reform resonates with the majority of people. Even in the chorus in favor of the reform, there may be "Mr. Nanguo" who is there just to make up the number or those who deliberately sing out of tune. However, this cacophony of voices does not prove that the reforms are wrong, but rather that it is necessary to solve these problems through reforms (Guangming Daily 2014).

Currently, the curtain of comprehensively deepening reforms has been raised. Three points should be noted in rebuilding the reform consensus. First, we must have a sense of historical responsibility and realize the importance of reforms to the present and future development of China and to the rejuvenation of the Chinese nation. If no reform is made at present, we will have to bear the resulting historical responsibilities in the future. Second, we must enhance the awareness of reform opportunities and the initiative consciousness. The current period still provides a strategic opportunity for China to make great progress and is a window period for reforms. The only way to break through the difficulties and cross over the middle-income trap is to take the initiative to make reforms. Third, we must take the reforms as a guide, use the reform mindset to plan the work, and precisely put the reform tasks into practice.

### *2.3.2 Improving Reform Impetus Mechanism*

All of the breakthroughs and evolution in the understanding and practice of the reform and opening-up have come from the practice and wisdom of the people. The passion of the local governments, grass-root cadres and the people is the impetus of reforms. It is necessary to encourage local governments, grass-root cadres and the people to emancipate their minds and make active exploration, encourage different regions to carry out differentiated pilot projects, take the concerns of the people and the difficulties of their lives as the priorities of reforms, and promote the positive interaction and organic combination between the top-level design and the grassroots' exploration.

However, the current reform impetus mechanism needs to be strengthened. This round of reforms is characterized by a top-down approach to promoting the top-level design proposed by the central government. This approach has the advantage of comprehensive and thorough implementation, but requires an active response from all levels of society for it to work. Now, the enthusiasm of many local governments and public officials have not yet been brought into play. By and large, provincial governments and officials take a wait-and-see attitude, while county and municipal governments and officials take for granted that reforms are not yet on their respective agendas and that reform measures are at least two years away from being implemented at the grassroots level. Ministries and departments at all levels merely muddle through and almost have not issued the specific reform programs. Even if some preliminary drafts are released, they still focus on alleviating local difficulties. The public at large feels that there is a gap between the expected and actual process of the reforms, which results in a decrease in their enthusiasm for reforms. Obviously, without the local participation and the people's enthusiasm, the reforms designed solely by the central government, written in the documents and discussed in the meetings cannot be put into practice.

First, the people should be motivated for participation. The key to motivate the people's enthusiasm for reforms is that the participants can benefit from the reforms. The fundamental reasons why the previous reforms were rolled out rapidly and advanced step by step was that they brought tangible benefits to the people, provided fair participation and development opportunities to the people, and gained the support of the people, which was the underlying impetus of the reforms. To comprehensively deepen the reforms, we should start from and end on the promotion of social fairness and justice and the enhancement of people's well-being. Therefore, it is necessary to establish fair and effective systems and mechanisms so that the reform dividend and the development fruits can be shared by the people. At present, there are indeed many unreasonable areas in the distribution of interests, so adjustments are required. However, when it comes to the adjustments of interests distribution, we should not only cut the "cake" of the existing interests from a static perspective, but more importantly, use a dynamic and developmental perspective to focus on the increment of interests, i.e., to make the "cake" bigger while properly cutting the "cake." Simple egalitarianism is not appropriate even for the adjustments of the existing interests distribution. First, the interests of the poor and low-income people should be protected and safeguarded so that they can have more development opportunities in the reforms. Second, the middle-income class should be allowed to expand over time so that they can have more room for development. Third, the legitimate interests of high-income people should be protected so that they can invest more and set up businesses without worries, thus creating a better development environment. It is important to allow different social groups to develop their abilities and play their roles, so that all the vitality in terms of labor, knowledge, technology, management and capital can burst forth and all the sources that create social wealth can come into full play, thus forming a pattern where all classes of people are widely involved in and support the reforms in all aspects.

Second, the exploration of reforms at the grassroots level should be promoted. At present, the lack of motivation for reform at the grassroots level in some cases needs to be given high priority. In fact, the reform difficulties are often concentrated at the grassroots level, where the call for reforms is the loudest and strongest. These difficulties include the "last mile" problem regarding implementation and execution, as well as new situations and problems that emerge in the development process. Without the exploration at the grassroots level, the solutions to these difficulties often become ineffective. Currently, there are many obstacles to the reform exploration at the grassroots level, including the "performance-based governance" of local government leaders who remain accustomed to pursuing good GDP figures, their attachment to vested interests, and their inability to make reforms due to limited competence Among these obstacles, the most critical one is that many local governments do not know where the reform boundaries lie and are concerned that their "exploration" may violate the laws or the rules, thus triggering various risks. As such, when advocating exploration at the grassroots level, we should also vigorously create a reform atmosphere, rationalize systems and mechanisms, improve the performance assessment system for local leaders and cadres, and systematically activate local vitality to fill the grassroots level with the energy of reforms. For example, for some local governments and grassroots organizations that have been at the forefront of the development, they should be given more room for reforms and more authorizations, so that they can be encouraged to provide more "reform templates" for solving some difficult issues, instead of just counting on top-level design. Meanwhile, some policies and measures for encouraging the reform exploration at the grassroots level should be studied and formulated in due course, and a fault-tolerance mechanism which encourages success and tolerates failure should be established for grassroots-level reformers, thus truly clearing up their worries in bold attempts and brave innovations and giving them sufficient confidence and motivation in carrying out the reforms. Now that we have entered uncharted waters of reforms, every single reform will definitely affect the whole structure, and if we only rely on the "boldness" and "fearlessness" of individual leaders, it is difficult to effectively promote the reforms, and the potential negative impact of the reforms is also not something that can be ignored. Nowadays, the bigger test for reformers should be how to ensure the people's participation in the reforms for maximizing the reform consensus and reform impetuss. Along with the continuous improvement of the laws, the deepening of reforms and the increasingly complex interest balancing among parties, it is obvious more important for reformers to listen to the people's opinions and make use of their support to ensure the smooth advancement of reforms in the desired direction. After all, the past reforms made unilaterally and suddenly have not only less and less room, but also diminishing marginal effects. It can be said that the most urgent task of reforms is to follow procedural justice, to bring government actions back to the legal framework of "not doing things not authorized by law," and to involve the people's power in the reform process so as to ensure that the reforms can be corrected at any time during the process. The only way to awaken the government officials' enthusiasm for reforms and innovation is to truly promote the restructuring of the reform evaluation and participation mechanism, i.e., to stimulate officials' intrinsic motivation for reforms and innovation in terms of power assessment and reciprocity of power and responsibility.

To sum up, when promoting the reforms, it is necessary to continuously motivate the enthusiasm of all parties, including fully motivating the enthusiasm of the people, the central and local governments, as well as motivating the enthusiasm, initiative and creativity of entrepreneurs, innovative talents and cadres at all levels.

### *2.3.3 Reform Interests Balancing and Incentive Compatibility*

Reform impetus comes from incentives. Only when reform participants believe that they can benefit from reforms will they be motivated to call for reforms, participate in reforms, and promote reforms.

Reform involves various relations of interests, and the practical path of reforms is in fact a slow advance in dealing with various complex mechanisms of interests. Therefore, the interests of all parties should be taken into account as much as possible in the design of further reforms. In other words, when promoting the reforms, we should pay more attention to rebuilding a pattern of balanced interests rather than just focusing on the solutions, and should consider in advance the issue of compensation for those whose interests have been damaged.

The rationalization of the interest mechanisms is actually about the so-called incentive compatibility. Incentive compatibility means how to ensure that, in the presence of moral hazard, the party with the information advantage ("agent") acts in accordance with the wishes of the other party to the contract ("principal") so that both parties tend to maximize utility. In simple terms, no one can maximize his or her own interests by compromising the collective interests. Individual and collective interests are aligned, as each individual strives for the goal of achieving his or her own interests, and this also leads to the maximization of collective interests. The theory and practice of modern economics show that the implementation of the incentive compatibility principle can effectively solve the conflicts between individual interests and collective interests, so that the actors' behaviors and the results are in line with the goal of maximizing collective values, i.e., the two objective functions of individual values and collective values can be aligned, or in other words, the objective function of individual values and the objective function of collective values are aligned. When the participants' rational strategies for maximizing individual interests are aligned with the strategies desired by the mechanism designers, the participants will voluntarily act in accordance with the strategies desired by the mechanism designers.

Now, we can think about the incentive compatibility of the reforms from the perspective of the central-local relationship. In this round of reforms, a key part is reshaping the central-local relationship. The current central-local relationship has problems of power asymmetry and interest asymmetry (Hu et al. 2014). The power asymmetry is reflected in the prominent problems of both over-centralization in line-like dictatorship and over-decentralization and fragmentation in block-like dictatorship; it is also reflected in the problems of both bureaucracy in the higher departments and the non-serious implementation in the lower departments. The interest asymmetry includes the damage to local interests and the lack of motivation for reforms caused by such measures as the "replacement of business tax with value added tax," and the complaints about the mismatch between local authority of affairs and financial resources. In particular, the interests of the central and local governments are not fully aligned with regard to their concerns about long-term issues, overall issues, and sustainable development issues. To stimulate the enthusiasm of both the central and local governments, to make the incentives of the two compatible, and to align and maximize the objective functions, it is necessary to clarify how to divide the functions and responsibilities between the central and local governments, and generally form a cooperative system and incentive compatible mechanism in which the central government makes the decisions, the state makes plans, the departments provide guidance, the provincial governments assume the overall responsibility, and the regional and municipal governments put things into practice.

### *2.3.4 Reform Mechanism Design*

Currently, the departmental interests and the vested interests are among the biggest obstacles to China's reforms. Looking back at the reforms over the past 30 years, we find that all the reforms led by government departments in their own fields often tended to stagnate or became stagnant due to limitations on the grounds of the "specificity" and "complexity," while most of the reforms that were not led by the government departments have progressed smoothly and achieved remarkable results. For example, the industrial sectors were the most thoroughly reformed because it was not the industrial departments that made their own decisions on the direction of the industrial system reform. Unfortunately, the government's industrial management departments were abolished, while the powers of other government management departments making reforms in their own fields (such as the Development and Reform Commission and the Ministry of Education) were strengthened. This actually runs counter to the direction of market-oriented reforms with less government intervention. Therefore, it is essential to construct an effective check-and-balance mechanism to effectively promote the reforms and curb the expansion of the powers of the government departments in the reform process. In this regard, we can draw on the "Veil of Ignorance," a concept that allows reform designers to design reform programs without knowing their interests. In other words, not only should the cadres of the relevant departments of the government be actively involved in the reforms to bring into play their advantages of high-level qualifications, experience and knowledge, but they should also be decoupled from departmental interests when participating in the reforms. To do this, the reform designers must design the reform programs without knowing where his or her own interests lie, or without knowing which department he or she will be working for in the new system. Actually, this means to set up a "veil of ignorance" in the reform mechanism. The simplest approach is to select outstanding cadres from relevant management departments and form a reform working group together with experts who have no direct interests to design reform programs. In parallel, it must be made clear that after the reform programs are completed and adopted, the reform designers are not allowed to return to their former departments, but are appointed to other important positions by the organization department. What matters is to leave the future appointment of the reform designers in uncertainty in order to make it possible to exclude interest-related interference in the design process. In this way, the administrative department's advantages in talent, business and information are given into full play, and the administrative departments are prevented from using these advantages to defend its own interests in the reform design process (Jin 2013). Apart from the checks and balances of interests, the implementation capabilities should also be taken into account in the reform mechanism design process. For coordination and overall advancement of the top-level reforms, a high-level coordination committee should also be established to ensure that the feedback from all parties (especially from ministries, departments and local governments) is heard and that sufficient authority is available to coordinate and handle different opinions. Currently, the working group for deepening system reforms, led by General Secretary Xi Jinping, intends to play a leading role.

### 2.3.5 Combination of Top-Level Design and "Crossing the River by Feeling the Stones"

At the early stage of reforms, we mainly crossed the river by feeling the stones because of unclear reform blueprints and lack of experience, which made the role of "top-level design" relatively weak. As we promote the reforms, especially as we enter uncharted waters, the top-level design becomes especially important. The exploration at the grassroots level is confined to the local area, which has the benefit of adapting reforms to local conditions, but also tends to result in fragmented, non-systematic and uncoordinated reforms. Therefore, a top-level design is needed for overall coordination. The top-level design involves the theoretical preparation for reforms, the overall layout of reforms, and the design of reform mechanisms. The emphasis on the top-level design does not mean that we will not "cross the river by feeling the stones." At the current stage, the reform context (such as the reforms on mixed ownership and state-owned enterprises) is very complex, so we have to explore the path and accumulate the experience through "crossing the river by feeling the stones." For the major reforms that must make a breakthrough but still have uncertainty, we should encourage and support some places with the conditions to carry out the pilot projects, in order to keep the risks and impacts within the local scope.

As the reforms have come to the current stage, there is a real need for a top-level design to ensure the correct direction of the reforms and no major problems in the key relationships and key links. After years of exploration and practice, China has accumulated rich experience in reforms and has the ability to make a good top-level design. We should start from the strategic overall situation, carefully carry out the top-level design and overall planning, make different reform measures supporting and connecting with each other and promote the reforms in a comprehensive and coordinated manner.

Modern market economy is a huge, complex and sophisticated system. We cannot design the modern market economy while constructing it, nor can we create it like a crude and simple pair of straw sandals which don't need advanced design; otherwise, the various subsystems will be unable to interconnect with each other and interact in a coordinated manner. Under the huge system of market economy, each local government and department often looks at their own work convenience and interests to make the institutional arrangements in favor of local interests. If the systems designed at the grassroots level are combined into a whole, such a whole system will certainly fail to operate in a coordinated manner.

When it comes to the top-level design, it means that we should take into account the new characteristics of China's overall reforms, make an integrated design for economic, political, cultural, social, and ecological systems instead of the previous one-sided and abrupt reform model, strengthen the research and analysis of the correlation among various reforms, so as to align the whole picture with the local situations, combine permanent solutions with temporary solutions, and promote gradual progress with breakthroughs. We should adopt a holistic reform strategy to grasp the systemic, interrelated and complementary nature of the reforms. The top-level design of the reforms involves three aspects:

First, we should increase reform researches and make adequate theoretical preparation. Objectively, the third plenary session of the 18th CPC Central Committee has theoretically drawn an overall blueprint of socialist market economy for us and roughly outlined the basic path to achieve this ideal blueprint. However, on the one hand, it is still an arduous task for us to educate the people with this theory and to further enrich this theoretical system by widely absorbing the people's suggestions, as the reforms are great undertakings participated by millions of people; on the other hand, the reforms involve an extremely wide range of areas, and our theoretical preparation for certain areas are somewhat inadequate. Therefore, motivating various social forces as well as strengthening research on reforms (for example, on how to play the decisive role of the market in the reform of state-owned enterprises and the financial system requires serious discussions, full debates and bold experiments) can help continuously improve our reform theories and strategies, so as to find more effective reform paths. Through this process, we can also increase the public's participation in the reforms and stimulate the public's enthusiasm for participating in the reforms.

Second, we should take a holistic approach to the reforms, design them systematically, promote them comprehensively, and avoid fragmentation. Although the decision of the third plenary session of the 18th CPC Central Committee has made an overall and systematic deployment of various reforms, the reform programs in all fields are required to be further improved and refined, because the reforms cover a wide range of areas and must be practiced before the effects can be known. In particular, the subsequent overall advancement plans need more explicit and specific thoughts. In the next step, we should grasp the reforms in a holistic manner to avoid fragmentation, and put forward clear goals and roadmaps for each reform. In the reforms, the rules should be simplified and the cumbersome administrative procedures should be reduced. The transparency should be improved, the reconstruction of social rules should be promoted, and the implementation of the reforms should be advanced under more open and transparent social rules. Since gradual reforms take a one-by-one and step-by-step approach, they are advanced in a non-systematic and non-synergistic manner, which often leads to mutual constraints among systems. Masahiko Aoki points out in his book *Toward a Comparative Institutional Analysis* that various institutions are strategically complementary in a system, and a change in one or more institutions may result in other institutions either being changed accordingly or having difficulty in working with the new institution, thus creating obstacles to the implementation of the new institution (Aoki 2001). In essence, therefore, institutional reforms should be advanced as a whole and can be implemented in steps; otherwise, we have to bear huge costs for operating the institutions. The reform and opening-up has brought about profound and all-round social changes, with each reform having a significant impact on other reforms, and each reform requiring the synergistic cooperation of other reforms. Therefore, the reform and opening-up is a systematic project that must be comprehensively promoted under the synergy of various reforms. Without the top-level design, the reforms will definitely get nowhere.

Third, we should strengthen the mechanism design of the reforms. The top-level design of the reforms must be done by a high-level authoritative body that stands above the local interests to carry out the top-down design planning and supervise the plan implementation under the support of grassroots innovation. The top-level design must involve more people and listen to the reform demands of the people and the political innovations of the grassroots governments. The basic idea behind the reform mechanism design is that a watermelon will be cut equally if the person who cuts it is the last person to take a piece. Such a mechanism also applies to the top-level design of reforms, which means that the reform design should not be turned into a pre-cutting of reform benefits, but should be such that all those involved in the reforms can see a hope of the fair sharing of reform benefits and the practical mechanism guarantee.

Of course, the emphasis on the top-level design does not mean that we will not "cross the river by feeling the stones." As a large country, China should neither make devastating mistakes on fundamental issues that, when they occur, would lead to irreparable and irremediable losses, nor maintain everything unchanged and unaltered. A pilot-based, stone-throwing approach should be adopted to clear the roads, explore the methods, gain the experience and reach the consensus. When the road ahead is clear, we can roll the reforms out on a wide scale to turn a small victory into a big one. China is a vast country with a wide variety of conditions, and the complexity of the current stage of reforms makes it difficult to anticipate many situations in advance. For the major reforms that must have a breakthrough but are still not in certainty, we should encourage and support some qualified places to carry out pilot projects, or to conduct explorations in the reform pilot zones. In case of successful pilots, such reforms should be rolled out in a timely manner; in case of failure, the mistakes should be corrected in a timely manner and the risks and impacts can be controlled within a local scope. Such an approach can ensure advance the reforms are advanced in an effective, positive and steady and smooth manner. In the future reform process, we should not only strengthen the macroscopic thinking and the top-level design and pay more attention to the systemic, holistic and synergistic nature of the reforms, but also continue encouraging grassroots innovation, bold experiments and pioneering breakthroughs, and keep leading the reform and opening-up to the depths.

### 2.3.6 Allowing the People to Obtain a Reform Dividend

In 2015, the Central Economic Work Conference further underlined that "reform policies should be practical," which meant that more efforts should be made to put the reforms in practice. It is necessary to improve the implementation mechanism, take advantage of the reform pilots, strengthen the overall coordination, stimulate the local enthusiasm, allow for local differentiated exploration, and give play to the grassroots-level innovation spirits. We must dare to undertake difficult tasks, dare to solve difficult problems, and strictly put the reform measures into practice, so as to constantly bring about effective results and provide more benefits to the people.

In early 2016, the 20th meeting of the Central Leading Group for Comprehensively Deepening Reforms further emphasized the need to bring reform policies into practice. In other words, the reforms cannot stop at documents, meetings or slogans, but must be put into practice, so as to effectively promote all the work and allow the people to obtain the reform dividend.

How to put the reforms into practice?

First, we should adhere to the problem-oriented approach and pinpoint the key links. The reforms are a systemic project, and it is important to hit the nail on the head and seize the key points in order to activate and promote the whole process. Only by following the general guiding principle of the five concepts for development, strengthening the overall assessment of reforms in various fields, adhering to the problem-oriented approach, and pinpointing the key links can we find the entry points and rallying points of the reforms. On the one hand, we should clearly mark out the reforms in various fields that underpin the main framework, and promote them with priority. In particular, we should pay close attention to the reforms have a leading role, such as the reforms of state-owned enterprises, taxation and finance, science and technology innovation, justice and other areas, so as to grasp the "bull's nose" of the reforms and give the supporting role of the key areas reforms into full play. On the other hand, as the reforms keep advancing in wider operating surfaces and deeper digging areas with increasing difficulty, we must adhere to the correct methodology. Through the methodology of "overall reforms led by key areas, mutual promotion between temporary and permanent solutions, as well as connection of key breakthroughs and gradual advancement," we can make precise and sustained efforts to push forward the reforms and continuously achieve new results.

Second, we should assign responsibilities to concerned parties, clarify the responsibility chains, tighten the responsibility screws, and improve the effectiveness of responsibility performance. Whether the reform work can be put in place is predicated on a clear definition of the responsible parties, and the assignment of responsibilities is the key. In reality, some local governments carried out the reforms in the form of "nine dragons ruling water," which resulted in all responsibilities being mixed together without clear assignment, and the frequent phenomenon of "middle blockage"; some local governments failed to keep up with and follow up on the central deployment, resulting in the obvious contrast between the central government's enthusiasm for reforms and the local governments' indifferent attitude; some local governments used to implement reforms in documents, and failed to take substantive measures, so the people reflected that only the voice of reforms was heard but no reform measures were put in place. The meeting of the Central Leading Group for Comprehensively Deepening Reforms has clearly assigned responsibilities and task requirements for each "front army" of comprehensively deepening reforms. The special task groups should make good coordination and deployment, and monitor and check how the reform are implemented; the departments leading the reforms are responsible for implementing the specific reform tasks deployed by the central government, and the key leaders of such departments have the direct responsibility for coordinating reforms, improving program quality, adjust interests and monitoring reform implementation; the local party committees bear the main responsibility for comprehensively deepening reforms in their areas; the party secretaries, as the first responsible person, should both take command and personally work on the reforms. Only when each local government and department live up to their own responsibilities and tighten each screw, the chain of responsibilities for reforms can run smoothly. By increasing the efforts of inspections, and setting rigid requirements for each link that can be implemented and verified, it will be possible to connect the joints, unblock the congestion, improve the quality, and continuously enhance the people's satisfaction with the reforms.

## 2.4 Summary: Enhance Reform Determination and Maintain Reform Tenacity

General Secretary Xi Jinping pointed out in his keynote speech at the 15th meeting of the Central Leading Group for Comprehensively Deepening Reforms that we should enhance reform determination, maintain reform tenacity, strengthen ideological guidance, focus on studying new situations and new problems encountered in reforms, improve the ability to precisely design and accurately implement reforms in a spirit of perseverance and resilience, and firmly put reform measures into practice.

The current reforms are unprecedented in terms of breadth, strength and depth, and relate to deep-rooted problems in China's political, economic, social, military and diplomatic fields. They are not useless attempts, but will bring far-reaching effects. However, the difficulties and resistance to reforms, as well as the stubbornness, ferocity, complexity and weirdness of the forces that do not adapt to or even oppose the reforms, may exceed our imagination. For these reasons, it is particularly critical to enhance reform determination and maintain reform tenacity.

If we put China's reform in the context of global institutional competition and reform competition, it is all the more important for us to maintain the determination and tenacity of reforms. Reform is an ongoing process that never ends, which is apparently true not only for countries with immature and undefined systems like China. As a matter of fact, reforms are ongoing even in mature market economies such as the US On a global scale, the institutional competition and the reform competition for the purpose of gaining institutional advantages will become the norm. From an institutional economics perspective, the factors that drive the evolution of intrinsic and extrinsic institutions are not only reactive responses to international trade and factor movements, but also proactive adjustments to institutions for gaining a larger market share and activating the production factors. Globalization has brought about the "competition over institutions (or systems)" (Ke and Shi 2000). It is especially important to note that since the global financial crisis in 2008, re-balancing, structural adjustments and reforms have become the main themes of global development. The third, fourth and fifth plenary sessions of the 18th CPC Central Committee have made comprehensive deployments for China's reforms and development, while the US, Europe and Japan have also rolled out structural reform plans and long-term growth strategies. Therefore, the reform competition has been kicked off in silence.

In fact, whether reforms can be continuously advanced is a reflection of a country's capacity. Edmund Burke (1790) said in *Reflections on the Revolution in France* that "A state without the means of some change is without the means of its conservation. Without such means it might even risk the loss of that part of the constitution which it wished the most religiously to preserve." It reveals what is the driving force of reforms at the deepest level, that is, we are continuously reforming exactly for the purpose of preserving the nature of the socialist system. In the context of global institutional competition and reform competition, China's continuous efforts in reforming itself can be said the most important logic of its reforms. In the 1980s, Comrade Deng Xiaoping said that the significance of reforms was to lay a good foundation for sustained development in the next decade and the first fifty years of the next century, and without reform there would be no sustained development in the future, so reforms were imperative, and not just for the next three or five years, but for the next twenty years and the first fifty years of the next century (Deng 1993).

## References

Aoki, Masahiko (2001), Toward a Comparative Institutional Analysis, Shanghai Far East Publishing House, Edition 2001.

Building a Consensus for Reform: One of the Series on Comprehensively Deepening Reforms Discussion, Guangming Daily, March 24, 2014.

Deng Xiaoping (1993), Selected Works of Deng Xiaoping (Volume III), People's Publishing House, Edition 1993, pp. 118.

Hu Angang et al. (2014), The Modernization of State Governance in China, China Renmin University Press, Edition 2014.

Jin Bei (2013), Building a Veil of Ignorance on Reform Mechanisms, China Business Journal, March 11, 2013.

Ke Wugang and Shi Manfei (2000), Institutional Economics: Social Order and Public Policy, The Commercial Press, Edition 2000.

# Chapter 3
# Enhancing Total Factor Productivity Through Comprehensively Deepening Reforms

**Zhang Ping and Yuan Fuhua**

**Abstract** Based on the economic growth calculation framework, the latest estimates show that the "structural slowdown" remains a serious challenge: (1) The growth of capital and labor supply will decline to single digits; (2) The industrial structure changes inefficiently; (3) The contribution of the total factor productivity (TFP) to economic growth has declined from about 30% at the peak growth period to the current 17%; (4) There is a shift in the distribution coefficients, with labor output becoming more elastic and capital output becoming less elastic; (5) As the people's income increases, the percentage of food consumption in the consumption structure decreases, the percentage of material consumption and general service expenditure decreases, while the percentage of residents' consumption in cultural, educational and lifestyle service sectors, such as the science, education, culture and health sector, sports sector and finance sector, increases rapidly. Only by breaking the current calculation and the present institutional barriers can we truly shift from the economic slowdown and downturn to the path of endogenous growth. Obviously, we should: (1) increase human capital while boosting the consumption of "broad-sense human capital"; (2) improve TFP, increase the innovation level and adjust the resource misallocation; (3) raise the productivity of the tertiary sector significantly, and thus enhance the overall consumption level; (4) We should further improve the level of income distribution to build a moderately prosperous society in all aspects. These rely on institutional reforms: (1) improve the development space and efficiency of the tertiary sectors through the reforms of the systems of the science, education, culture and health sector and other tertiary sectors; (2) correct resource misallocation and improve efficiency through the reforms of government administrative systems and state-owned enterprises supported by monopolistic, administrative or selective industrial policies;(3) promote a shift from a supply-oriented to a demand-oriented economy through the reforms that improve distribution and increases consumption.

---

Z. Ping (✉) · Y. Fuhua
Institute of Economics, Chinese Academy of Social Sciences, Beijing, China



X. Zhang (ed.), *Exploration on China's Economic System Reform under New Normal of Development*, https://doi.org/10.1007/978-981-95-2461-7_3

In recent years, the global discussion on international empirical comparison and analysis such as "mean reversion," "economic slowdown" and "long-term stagnation" in developed countries has started again. Chinese scholars have also done a great deal of empirical analysis and have proposed a number of interesting concepts: (1) The slowdown point is determined, for example, by a slowdown of at least 2% points in the seven years before and after the high growth period to the slowdown period; (2) The frontier gap and the time to convergence, i.e., the gap between late-developing countries and advanced frontier economies determines the "time" for economic growth to revert to the mean; (3) The principle of interactivity between the catching up of large countries and the mean reversion. Since the catching-up of large countries causes a global rebalancing, it is not advisable to use data on the rise of effects for direct comparisons, but the principle of interactivity should be followed; (4) Stage-based stagnation hypothesis. When economic growth reaches a certain stage, it will inevitably cause stage-based stagnation, with some countries breaking through the stagnation and some countries staying in the "poverty trap," "middle-income trap" and "long-term stagnation for the developed countries." These empirical comparisons have relatively large gaps in findings due to the choices of different sample points, and their use in the analysis of China will lead to even more uncertain prediction results.

In fact, the same is true for the estimates derived from the growth calculation framework. Both capital and labor inputs have diminishing marginal returns and converge gradually in an equilibrium trajectory, so that any country that reaches any stage of development will encounter the problem of "stagnation." However, only technological progress is assumed to be exogenous. In other words, the only way to break out of the current equilibrium is to rely on technological revolution and innovation; otherwise, the threat of development slowdown exists at every stage of development. The fundamental way to break through the trap is to keep innovating. In essence, the "structural slowdown" in factor calculations, the empirical exploration of "mean reversion" in international comparisons, and the research on TFP and institutional analysis are all seeking new paths to break through the stagnation in various development stages, and have all pointed out that only innovation-driven development can overcome the "traps." These empirical comparisons have large gaps in findings due to the different sampling sizes, and their prediction is even more uncertain when used in analyzing China.

However, the TFP is a "black box." How to truly construct new growth facts, statistics, theories and possible policies to break through stage-based stagnation has become the most important field among economic growth researches across the world. Currently, a number of exploration directions have been developed: (1) The construction of new facts. For example, the New Kaldor Facts have been proposed to explore the so-called "new factors," i.e., the factors with increasing returns to scale, such as knowledge, education, information, creativity, institutions, and scope. Whether these factors can resist the traditional issue of diminishing returns to scale is the key to achieving a breakthrough in economic growth; (2) Technological innovation paths. Most of the exploration focuses on an endogenous economic growth framework based around human capital and Joseph Alois Schumpeter's technological innovation process, where the establishment of a human capital-knowledge production sector and its transmission through the technology production chain to intermediate sectors for horizontal and vertical technological innovation is proposed; (3) Institutional improvements for resource misallocation. It aims to introduce the institutional factors that cause resource misallocation and suggests making institutional improvements to enhance the contribution of technological progress; (4) The progress in statistics. A new statistical system associated with knowledge production has also begun to emerge. In 2008, the World Bank launched a new SNA system for GDP calculation, which introduced the most important concepts of "legal property rights" and "economic owner"; included intellectual property products in GDP, and clarified five categories (including R&D, mineral exploration and evaluation, computer software and database, literature and original artwork, and others). Many products that people consume in their spiritual life are excluded from the items of consumption and included in the items of supply. All these have clarified the process of integrating knowledge consumption and production, and also made a breakthrough in the new transformation assessment. The introduction of "employee stock options" has aligned the option accounts with the labor remuneration system and also reflected the human factors in the new economy by transforming the original asset income into human capital income, etc. Of course, the whole system reform is complex, but the core is the redefinition of knowledge production.

Given the current progress, it is necessary for China to make a breakthrough analysis of reality and theory in three aspects: (1) We should actively introduce the supply of new factors in the theoretical analysis; (2) We should fully understand and expand the "knowledge production" in reality, which it will drive China's transformation from a traditional "general technology producer" to an "innovation-driven" country, so it is necessary to carefully analyze the nature of knowledge production and its characteristics for growth; (3) Institutional reforms and resource misallocation. Institutional reforms and resource misallocation. As the allocation efficiency decreases after catching up, and the traditional catching-up systems are greatly suppressing innovative activities and resulting in serious resource misallocation, it is necessary to make institutional arrangements that respond to the provision of new factors for growth and the creation of new knowledge production in order to achieve a breakthrough in the development stage.

## 3.1 Calculation of China's Growth

Based on the economic growth calculation framework, a "structural slowdown" in the growth process is proposed and used as a basis to track China's economic growth trajectory (Blue Book of China's Economy 2015). According to the latest calculations, the "structural slowdown" remains a serious challenge: (1) Both the growth of capital and labor supply and the marginal productivity of factors are declining. In particular, the growth of labor supply was negative during the 13th Five-Year Plan period (2016–2020), while the growth of capital supply is expected to decline to single digits due to the advancement of urbanization. (2) The industrial structure changes inefficiently. With China's modernization of its industrial structure (the added value of modern sectors such as industrial and service sectors accounts for approximately 93% of GDP, when calculated at comparable prices), the economic structural allocation through the transfer from the rural sector to the modern sector has become less efficient, while the modern sectors have suffered an inefficient structural allocation due to the lower labor productivity of the tertiary sectors compared to the secondary sectors, resulting in a decline in overall labor productivity in China. (3) The contribution of TFP to economic growth has declined from a level of about 30% at the peak growth period to the current level of 17%, due in large part to the declining market-based institutional improvements, as well as to the gradual reduction in the contribution of technological progress resulting from the introduction of advanced equipment through "learning by doing." (4) The factor distribution tends to be labor-oriented. With the arrival of the Lewis turning point, the labor output elasticity has increased to the level of 0.5, which has accelerated the slowdown trend. (5) With the increase in people's income, the percentage of food consumption in the consumption structure has been decreasing, and the percentage of material consumption expenditure has also been decreasing; the percentage of general service consumption expenditure has been decreasing, while the percentage of the people's consumption in cultural, educational and lifestyle service sectors, such as the science, education, culture and health sector, sports sector and finance sector, has been increasing rapidly, which can be concluded that the income consumption elasticity of the sectors for "general production and services of universal technologies" is less than 1%, with a declining proportion of consumption expenditure in the future. However, the elasticity of consumption demand for production and services related to human quality or "broad-sense human capital and quality improvement," is greater than 1%, and the percentage of consumption has been increasing, which has led to the transition from an industrialized material production economy to a knowledge economy.

### *3.1.1 Demographic Changes and Declining Labor Supply*

The demographic transition and the accompanying decline in the growth rate of the working age population are stylized facts that have been common in countries around the world since World War II, albeit with a temporal sequence. According to WDI data, the growth rate of the working age population in the high-income group of high-income countries has been declining steadily from 1.2% before the 1980s to 0.6% at the current stage; similar trends have been observed in the groups of lower-middle-income countries, middle-income countries and upper-middle-income countries, but their declines were significantly slower than that in the group of high-income countries. Up to now, the growth rate of the working age population in the group of middle-income countries has remained at 1.5% to 2%. From 1960 to 2000, the group of low-income countries witnessed an acceleration of the demographic dividend, but since 2000, there has been a convergence toward the top of the S-shaped curve, with the growth rate of their working age population ranging from 2.5% to 3%. From a regional perspective, the demographic transition has been particularly notable in the newly industrialized countries in East Asia and the Pacific region, while China is also facing a rapid decline in the growth rate of its working age population.

China's large-scale industrialization since the 1980s was fundamentally thanks to its advantageous demographic structure. The high economic growth over the past three decades coincided with the demographic dividend window, while the current structural slowdown is also closely related to the closing of the demographic dividend window. The growth rate of China's working age population declined from 1.58% in 1985–2007 to 0.61% in 2008–2015 and will further decline to -0.4% in 2016–2020 based on the age-moving method. Meanwhile, as the problem of population aging emerges, the affluent population tends to pursue leisure, and the education years of the young working age population increase, the ratio of labor supply to the working age population, or the labor force participation rate, also shows an increasingly significant downward trend. For example, the growth rate of labor force participation in China was −0.07% in 1985–2007, −0.24% in 2008–2015, and is estimated to be −0.50% in the next five years. The decline in both the working age population and the growth rate of labor force participation has directly resulted in changes in labor supply. The growth rate of labor inputs in China declined from 1.5% in 1985–2007 to 0.36% in 2008–2015 and is estimated to further decline to −0.9% in 2016–2020.

### *3.1.2 Economic Development Stages and Capital Input Changes*

In the process of rapid advancement of industrialization, there were two bases on which large-scale investment behaviors occurred: (1) low labor costs facilitated industrial investment expansion; (2) productive infrastructure such as transport infrastructure was built. These two types of investments complemented each other, making the investments profitable and the investment willingness stronger in the industrialization period. For example, in 1985–2007, China's society-wide fixed-asset investments grew at an average annual growth rate of more than 20%, and the society-wide capital formation rate was nearly 40%. At the same time, the capital stock grew at a rate of 11% and the capital per capita grew at a rate of 9.4%, fully reflecting the capital-driven, high-growth mode of industrialization.

After 2008, the favorable conditions for large-scale industrial investments gradually disappeared. With China's demographic transition, the rising costs of labor squeezed the returns on investment, and the investments in infrastructure such as transport infrastructure during the urbanization period increasingly focused on the convenience of life, which triggered the problem of diminishing returns on investment. At the same time, the expansion of the investments in social infrastructure, such as those for science, education, culture, health and social security, further squeezed the returns on investment and therefore weakened the private enthusiasm for investments. As seen from the data, China's high investments in 2008 were mainly driven by infrastructure and real estate, with more government intervention than ever before.

However, a basic conclusion based on China's urbanization development trend is that after nearly 20 to 30 years of large-scale development, the climax of investments in China's urban infrastructure is coming to an end. After China's urbanization rate exceeded 50% in 2011, China began to move towards the maturity stage of urbanization, and the capital accumulation rate in the industrial and service sectors will continue to decrease. Based on the inverted U-shaped relationship between the urbanization rate and the investment growth rate, the capital stock growth rate in China is estimated to be 9.5% in 2016–2020.

### *3.1.3 TFP*

In China's capital-driven large-scale industrialization process, the contribution of TFP to economic growth showed a systemically downward trend. The contribution was close to 30% in 1985–2007, but dropped to less than 20% in 2008–2015. This systemically downward trend in the contribution of TFP was the result of China's low-cost industrialization model.

From the perspective of efficiency improvement, the increase in labor productivity relied mainly on capital deepening, while the TFP growth relied on "learning by doing" rather than endogenous factors of technological progress. Efficiency gains by "depleting" the cheap labor force but not by "nurturing" human capital are the hallmark of this model. According to WDI data, China's human capital is typically characterized by secondary-education-led growth when compared to developed countries. The proportion of the higher-education workforce in China is significantly lower than that in both developed and other newly industrialized countries, which is a major problem that prevents China from transforming its growth in a relatively short period of time (Table 3.1).

### *3.1.4 Industrial Structure Changes and Efficiency Changes*

The changes in factor structure and productivity are closely linked to the changes in industrial structure. The overall trend is that as China's economic growth stage evolves, the service sector, with its high employment absorption capacity, is increasingly dominant in the urbanization period. Meanwhile, since the traditional service sector weighs heavily in China, it is impossible for the concentration of labor and capital in the service sector to achieve as fast a labor productivity growth rate as that in the large-scale industrialization period, so a structural slowdown is inevitable.

It is fair to say that China's efficiency growth in the industrialization stage relies on a large scale and low costs, and the efficiency maintenance in the urbanization stage

**Table 3.1** Production function decomposition and trend forecasts

| | Past (peak-peak: 1985–2007) | Current (2008–2015) | Forecast 2016–2020 |
|---|---|---|---|
| [1] [Three factors of potential growth (production function fitting)] | 10.10% | 8.54% | 6.20% |
| [2] Capital input (K): Elasticity | 0.6 | 0.6 | 0.5 |
| [3] Capital contribution = [2] ([8]) / [1] | 68.72% | 82.20% | 76.60% |
| [4] Labor input (L): Elasticity | 0.4 | 0.4 | 0.5 |
| [5] Labor contribution = [4] ([11]) / [1] | 6.17% | 1.69% | -7.25% |
| [6] TFP: Growth rate | 2.82% | 2.60% | 1.96% |
| [7] TFP contribution=100-[3]- [5] | 27.94% | 16.16% | 30% |
| [Factor Breakdown] | | | |
| [8] Capital input growth rate (*k*=*dK*/*K*)=[9]([10] | 11.13% | 11.70% | 9.50% |
| [9] (Net) investment rate (*I/Y*) | 21.32% | 36.00% | |
| [10] Capital efficiency (*Y/K*) | 0.52 | 0.34 | |
| [11] Labor input growth rate (*l*=*dL*/*L*)=[12]+[13] | 1.50% | 0.36% | -0.90% |
| [12] Working age population growth rate ($pop_l$) | 1.58% | 0.61% | -0.40% |
| [13] Labor force participation change rate ($\theta_L$) | -0.07% | -0.24% | -0.50% |
| [14] Labor productivity growth rate | | | |
| [15] Labor productivity (*y*=*Y/L*) growth rate=[16]+[17] | 8.54% | 8.16% | |
| [16] Capital efficiency (*Y/K*) growth rate | -0.89% | -4.19% | |
| [17] Capital per capita (*K/L*) growth rate | 9.43% | 12.35% | |
| [Urbanization] | | | |
| [18] Urbanization rate | 33% | 50.5% | 0.58* |

*Notes* (1) * The capital input growth rate is calculated based on the inverted U-shaped relationship between the urbanization rate and the investment growth rate
(2) The data in the table are processed with errors within the tolerance range

relies on human capital and corresponding innovation. At this point, the link between production innovation and consumption innovation becomes closer. It is no longer feasible for industrial structural changes to be driven solely by previous supply-side factors. Demand-side innovation and diverse capabilities emerge as key axles in the tertiarization period, provided that human capital accumulation and human capital externalities are enhanced in inter- and intra-industry linkages.

According to our estimates, labor productivity growth rates in the secondary and tertiary sectors declined in both the periods 1985–2007 and 2008–2015, with a consequent decline in society-wide labor productivity. This proves the consensus that China's rapid increase in labor productivity over the past 30 years is attributable to the effects of "learning by doing" and "learning by investing" in large-scale industrialization, but the decline in social labor productivity is inevitable as the industrial structure becomes service-oriented. Without effective improvement in human capital accumulation capacity, it is expected that the growth rate of society-wide labor productivity will continue to decrease to below 8% during the 13th Five-Year Plan period (2016–2020) (Table 3.2).

**Table 3.2** Decomposition of labor productivity factors

| | Past (peak-peak: 1985–2007) | Current (2008–2015) | Forecast 2016–2020 |
|---|---|---|---|
| Labor productivity ($y=Y/L$) growth rate | 8.54% | 8.16% | 7.70% |
| Primary industry labor productivity growth rate | 4.42% | 9.10% | 9.00% |
| Employment percentage change rate | -1.92% | -4.33% | -5.18% |
| Added value percentage | 0.18 | 0.09 | 0.08 |
| Secondary industry labor productivity growth rate | 9.21% | 7.41% | 7.00% |
| Employment percentage change rate | 1.35% | 1.18% | 1.00% |
| Added value percentage | 0.49 | 0.49 | 0.45 |
| Tertiary industry labor productivity growth rate | 5.99% | 5.00% | 5.00% |
| Employment percentage change rate | 3.11% | 3.31% | 3.00% |
| Added value percentage | 0..33 | 0.42 | 0.48 |
| (Reference indicator - taking 1978 as the base year): 2013 | | | |
| Secondary industry labor productivity growth rate: 8.1% | | | |
| Tertiary industry labor productivity growth rate: 2.1% | | | |

*Note* (1) Labor productivity ($y=Y/L$) growth rate=Primary industry added value percentage × Primary industry labor productivity growth rate+Primary industry employment percentage change rate)+Secondary industry added value percentage × (Secondary industry labor productivity growth rate+Secondary industry employment percentage change rate) +Tertiary industry added value percentage × (Tertiary industry labor productivity growth rate+Tertiary industry employment percentage change rate)
(2) The data in the table are processed with errors within the tolerance range

### 3.1.5 *Potential Growth in 2016–2020*

Through the decomposition of labor productivity factors and the calculation of the production function, China's potential growth rate in the 13th Five-Year Plan period (2016–2020) will be roughly maintained at 6%, which implicitly includes a number of assumptions such as population, labor productivity, and distribution effects. However, China's economic performance in recent years has shown that many factors are actually more severe than we assumed. Declining investment growth caused by low returns in the real economy, blocked innovation paths caused by oversupply of medium human capital, and overall inefficiencies in the service sectors are all threats to exacerbate the structural slowdown of the economy.

## 3.2 TFP Decline and Resource Allocation Inefficiencies

In this section, we have provided the necessary data to evidence the inefficiencies and human capital misallocation during the growth stage transition, with the aim of demonstrating the following points: (1) China's economic efficiency problems are clearly revealed under a biased investment approach as the growth stage I comes to an end; (2) The investment-driven economic growth stage I neglects human capital accumulation, and the segmented approach to developing labor resources distorts human capital resource allocation and becomes a major obstacle to slowdown governance. Thus, the basic understanding is clear: under the trend of urbanization dominated by economic slowdown, and under the pressure of the disappearing investment growth impetus, the decreasing labor force growth impetus and the diminishing learning-by-doing effect, the key to sustained growth is improving resource allocation efficiency and unleashing human capital potential.

### 3.2.1 *Capital Misallocation and TFP Decline*

In terms of capital stock per capita, China is still at a stage of relatively low development, close to the level of Korea in the 1980s (Zhang Ping and Lu Mingtao, 2013), and there exist relatively prominent misallocation phenomena (Yan Ping., 2012). This capital misallocation is not only reflected in enterprises with different ownership, but also in different industries. In the following paragraphs, we have compared the investment status of several categories of sectors, including industrial and other sectors, other service sectors, economic infrastructure, social infrastructure and real estate sectors.

First, we want to explain the classification of economic and social infrastructure sectors. Following the approach of Jin Ge (2012), we have given the following settings for the economic and social infrastructure sectors: (1) According to the classification of 16 sectors in the *Statistical Yearbook of the Chinese Investment in Fixed Assets*, in 1979–2002, there were three economic infrastructure sectors, i.e., "electricity, gas and water production and supply," "geological prospecting, water conservancy management," and "transport, warehousing and post and telecommunications"; and there were three social infrastructure sectors, i.e., "health, sports and social welfare," "education, culture, art, radio, film and television," and "scientific research and comprehensive technical services." (2) According to the classification of 20 sectors in *China Statistical Yearbook*, in 2003–2010, there were four economic infrastructure sectors, i.e., "electricity, heat, gas and water production and supply," "transport, warehousing and postal services," "information transmission, software and IT services," and "water conservancy, environment and public facilities management"; and there were four social infrastructure sectors, i.e., "scientific research and technical services," "education," "health and social work," and "culture, sports and entertainment."

Meanwhile, the industrial sectors that exclude water, electricity and gas production (i.e., extractive sector, manufacturing sector and construction sector) are classified as "industrial and other sectors"; the real estate sector is classified as a separate sector, and the real estate sector and other service sectors that are not included in the economic infrastructure sector and social infrastructure sector are combined as "other service sectors." From the year-by-year trends in the proportions of fixed assets investment in "industry and other industries," "other services," "economic infrastructure" and "social infrastructure" in each year, we can find the following results: (1) The proportion of investment in industrial and other sectors continued decreasing in 1979–2002, and then increased after 2003 due to the advancement of heavy chemical industrialization, which led to a decrease in the proportion of investment in other services. (2) In 2003–2012, the proportion of investment in the real estate sector to the total society-wide fixed investment averaged 24%, and the proportion of investment in the real estate sector to the investment in the service sectors was 50%. During this period, the real estate sector was characterized by an abnormally high growth rate of investment, resulting in a leap forward in development over the course of more than a decade; China's fundamental problem of investment distortion at the current stage is largely reflected in this explosive growth of investment. (3) Accordingly, the investment in economic infrastructure decreased, and the investment in social infrastructure was kept at a low level (Fig. 3.1).

Based on the above classification in terms of investment, we used the following approach to examine the growth trends in China's overall capital stock: (1) Taking the year 1978 as the base year, we separately estimated the fixed asset investment in two major categories of sectors (the first category refers to the investment in real estate, economic infrastructure and social infrastructure, and the second category refers to the investment in industrial and other sectors excluding the above three sectors). (2) We assumed that the depreciation rate of the first category of fixed assets investment is 2%, and the depreciation rate of the second category of fixed assets investment

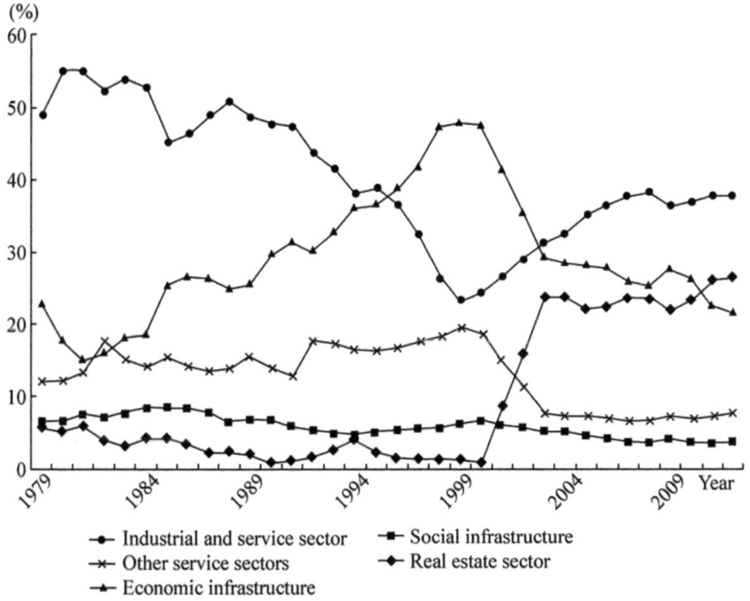


**Fig. 3.1** China's investment proportion by sector, 1979–2012. *Data source* The *China Statistical Yearbook* and the *Statistical Yearbook of the Chinese Investment in Fixed Assets* released in previous years

is 7%.[1] (3) The initial capital stock of the two categories of sectors is estimated as follows: Given the availability of data, we obtained that the initial capital stock of the first category of sectors is RMB 145.13 billion and the initial capital stock of the second category of sectors is RMB 312.20 billion by adding the depreciation rate of the two categories of sectors respectively with the GDP growth rate in 1978 and subtracting the fixed asset investment in the two categories of sectors in 1978. For the discounting of nominal fixed asset investment, the data from this research group (2013b) was used. (4) The capital stock series of the two categories of sectors in 1978–2012 were calculated based on the perpetual inventory method, and then the society-wide capital stock series were obtained through summation.

The labor input series and GDP series were also taken from this research group (2013b). For estimating TFP changes, we took the following steps: (1) For capital elasticity and labor elasticity, our estimates were made using the ratio of the sum of labor compensation in each province to the sum of GDP in each province (i.e., the proportion of labor compensation). (2) Technological progress was expressed as the difference between GDP growth and factor-elasticity weighted capital stock growth and labor input growth.

[1] ①We also estimated the capital stock series with a 3 percent depreciation rate for the first category of fixed assets and a 5 percent depreciation rate for the second category of fixed assets, and the growth rate of this series is essentially identical to the growth rate of the capital stock series yielded with 2 percent and 7 percent depreciation rates.

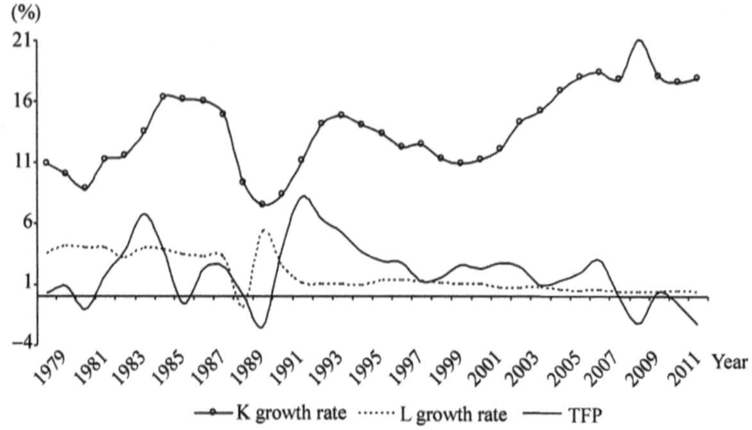


**Fig. 3.2** Change trends in growth factors, 1979–2012. *Data source* The *China Statistical Yearbook* released in previous years

The estimations revealed that there was a continuous decline in technological progress in China's economic growth in 1993–2012, and this decline was closely related to the continuous increase in the rate of capital growth; especially after 2008, the abnormally high growth rate of capital stock (around 18%) led to the negative growth of TFP. This negative TFP growth was strongly associated with the bias of investment distribution toward the real estate sector in recent years.

Therefore, the following issues have become increasingly prominent in China's economy: First, China's investment-driven trends have not fundamentally changed, but the investment distortions (especially the over-reliance on real estate) carry the risk of an overly rapid economic slowdown, as the real estate investment leapfrogging is unlikely to maintain a continuously high rate. Second, it is clear that the growth rate of China's labor force will also continue to decline. Third, the role of technological progress has not been played. In light of this, the above-mentioned triple structural shocks have placed China in great danger of an excessive economic slowdown (Fig. 3.2).

### 3.2.2 *Slow Growth of Human Capital*

It is commonly believed that human capital is accumulated mainly through education and the average education years are used as an important measure of human capital. Barro and Lee (2010) provided detailed data on the education level of the population in each country. When comparing China's average education years of its population aged 15 or above with those of developed countries such as the US, Japan, and developing countries in Latin America, it can be seen that China is not only far behind developed countries in terms of education years per capita, but also has a significant gap with many newly industrialized economies. Furthermore, in terms of the increase in education years per capita in 1970–2010, nine Latin American countries, Indonesia, Malaysia, the Philippines, Thailand, India, and China increased by 1.1 times, 1.7 times, 1.5 times, 0.8 times, 2.2 times, 2.9 times, and 1.1 times, respectively, and the growth of human capital in China was relatively low.

If we further compare the average education years of the population aged 15 or above with the GDP per capita, more meaningful insights can be obtained. By extracting the data series of the average education years of the population aged 15 or above in each country and the GDP per capita of each country in 2010 from Barro and Lee (2010) and the World Development Indicators, we created a scatter chart. It can be observed that China's education years per capita is not only less than that of most countries with higher GDP per capita, but also less than that of many countries with lower GDP per capita.

From the above worldwide comparison, it can be found that during the period when industrialization was structurally accelerated, China's capital-driven growth model neglected the role of technological progress on the one hand, and the cultivation of human capital on the other. In other words, these two factors, which are crucial for endogenous growth, have played a relatively insignificant role in China's long-term growth process, and such a situation, if not corrected, will make it difficult to offset the risk of an excessive economic slowdown (Table 3.3 and Fig. 3.3).

The efficient allocation of human capital is also essential for economic growth. Based on the data from the *China Statistical Yearbook* and foreign social surveys, we compared the differences in human capital allocation between China and developed countries. Detailed industry information of respondents is provided by the US General Social Survey (GSS). To enhance comparability, we selected the GSS survey data for the year 2012 (GSS 2012). Since the industry classification in GSS 2012 is based on four-digit codes adopted by North American Industry Classification System

**Table 3.3** Average education years of the population aged 15 and above by country

| Year | 1970 | 1975 | 1980 | 1985 | 1990 | 1995 | 2000 | 2005 | 2010 |
|---|---|---|---|---|---|---|---|---|---|
| US | 10.8 | 11.5 | 12.0 | 12.1 | 12.2 | 12.6 | 12.6 | 12.9 | 13.2 |
| Japan | 7.8 | 8.4 | 9.1 | 9.6 | 9.8 | 10.5 | 10.9 | 11.3 | 11.6 |
| Nine Latin American countries | 4.0 | 4.2 | 4.6 | 5.3 | 6.0 | 6.7 | 7.3 | 8.0 | 8.5 |
| Indonesia | 2.8 | 3.2 | 3.6 | 3.9 | 4.2 | 4.6 | 5.2 | 6.4 | 7.6 |
| Malaysia | 4.2 | 4.8 | 5.8 | 6.7 | 7.0 | 8.4 | 9.1 | 9.7 | 10.4 |
| Philippines | 4.7 | 5.5 | 6.2 | 6.6 | 7.1 | 7.6 | 7.9 | 8.2 | 8.4 |
| Thailand | 2.5 | 3.0 | 3.6 | 4.2 | 4.9 | 5.5 | 5.7 | 7.0 | 8.0 |
| India | 1.6 | 2.0 | 2.3 | 2.9 | 3.5 | 4.1 | 5.0 | 5.6 | 6.2 |
| China | 3.6 | 4.1 | 4.9 | 5.3 | 5.6 | 6.3 | 6.9 | 7.3 | 7.5 |

*Note* The data for nine Latin American countries is calculated as a population-weighted average; the nine countries include Uruguay, Peru, Paraguay, Mexico, Ecuador, Colombia, Chile, Brazil and Argentina
*Data source* Barro and Lee (2010)

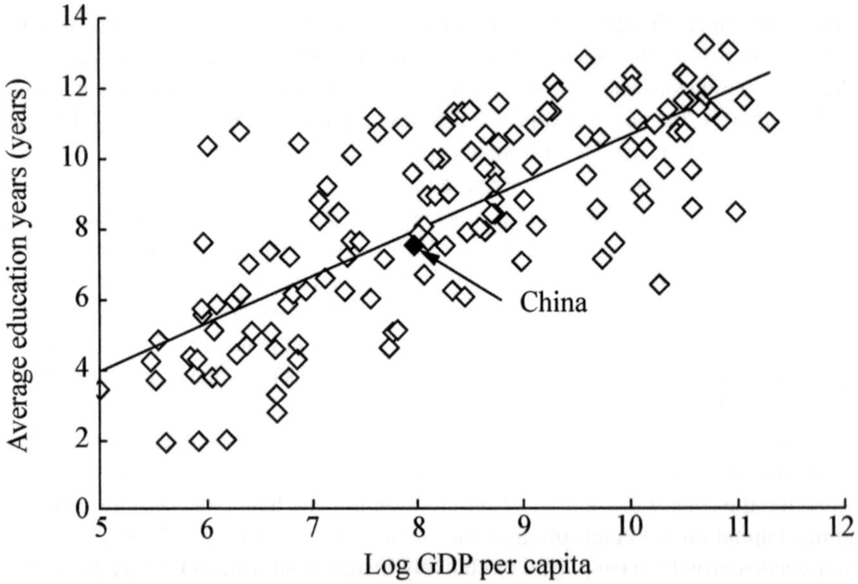


**Fig. 3.3** Scatter chart of GDP per capita and average education years in China and 144 countries. *Note* For the average education years, the statistical scope is the population aged 15 years and above. *Data source* Barro and Lee (2010), World Development Indicators 2014 (World Bank, 2014)

2007 (NAICS 2007), this book converts it into the classification of 20 sectors in accordance with the GB/T4754-2011, so that they are consistent with China's statistical specifications. Similarly, we took data from the sixth round of the European Social Survey (ESS Round 6) in 2012 and transformed it into the classification of 20 sectors for a comparison between China and major European countries.

First, a comparison is made between China and other countries in terms of the education years of laborers in various sectors. Broadly speaking, the education years of Chinese laborers in all sectors are lower than those in Russia, the 10 European countries, and the US, and it is consistent with the observation that the education years of the Chinese workforce are relatively low. However, if the marketization level and human capital differences among sectors are considered in the global comparison, some subtle facts are worth noting. For example, in sectors with low-level marketization such as "water conservancy, environment and public facilities management," "education, health and social work," and "culture, sports and entertainment," the gap between Chinese and foreign laborers is small, and Chinese workers in public administration, social security and social organizations have even slightly more education years than those in other countries, while in sectors with high-level marketization, China's human capital level is generally lower than that in other countries.

The core of the matter is that there is a serious human capital misallocation in China's sectors given the relatively low level of human capital. For obtaining comparable indicators, we used the population weights designed by the surveys and weighted the GSS and ESS samples. Based on this, we calculated the number of laborers with a bachelor's degree or higher and the total number of laborers in each sector and then estimated the distribution and proportion of laborers with a bachelor's degree or higher in each sector. These results were used to give a comparative description of the extent to which human capital is misallocated across sectors in China. For example, for the US, 10 European countries and Russia, their laborers with a bachelor's degree or higher are similarly proportioned across sectors and are relatively well distributed in manufacturing, wholesale and retail, education, health and social work, and public administration sectors. In contrast, China's laborer distribution curve is quite different. The sectors that have the most laborers with a bachelor's degree or higher are as follows in descending order: scientific research and technical services; education; public administration, social security and social organizations; health and social work; finance; and culture, sports and entertainment. Most of these sectors are poorly market-oriented and highly government-regulated in China. Even the finance sector is highly dominated by state-owned capital and subject to extensive government intervention. Moreover, unlike other countries where the manufacturing, wholesale and retail sectors attract a high percentage of laborers with a bachelor's degree or higher, China's university students are less frequently deployed in the manufacturing, wholesale and retail sectors (Fig. 3.4).

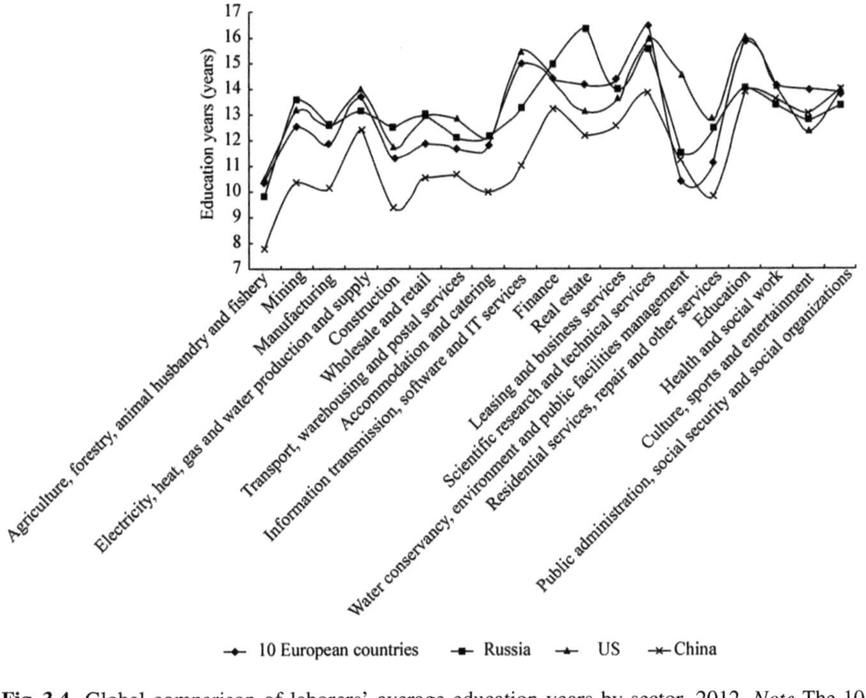


**Fig. 3.4** Global comparison of laborers' average education years by sector, 2012. *Note* The 10 European countries are Belgium, Switzerland, Germany, Spain, France, UK, Italy, Netherlands, Norway and Sweden. *Data source* GSS2012; ESS Round6; *China Statistical Yearbook*

Furthermore, we defined the sector human capital intensity by linking the sector human capital distribution to the sector added value distribution: the proportion of the workforce with a bachelor's degree or higher in each sector is divided by the proportion of added value to GDP in that sector. A higher human capital intensity means a more intensive use of human capital in that sector. Due to the limitation of data sources, we only compared China with France, Italy, the UK and the US. For example, (1) the human capital intensity in China's agriculture, forestry and fishing, manufacturing, wholesale and retail, and accommodation and catering sectors is far below that in other countries, and these sectors actually lack the human capital that is necessary for efficiency improvement. (2) China's public institutions or sectors (especially those under administrative control, such as cultural, sports and entertainment sectors) have a very high human capital intensity compared to other sectors in China and to similar sectors abroad. Through these comparisons, it is further revealed that there are human capital misallocation phenomena between productive and unproductive sectors in China (Fig. 3.5).

The pattern of government intervention that formed during China's economic catching-up period was mainly reflected in the government's vertical or top-down

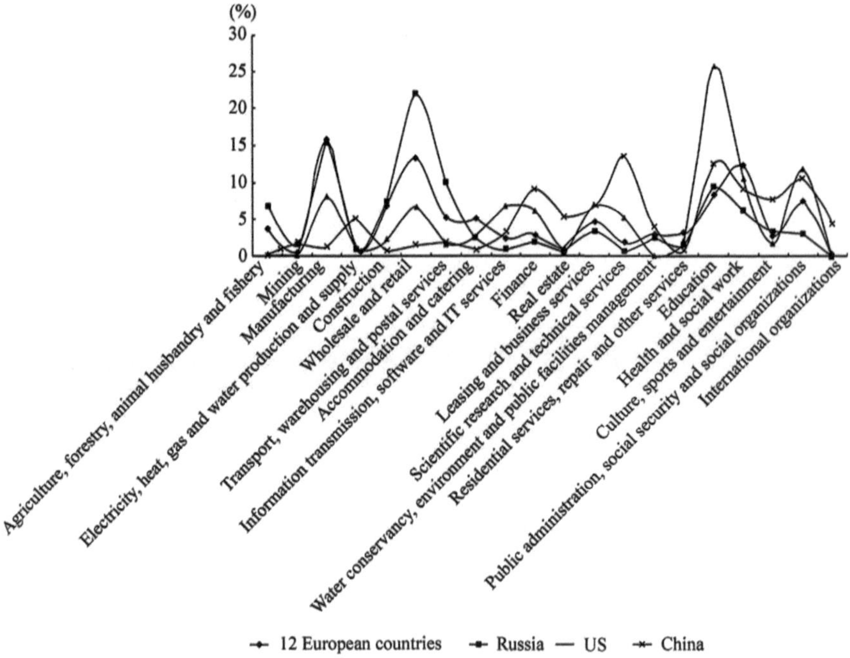


**Fig. 3.5** Global comparison of the distribution of laborers with a bachelor's degree or higher by sector, 2012. *Note* The 12 European countries are Belgium, Switzerland, Germany, Denmark, Spain, France, the UK, Italy, the Netherlands, Norway, Portugal and Sweden. *Data source* GSS2012; ESS Round6; *China Statistical Yearbook*

intervention in resource allocation, with details as follows: (1) Based on the production organization system under vertically integrated production arrangements, the government vertically divided the market's resource allocation functions, with functional ministries and departments as the lead. For example, the affiliation of each development zone can be figured out from the name alone: the high-tech development zone is affiliated with the Ministry of Science and Technology and the business zone is affiliated with the Ministry of Commerce. The horizontal connections were cut off, a large number of government approvals served this vertical institutional division, and market competition and the horizontal flow of resources were severely inhibited. (2) The government supported the enterprises above the designated size through various macro policies, including industrial and trade policies, fiscal subsidies, and the so-called "selective financing" (Shinohara, 1970), and encourage the sectors and enterprises defined as dominant by the government by setting institutional thresholds and policy subsidies. (3) For industrialization development, the government simply regarded the service sectors as a result of the division of labor in industrialization, reduced the costs of using public service facilities and allowed certain industrial sectors to access the public service facilities at a low price with subsidies or even for free (Research group, 2013a). (4) In China's economic catching-up process, the technological progress relied only on "learning by doing" with the imports of equipment, but not on independent research and development and knowledge innovation through "education and science." The scientific, educational, cultural, health and sports institutions, many public service departments, and trade associations were public institutions not included in the market and not added to the production system as innovative factors. Such a resource allocation pattern under the "vertical" division was a typical institutional feature of the government-intervention-based system during the catching-up period (Table 3.4).

In this production organization model, growth and efficiency have been placed under the divided institutional structure: The first category refers to the market-based sectors, mainly represented by productive SMEs. The second category refers to the policy-supported sectors where the government's industrial and financial policies support their scale expansion. The third category refers to government-regulated and subsidized sectors, which often have a natural monopoly nature, provide socialized universal services and have the qualification of quasi-public institutions, such as public infrastructure services, universalized education and healthcare, etc. The fourth category refers to the public institutions, which are non-market participants represented by the science, education, culture, health and sports sectors in the social service system, are purely funded by the government, and can earn revenue from the market in case of insufficient fiscal allocation. Despite their position as public institutions, such sectors bring together all the elements of national innovation – research, human capital, culture, etc. The above participants have different objective functions depending on their nature. In terms of objectives, the market-based sectors focus on profitability, the policy-supported sectors focus on scale expansion, the quasi-public institutions focus on receiving subsidies, and the public institutions focus on cost maximization. The widespread presence of the non-market sectors is what has caused the lack of endogenous growth impetus as described above. It is because

**Table 3.4** Global comparison of human capital intensity, 2012

| Sector | China | France | Italy | UK | US |
|---|---|---|---|---|---|
| Agriculture, forestry, animal husbandry and fishery | 0.004 | 2.777 | 3.696 | 2.070 | 0.176 |
| Manufacturing | 0.040 | 1.465 | 1.206 | 1.222 | 0.661 |
| Electricity, heat, gas and water production and supply | 2.235 | 0.595 | 0.651 | 0.435 | 0.502 |
| Construction | 0.125 | 1.401 | 1.098 | 1.307 | 0.563 |
| Wholesale and retail | 0.304 | 1.140 | 1.282 | 1.452 | 0.580 |
| Transport, warehousing and postal services | 0.817 | 1.264 | 0.633 | 1.269 | 0.553 |
| Accommodation and catering | 0.080 | 1.561 | 2.071 | 2.473 | 0.900 |
| Information transmission, software and IT services | 1.651 | 0.322 | 0.362 | 0.439 | 1.031 |
| Finance | 1.700 | 0.690 | 0.388 | 0.426 | 0.945 |
| Real estate | 0.944 | 0.073 | 0.006 | 0.093 | 0.084 |
| Leasing and business services | 3.449 | 0.363 | 1.120 | 0.314 | 2.808 |
| Scientific research and technical services | 9.197 | 1.351 | 0.113 | 1.697 | 0.556 |
| Residential services, repair and other services | 0.594 | 3.026 | 0.785 | 1.091 | 1.102 |
| Education | 4.129 | 1.364 | 1.675 | 1.648 | 23.647 |
| Health and social work | 5.794 | 0.976 | 1.503 | 1.757 | 1.469 |
| Culture, sports and entertainment | 12.230 | 1.304 | 2.737 | 1.535 | 1.654 |
| Public administration, social security and social organizations | 2.772 | 1.048 | 1.114 | 1.395 | 0.878 |

*Data source* GSS2012; ESS Round 6; UNdata; *China Statistical Yearbook*

state-owned enterprises, public institutions, and quasi-public institutions have pooled talents by virtue of their policy supports, government controls, high salaries and generous welfare, but their inefficiency has led to human capital misallocation.

As China entered the middle- and high-income development stage, its urbanization rate exceeded 55%, with the emergence of characteristics unlike those of the industrialization period, and the "structural frictions" appeared due to the incompatibility of the previous motivation system with the previous demand. The three most prominent frictions are as follows: (1) The level of "science, education, culture and health," information services, and urban public service facilities cannot meet the needs of scientific and technological innovation and the people's increasing spiritual needs and the consumption needs of urbanization. The mismatch between the demand and supply is fully reflected in such phenomena as the difficulty in enrolling in schools, the difficulty in visiting doctors, the occupation of mainstream channels by "weird TV dramas," the difficulty in parking, and the after-rain flooding in Beijing, Shanghai and Shenzhen. The sectors with insufficient supply are all sectors in the third or fourth category, and more of them are sectors that are largely made up of public institutions. (2) There is severe overcapacity in the heavy chemical sectors. Heavy chemical overcapacity resulted from government policy support during industrialization. Selective financing, industrial policies, and regional chain extension strategies were the core policies and theories that fueled the development of heavy industry, which complemented China's VAT-based incentive model. However, at present, the enterprises with severe overcapacity have not reduced the excessive capacity under the support of the government and banks, and many of them have become "zombie" enterprises. (3) Housing prices are rising, the overall labor productivity efficiency and TFP contribution is declining, and the resources have been over-allocated to the real estate sector. The profitability level and labor productivity of enterprises are directly lowered as a result of regulatory controls and high operating costs. Enterprises have increasingly found it difficult to accumulate revenues to support research and development for innovation.

The mechanism for distributing benefits among the four categories of sectors in the dynamic competition process has led to the inevitable lack of innovation impetus. Despite the economic slowdown, policy-supported enterprises can increase their debt ratios instead of being cleaned up by the market, thus leading to the emergence of many "zombie" enterprises. However, small enterprises and private sectors, which are more market-based, are facing the risk of bankruptcy at all times. The government-subsidized sectors can cover the shortfall of financial subsidies by raising prices, so that the overall costs of society are raised. The public institutions can maintain stable by relying on the state to raise taxes, regardless of the economic environment, so that the overall costs of the market are raised. In essence, these subsidies or taxes undermine the competitiveness of the market-based sectors. Therefore, the inefficient non-market-based sectors can still survive well during the slowdown, while the consequences of the slowdown are all absorbed by the market-based sectors, which drives further concentration of human capital to the inefficient sectors and makes innovation impossible. This institutional structure is not only detrimental to the elimination of inefficient sectors by the economic slowdown, but also, more importantly, does not stimulate innovation and optimize human resources.

The spatial agglomeration and innovation activities of enterprises in cities are based on the "horizontally linked agglomeration and innovation model," including the innovation mechanisms of face-to-face communication, labor mobility, entrepreneurial agglomeration and college knowledge spillover. This model is quite different from the original vertically integrated agglomeration powered by industrialization. The profits of innovation can be obtained as long as the institutional division fence can be surmounted. Whether for the resource allocation model based on government intervention or for various economic entities such as financial enterprises, technological innovation enterprises, internet companies, vocational training institutions, development zones and even hospitals, there is an urgent need for institutional reforms to break down the divisions, improve production efficiency and promote innovation development.

## 3.3 TFP Increase Through Reforms

Based on the previous analysis, the TFP and human capital factors are essential to offset the risk of excessive slowdown and to make growth sustainable. However, the problem is that the "vertical" intervention system during the traditional catching-up period has blocked the pathway for technological progress and human capital accumulation, and the slowdown trend inherent in the factor-driven or extensional growth model cannot be compensated for by efficiency, thus raising the urgency of slowdown governance. System changes are at the core of slowdown governance, while the key to slowdown governance is the cleanup mechanism, or "disruptive creation." We should gradually reduce and remove barriers to innovation and human capital accumulation through institutional reforms, while correcting the behaviors of micro-entities and forming a slowdown governance mechanism based on "horizontal" market competition and incentives. We should accelerate stock adjustments to release economic vitality, cushion the negative impacts of the economic slowdown, and improve resource allocation efficiency. In the new round of technological revolution, we should improve China's productivity and innovation level, and smoothly push China's economy from a high-speed growth stage to an efficient growth stage.

### *3.3.1 Changing from a "Vertical" Government Intervention System to a "Horizontal" Market Competition Mechanism*

The vertically divided government intervention and resource allocation system is a product of both the industrialization catching-up period and a long-standing problem that has plagued China's economic reforms. The key to the change is that (1) the government should reform itself, transform its functions, effectively streamline administration and decentralize power, and completely separate government functions from enterprise management. (2) The market should be allowed to play a decisive role, thus promoting the formation of a unified market in China as soon as possible. The focus should be on solving the problem of higher-level opening (i.e., the opening of factor markets) and the problem of fragmentation in areas such as capital markets, human mobility, infrastructure, and information. The status quo of the "division by strips and blocks" has affected the efficiency of resource allocation in space and also protected backwardness, thus making the inter-regional trade volume decrease or shrink. However, a unified, open, competitive and orderly market system can not only make social circulation more efficient to benefit both producers and consumers, but also stimulate the potential of domestic demands despite the structural adjustment and transformation at an accelerated pace in the context of the current economic slowdown. (3) We should strengthen the rule of law and improve the series of standard systems and regulations to regulate the order of the market economy. In this regard, it is crucial for the government itself to abide by the law.

Fundamentally, the emphasis and essence of marketization are government reforms, breaking the administrative system divided by strips and blocks, streamlining administration and decentralizing power, and returning benefits to the people. For this purpose, there are two measures: (1) the fiscally-supported staff as a percentage of GDP; and (2) macro taxation. In China, about 10 people are fiscally supported per USD one million of GDP, equivalent to 10 times that in Japan and more than five times that in the US and Germany. When it comes to streamlining administration and decentralizing power, we should not only simplify the approval procedures, but more importantly, reduce the people behind the administration and power. If these people are not reduced, we will certainly go back to the old path of "setting jobs for people." Over the past three decades, the Chinese government has launched seven rounds of institutional reforms in an attempt to streamline its huge fiscally-supported staff, but each effort has suffered a strong backlash, ultimately resulting in larger institutions, more officials, and greater power after the reforms. Even though the government institutions are streamlined, the civil servants who are laid off eventually find positions in public institutions. The public sectors and public institutions except for Party Caucus, Labor Union, Communist Youth League, and Women's Federation have increasingly expanded, and the total number of fiscally-supported staff has not decreased in the end. Currently, China's macro taxation has reached 35% to 40% and there seems no sign of tax reduction, which indicates that the government's decentralization to the market is insufficient. In the face of the economic slowdown, it has become very urgent for China to reorganize all kinds of relationships through stock reforms, and to shift from a "vertical" government intervention system to a "horizontal" market competition mechanism. Only when the power is decentralized can the market truly move forward.

### 3.3.2 *Drawing on International Experience to Promote Stock Reforms*

There is plenty of international experience on stock reforms worth learning from, such as the South Korean experience. South Korea adopted an economic catching-up strategy and developed an accompanying government-motivated market system to take full advantage of the demographic dividend at that time. However, upon completion of industrialization in the 1980s, South Korea began to face the danger of losing its economic growth impetus and was therefore forced to make a change in its growth pattern. This was because, on the one hand, foreign companies were increasingly reluctant to transfer their core technologies to South Korea, resulting in a sharp increase in the costs of technology introduction, and, on the other hand, South Korea lost its comparative advantage in terms of cheap skilled workers as the demographic dividend disappeared after the early 1980s, making it urgent to develop its own technological capabilities. With the Asian financial crisis in 1998, South Korea found an opportunity to make a real change in its economic growth.

Under the pressure of the crisis, it accepted the reform package proposed by the International Monetary Fund (IMF) and fully liberalized its capital markets, foreign direct investment and trade to become an almost completely open economy, thus ensuring a more stable and transparent business environment for enterprises and reshaping a fair and competitive market environment. The more competitive market environment can not only increase labor market elasticity and reduce the labor costs of innovation, but also stimulate enterprises of different sizes, including newly established SMEs, to participate in technological progress, thus creating favorable conditions for innovation spillovers to take effect. Using the micro data of 216 South Korean enterprises in 1985–2007, Taegi Kim and Keun-Yeob Oh (2012) confirmed that knowledge growth, as measured by levels of R&D expenditures and the increase in the number of patents, had a significant positive effect on the TFP of South Korean manufacturing enterprises during this period. After the post-crisis market-oriented reforms, South Korea achieved some success in transforming its economic growth and made a smooth transition into an advanced economy.

In the process of deepening reform, China must adjust the interest structure that already exists in China and reform the stock. Currently, one of the efforts in this regard is the market-oriented reform of the public sectors and public institutions. We should break the monopoly of resources and power, change the priority of the provision of public goods, build an open, competitive and fair order and environment, improve supply capacity and service efficiency, and activate market demands and consumption potential. Another effort is to revitalize stock assets. Currently, China has a lot of stock assets, but maturity mismatch, structural mismatch and directional mismatch have led to a huge amount of non-performing assets, idle assets and sunken assets. In particular, after the global financial crisis and since the economic slowdown, the Chinese government, enterprises and individuals have been leveraging up in order to maintain growth. This is an important reason for the current inefficient economic growth, financial inefficiency and high fiscal and financial risks. Only by accelerating de-leveraging, cleaning up debts and non-performing stock assets, and revitalizing the stock assets that flow into the virtual economy or overcapacity areas and turn into non-performing assets can China's economy move forward.

### *3.3.3 Removing Structural Barriers to Capital Allocation*

In terms of physical capital, excessive capital in China has gone into government-led sectors such as raw materials and heavy industrial sectors, as well as real estate and physical infrastructure sectors, resulting in the prominent phenomenon of inefficient capital allocation. While China's society-wide capital stock per capita is still well below that of South Korea in the 1980s, many industries have become over-invested. Under the government-led investment and financing system, the restricted access to finance and capital controls resulted in the state-owned sectors absorbing large amounts of capital and the private productive sectors facing severe financing limitations, which led to a coexistence of low returns in the capital market and high financing costs for the private sectors (Song, et al., 2011). Therefore, we must remove structural barriers to capital allocation, realize the free flow of capital among production sectors, and bring into play the role of capital in enhancing the production efficiency of the industrial manufacturing sectors, so that we can provide the necessary capital accumulation for China's future structural changes. The key to this process is the transition from the bank-dominated indirect market to the capital market. The bank-dominated approach to resource allocation, based largely on corporate mortgages, was very conducive to the economies of scale during the catching-up period. However, as we enter the innovation era, this approach has prevented many asset-light innovative enterprises from being financed and instead requires the capacity-discounted equity market to complete financing. China is actively transforming itself, but this transformation requires a series of reforms based on the rule of law. Without a strong legal system, there will be no guarantee that the equity market, which is discounted by future expectations, will play its role in allocating resources.

### *3.3.4 Reallocation and Effective Use of Human Capital*

The misallocation of human capital hinders the effective use of human capital. A large number of laborers with college degrees or above have entered and been employed in the service sectors, mainly in the public institutions related to science, education, culture and health, and in the highly-regulated sectors related to telecommunications, finance, transport and public services. However, the systems and controls in the public institutions have constrained the production efficiency of human capital, resulting in a phenomenon that not only the average education level of the whole society is low but also some industries are over-educated. The relatively low allocation of human capital in productive sectors has hindered the upgrading of industrial structure and the improvement of economic growth quality. In addition, the concentration of human capital in non-market-based sectors has undermined the remuneration level of human capital, thus discouraging residents from investing in human capital. It is not conducive to the development of modern service sectors and the promotion of structural changes. Therefore, we must make reforms in public institutions, regulatory reforms in modern service sectors such as telecommunications and finance sectors, and regulatory reforms in public service sectors, so as to attract social capital to the service sectors, optimize the allocation of human capital, increase the market-oriented degree of human capital pricing, and ultimately improve the mechanism that drives economic growth and structural changes.

### 3.3.5 Opening up New Space for Knowledge Production and Consumption in Science, Education, Culture and Health Sectors Through System Changes

Along with the development of urbanization and the increase of residents' income level, the proportion of material consumption in people's total consumption has been decreasing while the proportion of service sectors has been increasing. After 2014, the share of service sectors in China overtook the share of the secondary sector, and in 2015, this share is still growing. Tertiarization has gradually become an economic trend in China, but the supply and demand of the service sectors do not match, with high growth and low efficiency coexisting in the service sectors. The knowledge production related to broad human capital is limited by traditional systems, and China lacks a market-based impetus for knowledge innovation. It is reflected in the following aspects: (1) Inefficiency. In other words, both the general production service sectors (e.g. warehousing and logistics) and the low-level life service sectors (e.g. restaurants) are market-based sectors with considerable competition and declining profits, so they are no longer the future development direction of the service sectors. However, at the current stage, human resources can only be allocated in this direction, and accordingly, the phenomenon of excessive market demand (e.g., young people dropping out of school to work in cities) has surfaced. It is not conducive to the development of human resources and revenue sharing in China, and also not conducive to innovation and continuous efficiency improvement. (2) The new growth space of service sectors is governed as public institutions in fiscally-subsidized or fully funded sectors under the traditional catching-up system, so the modern service sectors such as science, education, culture and health sectors cannot meet the market demands. (3) The knowledge production sectors such as science, education, culture and health sectors, which relate to the consumption of broad human capital, have not been stimulated by the market, their innovation incentives are insufficient, and the concentration of a large number of talents in these sectors has prevented them from having a social effect. Therefore, China lacks the most valuable factors needed for both urbanization and knowledge economy. For innovation and efficiency improvement, we are in urgent need of system changes to open up the modern service sectors' development space that has been held down by our institution. There is no time like the present to reform the management system of the science, education, culture and health sectors. Only in this way can China move towards innovation and gain a new competitive advantage in the international game.

# Chapter 4
# Measurement of Reform Dividend and Priority Areas for Reform

**Lu Yang and Cai Fang**

**Abstract** In contrast to other research findings, we argue that the disappearance of the demographic dividend, characterized by a declining working age population and an increasing population dependency ratio, is the main cause of China's declining potential growth rate. Therefore, as China's demographic dividend gradually disappears, the reform dividend will become a key driver of China's economic growth. By simulating possible reform areas within the growth calculation equation, we have the following findings: (1) Both the increase in labor force participation rate and TFP can boost the potential growth rate, but the effects are different in the short and long term (i.e., the labor force participation rate has a stronger short-term effect and a decreasing long-term effect; while the TFP has a monotonically increasing effect on growth. It reveals that China's economic growth will rely more on TFP increases rather than traditional factor inputs. (2) Unlike the diminishing effect of increasing education rates on growth, increasing human capital by means of training can significantly boost the potential growth rate. If each employee has the opportunity for one-year training and further studies after every 10 years of service, China's potential growth rate will increase by 0.3 to 0.4 percentage points. (3) By relaxing its population fertility policy, China will increase its long-term potential growth rate while improving its demographic structure. (4) Comprehensive reforms will result in an average of 1–2 percentage points of future reform dividend for China.

## 4.1 Introduction

From 1978 to 2011, China's economy achieved an average annual real growth rate of 9.8%, ranking as the best growth performance in the world during the same period. The World Bank and the IMF estimated that China would overtake the US as the world's largest economy in terms of economic aggregate measured by purchasing power parity (PPP) by about 2014 or 2015 (IMF 2014). However, China's economic growth rate began to decrease dramatically in 2012, and this decrease is widely

---

L. Yang (✉) · C. Fang
Institute of Population and Labor Economics, Chinese Academy of Social Sciences, Beijing, China

 
X. Zhang (ed.), *Exploration on China's Economic System Reform under New Normal of Development*, https://doi.org/10.1007/978-981-95-2461-7_4

recognized by authorities and economists as a trend of the "new normal." At that time, there were different and divergent opinions about China's future economic growth forecasts, and the fundamental reason was that there was no consensus on the causes of the slowdown after 2012, given China's rapid growth after its reform and opening-up.

Generally, the forecasts of economic growth rates are often based on a methodology. Of course, the commonly used methodology is the traditional extrapolation method, in which the past growth rates are used to extrapolate the future growth rates. For example, Robert William Fogel (Fogel 2009), an American economist, listed a number of factors that China had shown to be conducive to its economic growth and forecasted that in 2040 China's economic aggregate, when measured by PPP, will reach USD 123.7 trillion, representing 40% of the world's total GDP and 2.95 times that of the US. Based on the forecasted population of China and the US, China's GDP per capita will also exceed that of the US by that time.

A fundamental problem with this methodology for forecasting economic growth is that it does not take into account the fact that different countries are at different stages of economic development and that many developing countries will witness changes in their development stages, and thus a number of parameters that affect the growth rate will also change. For this reason, it can be found that the more developed countries grow at a slower rate, while the catching-up countries can achieve a faster growth rate. With the arrival of Lewis turning point in 2004, which was characterized by labor shortages and increasing wages, and the disappearance of the demographic dividend in 2011, when the working age population began to grow negatively, China has undergone a substantial change in its economic development stage. Therefore, the traditional forecasting methodology can no longer accurately tell China's future economic growth rate.

Some noteworthy studies based on different methodologies have emerged in the recent literature as a modification of the above-mentioned traditional methodology. At the forefront are the forecasts of China's economic growth rate based on the "convergence" hypothesis of economic growth. Based on the convergence hypothesis of the neoclassical growth theory and the hypothesis of the latecomer advantage theory, these studies have used GDP per capita as a reference standard and compared China's current situation with that of other developed economies (especially that of East Asian economies) for a specific period of time to forecast the growth rate that China may achieve in a similar period in the future. For example, China's GDP per capita in 2008 was only 21% of that of the US, while based on the experience of some forerunner countries and regions (including Japan, which reached a similar level of development in 1950, Singapore, which reached a similar level of development in 1966, Taiwan region of China, which reached a similar level of development in 1975, and South Korea, which reached a similar level of development in 1976), it was found that all these economies achieved high rates of economic growth approximately 20 years after they reached the similar levels, and therefore these studies expected that China could rely on its latecomer advantage to achieve a high rate of catching up as well (Lin Yifu 2013).

The forecast results based on this methodology are informative as an expectation of the potential economic growth, but they have not told us what "potential" factors are included in the results and how to explore such factors. As a result, the forecast results often lead to the misconception that China can achieve such growth rates unconditionally. These economic growth forecasts based on the convergence hypothesis have certainly remedied the defect of the traditional extrapolation method which failed to take into account the changes in economic development stages, but they also have methodological flaws by treating GDP per capita as the only criterion for economic development stages. Since what we are considering is the potential rate of economic growth, it is obvious that GDP per capita alone cannot fully characterize the development stage of an economy. In particular, the demographic transition must be taken into account when comparisons are made with East Asian economies, which have been known for their demographic dividend for economic growth. For example, if the demographic transition point at which the working age population stops growing and the dependency ratio turns from a downward trend to an upward trend is taken as a reference standard, China's current development stage is roughly equivalent to that of Japan in the early 1990s, since when Japan's GDP has grown at an average annual rate of less than one percentage point.

Recently, an influential forecast of China's economic growth is based on a statistical rule called "regression to the mean." This statistical rule holds that any unusually strong economic growth will eventually return to the world average. According to this statistical rule, some scholars estimated that China's average annual growth rate would be only 5.01% in 2013–2023 and further decrease to 3.28% in 2023–2033 (Pritchett and Summers 2014). However, the fancy rule used in these forecasts is at best a statistical phenomenon and cannot be applied to all countries, so it is difficult to make a scientific and reasonable economic explanation for the slowdown derived from these forecasts. The forecasts of a significant slowdown in China may be justified by the disappearance of China's demographic dividend, but it does not make sense, at least in theory, to use this rule of "regression to the mean" to forecast a slowdown in India, a country that is still in the stage of harvesting the demographic dividend. Goldman Sachs, for example, predicted that India's economy would grow faster than China's in 2016–2018 (Kong Jun 2014).

Another highly cited study (Eichengreen et al. 2011) is based on a similar methodology and seems to provide an analysis of the reasons for the slowdown, which fills the gap in the previous studies. This study argues that the high growth rate comes to an end at a particular level of economic development. Based on extensive data on countries, the authors of the study found that in general, when the GDP per capita measured by PPP in 2005 reached USD 17,000, the high economic growth rate came to an end and there was a significant slowdown from an average growth rate of 6.8% in the past seven years to an average growth rate of 3.3% in the next seven years. Since China is expected to reach this threshold in 2015, the slowdown in China's future growth rate is predictable. Despite the authors' many analyses (especially for China) regarding the causes of the slowdown, this statistical study has also failed to find a consistent explanation for the slowdown because it includes a large number of countries at different stages of development.

As a matter of fact, how we interpret the high growth rate in the past will inevitably affect the analysis of the current economic growth slowdown and the expectation of the future economic growth rate. In contrast to the above study methods, we argue that the demographic dividend has been an important driver of China's high economic growth over the past 30 years. According to our calculations, China's demographic dividend has contributed to a quarter of its high economic growth as the working age population increased, the dependency ratio decreased, and educational attainment increased. However, following the demographic changes, China's demographic dividend is gradually diminishing, and there will even be a "demographic onus" in the future. It can be concluded that it is the end of the demographic dividend that causes the slowdown of China's high economic growth since 2012.

In the economics literature, the demographic dividend is usually defined as the positive effects of specific demographic characteristics on economic growth. Specifically, when a country sees a decline in the population dependency ratio and a rise in the working age population, the supply of factors required for economic growth (e.g. labor) will increase rapidly, the returns on capital will remain high, and the labor migration will bring about efficiency in resource reallocation, thus creating a demographic dividend for the growth of an economy. In fact, economic development leads to three stages of population growth: (1) the stage of "high birth rate, high mortality rate, and low growth rate"; (2) the stage of "high birth rate, low mortality rate, and high growth rate"; and (3) the stage of "low birth rate, low mortality rate, and low growth rate." The demographic dividend usually occurs during the transition from the second to the third stage. According to the historical experience of many countries, a particular stage of their economic development was usually accompanied by a demographic dividend (Williamson 1997).

With the advent of an era characterized by low birth rates, a demographic transition will be inevitable. After that, the demographic dividend will eventually disappear as the absolute working age population decreases and the population dependency ratio rises. It should be noted that the demographic dividend disappears mainly in the form of a decrease in the supply of production factors, especially the absolute supply of laborers; meanwhile, the marginal rewards of other production factors diminish; in addition, the TFP growth rate decreases when the agricultural laborers no longer continuously migrate to cities. Therefore, when a country's demographic dividend disappears, its potential growth rate decreases as well.

In 2011, China's working age population aged between 15 and 59 began to decline, and in 2013, China's working age population aged between 15 and 64 also began to decline, with a corresponding increase in the population dependency ratio. According to Cai and Lu (2013b) and the estimates of Lu Yang and Cai Fang (2014), China's potential economic growth rate will gradually decline to a level of 6–7% over the next decade from the previous level of around 10%. It's clearly not a phenomenon unique to China. In an empirical analysis that used multi-country data, Eichengreen et al. (2011) found that when the income per capita reached USD 17,000 (based on 2005 constant international prices, PWT 6.3 data), the real economic growth rate would drop sharply by at least 2 percentage points. Based on this, China may see an economic slowdown around 2015. However, they pointed out in their study that a number of economic factors could delay or advance the point of slowdown. One of these factors is that higher aged dependency ratios may increase the likelihood of economic growth slowdown, as higher aged dependency ratios are associated with lower savings rates and slower labor force participation rates. For China, the characteristic of "getting old before getting rich" will undoubtedly lead to an early slowdown in economic growth. Nonetheless, Eichengreen et al. (2011) also emphasized that the economic slowdown was not an inexorable law, the relationship between income per capita and economic slowdown could not be mechanical, and how long the high economic growth rate could be maintained also depended on economic policies. For example, such countries and regions as Argentina, Hong Kong region of China, Ireland, Israel, Norway, Portugal, and Singapore have witnessed another period of rapid economic growth through economic reforms.

We know that the increase in the supply of production factors and TFP is hindered by the institutions. Therefore, removing these hindrances through reforms will facilitate the increase of the potential growth rate. The greater institutional hindrances and the more thorough reforms will lead to more significant effects on increasing the potential growth rate. This is called the "reform dividend." In this paper, we will simulate the possible effects of various institutional reforms on economic growth. In other words, we will use the growth calculation equation to model the extent to which the potential growth rate can be increased by reform measures and which reform measures are more effective in the short and long run. Finally, we intend to answer two questions: (1) After the demographic dividend disappears, how can China shift from the demographic dividend to the reform dividend to sustain long-term economic growth? (2) To what extent China's reform dividend will contribute to economic growth? The overall structure of this paper is as follows: Sect. 4.2 focuses on the theoretical logic of the reform dividend. Section 4.3 presents the model and specific methodology for estimating the reform dividend, based on which we will estimate the size and long- and short-term effects of the reform dividend by mainly estimating the growth effects resulting from relaxing the population fertility policy, increasing the education years and training, raising the labor force participation rate, and increasing the TFP. Section 4.4 provides policy recommendations including key areas of reform and reform priorities based on the reform dividend estimation results.

## 4.2 Theoretical Logic of Reform Dividend

Empirically, it has been confirmed that the disappearance of the demographic dividend would affect the potential growth rate. For example, Louis Kuijs (Kuijs 2010) predicted that China's potential GDP growth rate would decrease from an average of 9.9% in 1978–1994 to an average of 9.6% in 1995–2009 and 8.4% in 2010–2015, although he did not specifically emphasize the role of demographic factors. Given the changed demographic structure, Cai and Lu (2013a) argue that China's potential growth rate will decline from 10% in the previous period to 7.3% in the 12th Five-Year Plan period (2011–2015) after the demographic dividend disappears. If the human capital factor, the impact of the population dependency ratio on the capital formation rate, as well as the impact of demographic changes on the labor force participation rate and the natural unemployment rate are taken into account, China's potential growth rate will be 7.75% on average during the 12th Five-Year Plan period (2011–2015) (Lu Yang and Cai Fang 2014). However, this estimate is based on the fact that labor supply continues declining and the assumption that the TFP growth rate remains constant. In other words, it is an estimate of the impact of changes in the demographic dividend factors on China's future potential growth rate under the assumption that the institutional hindrances to the supply of factors and the rise in productivity have not been broken. However, the potential growth rate can also be increased by reforming the labor supply and labor quality, etc. Besides, if the institutional hindrances that prevent full competition are removed and the TFP is increased, there is a possibility that China's potential growth rate will further increase in the future.

Much of the discussion on China's reforms suggests that there is a trade-off relationship between China's reforms and its economic growth rate, which means that reforms will be promoted at some sacrifice of the economic growth rate. However, another view is that the reforms will support economic growth. According to the institutional change theory, an institutional change usually occurs only when the benefits of such a change outweigh the costs (i.e. the net benefits are greater than zero). Of course, this theory aims to determine the political costs and benefits associated with the implementation of reforms considered by policymakers, i.e. whether the political support (benefits) generated by reforms outweighs the political opposition (costs). Generally, if the benefits outweigh the costs in an economic sense, it makes a strong case for convincing policymakers to implement a particular reform. It can be said that the effects of China's reforms in the relevant areas are very similar to this theory. The reforms that are designed to increase the resource allocation efficiency, improve income distribution, and enhance the equalization of basic public services not only serve the goal of a more equitable society, but also can bring direct and indirect reform dividend. Specifically, if we know the reasons for the current slowdown in China's economic growth, we can also expect which areas of reforms will have a direct effect on increasing the potential growth rate, as well as other indirect effects that will benefit economic growth.

The correct understanding of the benefits or the reform dividend that reforms can deliver is not only essential for the formation and building of reform consensus, but also can increase the options of reform approaches and strategies and strengthen the reform impetus. Despite the net benefits of reforms, both costs and benefits are asymmetrically apportioned among parties. For maximizing the incentive compatibility of reforms, there are usually two approaches: (1) "Pareto improvement," in which the reforms can be promoted without harming any vested interests; and (2) "Kaldor-Hicks improvement," in which, although some parties are harmed by the reforms, we can take a portion of the large net benefits of the reforms to compensate the harmed parties. The current reform tasks are rarely characterized by "Pareto improvement," but if we recognize and capture the reform benefits, the "Kaldor improvement" can be appropriately applied to reduce the reform resistance. In this chapter, the simulation results will show that the reform can generally bring benefits and directly increase the potential growth rate. China's reforms are "boosting" rather than "substituting for" the economic growth rate. This is exactly the economic rationale behind Premier Li Keqiang's statement that "we should obtain growth momentum from deepening reforms."

## 4.3 Simulation of Reform Dividend

### *4.3.1 Model*[1]

We use the production function method (PF) to estimate the potential GDP growth rate. We add the human capital stock to the standard Cobb-Douglass production function.

$$Y = AK^{\alpha}(hL)^{1-\alpha} \tag{4.1}$$

Specifically, Y represents the real GDP, A represents the TFP, K represents the capital stock (estimated using the perpetual inventory method based on historical capital formation), L represents the number of workers, and h represents the human capital, and Y/hL is obtained by dividing both sides of the equation by hL.

$$Y/hL = A(K/hL)^{\alpha} \tag{4.2}$$

The average labor productivity Y/hL after adding the human capital level (subsequently expressed by y) is a function of the TFP A and the capital-to-labor ratio K/hL after adding the human capital ( subsequently expressed by k), thus $y = Ak^{1-\alpha}$. By taking derivatives of both sides simultaneously for time t, the capital contribution factor $\alpha$ and labor contribution factor $(1 - \alpha)$ can be obtained through an estimation in Eq. (4.2).

$$\Delta y_t / y_{t-1} = \Delta A_t / A_{t-1} + \Delta k_t / k_{t-1} + \varepsilon_{t-n} \tag{4.3}$$

We substitute the estimated value α, the growth rate of capital-to-labor ratio $(\Delta k_t/k_{t-1})$ and the average labor productivity growth rate ($\Delta y_t/y_{t-1}$) in previous years into the Eq. (4.3) and obtain $\Delta \hat{A_t}/A_{t-1} + \varepsilon_t = \Delta y_t/y_{t-1} - \alpha\Delta k_t/k_{t-1}$, which is the TFP including the residual term εt. We remove the random disturbance factor $\varepsilon t$ by using the HP filtering method and finally estimate the TFP growth rate in previous years $(\Delta \hat{A_t}/A_{t-1})$. The result from the above process is identical to the TFP growth rate calculated using the Solow residual method in the literature.

[1] ①For the model sectors, we used the same approach as that of Lu Yang and Cai Fang (2014).

Based on the basic model parameters, the potential GDP growth rate is calculated by substituting the number of jobs at "full employment" *(i.e.* $Lt^*$*)*, and $Lt^* = population_{15+,t} \times Tr_{15+,t} \times (1 - NAI\text{-}RU_{15+,t})$. Specifically, $population_{15+,t}$ represents the population aged 15 or above in China in year t, and $Tr_{15+,t}$ means the potential labor force participation rate of the population aged 15 or above (obtained with HP filtering). Therefore, $population_{15+,t} \times Tr_{15+,t}$ means the potential economically active population aged 15 or above. $NAIRU_{15+,t}$ is the natural unemployment rate, and the potential employment $L_t^*$ can be calculated based on the population aged 15 or above, the potential labor force participation rate, and the natural unemployment rate.

We can calculate the average potential capital-to-labor ratio growth rate of the additional human capital $\Delta k_t^*/k^*_{t-1}$ and the average potential labor productivity growth rate of the additional human capital $\Delta y_t^*/y^*_{t-1}$ by substituting $h_tL_t^*$ into the model. Therefore, $\Delta y_t^*/y^*_{t-1} = \Delta A_t^{\wedge}/A_{t-1} + \widehat{\alpha}\, \Delta k^*_t/k^*_{t-1}$, in which $k_t^* = K_t/h_tL_t^*$, $y_t^* = Y_t^*/h_tL_t^*$, and $Y_t^*$ is the potential GDP in year t. With the known $\Delta y_t^*/y_{t-1}^*$ and $h_tL_t^*$, the following identical equation can be derived

$$\Delta Y_t^* / Y_{t-1}^* = \left(\Delta y_t^* / y_{t-1}^* + 1\right) \times \left(h_t L_t^* / h_{t-1} L_{t-1}^*\right) - 1 \tag{4.4}$$

Specifically, $\Delta Y_t^*/Y^*_{t-1}$ is the potential GDP growth rate in year t. It is obvious from the model that the potential GDP growth rate is influenced by four factors: the potential capital-to-labor ratio growth rate of the additional human capital, the potential employment growth rate, the human capital growth rate, and the TFP growth rate. It is worth noting that demographic changes will affect the first three factors directly or indirectly, while the TFP growth rate is largely related to institutional factors, such as migration system, household registration system, and technological progress.

## 4.3.2 *Data Sources*

### 4.3.2.1 GDP and Capital Stock

The data for real GDP and real capital stock K (in USD, based on 2005 constant prices) are from the Penn World Table (PWT8.0). However, as we do not know the value of China's capital stock in 2011–2050, we use the perpetual inventory method to estimate the future capital stock, i.e., $K_t = I_t + (1 - \delta_t) K_{t-1}$, in which $K_t$ is the actual capital stock in year t; $K_{t-1}$ is the actual capital stock in year t-1; $I_t$ is the actual capital formation in year t; and $\delta_t$ is the capital depreciation rate of 5% in year t. It can be seen from the equation that the current capital stock is determined by a combination of the initial capital stock and the new capital formation in subsequent years.

The capital formation rate (i.e., capital formation as a percentage of GDP) varies from country to country and depends on the stage of economic development, demographics, and "habits" of a country. Here, we assume that the capital formation rate is a function of the population dependency ratio. Specifically, a rise in a country's population dependency ratio implies a relative increase in the dependent population (young children aged 15 or below and older people aged 65 or above), which, in terms of the expenditure method for measuring the GDP, also means that the proportion of consumption in the new wealth created each year (GDP) will rise and the capital formation rate (and savings rate) will decrease. Therefore, based on historical data, we find the following correlation between the two: $C_t=62.733–0.399D_{t\text{-}1}$, where $C_t$ is the current period's capital formation as a percentage of the previous year's GDP and $D_{t\text{-}1}$ is the total population dependency ratio with a one-year lag. The historical data on the capital formation rate is obtained from the WDI database. As a final step, we calculate the population dependency ratio using the forecasted population data by age and gender and further forecast China's capital formation rate for 2011–2050.

#### 4.3.2.2 Potential Employment

The population and employment data for China from 1980 to 2010 is obtained from the *China Statistical Yearbook*. The forecasted population data by age and gender for 2011–2050 is from Guo Zhigang (2013). Based on the historical data, we can calculate the labor force participation rate of China's population aged 15 or above (i.e., the ratio of the economically active population to the total population aged 15 or above) in 1980–2010, and the natural unemployment rate for the same period is obtained from the estimation results of Du Yang and Lu Yang (2011). The potential employment is determined by three factors: the population aged 15 or above, the labor force participation rate, and the natural unemployment rate, so $L_t^*=population_{15+,t} \times Tr_{15+,t} \times (1-NAIRU_{15+,t})$.

In fact, both the labor force participation rate and the natural unemployment rate are functions of population ages, which means the trends in the labor force participation rate and the natural unemployment rate when the demographic structure changes and other factors remain unchanged. Therefore, the values of labor force participation rate and natural unemployment rate in China for 2011–2050 are calculated based on the labor force participation rate and natural unemployment rate by age and gender in China in 2010 and the population size by age and gender forecasted by Guo Zhigang (2013). The resulting equation for China's potential employment in 2011–2050 is as follows:

$$L_{i,t}^* = \sum_{n=16}^{n=95} population_{n,i,t} \times Part_{n,i,t} \times \left(1 - NAIRU_{n,i,t}\right)(i = 1, 2;\ 16 \le n \le 95)$$

$$L_t^* = \sum_{i=1}^{i=2} L_{i,t}^* \tag{4.5}$$

Specifically, $n$ represents age ($16 \le n \le 95$) and i represents gender ($i = 1$ for male and $i = 2$ for female); population$_{n,i,t}$ is the population of males (or females) aged n in year t; $Part_{n,i,t}$ is the labor force participation rate of males (or females) aged n in year t; $NAIRU_{n,i,t}$ is the natural unemployment rate of males (or females) aged n in year t; $L^*_{i,t}$ is the number of the potential employment of males or females in year t; and $L^*_t$ is the potential employed population in China in year t.

#### 4.3.2.3 Human Capital

The human capital data is obtained from the human capital index hc provided in Penn World Table (PWT 8.0), and this index is an adjustment of the average education years by Barro and Lee (2012) based on the rate of return to education estimated by Psacharopoulos (1994). We add the average education years at 5-year intervals in 2015–2050 using a similar approach to Barro and Lee (2012), and then add the average education years and the human capital index for 2011–2050 using an average trend approach.

### 4.3.3 Simulation Results

#### 4.3.3.1 Short-Term and Long-Term Effects of Population Fertility Policy Relaxation

In demography, the total fertility rate (TFR), or the average number of children per woman of childbearing age, is commonly used to measure the birth rate of a country. This index determines the total population and demographic structure of a country in the future. According to historical experience, when the economic development of a country goes beyond a certain stage, the people will change their concept of marriage and childbirth, and in general, gradually delay the age of marriage and childbirth with fewer births, resulting in a continuous decline in the birth rate. When the TFR decreases below 2.1, it means that the population size of the new generation cannot replace the population size of the old generation and the total population will decrease sooner or later. This is a common phenomenon in the economic development process, for example, in European countries and in Japan and South Korea in Asia. Unlike those in other countries, the demographic changes in China are influenced not only by its economic development, but also to a large extent by its unique one-child policy. According to international experience, even without the constraints of the population fertility policy, China's fertility rate will decrease sooner or later, but the process will be slow. The growth effect generated from the "demographic dividend" and the "demographic burden" will diminish.

In our forecasts of China's potential growth rate for 2011–2050, we assume that the TFP remains unchanged, while other factors of production, including capital, labor, and human capital, change with demographic structure. In other words, the forecasted future population size by age and gender in China directly affects the potential growth rate. As a matter of fact, the future population is forecasted based on reality. Different TFRs will lead to different forecasts of the total population and population size by age and gender. However, under the current two-child fertility policy for couples where either the husband or the wife is from a single-child family, the TFR is theoretically not more than 2.1, which means that the fertility rate is not yet at a replacement level. Therefore, using the data of population size by age and gender as forecasted by Guo Zhigang (2013), we estimate the future trend of potential growth rate in China when the TFR is at the level of 1.6 or 1.77 or even 1.94, respectively. The estimated results are shown in I in Table 4.1, and the basic results of this simulation are the same as those of Lu Yang and Cai Fang (2014).

The impact of population fertility policy relaxation on the potential growth rate differs in the short and long terms. Under the influence of the population fertility policy, new births can only increase the population dependency ratio in the short term, but cannot increase the working age population. As a result, the savings rate will decline, the consumption rate will rise, and the capital formation rate will decline. In the short term, the population fertility policy relaxation can reduce the potential growth rate by reducing the capital supply. However, the newborn population will reach the working age after 15 years, and then the dependency ratio will decline and the labor supply will increase, so in the long term, the population fertility policy relaxation can increase the potential growth rate by increasing the capital and labor supply. This is also the mechanism by which the so-called "baby boom" affects the potential growth rate. Figure 4.1 shows the trends of potential growth rates corresponding to different TFRs. The simulation results are consistent with our theoretical expectations.

Based on this simulation, we further analyze the impacts of the labor force participation rate increase, the human capital level increase, and the TFP increase on the potential growth rate, respectively. Meanwhile, we also present the simulation results for the combination of various policies.

#### 4.3.3.2 Decreasing Effect of Labor Force Participation Rate

The related simulations are shown in Table 4.1 (II) and Table 4.2 (II). The simulation results in II.1 in Table 4.1 show the level of potential growth rate after increasing the labor force participation rate by one percentage point, two percentage points, and five percentage points, respectively, when other factors are held constant under the baseline scenario with TFR = 1.6. II.2 shows the observed level of potential growth rate following an increase in the labor force participation rate under the baseline scenario with TFR = 1.77. It can be seen that an increase in the labor force participation rate will lead to an increase in potential growth rate when TFR = 1.6 and TFR = 1.77. For example, when TFR = 1.6, the average potential growth rate in the 12th Five-Year Plan period (2011–2015) will increase by 0.2 percentage points if the labor force participation rate increases by 1 percentage point per year; and the average potential growth rate in the 12th Five-Year Plan period (2011–2015) will increase by one percentage point if the labor force participation rate increases by 5 percentage points per year. However, what we also find is that although it is possible

**Table 4.1** China's future potential economic growth rate under different policy simulations: 2011–2050 (Unit: %)

| Potential growth rate | | | 2011–2015 | 2016–2020 | 2021–2025 | 2026–2030 | 2031–2035 | 2036–2040 | 2041–2045 | 2046–2050 |
|---|---|---|---|---|---|---|---|---|---|---|
| II | I | Impact of population fertility policy adjustment on potential growth rate: 2011–2050 | | | | | | | | |
| | | TFR=1.6 | 7.73 | 6.64 | 5.87 | 5.40 | 5.05 | 4.60 | 4.17 | 3.84 |
| | | TFR=1.77 | 7.72 | 6.58 | 5.78 | 5.34 | 5.16 | 4.80 | 4.39 | 4.04 |
| | | TFR=1.94 | 7.71 | 6.50 | 5.66 | 5.23 | 5.29 | 5.08 | 4.65 | 4.25 |
| | II | 1. Impact of labor force participation rate increase on potential growth rate when TFR = 1.6: 2011–2050 | | | | | | | | |
| | | 1 percentage point increase | 7.92 | 6.68 | 5.90 | 5.43 | 5.07 | 4.61 | 4.19 | 3.85 |
| | | 2 percentage points increase | 8.11 | 6.71 | 5.93 | 5.45 | 5.09 | 4.63 | 4.20 | 3.86 |
| | | 5 percentage points increase | 8.68 | 6.82 | 6.01 | 5.52 | 5.15 | 4.68 | 4.24 | 3.90 |
| | II | 2. Impact of labor force participation rate increase on potential growth rate based on TFR = 1.77: 2011–2050 | | | | | | | | |
| | | 1 percentage point increase | 7.91 | 6.6 | 5.81 | 5.36 | 5.18 | 4.82 | 4.40 | 4.05 |
| | | 2 percentage points increase | 8.10 | 6.65 | 5.84 | 5.39 | 5.20 | 4.83 | 4.42 | 4.07 |
| | | 5 percentage points increase | 8.67 | 6.76 | 5.92 | 5.46 | 5.26 | 4.88 | 4.45 | 4.10 |
| III | III | 1. Impact of TFP increase on potential growth rate when TFR = 1.6: 2011–2050 | | | | | | | | |
| | | 0.5 percentage points increase | 8.30 | 7.32 | 6.62 | 6.20 | 5.88 | 5.44 | 5.03 | 4.71 |
| | | 1 percentage point increase | 8.87 | 8.01 | 7.37 | 7.00 | 6.72 | 6.30 | 5.90 | 5.59 |
| | III | 2. Impact of TFP increase on potential growth rate when TFR = 1.77: 2011–2050 | | | | | | | | |
| | | 0.5 percentage points increase | 8.28 | 7.26 | 6.52 | 6.13 | 5.99 | 5.65 | 5.25 | 4.92 |
| | | 1 percentage point increase | 8.85 | 7.94 | 7.27 | 6.93 | 6.83 | 6.52 | 6.13 | 5.80 |
| IV | IV | Impact of school enrollment rate increase on potential growth rate: 2011–2050 | | | | | | | | |
| | | TFR=1.6 | 7.84 | 6.73 | 5.94 | 5.47 | 5.11 | 4.64 | 4.20 | 3.86 |
| | | TFR=1.77 | 7.83 | 6.66 | 5.85 | 5.40 | 5.22 | 4.85 | 4.42 | 4.06 |
| V | V | Impact of increased training on potential growth rate: 2011–2050 | | | | | | | | |

(continued)

**Table 4.1** (continued)

| Potential growth rate | | | 2011–2015 | 2016–2020 | 2021–2025 | 2026–2030 | 2031–2035 | 2036–2040 | 2041–2045 | 2046–2050 |
|---|---|---|---|---|---|---|---|---|---|---|
| | | TFR=1.6 | 8.14 | 7.02 | 6.28 | 5.80 | 5.45 | 4.98 | 4.49 | 4.18 |
| | | TFR=1.77 | 8.12 | 6.96 | 6.18 | 5.73 | 5.54 | 5.17 | 4.70 | 4.37 |
| VI | VI | Combined simulation: 1 percentage point increase in labor force participation rate, 1 percentage point increase in TFP, and n increase in school enrollment rate | | | | | | | | |
| | | TFR=1.6 | 9.18 | 8.13 | 7.48 | 7.10 | 6.80 | 6.36 | 5.95 | 5.62 |
| | | TFR=1.77 | 9.16 | 8.06 | 7.38 | 7.03 | 6.91 | 6.58 | 6.18 | 5.83 |
| | | TFR=1.94 | 9.15 | 7.98 | 7.26 | 6.92 | 7.05 | 6.88 | 6.46 | 6.05 |
| VII | VII | Combined simulation: 1 percentage point increase in labor force participation rate, 0.5 percentage points increase in TFP, and an increase in school enrollment rate | | | | | | | | |
| | | TFR=1.6 | 8.60 | 7.45 | 6.72 | 6.29 | 5.96 | 5.51 | 5.08 | 4.74 |
| | | TFR=1.77 | 8.59 | 7.38 | 6.63 | 6.23 | 6.07 | 5.72 | 5.30 | 4.95 |
| | | TFR=1.94 | 8.58 | 7.30 | 6.51 | 6.12 | 6.21 | 6.01 | 5.57 | 5.16 |
| VIII | VIII | Combined simulation: 1 percentage point increase in labor force participation rate, 1 percentage point increase in TFP, and an increase in training | | | | | | | | |
| | | TFR=1.6 | 9.48 | 8.44 | 7.82 | 7.45 | 7.16 | 6.72 | 6.25 | 5.96 |
| | | TFR=1.77 | 9.46 | 8.37 | 7.73 | 7.37 | 7.25 | 6.92 | 6.47 | 6.17 |
| | | TFR=1.94 | 9.45 | 8.29 | 7.60 | 7.25 | 7.37 | 7.20 | 6.74 | 6.38 |
| IX | IX | Combined simulation: 1 percentage point increase in labor force participation rate, 0.5 percentage points increase in TFP, and an increase in training | | | | | | | | |
| | | TFR=1.6 | 8.90 | 7.75 | 7.06 | 6.63 | 6.31 | 5.85 | 5.37 | 5.07 |
| | | TFR=1.77 | 8.89 | 7.68 | 6.97 | 6.56 | 6.40 | 6.05 | 5.58 | 5.27 |
| | | TFR=1.94 | 8.88 | 7.60 | 6.85 | 6.44 | 6.52 | 6.32 | 5.84 | 5.47 |

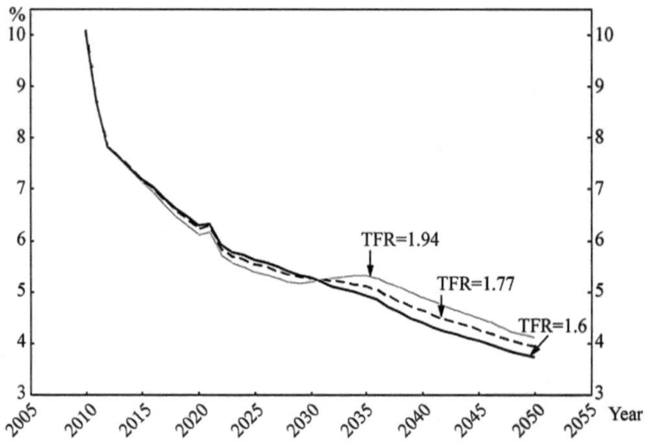


**Fig. 4.1** China's long-term potential growth rate under different TFRs

to increase the potential future growth rate by increasing the labor force participation rate (i.e., increasing the labor supply), the resulting effect is decreasing year by year (see Table 4.2). For example, if we assume that China's labor force participation rate increases by 5 percentage points each year during 2011–2050, then China's potential growth rate in the 13th Five-Year Plan period (2016–2020) will increase by 0.18 percentage points compared to the baseline scenario; however, by 2045–2050, the potential growth rate will only increase by 0.06 percentage points compared to the baseline scenario. At that time, the "growth effect" produced by the labor force participation rate will be reduced to one-third of its previous level. It is observed that the same degree of "treatment" will produce a decreasing "growth effect." We can conclude that the policy reforms focused on the labor force participation rate are not an "institutional dividend" that we can rely on in the long run, as visualized in Fig. 4.2.

#### 4.3.3.3 Increasing Effect of TFP

The related simulations are shown in Table 4.1(III) and Table 4.2(III). The simulation in III.1 in Table 4.1 shows the trend of the potential growth rate if the TFP increases by 0.5 or one percentage point from the original level and other factors are held constant under the future scenario with TFR = 1.6. The simulation in III.2 shows the impact of an increase in TFP on China's potential growth rate under the baseline scenario with TFR = 1.77. As we can see, the "growth effect" produced by the TFP is quite noticeable (see Fig. 4.3). For example, in the 12th Five-Year Plan period (2011–2015), if the TFP increases by 0.5 percentage points per year, the potential growth rate will increase by 0.568 percentage points compared to the baseline scenario; if the TFP increases by one percentage point per year, China's potential growth rate will increase by 1.136 percentage points compared to the baseline scenario in the

**Table 4.2** Net impact of various policy measures on China's future potential economic growth rate: 2011–2050 (Unit: %)

| 年份 | | | Year | | | | | | | |
|---|---|---|---|---|---|---|---|---|---|---|
| Potential growth rate: | | | 2011–2015 | 2016–2020 | 2021–2025 | 2026–2030 | 2031–2035 | 2036–2040 | 2041–2045 | 2046–2050 |
| I | I | Simulation of the impact on China's potential growth rate when TFR = 1.94 | | | | | | | | |
| | | Baseline scenario (TFR = 1.6) | -0.024 | -0.140 | -0.204 | -0.168 | 0.241 | 0.485 | 0.477 | 0.413 |
| | | Baseline scenario (TFR= 1.77) | -0.009 | -0.076 | -0.114 | -0.103 | 0.135 | 0.279 | 0.259 | 0.209 |
| II | II | 1. Simulation of the impact of labor force participation rate increase on potential growth rate when TFR = 1.6 | | | | | | | | |
| | | 1 percentage point increase | 0.190 | 0.036 | 0.029 | 0.025 | 0.021 | 0.017 | 0.015 | 0.014 |
| | | 2 percentage points increase | 0.381 | 0.072 | 0.058 | 0.050 | 0.042 | 0.033 | 0.029 | 0.027 |
| | | 5 percentage points increase | 0.952 | 0.177 | 0.142 | 0.123 | 0.101 | 0.080 | 0.071 | 0.064 |
| | II | 2. Simulation of the impact of labor force participation rate increase on potential growth rate when TFR = 1.77 | | | | | | | | |
| | | 1 percentage point increase | 0.190 | 0.036 | 0.029 | 0.026 | 0.021 | 0.016 | 0.014 | 0.012 |
| | | 2 percentage points increase | 0.381 | 0.071 | 0.057 | 0.052 | 0.042 | 0.031 | 0.027 | 0.024 |
| | | 5 percentage points increase | 0.951 | 0.176 | 0.140 | 0.126 | 0.101 | 0.076 | 0.065 | 0.059 |
| III | III | 1. Simulation of the impact of TFP increase on potential growth rate when TFR = 1.6 | | | | | | | | |
| | | 0.5 percentage points increase | 0.568 | 0.680 | 0.748 | 0.797 | 0.828 | 0.844 | 0.858 | 0.869 |
| | | 1 percentage point increase | 1.136 | 1.364 | 1.502 | 1.602 | 1.666 | 1.700 | 1.728 | 1.751 |
| | III | 2. Simulation of the impact of TFP increase on potential growth rate when TFR = 1.77 | | | | | | | | |
| | | 0.5 percentage points increase | 0.567 | 0.679 | 0.745 | 0.794 | 0.830 | 0.851 | 0.865 | 0.875 |
| | | 1 percentage point increase | 1.135 | 1.360 | 1.496 | 1.597 | 1.672 | 1.714 | 1.743 | 1.764 |
| IV | IV | Simulation of the impact of school enrollment rate increase on potential growth rate | | | | | | | | |
| | | TFR=1.6 | 0.111 | 0.084 | 0.077 | 0.069 | 0.059 | 0.047 | 0.032 | 0.019 |
| | | TFR=1.77 | 0.111 | 0.084 | 0.077 | 0.067 | 0.060 | 0.047 | 0.031 | 0.017 |
| V | V | Simulation of the impact of increased training opportunities on potential growth rate | | | | | | | | |

(continued)

**Table 4.2** (continued)

| 年份 | | | Year | | | | | | | |
|---|---|---|---|---|---|---|---|---|---|---|
| Potential growth rate: | | | 2011–2015 | 2016–2020 | 2021–2025 | 2026–2030 | 2031–2035 | 2036–2040 | 2041–2045 | 2046–2050 |
| | | TFR=1.6 | 0.404 | 0.381 | 0.408 | 0.402 | 0.400 | 0.383 | 0.319 | 0.344 |
| | | TFR=1.77 | 0.404 | 0.380 | 0.406 | 0.393 | 0.385 | 0.370 | 0.309 | 0.333 |
| VI | VI | Combined simulation: 1 percentage point increase in LFPR, 1 percentage point increase in TFP, an increase in TFR to 1.94, and an increase in school enrollment rate | | | | | | | | |
| | | When TFR=1.6 | 1.419 | 1.340 | 1.394 | 1.518 | 2.006 | 2.285 | 2.284 | 2.216 |
| | | When TFR=1.77 | 1.433 | 1.403 | 1.483 | 1.582 | 1.899 | 2.079 | 2.066 | 2.012 |
| VII | VII | Combined simulation: 1 percentage point increase in LFPR, 0.5 percentage points increase in TFP, an increase in TFR to 1.94, and an increase in school enrollment rate | | | | | | | | |
| | | When TFR=1.6 | 0.848 | 0.658 | 0.644 | 0.717 | 1.159 | 1.410 | 1.395 | 1.321 |
| | | When TFR=1.77 | 0.863 | 0.721 | 0.734 | 0.781 | 1.052 | 1.205 | 1.178 | 1.117 |
| VIII | VIII | Combined simulation: 1 percentage point increase in LFPR, 1 percentage point increase in TFP, an increase in TFR to 1.94, and an increase in training opportunities | | | | | | | | |
| | | When TFR=1.6 | 1.72 | 1.64 | 1.73 | 1.85 | 2.33 | 2.61 | 2.57 | 2.54 |
| | | When TFR=1.77 | 1.73 | 1.71 | 1.82 | 1.91 | 2.22 | 2.40 | 2.35 | 2.33 |
| IX | IX | Combined simulation: 1 percentage point increase in LFPR, 0.5 percentage points increase in TFP, an increase in TFR to 1.94, and an increase in training opportunities | | | | | | | | |
| | | When TFR=1.6 | 1.15 | 0.96 | 0.98 | 1.04 | 1.47 | 1.72 | 1.67 | 1.64 |
| | | When TFR=1.77 | 1.16 | 1.02 | 1.07 | 1.11 | 1.36 | 1.52 | 1.45 | 1.43 |

*Note* The baseline assumptions for human capital are the same as those from Lu Yang and Cai Fang (2014). We assume here that China's school-age children admission rate, elementary school admission rate, junior high school admission rate, and senior high school admission rate increase from the original 99.98%, 99.95%, 95%, and 90% to 99.999%, 99.999%, 98%, and 95%, respectively, by 2050 when other conditions remain unchanged. The data for other years is completed using the average method

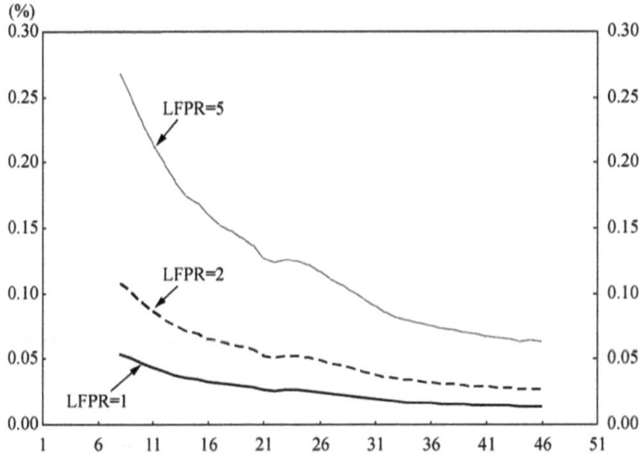


**Fig. 4.2** Effect of increasing labor force participation rate on potential economic growth rate (TFR = 1.6 under baseline scenario)

same period. It should be noted that, unlike the decreasing "growth effect" produced by an increase in labor force participation rate, the "growth effect" produced by the TFP is increasing. Under the two scenarios with different TFPs, China's potential growth rate will increase by 0.869 percentage points and 1.751 percentage points, respectively, by 2045–2050 compared to the baseline scenario, while the growth effect produced by the TFP in the 12th Five-Year Plan period (2011–2015) will be 0.568 percentage points and 1.136 percentage points, respectively. Figure 4.4 clearly shows the increasing "growth effect" brought about by the TFP.

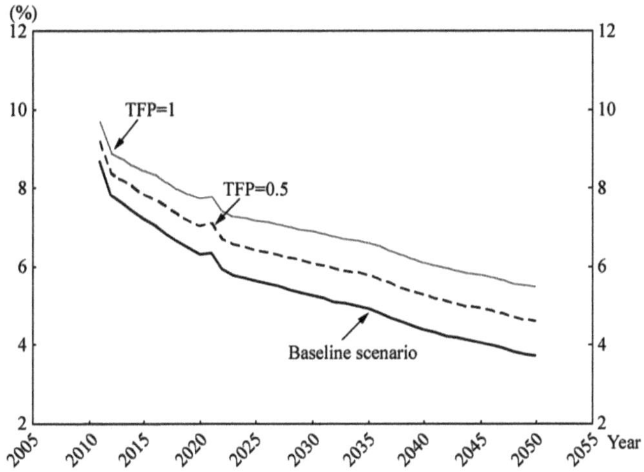


**Fig. 4.3** Effect of increasing TFP on China's long-term potential growth rate (under baseline scenario with TFR = 1.6)

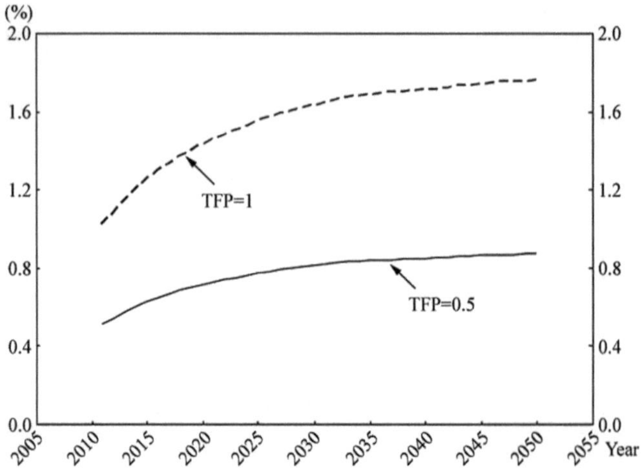


**Fig. 4.4** Effect of increasing TFP on potential growth rate (TFR = 1.6 under baseline scenario)

#### 4.3.3.4 Growth Effect of Human Capital: Higher School Enrollment Rate vs. Increased Training Opportunities

There are usually two options available to a country to improve its human capital level: education and training. However, it is a relatively long process to improve human capital by increasing the school enrollment rate (increasing the education years). The reason is that, in general, the human capital level (without taking into account training) will no longer increase with age when the individuals are older than a specific age of schooling. It can take years or even a decade for education policies targeted at younger populations to be reflected in the labor market. To compare the two ways of human capital improvement, i.e., education and training, we begin with an analysis of the impact of increasing school enrollment rate or admission rate on China's potential growth rate, without taking training into account.

In our simulations, it is assumed that the average schooling years of the population aged 25 or above remain constant. Based on this assumption, the change in human capital is only affected by the school enrollment rate or admission rate at each education level. Specifically, we assume that, compared to the baseline scenario, China's school-age children's admission rate, elementary school admission rate, junior high school admission rate, and senior high school admission rate increase from the previous levels of 99%, 99%, 95%, and 90%, respectively, to 99%, 99%, 98%, and 95% by 2050. The simulation results reveal that the human capital index hc tends to be monotonically increasing in general, but the magnitude of the increase is gradually decreasing; accordingly, the increase in human capital has a positive impact on China's potential growth rate, but the magnitude of the impact is also decreasing (see Figs. 4.5).

When the accumulation of human capital is considered merely from the perspective of schooling or admission rate at the education stages, it does have a very limited

**Fig. 4.5** School enrollment rate improvement and long-term potential growth rate increase (TFR = 1.6 under baseline scenario)

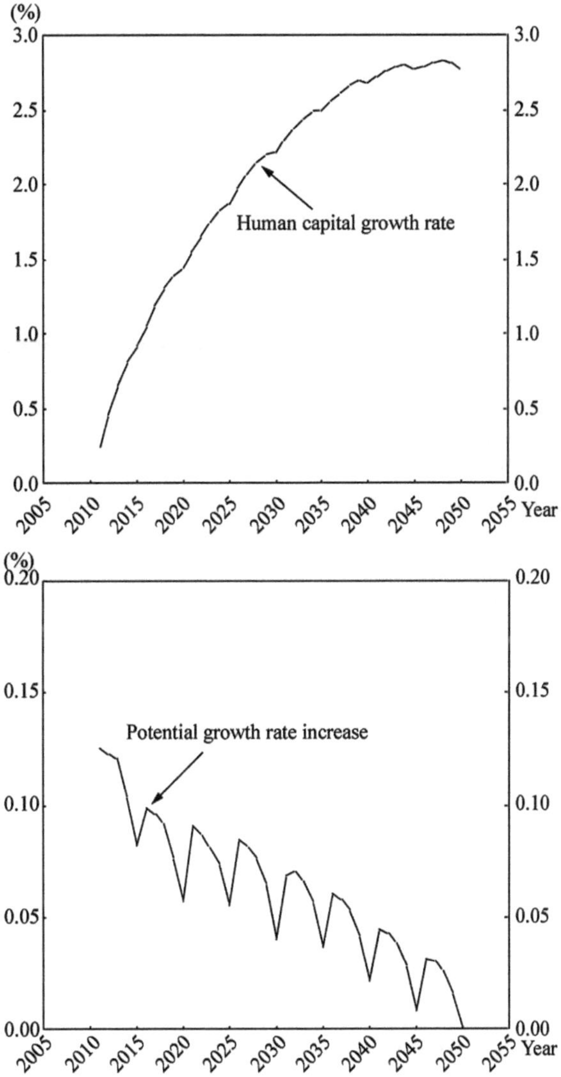


impact on the improvement of the potential growth rate. However, if the quality of human capital in the labor market can be improved through training and further studies, the magnitude of human capital improvement will be more pronounced. If the government and enterprises can provide employees with regular training and further study opportunities, improved human capital is likely to significantly boost the potential growth rate. To verify the findings, we make a simple assumption that under the baseline scenario, the workers in the labor market have an average of 1.2 months of training time per year. Therefore, it means that each year the average education years of every 10 workers in the labor market will increase by one year;

in other words, the average years of education of each worker will increase by one year after every 10 years of work. This assumption implies that different ages of the workforce enjoy the same probability of training, but in reality, the probability of training is unequally distributed across ages. For simplicity, we choose this assumption and extrapolate the average education years in China between 2011 and 2050, with the implicit hypothesis that training time is equivalent to education years.

According to the simulation results, providing more training opportunities in the labor market will have a stronger contribution to human capital and potential growth rate than the method of human capital improvement by raising the school enrollment rate. For example, if the workers in the labor market are trained for 1.2 months per year in the 12th Five-Year Plan period (2011–2015), the potential growth rate will increase by 0.404 percentage points (the baseline scenario takes 0 months of training per year because training is not considered). It should be noted that since the training acquired by the labor force in year t increases its own human capital (assuming that the duration of training is equal to the education years), the increased human capital (the increase in education years resulting from the training) can be substituted to year $t + 1$ and subsequent periods.

It is important to emphasize that the impact mechanism only involves young people, so the improvement of the future human capital level by means of increasing the school enrollment rate will be a slow process. This means that even if the school enrollment rate could be increased significantly in the short term, the extent to which the average level of human capital in a country could be increased would be very limited. However, training can be provided to the whole workforce, and if it is considered as another way to increase the education years, then it will significantly contribute to the potential growth rate. According to the simulation results, there is no significant decreasing trend in the growth effect of training. If the training program is implemented from 2011, the growth effect produced by training will be 0.344 percentage points by 2045–2050 (see Fig. 4.6). If the government and enterprises provide more training opportunities in the future, there will be a more significant impact of training programs on the potential growth rate.

#### 4.3.3.5 Growth Effect of Policy Mix

In the above paragraphs, the impact of increasing TFR, labor force participation rate, TFP, and human capital (increasing the school enrollment rate and training) on China's future potential growth rate is discussed. Although single-factor improvements have a limited impact on the potential growth rate, the government can choose a policy mix to amplify the "growth effect" of the policies. In Tables 4.1 and 4.2, we can see the effects of policy mix on China's potential growth rate in 2011–2050. If we assume that the TFR increases from 1.6 to 1.94, the labor force participation rate increases by one percentage point, the TFP increases by 0.5 percentage points, and the junior high school and senior high school admission rates increase by three percentage points and five percentage points, respectively, in 2050, then China's potential growth rate will increase by 0.85 percentage points in the 12th Five-Year

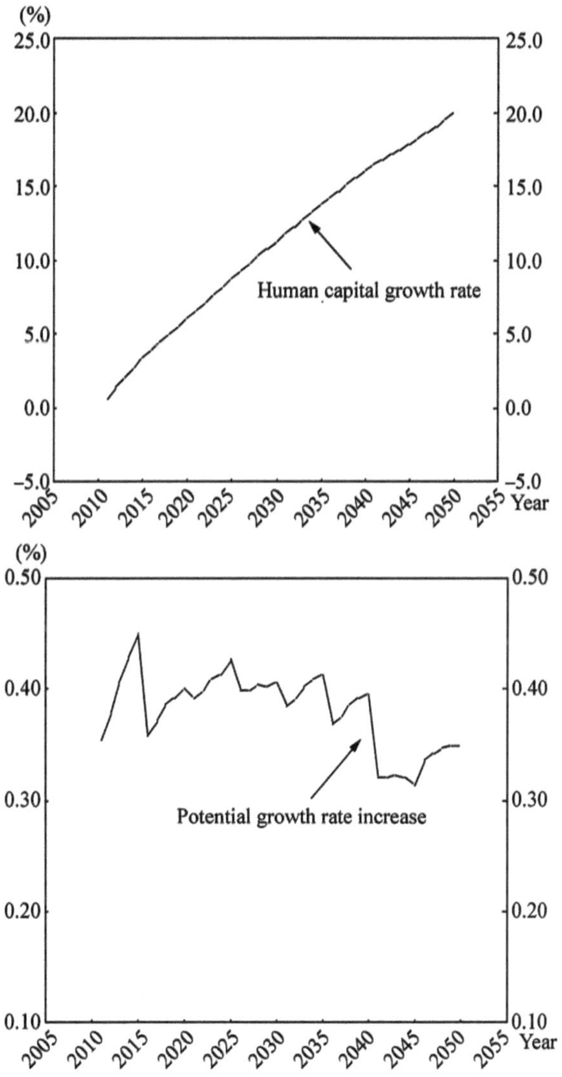


**Fig. 4.6** Increased training and long-term potential growth rate increase (TFR = 1.6 under baseline scenario

Plan period (2011–2015) and by 1.32 percentage points on average in 2045–2050 compared to the baseline scenario. If the contribution of training to human capital is taken into account, then the effect of policy mix will be even more pronounced. For example, if other assumptions remain the same (i.e., the TFR increases from 1.6 to 1.94, the labor force participation rate increases by one percentage point, and the TFP increases by 0.5 percentage points), and the government chooses to increase the human capital stock through training rather than by increasing school enrollment rate (i.e., the workers obtain an average of 1.2 months of training per year), then by 2045–2050, China's potential growth rate will increase from 3.84% to 5.47%, representing an increase of 1.64 percentage points.

Figure 4.7 shows the simulation results of several policy mixes with the baseline scenario: future trend of China's potential growth rate with TFR = 1.6 and without reform dividend. Scenario A: the trend of China's potential growth rate if TFR = 1.6, the labor force participation rate increases by one percentage point, the TFP increases by 0.5 percentage points, and the junior high school and senior high school admission rates in 2050 increase by 3 percentage points and 5 percentage points, respectively. Scenario B: long-term trend of China's potential growth rate if TFR = 1.6, the labor force participation rate increases by 1 percentage point, the TFP increases by 0.5 percentage points, and the human capital is improved by training rather than by raising the school enrollment rate. Scenario C has the same assumptions as Scenario B, with the only exception that Scenario C assumes an increase in China's future TFR from 1.6 to 1.94. The increase in TFR only affects the population dependency ratio in the short term, which will in turn reduce the capital formation rate and the total capital stock; however, as the new population reaches the working age, the labor supply will increase and the population dependency ratio will decrease, which in turn will increase the capital formation rate and the capital supply. Therefore, the short-term effect of increasing the TFR on China's potential growth rate is "negative," while the long-term effect is "positive."

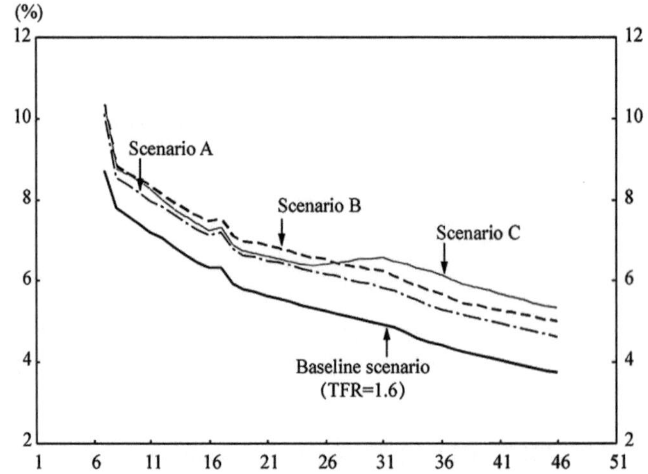


**Fig. 4.7** Impact of policy mix on China's long-term potential growth rate (TFR = 1.6 under baseline scenario)

## 4.4 Reform Priority Areas and Reform Approach

The disappearance of demographic dividend, characterized by a decrease in the absolute size of the working age population and an increase in the population dependency ratio, has led to a natural downward trend in China's potential growth rate. However, it doesn't mean that the government can do nothing in the face of the declining potential growth rate. For China, the key to sustainable economic development is to take a series of reforms to remove the institutional hindrances that impede factor supply and productivity gains and to mitigate the downward trend in potential growth rate. The results of the reform dividend simulations also help us to prioritize the reforms and choose the reform path and approach.

First, the government should continue to adjust and improve its fertility policy. Although the population fertility policy relaxation has no immediate growth effect or even a negative effect, such as the negative effect of the two-child fertility policy on the potential growth rate in the first 15 years compared to the one-child policy, this negative effect is very limited. In the long run, the relaxation of the population fertility policy is conducive to forming a reasonable demographic structure and increasing the size and proportion of the working age population in the future, which can have a positive impact on the potential growth rate. However, we must understand that while the population fertility policy affects the TFR, the decline in population fertility is the result of economic and social development. As the economy develops, there is a trend of lower fertility desires, and no significant reversal is expected. Early adjustments to the policy will have a more pronounced effect. Therefore, we should make a transition from the "two-child fertility policy for couples where either the husband or the wife is from a single-child family" to the "full liberalization of the two-child policy" as soon as possible, and should further adjust the fertility policy according to the reality of population development.

Second, the system and mechanism for allocating resources in the market should be improved to create a competitive environment for equal entry and exit. When it comes to improving the TFP, there is another important area that still holds great potential, that is, the large productivity differences among enterprises within an industry. It is possible to increase the productivity levels of industries and the whole economy by encouraging more efficient enterprises to survive, expand and thrive, and by eliminating the enterprises that have not improved their efficiency over time. Some studies show that the US has realized a 30–50% contribution to the TFP increase by adopting the creative destruction mechanism of entry, exit, survival and elimination of enterprises within each sector (Foster et al. 2008, 2001). Furthermore, some studies reveal that China's TFP will be increased by 30–50% if the large productivity differences among enterprises within each sector can be reduced to the US level (Hsieh et al. 2009). Why is it 30–50% in both of the above cases? It means that this type of source for increasing the TFP has not been available to China so far. Therefore, the relevant reforms will be the areas where significant gains can be achieved as well.

In fact, through the mixed ownership reform, it is possible to give more opportunities for the non-public economy to enter the competitive sectors and break the monopoly of state-owned enterprises through competition, which allows us to obtain the aforementioned reform dividend. In other words, the TFP can be boosted by increasing the factor mobility, and then the potential growth rate can be increased. In addition, we can also improve the efficiency of factor allocation through financial system reforms. The focus of the financial system reforms should be on the advancement of interest rate liberalization. Only with market-based interest rates can we improve the efficiency of capital allocation. Under the conditions of non-market-based interest rates, the interest rates cannot float with the returns on capital, and production and allocation efficiency are below optimal levels, leading to a decline in the TFP.

Third, the citizenship of migrant workers should be promoted through the household registration system reform. Through public policy reform, we can promote the further migration of surplus rural labor and the citizenship of migrant workers. In this way, we can not only increase the potential growth rate by expanding labor supply but also continue to create efficiency in resource reallocation by removing institutional hindrances and unblocking labor mobility channels, thus continuously increasing the TFP. In addition, this reform can ease the pressure of excessively rapid wage increases and gain time for enterprises to upgrade their industrial structure. By following three parallel paths – absorbing migrant workers into the urban household population, providing the same basic public services for migrant workers who are not yet qualified to become urban residents as those provided to urban residents, and achieving full coverage of the social security system for urban and rural residents, the household registration system reform will be a typical area for harvesting the reform dividend. Therefore, the top-level design of the reform should address the issue of sharing the reform costs between the central government and local governments, so as to form incentive compatibility.

Fourth, the government and enterprises should provide diverse training programs for employees. Enterprises have concerns about providing training to employees due to employee mobility, but China's future economic development will depend on human capital. Similarly, enterprises need to rely on human capital if they want to boost productivity and technological innovation. In terms of providing training, enterprises want their employees to be stable, and employees want to maximize their benefits through mobility between enterprises. Therefore, apart from training programs provided by enterprises, the government needs to provide more training programs in order to increase human capital and ultimately significantly improve the potential growth rate. For example, in our simulation results, if each employee has the opportunity for one-year training and further studies after every 10 years of service, China's potential growth rate will increase by 0.3 to 0.4 percentage points.

Fifth, when faced with a package of reform programs, the government should pay more attention to reform priorities. Currently, economists have opinions on reform priorities such as "easy reforms first," "reforms with a consensus first" and "the smallest 'package' of reforms." In fact, we can choose reforms that have a more pronounced "growth effect," such as gradually promoting the reform of the citizenship of migrant workers, gradually shifting from a two-child fertility policy for couples where either the husband or the wife is from a single-child family to a fully liberalized two-child policy, reforming the financial system and deepening the reform of state-owned enterprises to achieve efficiency in resource allocation. In addition, we can increase human capital in the labor market through more training programs, thus contributing to better productivity and innovative capacity. This is also in line with Premier Li Keqiang's view that "reforms should start from the most prominent problems that restrict economic and social development."

## References


Cai Fang and Lu Yang (2013), Advancing Reforms to Improve Potential Growth Rate, Comparative Studies, Issue 1.

Cai Fang and Lu Yang (2013), Population Change and Resulting Slowdown in Potential GDP Growth in China, China & World Economy, Vol. 21, Issue 2, pp. 1–14.

Du Yang and Lu Yang (2011), "Natural Unemployment in China and Its Implications," The Journal of World Economy, Issue 4.

Eichengreen, Barry, Donghyun Park and Kwanho Shin (2011), When fast growing economies slow down: International evidence and implications for China, NBER Working Paper No.16919, National Bureau of Economic Research, Cambridge, MA.

Fogel, Robert W (2009). The Impact of the Asian Miracle on the Theory of Economic Growth, NBER Working Paper 14967, 2009.

Foster, Lucia John Haltiwanger and C.J. Krizan (2001), Aggregate Productivity Growth: Lessons from Microeconomic Evidence, in New Developments in Productivity Analysis, NBER/University of Chicago Press.

Foster, Lucia John Haltiwanger, and Chad Syverson (2008), Reallocation, Firm Turnover, and Efficiency: Selection on Productivity or Profitability?, American Economic Review, Vol. 98, pp. 394–425.

Guo Zhigang (2013), China's Population Forecast 2011–2050, working paper.

Hayashi, Fumio and Edward C. Prescott (2002), The 1990s in Japan: A Lost Decade, Review of Economic Dynamics, Vol. 5, No. 1, pp. 206–235.

Hsieh, Chang-Tai and Peter J. Klenow (2009), Misallocation and Manufacturing TFP in China and India, The Quarterly Journal of Economics, Vol. CXXIV, Issue 4, November, pp. 1403–1448.

IMF (International Monetary Fund) (2014), People's Republic of China: 2014 Article IV, Consultation – Staff Report, IMF Country Report No. 14/235.

Kuijs, Louis (2010), China Through 2020—A Macroeconomic Scenario, World Bank China Research Working Paper No.9.

Lu Yang and Cai Fang (2014), The Impact of Demographic Changes on Potential Growth Rate: A Comparison between China and Japan, The Journal of World Economy, Issue 1.

Lu, Yang and Cai Fang (2014), China's Shift from the Demographic Dividend to the Reform Dividend, in Ligang Song, Ross Garnaut, and Cai Fang (eds) Deepening Reform for China's Long Term Growth and Development, ANU E Press.

Pritchett, Lant and Lawrence H. Summers (2014), Asiaphoria Meets Regression to the Mean, NBER Working Paper, No. 20573, 2014. http://www.nber.org/papers/w20573.

Williamson, Jeffrey (1997), Growth, Distribution and Demography: Some Lessons from History, NBER Working Paper Series, No. 6244.

# Chapter 5
# Sci-Tech System Reform Under Innovation-Driven Development Strategy

**Li Ping, Wang Hongwei, and Cai Yuezhou**

**Abstract** Combining the theories of innovation economics and development economics as well as China's practice of sci-tech system formation and reforms, this chapter analyzes and outlines the relationship between the sci-tech system and sci-tech innovation, the changes in China's sci-tech system, the main problems in the sci-tech innovation before the 18th CPC National Congress, and the sci-tech system reforms after the 18th CPC National Congress. The implementation of an innovation-driven development strategy is the inevitable choice of the times, its core is to accelerate sci-tech innovation, and its success depends on the sci-tech system reforms. The in-depth sci-tech system reforms launched after the 18th CPC National Congress have shown initial results in promoting sci-tech innovation. Under the context of the new round of technological revolution and industrial changes, a new technology-economy paradigm is taking shape, and the role of sci-tech innovation in supporting economic and social development is increasingly prominent. China should follow the trend of the times, continue deepening the sci-tech system reforms, and reduce the constraints and obstacles to sci-tech innovation.

## 5.1 Sci-Tech System Reform Affects Innovation-Driven Development

### *5.1.1 Mode Shift and Structural Adjustment Require Innovation Drive*

China's rapid growth over the past 30 years since its reform and opening-up has been largely a kind of factor-driven growth based on the expansion of factor inputs, especially the expansion of investment and capital accumulation. The factor-driven model is consistent with the idea in classical and neoclassical economics that "capital accumulation is the impetus of economic growth"; it is also a developmental

L. Ping (✉) · W. Hongwei · C. Yuezhou
Institute of Quantitative and Technological Economics, Chinese Academy of Social Sciences, Beijing, China

 
X. Zhang (ed.), *Exploration on China's Economic System Reform under New Normal of Development*, https://doi.org/10.1007/978-981-95-2461-7_5

stage that an economy must go through in order to take off.[1] In 2010, China's GDP per capita exceeded USD 4,000, making China basically stride over the "take-off stage" of economic growth and officially become an upper-middle-income country. According to international experience, after reaching the middle-income level, some economies such as Japan and South Korea have continued high growth and successfully entered the ranks of developed economies, while others such as many Latin American countries have experienced long-term economic stagnation or slack and fallen into the so-called "middle-income trap." Economies falling into the "middle-income trap" usually face a dilemma: on the one hand, they are less competitive in the low-end manufacturing sectors due to rising labor costs brought about by the higher income levels; on the other hand, they are unable to compete with the developed economies in the high-end sectors due to insufficient technological innovation capabilities.

For China, when it comes to achieving the goals of sustainable economic and social development and building a moderately prosperous society in all aspects, it is faced with more complex internal and external conditions. First, the precondition for the sustainability of the factor-driven model is the "demographic dividend" brought about by the declining population dependency ratio. With the advent of the "Lewis turning point" that is characterized by labor shortages and continuously rising wages, it is no longer sustainable to rely on large-scale government-led investments to support the economic growth rate. It is imperative for China to adjust its policies to derive greater efficiency from technological progress and institutional improvements and to sustain its economic growth (Cai Fang 2013). Second, as the level of economic development increases and the industrial and sector technologies mature, the dividend of the technology gap as a latecomer advantage has been diminishing. Third, the deterioration of the ecological environment, the prominent constraints on resources and energy supply, and the serious overcapacity have made the traditional factor-driven growth model unsustainable. Fourth, the international economy has struggled to recover from the global financial crisis and the European sovereign debt crisis, and the demand in the international market continues to shrink. Fifth, knowledge creation and technological innovation has accelerated significantly worldwide, with the rapid emergence of a new round of global sci-tech revolution and industrial change based on new technological breakthroughs, and all countries in the world are speeding up the transformation of economic and social development, in an effort to gain the initiative in the future international competition.

Under such a complex domestic and international environment and background, innovation-driven development is an essential way for China to accelerate the transformation of its economic growth model, solve the deep-rooted conflicts and problems in economic development, and enhance the endogenous impetus and vitality of economic development. As General Secretary Xi Jinping has emphasized on different occasions, "Innovation is always a key force that drives a country and a nation

[1] ①W.W. Rostow (2001), an economic historian, defines the "five stages of economic growth": (1) traditional society, (2) preconditions to take-off, (3) take-off, (4) drive to maturity and (5) age of high mass consumption.

forward... To grasp innovation is to grasp development, and to seek innovation is to seek the future. If we don't innovate, we will fall behind, and if we innovate slowly, we will also fall behind... We should vigorously promote the strategic adjustment of economic structure and put innovation in a more prominent position."[2]

### *5.1.2 Innovation-Driven Development Strategy Focuses on Sci-Tech Innovation*

According to Joseph Alois Schumpeter's definition, innovation is breaking the circular flow equilibrium of the economic system and recombining some of the factors of production in the economic system; only this recombination of factors can be called "economic development" and can be profitable through a monopoly position (Schumpeter 1994). Peter F. Drucker (2009), a management expert, points out that anything that enables a change in the wealth-producing potential of the existing resources is sufficient to constitute innovation; innovation is about production and about providing value and satisfaction to customers by changing products and services.[3] The essence of innovation, as defined by Joseph Alois Schumpeter and Peter F. Drucker, is to acquire a monopoly position and enhance core competitiveness through the recombination of factor resources; to achieve monopoly profits or value appreciation at the micro level and to provide a driving force for economic and social development at the macro level. Innovation can be divided into different types including sci-tech innovation (technological innovation), model innovation, and institutional innovation, but people are used to associating innovation with sci-tech and consider sci-tech innovation (technological innovation) as the equivalent of innovation on many occasions. For example, both the first and second editions of the OECD Guidelines for Collecting, Reporting and Using Data on Innovation (i.e., the Oslo Manual) focused exclusively on sci-tech innovation (technological innovation). The reasons behind it may be that sci-tech innovation requires scientific research and knowledge creation as the basis, and covers many aspects such as product development and market development, so sci-tech innovation features greater difficulty and uncertainty, and is not easy to be imitated. Besides, model innovation and institutional innovation are mostly products derived from successful sci-tech innovation.

The implementation of the innovation-driven development strategy indicates that China places the utmost importance on sci-tech innovation. The 18th CPC National

---

[2] ②The three different occasions when innovation was talked about were (1) the seventh meeting of the Central Leading Group for Financial and Economic Affairs on August 18, 2014; (2) the symposium of comrades in charge of some provincial and regional party committees held in Changchun on July 17, 2015; and (3) the symposium of comrades in charge of some provincial, regional and municipal party committees held in Guizhou on June 18, 2015.

[3] ③Joseph Alois Schumpeter and Peter F. Drucker were both Austrian-Americans. When Peter F. Drucker was young, he visited and sought advice from Joseph Alois Schumpeter, whom he was deeply influenced by. For this reason, Peter F. Drucker's definition of innovation is clearly inherited from Joseph Alois Schumpeter's idea.

Congress clearly stressed that sci-tech innovation is a strategic pillar for boosting social productivity and comprehensive national strength and therefore must be placed at the heart of the country's development. Since the 18th CPC National Congress, General Secretary Xi Jinping has repeatedly talked about innovation during inspections or meetings, with a strong emphasis on sci-tech innovation. "At present, the whole Party, the whole country and people of all ethnic groups are united in the struggle to build a moderately prosperous society in all aspects as well as to realize the Chinese dream of the great rejuvenation of the Chinese nation. We need a strong force of sci-tech innovation more than ever before. The old path is no longer possible, and the new path is based on sci-tech innovation and on accelerating the shift from factor-driven and investment-scale-driven development to innovation-driven development."[4] "The country that grasps the 'bull's nose' of sci-tech innovation and takes the first move of sci-tech innovation will be able to dominate and win the advantage."[5]

### 5.1.3 Sci-Tech System Constrains the Role of Sci-Tech Innovation

The sci-tech innovation activities cover multiple steps from theoretical research, basic and applied research to product development and commercial application; these steps have obvious succession characteristics, and there are feedback and interaction mechanisms. In a sense, sci-tech innovation activities can be broken down into three distinctly different but closely related functions: scientific function, technological function and innovation function. Specifically, the scientific function is mainly reflected in various theoretical research, major discoveries, basic applied research and major inventions without specific application value; the technological function includes applied research in universities and institutes and R&D activities in industries; the innovation function is more reflected in product development, production organization, model innovation and marketing based on R&D activities, with its core being the realization of large-scale commercial application. From the perspective of linear innovation theory, the three functions are logically successive, which means that the scientific function is usually the basis of the technological function, and the innovation function is based on the technological function; meanwhile, the feedback from the subsequent steps often affects the orientation and direction of the preceding function, especially the interactive feedback between the innovation function and the technological function is more prominent; the three functions constitute a complete chain and closed-loop system (Fig. 5.1).

[4] ④Excerpted from the important speech "Firmly Innovate and Re-innovate, Accelerate the Pace of Building an Innovative Country" delivered by General Secretary Xi Jinping at the General Conference of Academicians of the Chinese Academy of Sciences and the General Conference of Academicians of the Chinese Academy of Engineering on June 9, 2014.

[5] ⑤Xi Jinping's speech during his inspection and investigation in Shanghai on May 24, 2014.

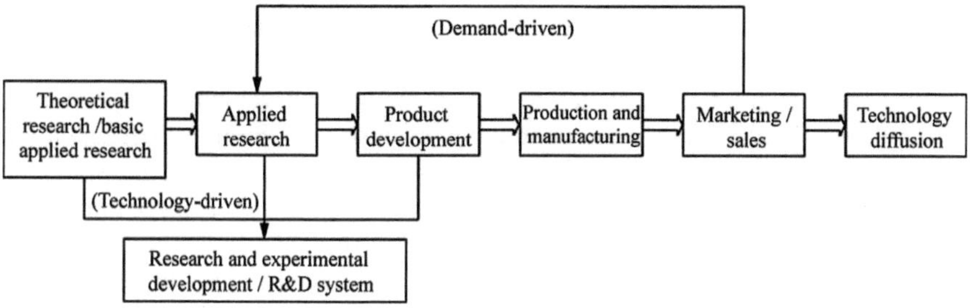


**Fig. 5.1** Division of sci-tech innovation activity steps based on the linear innovation model. *Data source* Compiled from relevant literature of Rothwell (1994) and Godin (2006)

Sci-tech innovation activities are typically characterized by market failures, which are reflected in both the knowledge spillover and the risks that exist in various aspects of sci-tech innovation.

Sci-tech innovation activities are, first of all, the process of creating and producing various innovative knowledge. Knowledge is a kind of information, which naturally has the characteristics of mobility and diffusion, and also has the properties of public goods such as non-rivalry and non-exclusivity. Therefore, innovation knowledge generated from sci-tech innovation activities will inevitably spill over or spread from the innovators to the outside world. In addition, innovation knowledge will be materialized as various innovation products in the product innovation process, and the sales and marketing of innovation products will also bring innovation knowledge spillovers.

Innovation knowledge spillovers are in essence the commercial returns that innovators deserve from their innovation activities and are shared by other members of society through the flow and diffusion of innovation knowledge. Innovation knowledge spillovers can be divided into rent spillovers and pure knowledge spillovers according to the different ways of sharing innovation returns. Rent spillovers refer to the phenomenon that when innovation knowledge is materialized as new products for external sales, the market prices of these products usually fail to fully reflect the improvement in product quality and performance brought about by the innovation, or are lower than the true value of the innovation knowledge. The final products developed by downstream enterprises in the industrial chain by using the innovation products of upstream enterprises as intermediate inputs will also gain additional commercial value due to the improved quality or performance. In essence, the additional revenue gained by downstream enterprises is the result of spillovers from upstream innovation activities and the transfer of the innovation rents not fully captured by upstream innovation products to downstream enterprises, hence this kind of spillover is called rent spillovers. Pure knowledge spillovers refer to the phenomenon that innovative knowledge is gradually acquired by enterprises other than the innovators due to personnel exchange, talent mobility, and R&D cooperation, and these enterprises develop competitive products through imitation and jointly share the market rents generated by innovative activities. No matter what kind of innovation knowledge spillovers, the ultimate result is that other members of society can enjoy the positive externalities brought by innovation achievements, which has a positive effect on promoting economic growth and social development. Specifically, rent spillovers will stimulate the continuous extension of the industrial chain and expand the overall scale of the industry vertically, while pure knowledge spillovers will directly bring about a horizontal expansion of the industry scale. For innovators, neither kind of innovation knowledge spillover is avoidable. In the process of rent spillovers, innovators can obtain considerable commercial returns through market mechanisms, so this kind of spillover is acceptable to innovators. In contrast, the process of pure knowledge spillovers not only prevents innovators from obtaining commercial returns, but also results in the rapid sharing of the excess profits and social gains generated by their innovations among a large number of competitors. All innovation activities require large amounts of investment, while excessive pure knowledge spillovers will surely lead to the inability of innovators to cover their innovation costs with their innovation gains, which will in turn cause a serious shortage in the supply of innovation activities on a society-wide basis.

High risks and uncertainties in the sci-tech innovation process are also important reasons for the market failures of sci-tech innovation activities. According to Arrow (1962), innovation itself is a risky activity with a constant possibility of failure. Innovation decisions are usually made in a state of high uncertainty. It is difficult to forecast the future direction of knowledge and sci-tech development, the market positioning, the product demand and the potential usage of technologies; there is also uncertainty in product innovation, process innovation, market innovation and organizational innovation. Meanwhile, each step in the sci-tech innovation process, including basic research in the early stage, technology development in the middle stage, and marketing in the later stage, requires high investments; even the collection of relevant information in the early stage is very time-consuming and costly. Therefore, the high-risk characteristics of innovation are self-evident. Radical technological innovation is even more exposed to ubiquitous risks. The possibility of failure is high in every step of the process, from basic research to applied research and technology development, and then to production and manufacturing. Given the presence of existing technologies and the low maturity of new technologies, even if applied research and technology development is successful, there are still numerous risks in realizing commercial value, including "market (acceptance) risk," "operational management risk," and "government regulation risk." High risks and uncertainties can influence enterprises' innovation decisions, increase their difficulty in securing external funding for innovation, and as a result, reduce the innovators' willingness for innovation and the supply of innovation in society.

The market failure characteristic of sci-tech innovation activities makes it necessary for government departments to comprehensively use various policies and regulatory measures such as financial subsidies, tax exemptions, financial support and intellectual property protection for different steps of sci-tech innovation activities so that the additional risks and costs borne by sci-tech innovators in the process of implementing innovation activities can be hedged and compensated. The policies and regulatory measures for each step of sci-tech innovation activities, as well as the organizational structure and management mechanisms for formulating and implementing the policies and regulatory measures, have together constituted the current sci-tech system. Whether the sci-tech system can better adapt to the inherent characteristics and laws of sci-tech innovation and effectively solve the problem of market failure in sci-tech innovation activities will have a direct bearing on the activeness and ultimate effectiveness of sci-tech innovation activities, as well as the success of the implementation of innovation-driven development strategy. As General Secretary Xi Jinping pointed out, "In the implementation of the innovation-driven development strategy, the most fundamental task is to enhance the capability of independent innovation, and the most urgent task is to break down the institutional and system barriers to liberate and stimulate to the maximum extent the huge potential hidden in science and technology as the first productive force."[6] "We should…deepen the sci-tech system reform, enhance the vitality of sci-tech innovation, gather our strength to promote sci-tech innovation, and really put the innovation-driven development strategy into practice."[7]

## 5.2 Changes in China's Sci-Tech System Prior to the 18th CPC National Congress

From the founding of the People's Republic of China to the convening of the 18th CPC National Congress, China's sci-tech system went through three stages: (1) the sci-tech system during the planned economy period before the reform and opening-up in 1978; (2) the sci-tech system during the economic system reform and transformation period after the reform and opening-up until Deng Xiaoping's South China Speech in 1992; and (3) the sci-tech system during the period from 1992 to 2012 when the socialist market economy system was established and perfected before the convening of the 18th CPC National Congress.

### *5.2.1 Sci-Tech System During the Planned Economy Period*

After the founding of the People's Republic of China, the international political situation in which we found ourselves was tense and complex. Along with the flourishing cause of communism worldwide, the Western leading capitalist countries also entered

[6] ⑥Excerpts from Xi Jinping's speech "Accelerating the Shift from Factor-Driven and Investment-Scale-Driven Development to Innovation-Driven Development" at the General Conference of Academicians of the Chinese Academy of Sciences and the General Conference of Academicians of the Chinese Academy of Engineering on June 9, 2014, included in *Xi Jinping: The Government of China.*

[7] ⑦Xi Jinping's speech during his inspection tour at the Chinese Academy of Sciences on July 17, 2013.

a golden period of post-war economic recovery and development, with the US-led capitalist countries emphasizing the "Cold War" against the communist world. Despite its political independence, China was not only blockaded by the capitalist countries, but also still under the threat of wars, so there was an urgent need to establish a complete industrial system and a strong defense industry as soon as possible to lift itself out of poverty and backwardness. At that time, it became a natural choice for China to implement the catching-up strategy to rapidly strengthen its national power and get rid of the control and threat of developed countries. Meanwhile, the recovery of the national economy and the early completion of the socialist transformation also laid a solid economic foundation for the final and formal establishment of the catching-up strategy during the First Five-Year Plan (1953–1957). For catching-up under the conditions of insufficient human and material resources, it was important to make full use of the existing resources; the organized and planned promotion of sci-tech work became an inevitable choice under the historical conditions at that time.

Under the guidance of the catching-up strategy, China formulated and promulgated two major sci-tech plans, i.e., the *Long-term Plan for the Development of Science and Technology (1956–1967)* (hereinafter referred to as the "12-Year Plan"), which was prepared in October 1955 and approved for implementation in December 1956; and the *Outlines of the Plan for the Development of Science and Technology (1963–1972)* (hereinafter referred to as the "10-Year Plan), which was finalized in June 1963 and approved for implementation in December 1963. Through the implementation of two major sci-tech plans and the supporting sci-tech policies, China built up a sci-tech research system that met the actual needs of the national economy (socialist construction); it made systematic designs and arrangements for almost all aspects involved in sci-tech innovation activities, such as scientific research organization, human capital, knowledge diffusion, application and promotion, and incentive mechanism, thus forming a sci-tech system unique to the planned economy; it was also designed to rapidly establish a sci-tech system with a full range of sectors and organizations that can support industrial modernization and national defense modernization.

In the sci-tech system during the planned economy period, there was a clear division of labor and responsibilities among the various types of research institutions and innovators: (1) the research institutes, mainly led by the Chinese Academy of Sciences (hereinafter referred to as CAS), were responsible for the major part of basic theoretical research work; (2) the research institutions under the ministries and local governments were responsible for the research on generic technologies and various applications; (3) the higher education institutions were responsible for the cultivation of various types of sci-tech talents; (4) the research departments within the enterprises were responsible for product development. Based on the above division of labor and responsibilities, the State Science and Technology Commission, the State Planning Commission and other ministerial-level organs provided unified leadership and organization of sci-tech work, and worked with the Ministry of Higher Education under the State Council and various industrial transportation departments to coordinate and align the work of various types of research innovators. The sci-tech system formed under the catching-up strategy gave full play to the advantages of the planned system in mobilizing resources, accelerated the process of scientific research work and sci-tech output transformation through administrative measures, made major breakthroughs such as the "Two Bombs, One Satellite" and synthetic bovine insulin crystals, etc., and provided strong support for the construction of a modern industrial system with a full range of sectors, especially the national defense industrial system.

### *5.2.2 Sci-Tech System During the Reform and Transformation Period*

After the third plenary session of the 11th CPC Central Committee, China focused its efforts on economic construction, in which reform and opening-up became the basic national policy and raising people's living standards became the primary goal of economic and social development. China began to enter the economic system reform and transformation period characterized by changing the incentive mechanism and stimulating microscopic vitality. Although the planned system remained in place during the reform and transformation period, the commodity economy and market mechanism were gradually accepted and recognized. For the sci-tech system formed under the catching-up strategy, the coordination and cooperation among various parties and steps relied on administrative means and planned deployment, especially, there was no market incentive mechanism available for the transformation of sci-tech findings, so it was difficult to meet the requirements of economic and social transformation and to give full play to the role of sci-tech in supporting economic construction. Therefore, upon entering the reform and transformation stage, China continued promoting the sci-tech system reform in line with the adjustment of the overall goal of national sci-tech development, in an effort to explore the optimal path to liberation and development of sci-tech productivity. In fact, the main line of the sci-tech system reform during the transformation period was reflected as "promoting the integration of sci-tech with the economy to support and lead the economic and social development."

It was clearly stated at the National Science Conference held in 1978 that sci-tech was the productive force, intellectuals were part of the working class and sci-tech modernization was the key to the four modernizations. From then on, China regained its scientific prosperity. In 1980, the CPC Central Committee put forward the strategic policy that "economic construction must rely on sci-tech, and sci-tech must be oriented to economic construction," which set out a clear direction for the transition of the sci-tech strategic objectives. The *Plan for the Development of Science and Technology (1986–2000)* (hereinafter referred to as the "15-Year Plan"), which was drafted in April 1981 and formally approved in December 1982, followed the above guidelines: (1) The 15-Year Plan underlined the integration of sci-tech and economy, and promoted the sci-tech system reform under the strategic policy that "economic construction must rely on sci-tech, and sci-tech must be oriented to economic construction"; (2) it emphasized the need of formulating a unified technology policy and, for the first time, made it a key basis and component of planning so as to promote the rapid and extensive application of sci-tech fruits in production; (3) it also stressed the close combination of sci-tech development planning with technological transformation planning and economic development planning.

On March 5, 1985, the CPC Central Committee promulgated the *Decision on the Sci-Tech System Reform*, marking the official launch of the sci-tech system reform. The CPC Central Committee clearly pointed out that the fundamental purpose of the sci-tech system reform was "to make sci-tech achievements rapidly and widely applied to production, to give full play to the roles of sci-tech personnel, to greatly liberate the sci-tech productivity, and to promote economic and social development." It also gave clear instructions on how to reform the sci-tech management mechanism, sci-tech funding system and other aspects. This marked the entry of China's reform of scientific research institutions into a well-led, well-organized and well-planned stage of comprehensive implementation.

As the economic construction progressed and the sci-tech level improved rapidly in the late 1980s and early 1990s, China began to refine and adjust the objectives and contents of the 15-Year Plan. The *Ten-Year Plan for the Development of Science and Technology (1991–2000) and the Outline of the Eighth Five-Year Plan* (hereinafter referred to as the "8th Five-Year Plan Outline") was drafted in March 1991 and adopted in December 1991. The 8th Five-Year Plan Outline defined sci-tech development as key support for economic growth and upheld sci-tech as the first productive force; it further put forward the strategic deployment of "high-tech development and industrialization" on the basis of the strategic policy that "economic construction must rely on sci-tech, and sci-tech must be oriented to economic construction."

### *5.2.3 Sci-Tech System Under the Socialist Market Economy*

In early 1992, Deng Xiaoping visited southern China and delivered important speeches; in October of the same year, the report of the 14th CPC National Congress clearly proposed the reform goal of establishing a socialist market economy system. In 1993 and 1994, China implemented a series of major reforms in the grain circulation system, financial system, foreign trade system and fiscal and taxation system, which created a more favorable institutional environment for sci-tech development, and also put forward new and higher requirements for sci-tech progress. At the same time, the global political pattern after the Revolutions of 1989 made sci-tech underpinning economic competitiveness increasingly become a new focal and decisive factor in international competition; the ability to master and apply sci-tech, especially high-tech, emerged as a major measure of a country's comprehensive national power. In such a context, the State Science and Technology Commission started to prepare the *Ninth Five-Year Plan for the National Sci-Tech Development and the*

*Outline of Long-term Goals by 2010* (hereinafter referred to as the "9th Five-Year Plan Outline") in 1994. Although the 9th Five-Year Plan Outline was not finally released to the public, it highlighted the guiding ideology that "sci-tech is the first productive force and sci-tech should be integrated with the economy," and proposed the strategy of invigorating China through science and education on the basis of the strategic policy that "economic construction must rely on sci-tech, sci-tech must be oriented to economic construction, and efforts should be made to reach the peak of sci-tech." In May 1995, the CPC Central Committee held the National Science Conference and issued the *Decision on Accelerating Sci-Tech Progress*, which formally established the strategy of invigorating China through science and education. The strategy of invigorating China through science and education also became the main guideline for the sci-tech system reform in the mid and late 1990s; the goal of the sci-tech system reform at this stage was changed to "strengthening the construction of the national innovation system and accelerating the industrialization of sci-tech achievements." With the goal of accelerating the industrialization of sci-tech achievements, in 1998, the State Council decided to reform the management system of 242 research institutes affiliated to 10 national bureaus under the management of the State Economic and Trade Commission, and issued the *Decision on Strengthening Technological Innovation, Developing High-Tech and Realizing Industrialization* and the *Outline of the Report on the Piloting of the Chinese Academy of Sciences (Knowledge Innovation Project)*, which marked that the sci-tech system reform went into the stage of promoting the construction of a national innovation system with enterprises as the mainstay. After the National Technology Innovation Conference in 1999, a series of policies were introduced to enable enterprises to be innovators.

At the end of the twentieth century, China achieved the second strategic goal of socialist modernization ahead of schedule and began to enter a new stage of economic, social and sci-tech development. On a global scale, the process of economic globalization was significantly accelerated, the sci-tech development was rapid, and the knowledge economy began to take shape. The world economy was undergoing significant and profound changes, with a large-scale restructuring of the international division of labor and further resource allocation at the global level. The sci-tech innovation capability became the dominant factor in international competition. The world's major developed countries relied on their sci-tech advantages and seized the historical opportunity of imminent major breakthroughs in sci-tech innovation to rapidly secure the leading positions in terms of sci-tech in the twenty-first century, while the developing countries also actively adjusted their strategies to accelerate their sci-tech development in an effort to win the initiative in the future international political and economic landscape. Against this background, the *Tenth Five-Year Plan for the National Economic and Social Development and the Special Plan for the Development of Science, Technology and Education* (hereinafter referred to as the "10th Five-Year Plan for Sci-Tech and Education") was drafted in February 2000 and released in May 2001. In the 10th Five-Year Plan for Sci-Tech and Education, sci-tech competitiveness was regarded as the key to driving economic development, promoting social progress and maintaining national security, as well as an important factor in determining the future and destiny of the country. The 10th Five-Year Plan for Sci-Tech and Education defined the basic policy for sci-tech development that "We should know what to do and not to do, keep up with the international community in general, make breakthroughs in key areas, develop high-tech, realize industrialization, improve the capability of continuous innovation in sci-tech, and achieve the leap-forward development in technology" (hereinafter referred to as the "innovation and industrialization policy"). China aimed to keep up with the world's advanced level and narrow the gap with other countries in major fields, lead the world in some fields with comparative advantages, and achieve breakthroughs in certain areas that it had the potential, promote the strategic restructuring of the economy and achieve a qualitative leap in social productivity.

In November 2002, the report of the 16th CPC National Congress introduced the concept of building a moderately prosperous society in all aspects and put forward new requirements for sci-tech development. The advantages of developed countries in economy, sci-tech and other aspects made China faced with an international environment with increasingly fierce competition. "...It is more important than ever for us to rely closely on sci-tech progress and innovation to drive a qualitative leap in productivity and promote comprehensive, coordinated and sustainable economic and social development." For this purpose, China kicked off the preparation of the *Outline of the National Medium- and Long-term Plan for Scientific and Technological Development* (hereinafter referred to as the "Medium- and Long-term Plan Outline") in June 2003 based on unprecedented leadership specifications, research team size and time span, and officially released by the State Council in February 2006.

The Medium- and Long-term Plan Outline raised higher requirements for strengthening independent innovation capability, and made more detailed arrangements and deployments for building the national innovation system. First, it clearly pointed out that the improvement of independent innovation capability should be placed in a prominent position of all sci-tech work, and that original innovation, integrated innovation and re-innovation after technology introduction, digestion and absorption should be enhanced from the perspective of enhancing the national innovation capability. Second, the enterprises were fostered to become technology innovators, the modern research institute system was established, the sci-tech management system reform was deepened, and the construction of the national innovation system with Chinese characteristics was comprehensively promoted. Third, concrete supporting policies and safeguard measures related to fiscal taxation, finance, and public service platforms were introduced to enhance the independent innovation capability and build the national innovation system and other specific aspects. After the National Technology Innovation Conference was held in 2012, the State Council established a leading group on sci-tech system reform and innovation system construction. The group, with 26 departments and units as its members, coordinated the top-level design of sci-tech reform and development, provided organizational leadership, and identified 62 missions, 242 reform initiatives and 20 key reform tasks. In September 2012, the CPC Central Committee and the State Council issued *Opinions on Deepening Reform of the Science and Technology System and Accelerating the Construction of the National Innovation System* in order to fully implement the Medium- and Long-term Plan Outline and accelerate the building of a national innovation system and an innovative country.

## 5.3 Main Problems in Sci-Tech Innovation Prior to the 18th CPC National Congress

From the reform and opening-up in 1978 to the convening of the 18th CPC National Congress in 2012, China witnessed the continuous advancement of sci-tech system reform in these 34 years, which created a strong impetus to the improvement of the national sci-tech level and innovation capability. Thanks to the significant increase in its sci-tech innovation capability, China emerged as a major sci-tech power with significant global influence. China ranked 2nd in the world in terms of the quantity of scientific papers published internationally, and 4th in the number of citations to its papers. China ranked 1st and 2nd in the world in terms of invention patent applications and licensing, with 37.9% and 22.3% of the global invention patent applications and licensing, respectively. China took first place in the world in terms of the exports of high-tech industry as a percentage of exports of manufacturing, and third place in the world in terms of the added value of knowledge services. In 2013, China's society-wide R&D expenditure was RMB 1.1906 trillion, which ranked 3rd in the world and accounted for 2.09% of its GDP. China had a large pool of human capital, with its R&D staff leading the world in terms of full-time equivalents and accounting for 9.2% of the global total R&D staff. However, the problems in the sci-tech resources allocation, the principal position of enterprises, the industry-university-research collaboration, and the state-owned enterprise innovation still restricted the supporting role of sci-tech innovation on economic development.

### *5.3.1 Sci-Tech Resources Allocation Efficiency Needed to Be Improved*

Although sci-tech innovation activities cover many steps, they can generally be divided into two relatively independent parts, i.e. "scientific output" and "technological innovation." These two parts are closely related but have very different attributes and characteristics. The scientific output refers to the creation of public knowledge in theory and the development of technological achievements in application through the investment of human, material and financial resources in scientific research, so it solves the problem of macro supply of sci-tech as a factor of economic growth and has strong characteristics of public benefits. Technological innovation refers to the industrialization and large-scale transformation of technological achievements through product development and market promotion, so it solves the problem of integration of sci-tech with the economy and has obvious market-oriented characteristics. The key reason why the high-level sci-tech investments failed to support the economy as they should be at that time was that the prevailing sci-tech system adversely affected the efficiency of sci-tech resource allocation from the above two aspects.

In terms of scientific output, the prevailing sci-tech management system restricted the optimal allocation of sci-tech resources. First, the macro-level sci-tech management system was not rationalized, and the regulation and control capacity was obviously weak. The communication and coordination mechanism between the central government and local governments, between sci-tech departments, and between sci-tech departments and other departments was not well-organized, resulting in the phenomenon that departments acted on their own and the duplicated deployments of sci-tech resources without centralized and efficient utilization. Second, the mechanism for allocating sci-tech funds was unreasonable. The funds were not reasonably allocated between scientific research and technological research, and the proportion of inputs for scientific research was small. The scientific research funds were managed from multiple sources and divided into multiple parts, the scientific research projects overlapped with each other, and there was a severe waste of funds due to repeated applications from different departments. Third, the assessment and evaluation mechanism that pursued only short-term effects was detrimental to the exploration of basic theories and the creation of public knowledge in scientific research, and the excessive administrative intervention in scientific research projects also affected the creativity of researchers.

In terms of technological innovation, there was no healthy pattern that social resources were concentrated on innovation activities. First, the government interfered too much with the micro economy, and the government focused on production expansion and tilted more macro market resources to the heavy chemical industry, real estate industry and infrastructure industry, but failed to provide enough guidance and support to enterprise technological innovation and failed to give positive incentives to the micro entities engaged in technological innovation. Second, the distortions in factor markets and the non-marketization of high-level factors made it difficult to allocate resources to technological innovation. Third, given the gap between China and the world's cutting-edge technologies, Chinese enterprises tended to introduce, follow and imitate foreign technologies, with only low-level replication production capacity and were not willing to take the path of independent innovation with market risks. Fourth, the absence of a mechanism for the two-way mobility of scientific researchers across systems and departments directly affected the effective allocation of sci-tech human resources in the whole society. Besides, the phenomenon that departments acted on their own, lacked coordination and even impede each other made it difficult for various preferential policies to effectively play a role in encouraging and guiding technological innovation. For example, although the Ministry of Science and Technology introduced a policy of pre-tax additional deduction for R&D investment, it required the pre-filing with the taxation department in the implementation, and certain requirements for enterprise qualification were put forward, so the small and medium-sized technology enterprises could hardly benefit from this policy, and the guiding role of this policy on technological innovation of micro entities was restricted.

### 5.3.2 Enterprises' Principal Position Was Not Fully Established

After the reform and opening-up, the continuous sci-tech system reform boosted the enterprises' innovation capability and the role they played in sci-tech innovation. The main sci-tech innovators changed from research institutes and higher education institutions to enterprises. To be more specific, about 90% of R&D institutes were set up in enterprises, about 70% of R&D personnel were distributed in enterprises, more than 70% of R&D funds were used by enterprises, and more than 60% of invention patents were applied by enterprises. However, the *Opinions on Deepening Reform of the Science and Technology System and Accelerating the Construction of the National Innovation System* released shortly before the 18th CPC National Congress pointed out that the principal position of enterprises in technological innovation was not really established. In fact, the undertaking of most of the innovation activities was only a necessary but not a sufficient condition for enterprises to become the main technological innovators. To truly become the main technological innovators, enterprises must also have the ability to dominate and control the decisions related to innovation activities (Guo Tiecheng 2015). However, the enterprise-led industrial technology R&D and innovation system and mechanism were not fully formed.

First, the government still interfered too much with the micro-economy, which weakened the autonomy of enterprises in innovation decisions. Especially in regions with a strong tendency to GDP expansion, the local governments put more emphasis on economic volume but less guidance and support for enterprises' sci-tech innovation. Even when the government supported sci-tech innovation activities, enterprises were usually required to carry out specific implementation according to the government's wishes, so it was difficult for them to actually become the main innovators.

Second, the intrinsic impetus of state-owned enterprises to promote sci-tech innovation still needed to be further boosted. Given the attributes of property rights and the management mechanism, state-owned enterprises maintained close ties with the government and shared many social responsibilities for the government to a greater or lesser extent. In most cases, state-owned enterprises neither took the pursuit of commercial profit maximization as their primary goal nor assumed the risk of business failure and bankruptcy, thus resulting in their inertia in sci-tech innovation. The lack of motivation for innovation in state-owned enterprises also resulted, to a large extent, from the assessment system and the tenure system, in which the leaders of state-owned enterprises were more concerned with administrative promotions and current benefits.

Third, although private small and medium-sized enterprises had an enthusiasm for innovation, they lacked the ability and conditions to integrate innovation resources. Small and medium-sized enterprises had a greater tendency for innovation due to their institutional flexibility, strong market awareness and crisis consciousness. In China, 65% of invention patents, over 75% of technological innovation and over 80% of new product development were realized by small and medium-sized enterprises, and the enterprises' investment in innovation as a percentage of total innovation investment was increasing. However, the role of private small and medium-sized enterprises in promoting sci-tech innovation was also limited by such factors as unsound risk-sharing mechanism, difficulties in raising funds for innovation, lack of innovative talents, and limited R&D capabilities. In addition, some non-inclusive policies introduced by the governments at all levels enticed private enterprises to compete, which also to some extent undermined the enterprises' intrinsic motivation for innovation.

### *5.3.3 Inefficient Government-Industry-University-Research Collaboration Mechanism Resulted in Insufficient Transformation of Sci-Tech Achievements*

Insufficient transformation of sci-tech achievements mainly meant the lack of effective linkage between scientific output and technological innovation, which directly affected the supporting role of sci-tech innovation on economic and social development. In China, the insufficient transformation of sci-tech achievements was highlighted by the disconnection between universities and research institutes and industrial sectors. In 2012, the Institute of Quantitative & Technological Economics of Chinese Academy of Social Sciences made a survey on the transformation of sci-tech achievements among 29 universities in "Project 211." In terms of the willingness for industry-university-research collaboration, the enterprises and industrial sectors expressed a strong willingness to cooperate with universities (institutes) for collaborative R&D. However, the survey showed that the transformation of sci-tech achievements in universities was very unsatisfactory; About 80% of the universities had a patent transformation rate of less than 20%, and about one-fourth of them had a transformation rate of less than 5%. The low transformation rate of sci-technological achievements in universities was mainly attributed to the following reasons:

First, there were no smooth communication, exchange and cooperation channels between the academic community and the industrial sectors, and there were no links among universities, research institutes and enterprises. On the one hand, a large number of sci-tech achievements are put on the shelf, and they not only failed to be transformed into social productivity in time and effectively but also caused a serious waste of sci-tech resources; on the other hand, as the lack of communication channels, the universities' sci-tech achievements could not fully match with the demands of enterprises and markets, which made some of the sci-tech achievements have no value for market transformation.

Second, various parties in the government-industry-university-research collaboration mechanism had unclear responsibilities, and the government departments did not take up the responsibilities for guiding scientific exploration to match with the real needs and promoting the cooperation between universities and institutes and industrial enterprises. The governments at all levels failed to provide adequate public services, which prevented many sci-tech achievements from being effectively industrialized and weakened the role of sci-tech in supporting economic growth.

Third, there were no sci-tech intermediary service providers responsible for intermediary and coordination functions in the established innovation system. The responsibilities of various parties were unclear, and the collaborative relationship among the government, enterprises, universities and research institutes in technological innovation was misaligned. In addition, China's technology intermediary service providers for public welfare were weak, the technology service system and platform construction were outdated, and there were no applied technology R&D institutions to provide socialized services, especially the efforts in R&D of applied technology to serve small and medium-sized enterprises were seriously inadequate.

Fourth, the government lagged behind in regulating and supervising the industries, which was a major factor affecting the transformation of sci-tech achievements. Especially in some emerging industries, industrial regulation and supervision often failed to respond to the changing requirements of the development of emerging technologies and make timely adjustments, so the role of emerging technologies in supporting industrial development and economic growth was restricted. In the IOT industry, for example, the final products (services) were provided in the form of detailed and comprehensive solutions tailored to customer needs. The relevant regulations required that companies providing solutions must have associated qualifications, such as first-class qualification in system integration and computer software standards. However, most IoT companies had the advantage of expertise in RF chip research and development, and may lack other qualifications, which limited their related business activities. Similar problems also existed in the new energy vehicle industry. New energy vehicle technologies are centered on batteries, motors and electric controls, so it is easy for companies with technical advantages in batteries, motors or electric controls to enter the field of new energy vehicles. However, since new energy vehicles are part of the automotive industry, the relevant companies are subject to the special requirements associated with the industry qualifications. The Ministry of Industry and Information Technology has set a high entry threshold, and only companies with whole-vehicle production qualifications can engage in automobile manufacturing. Naturally, this entry threshold made it more difficult for companies in related industries to enter the field of new energy vehicles.

### 5.3.4 The Gap Between China and Europe and the US in Terms of Independent Innovation Capability Was Obvious

There was a large gap between China and developed countries in Europe and the US in terms of independent innovation capability. It was not only reflected in the basic scientific research level, but also reflected in the level of industrial technologies and the division of labor in the industrial value chain.

From 2010, the State Council issued a series of documents and measures in response to the requirements of the new round of the world's scientific and technological revolution and industrial change, with a view to accelerating the cultivation and development of strategic emerging industries and seizing a leading position in the future world in terms of sci-tech and economy. However, the National Development and Reform Commission conducted a survey on strategic emerging industries in 2012, and the results showed a pessimistic situation which was highlighted by the fact that the core aspects of the industries were heavily dependent on foreign technologies and most enterprises were only involved in the low-end aspects of high-end industries. From the perspective of output value alone, the strategic emerging industries in many regions accounted for a large proportion, but the core technologies and equipment in most industries relied on imports. For example, the battery production line, polysilicon ingot furnace, multi-wire cutting machine, high-power inverter in the photovoltaic industry, as well as the glass substrate in the flat panel display industry were mainly based on imports. Due to the lack of core technologies, most enterprises in the high-end strategic emerging industries were at the low end of the industrial chain, and were mainly engaged in assembly, processing and other labor-intensive and low-value-added activities.

From an objective point of view, the gap between China and Europe and the US in terms of independent innovation capability was determined by the different starting points of sci-technology innovation and the development stage they were at. Besides, the gap between China and the world's cutting-edge technologies caused that many enterprises chose to introduce, follow and imitate foreign technologies for cost and profit considerations, and have only a low level of replication production capacity, instead of being willing to take the path of independent innovation with huge market risks. Meanwhile, various low-tech, short-cycle and fast-profit projects, including real estate investment, mineral resources development and commodity speculation, were very attractive to entrepreneurs, and the demonstration effect brought by these projects seriously weakened the enterprises' motivation in innovation. Of course, the failure of government departments to take responsibility for intellectual property protection, industry regulation, and macro income distribution adjustment was also a major factor that hindered the improvement of enterprises' independent innovation ability.

### *5.3.5 The Social Atmosphere Advocating Innovation Was Far from Taking Shape*

The sci-tech system reform prior to the 18th CPC National Congress brought remarkable results in terms of clarifying the goal of sci-tech innovation to serve economic development, rationalizing the relationship and responsibilities among different parties such as government, enterprises and universities and institutes, and building a national innovation system. However, the high-level innovation culture and the social environment for innovation were not formed.

After all, the specific tasks of sci-tech innovation activities needed to be executed and completed by micro-individuals such as scientists, engineers, technicians and entrepreneurs. The recognition and preference of each micro-individual for R&D and innovation activities were directly related to the results and outcomes of each innovation activity, as well as to the overall implementation effect of the innovation-driven strategy. However, the preference and tendencies of micro-individuals in sci-tech innovation were largely dependent on the social environment where they were living.

After the entry of the twenty-first century, with the rapid advancement of urbanization and the dramatic increase in the speed of information dissemination and diffusion, the pace of people's life and work accelerated, and the whole society was full of fickleness; the myth of "overnight riches" as a result of certain system and policy loopholes in the process of economic transformation intensified the spread of fickleness in society and gave birth to the prevalence of utilitarianism and pragmatism. These value concepts ran counter to the spirit of down-to-earth and perseverance required by sci-tech innovation, and the extension of such value concepts would undermine the micro-social foundation for the implementation of the innovation-driven development strategy. Meanwhile, the guidance on evaluating science and technology was unreasonable, and the construction of scientific research integrity and innovation culture was insufficient, which prevented the enthusiasm and creativity of sci-tech personnel from being given full play. For this, it was necessary to create a social atmosphere advocating science and encouraging innovation through propaganda, education, assessment and incentives and to arouse the intrinsic motivation and enthusiasm of micro-individuals for engaging in activities and undertakings related to technological innovation.

## 5.4 Sci-Tech System Reforms and Initial Results After the 18th CPC National Congress

After the 18th CPC National Congress, the formal establishment of the innovation-driven development strategy led to a new round of sci-tech system reform in depth. The CPC Central Committee and the State Council issued several programmatic documents that provided a top-level design for deepening the sci-tech system reform. Focusing on strengthening the principal position of enterprises in innovation, improving the sci-tech management system, and optimizing the innovation and entrepreneurship ecosystem, the central and local governments introduced a series of policies and measures, with a view to continuously releasing the reform dividend and pushing forward the implementation of the innovation-driven development strategy.

### 5.4.1 Programmatic Documents and Top-Level Design

In November 2012, the report of the 18th CPC National Congress formally established the innovation-driven development strategy, and explicitly proposed "to deepen the sci-tech system reform, promote the close integration between sci-tech and economy, accelerate the construction of a national innovation system, and focus on building a technological innovation system with enterprises as the main body, with the market as the guide, and with industry-university-research as the basis."

In November 2013, the third plenary session of the 18th CPC Central Committee adopted the *Decision of the CPC Central Committee on Some Major Issues Concerning Comprehensively Deepening Reform* (hereinafter referred to as the "Decision"). The Section (13) of the Decision specifically elaborated on the issues related to the deepening of the sci-tech system reform, further clarified the objectives of the deepening of the sci-tech system reform in the new period, that is, "to remove the deep-rooted system and mechanism obstacles, improve the capacity of independent innovation, drive economic and social development with innovation, improve the national innovation system, and build an innovative country," and pointed out the main directions for promoting the sci-tech system reform: (1) establishing and improving the system and mechanism for encouraging original innovation, integrated innovation, and re-innovation after technology introduction, digestion and absorption; (2) enhancing the market-oriented mechanism of technological innovation and strengthen the principal position of enterprises in technological innovation; (3) strengthening the use and protection of intellectual property rights; and (4) integrating sci-tech plans and resources, and building an open and transparent national mechanism for managing research resources and evaluating projects.

In March 2015, the CPC Central Committee and the State Council issued the *Several Opinions on Deepening the Reform of Systems and Mechanisms and Accelerating the Implementation of the Innovation-driven Development Strategy* (hereinafter referred to as the "Several Opinions"). The Several Opinions proposed 30 reform measures in eight aspects such as creating an environment of fair competition, increasing financial support, establishing a market-oriented mechanism, stimulating the transformation of sci-tech achievements, improving the scientific research system, accelerating the training and mobility of talents, promoting open innovation, and strengthening overall coordination, with a view to rationalizing the allocation of innovation resources, stimulating innovation vitality, and boosting "mass entrepreneurship and innovation initiative."

On June 4, 2015, the 93rd executive meeting of the State Council adopted the *Opinions on Several Policies and Measures for Vigorously Promoting Mass Entrepreneurship and Innovation Initiative* (hereinafter referred to as the "Opinions on Mass Entrepreneurship and Innovation Initiative"). The Opinions on Mass Entrepreneurship and Innovation Initiative took a holistic view, put emphasis on reform, strengthened innovation, focused on following the laws of entrepreneurship and innovation, and aimed to promote the realization of "the capital chain guiding the entrepreneurship and innovation chain, the entrepreneurship and innovation chain supporting the industrial chain, and the industrial chain driving the employment chain," thus forming a flourishing development pattern of mass entrepreneurship and innovation initiative.

As China's programmatic documents for "deepening the sci-tech system reform and promoting the innovation-driven development strategy" after the 18th CPC National Congress, the above four documents not only clarified the goals of the deepening of the sci-tech system reform in the future but also provided the top-level design for the specific direction of promoting the sci-tech system reform. According to the specific descriptions and main spirit of the sci-tech system reform in the above four documents, the ultimate goal of the deepening of the sci-tech system reform was the comprehensive implementation of the innovation-driven development strategy to create a picture of "mass entrepreneurship and innovation initiative" and support the sustainable economic and social development, while the specific content of the reform focused on the prominent problems and obstacles in the field of sci-tech innovation, including strengthening the principal position of enterprises in innovation, improving the sci-tech management system, and building the innovation and entrepreneurship ecosystem.

### *5.4.2 The Principal Position of Enterprises in Innovation Was Strengthened*

Whether enterprises could really become the main sci-tech innovators was the key to the effectiveness of sci-tech innovation to support economic development, and was also the focus of the sci-tech system reform. After the closing of the 18th CPC National Congress, the National Leading Group for Sci-Tech System Reform and Innovation System Construction (hereinafter referred to as the "Leading Group for Sci-Tech Reform") held its second meeting to discuss the strengthening of the principal position of enterprises in technological innovation and the overall enhancement of their innovation capabilities. In January 2013, the General Office of the State Council issued the *Opinions on Strengthening the Principal Position of Enterprises in Technological Innovation and Comprehensively Enhancing the Enterprises' Innovation Capabilities*, which clearly proposed to deeply implement the national technological innovation programs as a key way to comprehensively promote the work related to enterprise technology innovation.

As a follow-up and implementation of the spirit of the above meeting and documents, the Ministry of Science and Technology in conjunction with 15 departments and units including the National Development and Reform Commission established a joint promotion mechanism in June 2013, with a focus on the implementation of "increasing the government's guidance on enterprise investment in research and development" and other five key areas of work to promote enterprises as the main technological innovators. In more than one year after that, the Ministry of Science and Technology and 57 national departments and units introduced more than a hundred inclusive policies to stimulate enterprise innovation and enhance their technological innovation capabilities, such as increasing the implementation of policies related to an additional deduction of R&D expenses and tax incentives for high-tech enterprises, expanding the scope of pilot policies in Zhongguancun, increasing financial and fiscal support for innovation in small and medium-sized enterprises, and concretely organized the revision of the *Law of the People's Republic of China on Promoting the Transformation of Scientific and Technological Achievements*. Meanwhile, local governments also rolled out specific policies and measures that were practical and more powerful, such as promoting the establishment of R&D institutions in large and medium-sized enterprises in Jiangsu Province, implementing income tax refunds for innovative enterprises in Anhui Province, and supporting the transformation of enterprises' major achievements in Sichuan Province, so as to stimulate the innovative vitality and innovation potential of enterprises.

### *5.4.3 The Prevailing Sci-Tech Management System Was Improved*

The sci-tech management system is the foundation of national sci-tech governance. The outstanding problems in the field of sci-tech innovation at that time, such as inefficient allocation of sci-tech resources, insufficient motivation of scientific researchers for innovation, and difficulty in transforming sci-tech achievements, were largely attributed to the rigidity of the sci-tech management system. Specifically, the research funding management system and the sci-tech evaluation system were the most criticized systems. After the third plenary session of the 18th CPC Central Committee, relevant reforms were pushed forward, aiming to establish the sci-tech management system in line with the laws of innovation.

On November 15, 2013, the Leading Group for Sci-Tech Reform held its fourth meeting and discussed the reform matters and work plans concerning the management of central government-funded scientific research projects and funds, the acceleration of the construction of a sci-tech reporting system, and the establishment of a national innovation survey system. After that, the Ministry of Finance and the Ministry of Science and Technology jointly issued the *Regulations on the Management of Post-Subsidy for National Sci-Tech Programs and Special Funds*, which introduced the post-subsidy mechanism in the management of national sci-tech programs and special projects under the authority of the Ministry of Science and Technology, and officially launched the reform in the management system of scientific research funds. In January 2014, the State Council issued the *Plan on Deepening the Reform of the Management of the Central Government-Funded Sci-Tech Programs (Key Projects, Funds, etc.)* (hereinafter referred to as the "Plan"), which made a comprehensive deployment for the reform of the management of the central government-funded sci-tech programs (key projects, funds, etc.), and aimed to solve the phenomena of duplication, fragmentation, closure and inefficiency of the existing sci-tech programs (key projects, funds, etc.), as well as the outstanding problems such as multiple parties applying funds for the same project and fragmented allocation of resources. The Plan had an arrangement to fully complete the reform by 2017, with the operations of sci-tech programs (key projects, funds, etc.) in accordance with the optimized and integrated five categories and the construction of an open and unified national sci-tech management platform.

In parallel with significant progress in the research fund management system reform, other aspects of the sci-tech management system was also been reformed in an organized manner.

In terms of sci-tech evaluation, the CAS took the lead in accelerating the reform of the sci-tech evaluation system, abandoned the quantitative evaluation and the purely paper-oriented approach, and established an evaluation system oriented to major achievements and outputs. In November 2013, the Ministry of Education issued the *Opinions on Deepening the Reform of Sci-Tech Evaluation in Higher Education Institutions*, which pointed out the need to establish classified evaluation standards and open evaluation methods, and to create a culture of innovation in the pursuit of truth and dedication to learning. In December 2013, the Organization Department of the CPC Central Committee and the Ministry of Science and Technology, together with the Propaganda Department of the CPC Central Committee and the Ministry of Education, carried out rectification work on scientific research projects, talents and institutional evaluation with a focus on simplifying the number of evaluation projects, which resulted in an overall reduction of 28% in the number of evaluation projects. In addition, the Ministry of Science and Technology further focused on the goals and priorities of the "sci-tech major projects" under its management, established a scientific mechanism for dynamic adjustment and elimination of projects, relied on third parties to carry out a mid-term evaluation, and developed an assessment and accountability approach.

In terms of sci-tech system construction, the Ministry of Science and Technology and other relevant departments started to push forward the establishment of the national sci-tech reporting system, the national innovation survey system and the unified national sci-tech management information system (i.e., "two systems + one system") in 2014, and took the open sharing of major research instruments and equipment as a pathway to establish and improve the sci-tech resources open sharing system. In January 2014, the Leading Group for Sci-Tech Reform reviewed and adopted the *Work Plan on the Establishment of the National Innovation Survey System*. In September 2014, the General Office of the State Council forwarded the Guiding Opinions on Accelerating the Establishment of the National Sci-Tech

Reporting System issued by the Ministry of Science and Technology. In December 2014, the State Council issued the *Opinions on the National Major Research Infrastructures and Large Research Instruments Opening to the Society* (GF [2014] No. 70).

### 5.4.4 The Innovation Ecosystem Was Optimized

The alignment between sci-tech innovation and the economy, between innovation results and the industries, and between innovation projects and actual productivity is impossible without a good innovation ecosystem. After the 18th CPC National Congress, the sci-tech system reform was promoted on all fronts, the policy and institutional environment for innovation and entrepreneurship was improved with the introduction of various laws, systems and policies, and the innovation ecosystem with Chinese characteristics was being constructed and optimized, as highlighted in the following aspects:

First, administration was streamlined, power was delegated to the lower levels, and the cost of innovation and entrepreneurship was reduced. On October 27, 2013, the executive meeting of the State Council made arrangements to promote the reform of the registration system of the registered capital of enterprises, reduced the cost of entrepreneurship and stimulated the vitality of social investment. On February 7, 2014, the State Council issued the *Notice on the Issuance of the Plan for the Reform of the Registered Capital Registration System* ([2014] No. 7). The three executive meetings of the State Council held on June 4, 2014, August 20, 2014, and December 12, 2014, discussed the matters concerning the streamlining of administration and decentralization of power, with an aim to stimulate social vitality and support innovation and entrepreneurship. The executive meeting of the State Council held on January 7, 2015, decided to standardize and improve administrative approval measures in order to legalize administrative power, create a business environment conducive to entrepreneurship and innovation, and stimulate social vitality and creativity. After that, the government established the principle of "multiplying" the enthusiasm for entrepreneurship and innovation by "subtracting" the government's power and further realized the streamlining of administration and decentralization of power by means of simplifying the commercial systems and increasing tax incentives for small and micro enterprises.

Second, efforts were made to create a market environment for fair competition. On September 3, 2014, the State Council issued the *Opinions on Promoting Fair Competition and Maintaining Regular Order in the Market* (hereinafter referred to as the "Opinions"). The executive meeting of the State Council held on November 5, 2014, made arrangements to strengthen the protection and use of intellectual property rights to help innovation and entrepreneurship and upgrade "Made-in-China." The Opinions set the primary task of the deepening of institutional and mechanism reform and the implementation of the innovation-driven strategy as "creating an environment for fair competition to encourage innovation," and provided detailed deployments in five aspects, i.e., implementing a strict intellectual property protection system, breaking industry monopolies and market segmentation as constraints to innovation, improving the entry management of new technologies, new products and new business models, improving industrial technology policies and management systems, and creating a mechanism for pushing innovation by factor prices. In addition, the introduction of inclusive policies in terms of taxation, finance and industry access, the revision of the Law on Promoting the Transformation of Scientific and Technological Achievements under the leadership of the Ministry of Science and Technology, and the creation, use, protection and management of intellectual property rights were all dedicated to creating a fair market environment for accelerating the pace of scientific and technological innovation.

Third, innovative sci-tech financing institutions and mechanisms were used to address the financing challenges of innovation and entrepreneurship. On January 7, 2014, the People's Bank of China, together with other five departments, issued the *Opinions on Vigorously Promoting the Innovation of Mechanisms and Institutions and Effectively Providing Financial Services for Sci-Tech* (YF [2014] No. 9), which innovated institutions and mechanisms in seven aspects (i.e., financial organization system, credit product and service model innovation, financing channels, insurance products and services, credit enhancement mechanism, in-depth integration of sci-tech and finance, and innovative policy and coordination and organization mechanism) in order to promote the in-depth combination of sci-tech and finance, and support the construction of the national innovation system and innovation ecosystem. On January 14, 2015, the State Council held an executive meeting and decided to set up the national emerging industry venture capital guidance fund to boost entrepreneurship, innovation and industrial upgrading.

Fourth, collaborative innovation and open innovation were vigorously promoted. With a good national innovation system and innovation ecosystem, various innovation resources and innovation factors can be effectively organized to bring about synergistic effects. For this reason, it was one of the key tasks of the new round of sci-tech system reform to "strengthen integrated deployment and collaborative innovation to improve the overall effectiveness of the innovation system." In April 2013, the Ministry of Education recognized the first batch of 14 collaborative innovation centers, pushed forward the implementation of the *Plan for Improving Innovation Capacity of Higher Education Institutions*, and promoted the formation of collaborative innovation centers between universities and key enterprises and research institutes. Meanwhile, the Ministry of Science and Technology, in conjunction with relevant departments, facilitated the construction of enterprise-led industrial technology innovation alliances, with 55 new national pilot alliances in 2013 alone. In response to the new trend of mass entrepreneurship and innovation initiative in the internet era, the General Office of the State Council issued the Guiding Opinions on Developing the Makerspace and Promoting Mass Innovation and Entrepreneurship on March 2, 2015, with a view to accelerating the development of new models such as the makerspace and providing an open service platform for innovation and entrepreneurship.

### 5.4.5 Initial Results of Sci-Tech System Reform

After the 18th CPC National Congress, the all-around top-level design and intensive roll-out of policies and measures in the sci-tech system reform brought about initial results, with specific results in the following areas:

First, China's national innovation capacity improved steadily. According to the Global Innovation Index (GII) compiled and published by Cornell University, INSEAD and the World Intellectual Property Organization (WIPO), the ranking of China rose steadily from 34th place in 2012 to 29th place in 2014; particularly, its ranking in the innovation output sub-index rose from 19th place to 16th place, and its ranking in the innovation input sub-index rose from 55th place to 45th place. The National Innovation Index Report (2014) released by the Chinese Academy of Science and Technology for Development also showed a steady increase in China's innovation capacity, as China further narrowed its gap with innovative countries and ranked 19th in terms of the national innovation index, the same as the ranking in 2013, but with a score 3.2 points higher than that in 2013; China ranked 20th in 2012.

Second, the principal position of enterprises in innovation and innovation capabilities was strengthened and enhanced. Currently, there are 676 innovative enterprises fostered and supported by relevant state ministries and commissions in various industries, leading to more than 8,400 innovative enterprises at the provincial level; there are 99 national key laboratories and 313 engineering centers built in enterprises, as well as 887 recognized national enterprise technology centers, so the foundation of enterprises' technology innovation capabilities has been strongly strengthened; 52.3% of the national major sci-tech projects, 38.7% of the National High-tech R&D Program (863 Program), 40% of the Sci-Tech Support Program, 44% of the special research projects under international sci-tech cooperation are led and undertaken by enterprises.

Third, social funds were effectively directed to the field of sci-tech innovation. In 2013, the size of the SME venture fund reached RMB 4.736 billion, with more than 30,000 sci-tech-based SMEs in total being supported; in 2015, China set up a new emerging industry venture capital guidance fund with a size of RMB 40 billion. Along with the operations of various innovation and entrepreneurship funds, social funds came into the field of sci-tech innovation rapidly. In 2012, the total angel investment in China was RMB 5.645 billion and increased to RMB 20.123 billion and 52.609 billion in 2013 and 2014, respectively, after the subsequent explosive growth.

## 5.5 Concluding Remarks and Related Advice

### 5.5.1 Concluding Remarks

Based on the detailed analysis and explanation from four aspects (i.e., the relationship between sci-tech system and sci-tech innovation, the changes in China's sci-tech system, the main problems in the field of sci-tech innovation before the 18th CPC National Congress, and the new round of sci-tech system reform after the 18th CPC National Congress), the following conclusions can be made:

First, the implementation of the innovation-driven development strategy is an inevitable choice given the current stage of China's economic development, its own factor endowment structure and the new round of global technological revolution and industrial changes. Sci-tech innovation should be based on scientific research and knowledge creation. Despite the difficulty and high risks as it covers many steps such as product development and market development, sci-tech innovation is the basis of other types of innovation and should be put in the core position of innovation-driven development strategy. The sci-tech system is an institutional system composed of various policies and mechanisms in the process of sci-tech innovation activities. Whether the sci-tech system adapts well to the intrinsic characteristics and laws of sci-tech innovation and effectively solves the problem of market failure in sci-tech innovation activities has a direct impact on the activeness and ultimate effectiveness of sci-tech innovation activities, and also on the success or failure of the implementation of innovation-driven development strategy.

Second, the sci-tech system, as an operational mechanism for the country to organize and manage sci-tech innovation activities, should be formed in compliance with national strategic needs. After the founding of the People's Republic of China, we witnessed different periods of economic and social development in China, including the planned economy period, the reform and transformation period, and the socialist market economy period, resulting in changes in the sci-tech system in line with the strategic goals of different periods. Prior to the 18th CPC National Congress in November 2012, China endeavored to build and improve a market-oriented and enterprise-dominated sci-tech system and a national innovation system.

Third, from 1978 to the 18th CPC National Congress in 2012, China continued its reform of the sci-tech system, and vigorously boosted the level of national sci-tech innovation, enabling China to become a major sci-tech power with significant global influence. However, there were still outstanding problems in the allocation of sci-tech resources, the principal position of enterprises in innovation, the industry-university-research collaboration, and the innovation of state-owned enterprises, which restricted the supporting role of sci-tech innovation in economic development.

Fourth, after the 18th CPC National Congress, the establishment of the innovation-driven development strategy marked the launch of the new round of sci-tech system reform. With the focus on strengthening the principal role of enterprises, improving the efficiency of sci-tech resource allocation and optimizing the innovation ecosystem, both the central and local governments introduced a series of extensive policies and measures aimed at deepening the sci-tech system reform and supporting innovation-driven development, and initial results were achieved.

### 5.5.2 Related Advice

Currently, the new round of global sci-tech revolution and industrial changes has just started. The general purpose technologies (GPTs) with the new-generation information technologies as the core is hastening the birth of a new mainstream technology system and promoting the shift of technology-economy paradigm. The emergence of new concepts such as "Industry 4.0," "Internet Plus" and "online-to-offline (O2O)" shows the signs of a paradigm shift. The sci-tech innovation plays a more important role than ever in supporting economic development. To this end, we must conform to the above trend, follow the principle of "making up for market defects and correcting market failures," define the government's responsibilities in sci-tech innovation, further deepen the sci-tech system reform, and reduce the restrictions and obstacles in sci-tech innovation as much as possible.

First, the government departments should not only continue streamlining administration, delegating power and strengthening the principal role of enterprises in innovation, but also continue increasing inputs in basic research. Although forward-looking basic research cannot be commercialized in the short term, it can provide inspiration for various applied research and development activities. In general, it is difficult for enterprises to invest heavily in basic research for reasons of survival and operations, so this function has to be undertaken by the government.

Second, we should strengthen the construction of various software and hardware infrastructure to provide more convenience for SMEs to be engaged in sci-tech innovation activities. (1) We should strengthen the construction of ICT infrastructure to facilitate entrepreneurship in various "Internet Plus" related industries; (2) given that SMEs, as principal innovators, generally face constraints in information, talents, as well as R&D conditions, we should focus on these constraints to organize the R&D of generic technologies, increase the construction of sci-tech infrastructure, build the generic platforms for various industries, so as to provide strong support for their innovation activities; (3) we should standardize the capital market, strengthen the regulation, reduce abnormal speculation, and make good use of platforms such as the National Equities Exchange and Quotations (NEEQ, known as the New Third Board) to channel more private funds into entrepreneurship and innovation activities.

Third, government departments should adhere to the principle of encouraging and supporting innovation, and focus on improving the level of regulation and supervision on the basis of their own scientific literacy and awareness. It is necessary to actively learn about the dynamics of the new round of sci-tech revolution and industrial changes, proactively adapt to the requirements of new technologies, new industries and new models, and make timely adjustments to various regulatory and access rules to minimize the hindrance brought by by outdated regulatory rules on entrepreneurship and innovation.

Fourth, we should establish an insolvency aid and protection mechanism for technology-based startups, so as to maximize the retention of the innovative resources and innovative capabilities accumulated by startups, encourage the failed ones to start a second business and create a fair competitive environment for them.

Fifth, we should create a favorable social atmosphere to stimulate micro-individuals to engage in innovative activities. After all, specific tasks of technological innovation activities need to be performed and completed by micro-individuals such as scientists, engineers, and entrepreneurs. The recognition and preference of each micro-individual for R&D innovation behaviors are directly related to the effectiveness and success of each innovation activity, and the general preferences and tendencies of most micro-individuals are related to the overall implementation results of the innovation-driven strategy. It is necessary to strengthen scientific popularization and education, spread the general knowledge of modern science, enhance the scientific literacy of the public, and, in particular, stimulate the interests and enthusiasm of the youth for scientific exploration and technological innovation.

## References

Arrow, Kenneth (1962), The Economic Implications of Learning by Doing, Review of Economic Studies, Vol. 29 (3), 155–173.

Cai Fang (2013), How China's Economic Growth Shifts Towards TFP-Driven, Social Sciences in China, Issue 1.

Cai Yuezhou (2015), Analysis on the Intermediary Factors of Intellectual Property Regime Influencing Technological Innovation, Forum on Science and Technology in China, Issue 8.

Drucker, Peter F. (2009), Innovation and Entrepreneurship Practice and Principles (Chinese translation version), China Machine Press, 2009 Edition.

Dutta, Soumitra, Bruno Lanvin, and Sacha Wunsc-Vincent (Ed.) (2015), The Global Innovation Index 2014: The Human Factor in Innovation, Conell University, INSEAD, and the World Intellectual Property Organization (WIPO).

Godin, Benoît (2006), The Linear Model of Innovation: The Historical Construction of an Analytical Framework, Science, Technology, &Human Values, Vol. 31 (6), 639–667.

Guo Tiecheng (2015), How to Make Enterprises Become the Main Technological Innovators, China Science Daily, June 26.

Li Ping and Cai Yuezhou (2014), Major Sci-Tech Plans and Construction of National Innovation System Since the Founding of New China, Seeking Truth, Issue 5, (Bimonthly).

OECD (2005), Oslo Manual: Guideline for collecting and interpreting innovation data (Third edition), A joint publication of OECD and Eurostat.

Rostow, W. W. (2001), The Stages of Economic Growth: A Non-Communist Manifesto (Chinese translation version), China Social Sciences Press, 2001 Edition.

Rothwell, R. (1994), Towards the Fifth-generation Innovation Process, International Marketing Review, Vol. 11, (1), pp. 7–31.

Schumpeter, Joseph A (1994), The Theory of Economic Development: An Inquiry into Profits, Capital, Credit, Interests, and the Business Cycle, Cambridge, MA: Harvard University Press.

# Chapter 6
# Demand for Human Capital and Education Reforms

**Cai Fang**

**Abstract** To adapt to and proactively lead the "new normal" of economic development, i.e. to correctly respond to the economic slowdown, accelerate the industrial restructuring and development mode transformation, and promote the shift to innovation-driven economic growth engine, it is necessary to accelerate the accumulation of human capital, thus realizing the advanced development of education. First, this chapter outlines the new characteristics of China's demographic transition, the new situation of labor supply and the new trend of labor productivity, and reveals the urgent need for human capital to maintain long-term sustainable economic growth. Second, this chapter describes the emerging race between human capital accumulation and robotics, points out that we can only win this race with improved quality of workforce, and further summarizes the characteristics of the human capital requirements for "mass entrepreneurship and innovation initiative" and the characteristics of the returns on all levels and types of education. At the end of this chapter, the author provides policy advice on education development and reforms in terms of resource allocation and individual, social, and governmental responsibilities in relation to China's current development stage and its challenges.

## 6.1 Introduction

The important judgment that China has entered a "new normal" in economic development is based on three characteristics of the specific stage of development that China has presented and will present. First, China is witnessing a structural slowdown in economic growth. With a fundamental change in the demographic structure when the working-age population aged between 15 and 59 reached its peak in 2010 after rapid-growth and slow-growth stages and subsequently entered a negative growth stage, the demographic dividend that had supported China's rapid economic growth for more than 30 years has been disappearing. China's potential economic growth rate, estimated based on the changes in labor supply, capital accumulation,

C. Fang (✉)
Chinese Academy of Social Sciences, Beijing, China

 
X. Zhang (ed.), *Exploration on China's Economic System Reform under New Normal of Development*, https://doi.org/10.1007/978-981-95-2461-7_6

human capital improvements, and productivity gains, has declined from about 10% on average during the period from reform and opening-up to 2010 to 7.6% on average during the 12th Five-Year Plan period (2011–2015), and will further decline to 6.2% on average during the 13th Five-Year Plan period (2016–2020) (Cai and Lu 2013). This reveals that the growth rate of gross domestic product (GDP) is well below the average level since the reform and opening-up, and shows a year-on-year downward trend, which is a characteristic of the "new normal" that has been shown.

Second, while the economic growth rate slows down, the sector structure adjustments, upgrading and optimization will be gradually accelerated. A structural slowdown means that the factors that had traditionally supported economic growth have weakened, with some of them having even disappeared or will gradually disappear. Given that economic growth is a constant and dynamic process, both industrial and technological structures will inevitably be adapted to the new context. Only enterprises, sectors and technologies that can survive based on new growth sources will emerge as winners in the end; otherwise, they will be eliminated by the competitive environment of creative destruction. After all, the future source of China's economic growth comes from this process of survival and elimination. The key elements supporting structural upgrading and optimization are the creativity and skills of laborers, which are directly related to the accumulation of human capital.

Third, for long-term sustainable economic growth, China needs to transform its engine of economic growth by adjusting its sector structure as above and by simultaneously shifting its mode of economic development. The transformation means that economic growth is no longer driven by capital, labor and land inputs, but by innovation and total factor productivity improvement. In the traditional development mode, it is true that the quality of the laborers is crucial and the contribution of human capital is significant. However, in the new development mode, human capital will not only be an increasingly important source of growth, but also a necessary condition for promoting innovation and productivity gains.

Economic growth is ultimately driven by the creativity of laborers, and increasingly widespread or deepened education is a necessary prerequisite for the creativity of modern society, a source of innovation and a guarantee of productivity. As China accelerates its economic restructuring, changes its mode of development and transforms its growth engine, the role of education development is crucial and irreplaceable. In addition, education also serves to enhance social mobility and prevent the widening of income disparities and the intergenerational transmission of poverty. Therefore, the development of education not only helps sustain economic growth, but also plays a key role in enhancing the shared nature of economic development.

Economists have discussed the formation and measurement of human capital over a long period of time. Currently, the measurement of educational outcomes in terms of school-age population enrollment rate, the population with specific educational qualifications as a percentage of the total adult population, and the average education years for the adult population (or labor force) have been proven as the surrogate measure of human capital with the most observable, easy-to-collect, and sufficient information. It means that, on the one hand, economists often use similar measures of education as surrogate variables of human capital in their analyses; on the other hand, policy makers and practitioners usually implement human capital accumulation strategies aimed at developing education in their practice of improving human capital. Therefore, the human capital challenges that China faces as its economic development enters the "new normal" are not only the emerging demand for education development but also new opportunities for education development.

The accumulation of human capital relies on the inputs of individuals, families, society and government, and requires the right market signals that stimulate human capital investment. At the current stage of development, China has various system and mechanism related obstacles that discourage the demand and supply of education, so we should deepen the reforms in related fields, especially the education system, to unleash the productivity of human capital accumulation and to ensure that China will not fall into the middle-income trap. This chapter discusses the new sources of growth that need to be tapped as China's economic development enters the "new normal," brings to light the serious challenges for human capital accumulation and the new characteristics of human capital under the "new normal," and further puts forward policy advice for education development and reforms.

## 6.2 Sources of Growth Under the "New Normal" of Economic Development

Many economists argued that if the average growth rate of the world economy was taken as the "mean," a GDP growth rate well above this mean would eventually decline, and they called this process as "reversion to the mean" (e.g. Pritchett and Summers 2014). Through statistical analyses, some scholars also found that an economy often faced a high probability of economic slowdown when its per capita income reached a specific level, for example, when its GDP per capita reached USD 17,000 (measured in international dollars in 2005) (Eichengreen et al. 2012). All of these "statistical regularities" hid the abundant growth practices of many countries over their long-term development beneath a set of panel data and, in particular, ignored the catching-up characteristics of developing countries and failed to explain why the former catching-up economies such as Japan, the "Four Asian Tigers" (i.e. South Korea, Taiwan, Hong Kong and Singapore) and China could achieve high economic growth in the past 30 years, so no convincing basis for the slowdown was provided. But at least, these studies revealed, on the basis of most phenomena, that a country's economic growth may shift from one normal to another for specific reasons.

Currently, China's economy and even the world economy are facing a downward trend. The right recognition of the causes of the economic slowdown is key to dealing with it and sustaining long-term growth. For the slowdown both in the world economy and in China, there is a common view that insufficient demand after the global financial crisis in 2008–2009 caused the downward cycle of sluggish economic growth. However, this may be incorrect as, on a long-term basis, the potential economic growth is ultimately underpinned by the supply of production factors and productivity gains, while the global deceleration in labor productivity growth occurred prior to the financial crisis. Therefore, the sluggish growth in all countries should not be explained by demand factors alone.

When it comes to China's economy, it was even in 2004, long before the financial crisis, that an important turning point (namely the Lewis turning point) of development was seen. In the ten years that followed, China experienced shortages of unskilled labor force and wage increases, as the concept foreshadowed. For example, the actual average wages of migrant workers, as representatives of the unskilled labor force, grew at an annual rate of 11% from 2004 to 2014. In addition, the wages of ordinary laborers in the labor-intensive manufacturing and construction sectors, as well as several agricultural sectors, grew at a relatively high rate. Currently, the wage levels of ordinary laborers in China are generally higher than those in developing countries in Asia, and more specifically, the wage levels in Beijing, Shanghai and Guangzhou are only lower than those in Japan, the "Four Asian Tigers" (i.e. South Korea, Taiwan, Hong Kong and Singapore) and other developed economies in Asia [Bank of Tokyo-Mitsubishi UFJ (China), Ltd., 2015]. More importantly, labor shortages and wage increases will continue due to demographic changes. If the absolute decrease in the working-age population from 2010 does not yet reflect the level of labor supply, the expected absolute decrease in the economically active population from 2017 will no doubt be a typical measure of labor supply. In other words, the labor shortage will become more and more severe at that time (Fig. 6.1).

The change in the basic nature of the infinite supply of labor in the dual economy and the gradual disappearance of the demographic dividend which fully supported China's economic development during the reform and opening-up period have not only negatively affected the economic growth rate in terms of labor supply constraints, but also have reflected in such results as slower improvements in the quality of labor force (human capital), lower returns on capital, and decelerating growth of TFP, all of which have reduced the potential growth rate. In fact, wage increases do not necessarily imply an impact on comparative advantages and result in a reduction in competitiveness. The factor that affects comparative advantages and competitiveness is the unit labor cost, or the ratio of wages to labor productivity. A direct relationship that we can find is that the extent to which the GDP growth is limited by the increase of the quantity of labor force actually depends on the labor productivity growth rate. In other words, even when the quantity of labor force stops increasing, the comparative advantages can be maintained and the desired economic growth rate can be sustained as long as the increase in labor productivity can offset the increase in costs caused by labor shortages.

There are three ways to increase labor productivity: (1) Increasing the capital-labor ratio. As the costs of labor increase, capital-labor substitution or machine substitution is bound to happen. However, this substitution cannot be achieved overnight because it is subject to the law of diminishing returns on capital. If the quality of laborers cannot meet the requirements for operating machines, the capital-labor substitution will get more kicks than halfpence. (2) Improving human capital. Improving the quality of operating workers and increasing the percentage of engineers are necessary

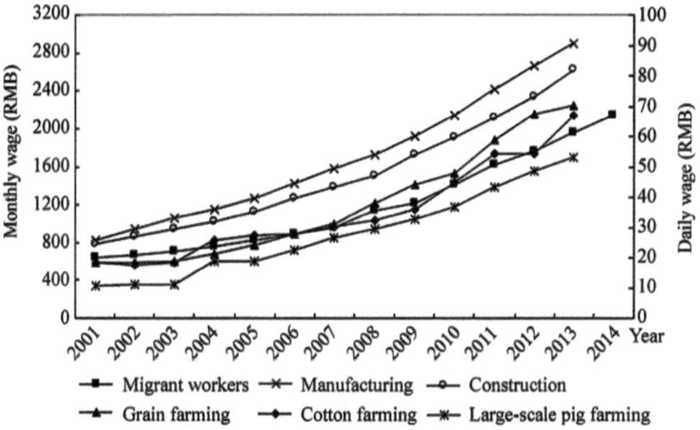


**Fig. 6.1** Trend of wage increases of migrant workers and some sectors. *Note* All wages are calculated at constant prices in 1998. *Data source* The daily wages of grain farming, cotton farming and large-scale pig farming sectors are sourced from the *National Agricultural Product Cost Benefit Information Compilation* for previous years authored by the National Development and Reform Commission's Department of Price and published by China Statistics Press; the monthly wages of manufacturing and construction sectors are sourced from China Labor Statistics Yearbook for previous years authored by the Department of Population and Employment Statistics of the National Bureau of Statistics and the Department of Planning and Finance of the Ministry of Human Resources and Social Security and published by China Statistics Press; the monthly wages of migrant workers are sourced from China Yearbook of Rural Household Survey for previous years authored by the Department of Rural Social and Economic Survey of the National Bureau of Statistics and published by China Statistics Press

for a small number of workers to operate a large number of machines and equipment. Therefore, if we lack well-qualified laborers who have improved skills, the ability to update skills and creativity, the process of substituting capital for labor will hardly have the desired effect. (3) Increasing TFP. The most essential and sustainable source of labor productivity is to increase TFP by applying new technologies, promoting innovation and improving resource allocation. It involves system reforms such as creating a competitive environment.

We found in the decomposition of the factors behind China's GDP growth from 1978 to 2010 that the contributions of physical capital accumulation, labor force quantity, workers' education level (human capital), population dependency ratio, and TFP were 73.7%, 7.1%, 4.2%, 6.7%, and 15%, respectively (Cai and Zhao 2012). Obviously, the contribution of human capital seemed less significant than expected. In fact, other research designed to explain the factors behind China's economic growth showed similar results. In this regard, it is particularly important to note two points:

First, the previous estimates did not take the education quality into account, resulting in an underestimation of the contribution of education to economic growth. According to a recent study conducted by economists including Manuelli, once the education quality is taken into account, the human capital will become a more complete and sufficient explanatory variable, such that, for statistical purposes, its contribution to economic growth will be larger and even greater than that of productivity growth (Manuelli and Seshadri 2005).

Second, the contribution of human capital to economic growth will become increasingly significant. In the above decomposition of economic growth factors, the contribution of physical capital accumulation will become increasingly weaker as the savings rate declines due to population aging and the marginal rate of returns on capital declines, while the demographic transition trend will inevitably cause the contribution of labor force quantity and population dependency ratio to become negative. Therefore, the only sustainable source of growth that we must rely on is human capital accumulation and TFP increase.

For example, John Whalley and others estimated a much higher contribution of human capital (Whalley and Zhao 2010). According to their estimates using a neoclassical growth accounting approach, among such factors as the physical capital size, labor force, human capital size measured by education years, and TFP, the contribution of human capital was 11.7% in 1978–2008; after considering the different levels of productivity contributed by different levels of education, they estimated that the contribution of human capital would increase to 38%. It has also been pointed out by John Whalley et al. and other scholars that human capital accumulation not only plays an important role in China's economic growth but also offsets the poor performance of TFP.

The neglect of the disappearing demographic dividend is manifested in phenomena such as a notable deceleration in the improvement of human capital. As a country that has made extraordinary leaps in both demographic transition and economic and social development processes, China mainly relies on the constant infusion of new labor force to improve its human capital size. Thanks to the extraordinary educational development during the reform and opening-up period such as the popularization of nine-year compulsory education and the expansion of higher education enrollment, the new labor force with more education years has significantly improved the overall human capital. However, as the growth of the new labor force becomes negative, the improvement of human capital will inevitably slow down.

In fact, the so-called new labor force is the sum of the number of dropouts and graduates who have failed to continue their studies at all levels and in all types of education. According to the population forecasts, the growth of the new labor force will be negative from 2014. If there is no significant change in education development, the trend shows that the growth rate of the average education years of the new labor force will stagnate, or even be negative after 2019. Accordingly, a negative growth trend will be seen in the incremental human capital each year, with the total size shrinking rapidly.

China's economy did not slow down immediately when it reached the Lewis turning point due to the labor shortages in 2004, mainly because: (1) Despite the emergence of labor shortages, especially the negative growth of the working-age population aged 15–59 after 2010, a slight increase in the labor force participation rate has kept the economically active population growing at a moderate rate. According to population forecasts, the economically active population will not peak until 2017 and will enter into a negative-growth period after that. (2) For a period of that time,

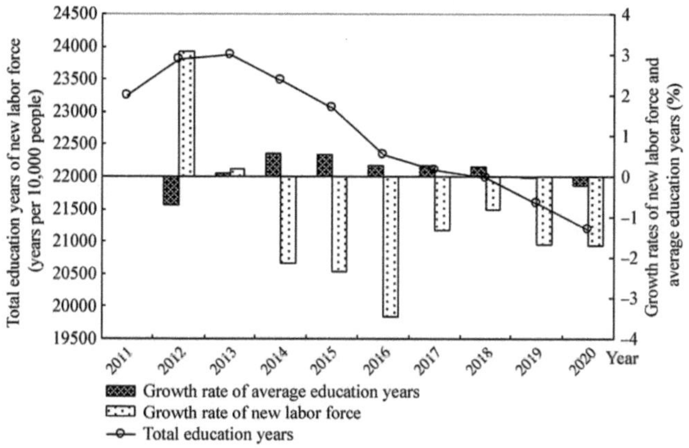


**Fig. 6.2** New labor force and incremental human capital. *Data source* Calculated based on Guo Zhenwei's forecasts of China's population age structure

the improvement of labor productivity was faster than the wage increases, and the latter had the nature of compensating the historical debt, which caused no significant increase in unit labor costs (Fig. 6.2).

However, in the second decade of the twenty-first century, there is a significant deceleration in the improvement of labor productivity. Based on the latest data from the Conference Board (The Conference Board 2015), China's average labor productivity growth rate declined from 9.5% in 2007–2012 to 7.3% in 2012–2013, and further declined to 7% in 2014. The new trend that the improvement of labor productivity lags behind the wage increases has led to an increase in unit labor costs. According to estimates by Du Yang (2014), as the wage increases have been faster than the improvement of labor productivity, the unit labor cost in China's manufacturing sector has been on an upward trend since 2004, and increased by 40% in 2004–2012.

The author does not believe that China's economic slowdown is the result of demand factors in the "new mediocre" of the global economy after the financial crisis, but the weak external demands of the particular period have indeed brought additional urgency to the inevitability of the slowdown caused by the change in the stage of development. For example, when it comes to the changes in the comparative advantages of labor-intensive products, the high wage costs associated with the labor shortages have reduced the comparative advantages and international competitiveness of the relevant sectors, but the potential international competitors (e.g. developing countries with an advantageous population age structure) cannot match Chinese workers in terms of labor quality in the short term, nor can they create a sufficient scale of supply to replace "Made in China." Therefore, the comparative advantages of Chinese products could have been maintained for a certain period of time and the economic slowdown could have occurred in a gradual manner. However, the global financial crisis and sluggish recovery have shortened this "buffer period," and the reality of accelerated economic slowdown has made the requirement for structural adjustment even more urgent.

## 6.3 Race Between Human Capital Accumulation and Robotics

The *Financial Times* reported the experience of an American entrepreneur who owned a factory and pointed to his workshop and said, "These manufacturing processes used to be done in China, and thanks to the use of robots, we have turned Made in China into Made in the US" (Fleming and Giles 2015). That's consistent with the US economy and the US jobs recovery. Michael Spence, a Nobel laureate in economics, concluded that it was industrial outsourcing that destroyed the US economy because he found that almost all of the increase in US employment between 1990 and 2008 came from the nontradable sectors and the middle- and low-end jobs in the tradable sectors flowed to the emerging economies (Spence and Hlatshwayo 2011). However, with the rapid development of automation and robotics on the one hand, and the rising costs of labor in China on the other, there is no doubt that some manufacturing jobs have been brought back to the US. Although this process has not brought the expected number of jobs back to the US, the jobs for Chinese workers will undoubtedly be substantially reduced.

The other side of this story is the challenges faced by unskilled labor in China: machine substitution. On the surface, it seems that machine substitution is a natural process that will not impact China's labor market. Well, what are the challenges? As China enters and adapts to the "new normal" of economic development, it is bound to result in two human resource-related changes: (1) The rising costs of labor will trigger a tendency for capital-labor substitution, and reduce low-end jobs. (2) The urgency of shifting to an innovation-driven mode will raise higher requirements for human capital and increase higher-end jobs. With today's global technology trends, the above changes pose particular challenges for China. The process of capital-labor substitution in the traditional sense (whether it is the replacement of workers by machinery and equipment or by the replacement of workers by old-generation robots) has been usually slow and gradual as a result of the law of diminishing returns on capital so that it could keep pace with the improvement of the quality of workers. However, the new-generation robots not only integrate physical capital and human capital, but also combine operational skills with cognitive abilities, so they will inevitably replace both the labor-intensive workers on the operation lines and gradually replace the knowledge-intensive workers. As a result, the law of diminishing returns on capital will be broken. As the chips that direct robots to work are updated at a much faster pace than the conversion of worker skills, the substitution will come to reality much faster than ever before.

In 2014, China overtook Japan as the world's largest market for robots, with growing imports and production volumes. According to media reports, the Guangdong government announced investing RMB 943 billion in the next three years for technological transformation, including "machine substitution" (People's Government of Guangdong Province 2015). If we assume that the current annual wage of frontline workers in the Pearl River Delta region is RMB 50,000, the investment expected to be made by the government is sufficient to employ 18.86 million workers, and even based on the maximum labor shortage of 600,000 workers after the Spring Festival, it will help meet the labor shortages for the next three years. Therefore, this ambitious investment plan must be made under the severe "bottlenecks" and constraints, and has stronger motives and longer-term expectations:

First, it arose from the plague of multi-year recruitment difficulties and rising labor costs. In 2004, the Pearl River Delta region was the first region in China that suffered from migrant worker shortages, following which the majority of export-oriented manufacturing enterprises in this region faced the most severe problems of labor shortages and rising wage costs. It was reported that the labor costs in Dongguan have been 10 times higher than those in Southeast Asia (Sohu.com 2015). According to Standard Chartered Bank survey, Guangdong Province's nine cities located in the Pearl River Delta region, despite accounting for only 0.6% of the country's area and 4.2% of the country's population, have contributed 27% of exports and attracted 20% of foreign direct investment and Hong Kong, Macao and Taiwan direct investment (Lau et al. 2015). Therefore, the plight of the Pearl River Delta region can fully reflect the plight of China's export-oriented manufacturing sector.

Second, it was inspired by the rapid advances in robotics. Traditional robots are still machines by nature, but the new-generation robots have the learning ability and have made, are making, and will make further and faster advances in intelligence. Currently, the applications of robots that can be seen or anticipated are far beyond what was previously imagined, including ordinary and complex operations by all kinds of machinery, home deliveries and crop tending by drones, self-driving cars and tractors, as well as medical care and complex surgery. The new-generation robots can do almost anything. More importantly, when product updates and industrial upgrades require workers to upgrade and switch skills, it is much faster and more efficient to reprogram robots than to train personnel (Reference News 2015). For this reason, machine substitution may be realized sooner than anyone expects. In fact, this is only what we can observe from our experience. In the wake of Moore's Law and Cooper's Law, another law related to artificial intelligence, Kurzweil's Law, points out the exponential growth nature of technological changes (Kurzweil 2001), and the development of the new-generation robotics will be a perfect embodiment of this law.

Third, it was stimulated by the increasingly intense international competition in the manufacturing sector. While China is witnessing an accelerated aging process and losing its demographic dividend, many developing countries will continue benefiting from the demographic dividend brought about by a growing working-age population and a declining population dependency ratio for decades. For this reason, many foreign economists have predicted that India would outpace China in terms of economic growth to become the fastest-growing country with a large population. In the face of competitive pressure, we should also understand that the problem is not simple. If the economic growth rate is determined by demographic factors alone, the countries with a demographic structure dominated by young people, such as India and Africa, still have a huge gap with China in terms of the education level of their workforce and will not be able to catch up with China in the near future. For example, for the population aged 35, the average education years in India (5.4 years) is 38.7% less than that in China (8.8 years). According to the law of education development, this gap cannot be filled in the short term.

The real competition that China faces is the developed countries on the cutting edge of technological innovation with significant advantages in human capital, as the development of robots and their reduction in costs are expected to rapidly eliminate any country's advantages in unit labor costs and reduce the differences among countries in this regard. In other words, what determines the future configuration pattern of the manufacturing sector is the ability of sci-tech innovation and the quality of labor force, but not the quantity of labor force and wage levels. Similarly, for the average education years of the population aged 35, the gap between China and the US (14.2 years) is the same as the gap between China and India. As such, the challenge for China is not that developing countries with low labor costs are taking away jobs, but that the race is on between human capital accumulation and robotics. Whether China will win this race depends on how quickly it improves its human capital.

In addition, based on the experience and lessons learned from developed countries such as the US, our failure to win the race through human capital accumulation will lead to social risks. In the new era of globalization accompanied by the development of the internet and robotics, new technologies have increased the demand for workers' creativity and skills, which will not only substantially increase the income of highly-educated workers, but also reduce the number of low-end jobs and lower the family income of low-end workers, with the ultimate result that, as seen in the US over the past two or three decades, poor families will not benefit accordingly from the globalization and new technological revolution, and the income distribution will deteriorate and the Gini coefficient will increase. Currently, the income distribution in China's society has been on a track of gradual improvement, with both the urban–rural income gap and the Gini coefficient on a decreasing trend since 2009. However, the trend of only a few years is not sufficient to prove that China has reached the "turning point" in a Kuznets curve for improving income distribution. Therefore, if we do not lay a solid and necessary foundation in the education field, there remains the risk of a widening income gap in the future.

## 6.4 Human Capital Required for Mass Entrepreneurship and Innovation Initiative

The new technological revolution that is emerging (if we cannot say it is happening) will not turn into a nightmare for unskilled and skilled workers, as feared by the original Luddites and neo Luddites. This means that the combination of new technologies and new forms of employment will not inherently make every worker impaired. The zero marginal costs that the internet, especially the mobile internet, is characterized by (Rifkin 2014) enable millions of workers to be employed according to demand and to share the fruits of the new technological revolution. Accordingly, the economic pattern will be increasingly sharing-based, leading to a glimmer of hope for reducing income inequality. More precisely, whether technological change will facilitate the sharing of the fruits of economic development depends on how the labor market responds and how the government makes relevant policies. The accumulation of human capital in connection with education, training and "learning by doing" is a key area for proper response.

In response to new technologies and the new economic model that has emerged, the Chinese government has vigorously promoted the strategy of "mass entrepreneurship and innovation initiative," which not only provides a platform for all people to share the fruits of the new technological revolution, but also places higher demands on the human capital of participants. Based on the theories and practices of human capital and the characteristics of new technologies, new business forms and new employment patterns, we have explained the characteristics of human capital required for embracing the "mass entrepreneurship and innovation initiative" strategy and its implications for education development as below:

Undoubtedly, the goal of education is, among other things, to develop the workers' skills. Skills are developed both through basic education for cognitive skills and through vocational education and training. Therefore, the education years can also be used as a surrogate measure of skills to some extent. With the upgrading and optimization of sector structure, the new demand for workers' skills also means higher requirements for the education level of the working-age population. In the current labor market, the demand for unskilled workers is relatively strong, thus sending a signal that discourages family and individual investment in education and resulting in a negative stimulus for human capital accumulation. This situation not only constrains the development of skills at the present stage, but also may pose a crisis of human capital in the future.

From the perspective of the education level of the rural labor force transferred to non-agricultural sectors: According to the survey data, the current average education years of migrant workers is 9.6 years. This level of human capital makes them well-suited to labor-intensive jobs in the secondary sector (which requires workers to have 9.1 years of education) and to labor-intensive jobs in the tertiary sector (which requires workers to have 9.6 years of education). However, there is a trend towards slower economic growth and faster industrial restructuring in China's economy in the future. In terms of the current human capital-related requirements for jobs, the capital-intensive jobs in the secondary sector require 10.4 years and the technology-intensive jobs in the tertiary sector require 13.3 years. If the industrial trend in the future is a significant increase in the capital-intensive and technology-intensive level of jobs, it can be predicted that the current education level of migrant workers is not yet sufficient to allow them to take up these new jobs.

From the perspective of the human capital matching of college graduates: A main reason for the college graduates' difficulty in finding jobs is that this group of laborers has a very limited scope of employment. By comparing the sector distribution of workers with a college degree or above in China and the US, we found that the majority of Chinese workers with a college degree or above are employed in finance, information, education and health, public administration and other sectors, and the proportion of employees with a college degree in these sectors is even higher in China than in the US. However, the proportion of employees with a college degree or above in the direct production sectors is much lower in China than in the US. For example, the proportion of employees with a college degree or above in agriculture sectors is 0.6% in China and 24.6% in the US; the proportion of employees with a college degree or above in the manufacturing sector is 10.3% in China and 30.0% in the US; the proportion of employees with a college degree or above in transportation sectors is 10.8% in China and 27.1% in the US; and the proportion of employees with a college degree or above in commerce, trade, catering and tourism sectors is 11% in China and 28.6% in the US (Hu Ruiwen et al. 2013).

It does not mean that we should encourage college graduates to work in these sectors of the real economy and that we can expect results. Actually, the low proportions of highly-educated workers employed in the above sectors can be explained by the fact that these sectors are still relatively at the lower ends of the value chains and there is no demand for employing many college graduates in these sectors. However, when a country is well prepared in terms of human capital conditions, it will overcome the "Productivity Paradox"[1] as early as possible and witness the extensive application of new technologies, which will lead to a new round of economic growth. Predictably, the future upgrading of these sectors will inevitably place higher demands on human capital, and whether China's higher education development will meet these demands depends on the foresightedness of our current choices.

Apart from developing skills, the more important role of education is to develop people's cognitive abilities. As creators or creative workers, people need to have the ability to process, store and extract the acquired information through the brain's thinking, so as to understand the composition, properties and interrelationships of things, as well as all kinds of relevant laws. Therefore, education is not only about imparting knowledge, but also about developing the ability of observation, memory, imagination and concentration, so that the educated group will consciously acquire

[1] ⑧Economists observed that the development of information technology did not bring a corresponding increase in productivity in a timely manner (Brynjolfsson 1993). In a broader sense, this paradox can also be interpreted as the fact that there is no natural causality between new technological developments and the economic growth that they are supposed to bring about, or that there is a time lag for this relationship to be triggered. Therefore, we have to create the necessary conditions for realizing this relationship.

new knowledge in the future and be skilled at transforming it into creativity and skills. Obviously, the examination-oriented education system that focuses on teaching knowledge and skills is often unable to develop cognitive skills. It also indicates that we need to develop vocational education, but cannot replace general education with it.

In an era of knowledge-based economy, the sector structure changes very rapidly, and as a consequence, specialized skills can quickly become ineffective. The experience of many developed countries shows that the current popular jobs and relevant skills did not exist 20 or 30 years ago, so it is not possible to learn them in vocational schools. However, workers with cognitive abilities are more adept at acquiring new skills and are less likely to be eliminated from the labor market. The current signals from the labor market discourage families from investing more money and extending their children's years of general education, but from a long-term point of view, the individuals and families with more education, especially higher education, will eventually come out on top. For example, while the difficulty in finding employment and high unemployment rates among young people is a global phenomenon, the situation in all countries shows that laborers with a college degree or above not only have lower unemployment rates, but also have faster wage increases in the long run, making them more likely to be part of the middle-income group.

In addition, education is increasingly having the function of developing non-cognitive abilities, which are mainly reflected in the stage of early childhood education. Non-cognitive abilities include emotional health, social adaptability, and interpersonal communication skills. If cognitive abilities are simply reflected by the "intelligence quotient," non-cognitive abilities are more reflected in "emotional quotient." Professor James J. Heckman's long-term research on early childhood education focuses on abilities such as mental health, perseverance, ability to concentrate, and self-confidence. These are considered important "soft skills" that help children perform better in schools and help adults succeed in society (Liu Libo 2012). More importantly, the new-generation robots are already equipped not only with human-like skills but also with human-like cognitive abilities. But at least for now, non-cognitive abilities are one of the human-specific advantages that robots have yet to reach for a certain period of time.

Under the "new normal" of economic development, the realization of "mass entrepreneurship and innovation initiative" requires the comprehensive cultivation of human capital in the above three areas through education development, so we need to understand the respective laws of education and economic implications. According to a large number of research findings that have reached consensus, among the three abilities that education must develop, vocational education and skill development in vocational training has the highest private returns, relatively low social returns, and relatively low market externalities. In contrast, cognitive abilities developed by general school education have higher social returns, greater externalities, and relatively lower private returns. Non-cognitive skills that are primarily developed in early childhood development and preschool education have the highest social returns, the most notable externalities, and relatively low private returns (Carneiro and Heckman 2003). As a result, economists ranked various types of education in

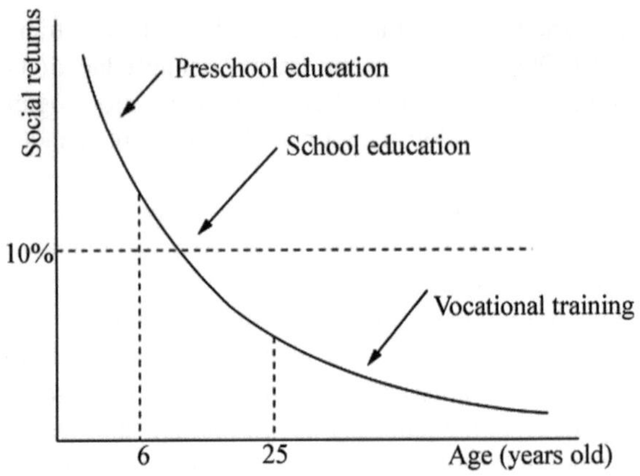


**Fig. 6.3** Ranking of all levels and types of education by social returns. *Data source* Carneiro and Heckman (2003)

order of social returns, and came up with such a priority order: (1) preschool education; (2) compulsory education; (3) higher education; and (4) vocational training. Undoubtedly, government inputs should also be prioritized accordingly.

A long-standing misconception about the returns on human capital is that people treat private returns on education as a measure of the returns on inputs and create incentives for education based on them. In fact, the social returns on education are more fundamental and sharing-based, but, given the externalities characteristic of education, the labor market signals tend to ignore or even hide the social returns, resulting in a failure to translate the signals of social returns into educational incentives. Recent studies evidenced the above misconception. In the early 1990s, James J. Heckman (later a Nobel laureate in economics) lobbied then-Assistant Secretary of the Treasury Lawrence Summers to ensure educational opportunities for children aged 3–4 from poor families, noting that the policy advice was not a benign and vague wish, but a practical investment that would bring tangible returns in the form of reduced social welfare spending, reduced crime and increased tax revenues (Fig. 6.3).

## 6.5 Education Development Sustainability and Reform Directions

From the experience of East Asian economic development, economist Masahiko Aoki (Aoki 2012) found that any country or region that had gone through a government-dominated economic development stage characterized by structural adjustments based on the Kuznets curve would inevitably enter an economic development stage driven by human capital. This turn from one stage to another that he described is what we call the "Lewis turning point." Human capital plays a vital and indispensable role in the process of industrial restructuring, and it will remain a key source of sustained economic growth in the future.

Based on our econometric model, it is estimated that a specific increase in the overall human capital level through the feasible development of education and training would increase its contribution to China's potential growth rate by about 0.1 percentage points in the future (Lu and Cai 2014). This increase in contribution may seem insignificant for any economy that can achieve double-digit growth, but it is not a negligible figure for China as a country strives to maintain medium-to-high growth and avoid a premature descent into medium or even low-to-medium growth under the "new normal" of economic development. Moreover, what is considered here is only the quantity of human capital. By adding the consideration of education quality, the contribution of human capital to economic growth will be significantly higher than the contribution of productivity, as shown in a study cited earlier (Manuelli and Seshadri 2005).

It is obvious that the urgent task for China is how to significantly improve the quantity and quality of education so that it can rely on human capital accumulation to maintain long-term sustainable economic growth. The key to improving education in terms of quantity is to increase the education years of the new-generation workforce. As a general rule, when the enrollment rate of compulsory education has already been high, it is more difficult to continue increasing the years of education. Therefore, the only way is to significantly increase access to preschool education, high-school education and higher education. The key to improving the quality of education depends on what knowledge and abilities are taught to students in what educational mode and with what degree of efficiency. For both the quantity and the quality of education, we must rely on reforms for educational development.

In terms of increasing access to preschool education, high-school education, and higher education, we are faced with a number of obvious cognitive barriers and policy obstacles, thus hindering the development of education quantity. We can look for answers from these barriers and obstacles, so as to propose policies to tackle them. One of the obstacles is the large gap in income levels and education availability between urban and rural areas, between regions and between residents. The absolute level and proportion of direct expenses borne by families for their children's education after the compulsory education stage remains high, which is beyond the reach of low-income families. Moreover, the trend of rising wages of migrant workers has resulted in rising opportunity costs of access to education, and the cost–benefit calculation that families make for their children's education is not conducive to the expansion of education. When there is a labor market failure or paradox of returns on education, one solution is to increase the years of compulsory education by extending the current 9-year compulsory education by three years forward (preschool education) or three years backward (high-school education), thus expanding the scope for the government to pay for education. However, when faced with many options regarding increased spending on people's livelihoods, the government may hesitate to make decisions, and in particular, raise the question of whether China has come to a development stage where preschool education and high school education should be included in free and compulsory education.

In fact, many developed countries have also not expanded compulsory education to this extent. However, a consideration of the characteristics of China's economic development can help us understand the need to surpass developed countries in education. First, different from the neoclassical growth of developed countries, China's economic development is a catching-up process under the conditions of a dual economy, which allows for both faster growth than developed countries and deceleration by a significant margin after the Lewis turning point and before entering the neoclassical growth (and higher-income stage). China must keep the development of education as fast as possible in order to prevent a decline in economic growth and even a fall into the middle-income trap. Second, China's demographic characteristics of "getting old before getting rich," when reflected in the labor market, have a strong negative incentive for education. The only way to break this market failure is to rely on government intervention (i.e. to increase the scale and proportion of public investment) to achieve the advanced development of education.

The next question is where will the money for increased government investment come from. Since 2012, the Chinese government's public investment in education has exceeded 4% of GDP, which is also a high percentage according to international standards. With the improvement of per capita income level, it is certainly necessary to further increase this percentage, but a more feasible and reasonable way is to reform the mechanism of inputs, adjust the structure of inputs, and improve the efficiency of inputs and outputs. The uneven distribution of government investment in education between rural and urban areas, between regions, and between all levels and types of education is currently observed and criticized from the perspective of equity. In fact, this uneven allocation of resources is also inefficient (Heckman 2005). For these reasons, on the one hand, we should first allocate public education resources to poor areas, rural areas and poor families, and on the other hand, we should use the policy priorities redefined by the social returns, namely: (1) preschool education, (2) compulsory education, (3) higher education; and (4) vocational training, as the principle for allocating public education resources, so that we can not only narrow the ability gap as well as the income gap and prevent the intergenerational transmission of poverty, but also significantly improve the efficiency of resources and solve the problem of insufficient investment.

If education is considered a production process that cultivates human capital, different paths should be used to improve the quality of education according to the externalities of different stages and categories of education. For a more equal allocation of resources in compulsory education, we can remove the bottleneck constraints of under-resourced links, improve the overall education efficiency through resource reallocation, and increase human capital outputs. Compulsory education is the key to laying a good foundation for lifelong learning and creating an equal "starting line" for children from urban and rural areas and from families with different income levels. The government should reduce the proportion of household expenditures on compulsory education and stabilize and improve the completion rate of compulsory education. By including preschool education in compulsory education, rural and poor children will not fall behind at the "starting line, which will greatly help to improve their completion rates at the stages of primary school and junior high school, and provide equal opportunities for them to continue their education.

We should substantially improve high school enrollment rates and promote access to higher education. High school and college enrollment rates have bi-directional cause-effect relationships. If high school enrollment rates are high, it means that the number of people with aspirations to attend college is large; if there are more chances to enter college, it also means a greater incentive for students to attend high school. The current share of government budgeted funds spent at the high school level is low, and for rural areas, especially poor rural areas, the disproportionate burden of family expenditures at the high school level, combined with the large opportunity cost and low success rate of college entrance, make this stage of education a bottleneck for education development in the future. For these reasons, in order to continue the rapid advancement of access to higher education, the government should make high school education free as soon as possible (even if it is not included in compulsory education). In contrast, higher education should be further developed based on the enthusiasm of running schools by society and making investment by families.

The improvement of the quality of higher education depends on competition, just as the quality of any product with a fully competitive market is ultimately assured by competition. In this regard, a series of reforms in the education system need to be pushed forward in order to create a fully and fairly competitive environment. The universities in developed countries also went through a long period of exploration and tough reforms before they were able to cultivate talents adapted to the needs of the knowledge economy. For example, European countries reformed their university systems with a focus on increasing competition, reducing regulation, increasing autonomy, and listening more fully to the views of stakeholders, after they saw that their universities were less competitive than those in the US (Kim 2015). China's education systems have problems that are similar to those of other countries and problems that are specific to special national conditions. Only when the commonalities and specificities are combined and analyzed can we come up with targeted reform policies and proposals.

It is actually not difficult to answer the famous "Qian Xuesen's question," "Why can't our universities produce outstanding talents." Each university president is able to list a variety of phenomena and can provide advice on reforms in such areas as curriculum, research systems, teaching quality, and the linkage to the labor market. However, after all, any good advice and perfect design need to be compatible with the incentive mechanism and need to be pushed by the pressure of competition before they can turn into reality. The administrative management of universities is a unique factor in the current system that hinders university competition in China, including their excessive reliance on government funding, their classification into various grades and ranks, and the administrative hierarchy defined for the universities and their administrators. Under the current system, some universities have administrative monopolies, and they rely on administrative ranks and their reputation as key universities to obtain sufficient funding for their operations and to recruit outstanding students. They do not have to rely on the improvement of teaching quality to compete for students and social resources. In contrast, the universities that are classified into lower ranks and categories are excessively market-oriented, blindly seek to meet market demand, and are not motivated to improve their teaching quality.

It is evident that strategies and education system reforms should be implemented according to the characteristics of different stages and categories, especially according to the relative significance of their social and private returns, so that the scale of education can be expanded and the quality of education can be improved. For education fields with relatively high social returns, the fairness of public resource allocation can ensure the efficiency of resource use and contribute to the increase in the quantity and quality of human capital, so these fields can be managed as the fields of public goods production. For education fields with relatively high private returns, we should correct the market signals, align the incentive mechanism, increase the proportion of market-based financing, and improve the competition mechanism, so that the quantity and quality of education can be boosted through reforms.

## References

Aoki, M. (2012), Five Phases of Economic Development and Institutional Evolution in China, Japan and Korea, Part I, in Aoki, M., T.Kuran and G.R.Roland, eds., Institutions and Comparative Economic Development, Basingstoke: Palgrave Macmillan.

Bank of Tokyo-Mitsubishi UFJ (China), Ltd. (2015), Foreign Investment Trends of Japanese Companies: Is it Possible for Japanese Companies to Fully Exit from China?, Japanese Economic Observation, Issue 42.

Brynjolfsson, Erik (1993), The Productivity Paradox of Information Technology: Review and Assessment, Communications of the ACM, Vol. 36 (12), 66–77.

Cai, Fang and Lu Yang (2013), The End of China's Demographic Dividend: The Perspective of Potential GDP Growth, in Ross Garnaut, Cai Fang, and Ligang Song (eds.), China: A New Model for Growth and Development, Australian National University E Press and Social Sciences Academic Press (China), pp. 55–74.

Cai, Fang and Wen Zhao (2012), When Demographic Dividend Disappears: Growth Sustainability of China, in Massa Aoki and Jinglian Wu (eds.), The Chinese Economy: A New Transition, Palgrave Macmillan, Basingstoke, pp. 75–90.

Carneiro, Pedro and James Heckman (2003), Human Capital Policy, in Hec km an, James, A. Krueger, and B. Friedman (eds.), Inequality in America: What Role for Human Capital Policies? Cambridge: MIT Press, pp. 77–239.

Du, Yang (2014), Labor Market Changes and New Sources of Economic Growth, China Opening Journal, Issue 3, 2014.

Eichengreen, B, D Park and K Shin (2012), When Fast Growing Economies Slow Down: International Evidence and Implications for China, Asian Economic Papers, Vol. 11, pp. 42–87.

Fleming, Sam and Chris Giles (2015), The Waiting Game, Financial Times, 26 May.

Global Trends in the Replacement of Human Labor by Robots. (2015). Reference News, February 12, 2015.

Guangdong Provincial People's Government (2015), Notice of Guangdong Provincial People's Government on Issuing a Three-Year Action Plan for Industrial Transformation and Upgrading of Guangdong Province (2015–2017), Official Website of the Department of Science and Technology of Guangdong Province: http://www.gdstc.gov.cn/HTML/zwgk/wscd/1427425587105-7597055140172415808.html.

Heckman, James (2005), China's Human Capital Investment, China Economic Review, Vol. 16 (1), 50–70.

Hu, Ruiwen et al. (2013), China's Education Structure and Talent Supply & Demand, Research Report, 2013.

Kim, Jaehoon (2015), Regulation of University Admission Quotas in Metropolitan Areas and the Competition between Universities, KDI Focus, No. 60.

Kurzweil, Ray (2001), The Law of Accelerating Returns, Kurzweil Accelerating Intelligence Website: http://www.kurzweilai.net/the-law-of-accelerating-returns, March 7.

Lau, Kelvin et al., (2015), PRD' s pain, China and ASEAN's gain, Global Research Special Report, Standard Chartered.

Liu, Libo (2012), Nobel Laureate James J. Heckman's Remarks on Investing in Disadvantaged Children, China Philanthropy Times, November 7, 2012.

Lu, Y. and F. Cai (2014), China's Shift from the Demographic Dividend to the Reform Dividend, in L. Song, R. Garnaut and F. Cai (eds.), Deepening Reform for China's Long Term Growth and Development, ANU E Press, Canberra, pp. 27–50.

Manuelli, Rodolfo E. and Ananth Seshadri (2005), Human Capital and the Wealth of Nations, Department of Economics, University of Wisconsin, Madison, May.

Pritchett, L and LH Summers (2014), Asiaphoria Meets Regression to the Mean, NBER Working Paper No. 20573.

Rifkin, Jeremy (2014), The Zero Marginal Cost Society, China CITIC Press, Edition 2014.

Sohu.com (2015), Dongguan Manufacturing Remains in Dilemma After the Replacement of People by Machines, http://mt.sohu.com/20150607/n414565573.shtml.

Spence, Michael and Sandile Hlatshwayo (2011), The Evolving Structure of the American Economy and the Employment Challenge, Maurice R. Greeberg Center for Geoeconomic Studies Working Paper, Council on Foreign Relations, May.

The Conference Board (2015), Productivity Brief 2015, http: //www.conference-board.org/data/eco nomydatabase/.

Whalley, John and Xiliang Zhao (2010), The Contribution of Human Capital to China' s Economic Growth, NBER Working Paper, No. 16592.

# Chapter 7
# Financial Reforms: From the Third Plenary Session to the Fifth Plenary Session of the 18th CPC Central Committee

**Yin Jianfeng**

**Abstract** Aligned with the demographic dividend characterized by high savings, high investment and high economic growth, China's financial system has evolved three key features after more than 30 years of development: (1) In terms of financial resource allocation, it is a constrained financial system in which the government plays a dominant role; (2) In terms of savings channels and investment channels, it is a bank-oriented system in which the (traditional) banking sector plays a major role; (3) In terms of the opening-up level of the financial system, China's financial system is still relatively closed. This financial system not only fails to adapt to the requirements of the "new normal" of the economy, but also is causing potential systemic risks. It can be seen that China's leverage level has reached or even exceeded those of the countries involved in the European sovereign debt crisis, and China's leverage level has continued to rise in 2016.

In the post-demographic dividend period, China needs to reform its financial system in three aspects in order to adapt to the new economic normal: First, the government-dominated constrained financial system should be shifted to a liberalized financial system in which the market plays a decisive role in the allocation of financial resources. As financial liberalization reforms are usually accompanied by an increase in financial risks, it is crucial to strengthen regulation. The current "One Bank–Three Commissions Regulatory Structure," under which the People's Bank of China (PBOC), the China Banking Regulatory Commission (CBRC), the China Securities Regulatory Commission (CSRC) and the China Insurance Regulatory Commission (CIRC) regulate different parts of the financial sector, requires major reforms. Second, the bank-oriented system should be shifted to a (capital) market-oriented system in which capital markets play a major role in the transformation of savings into investment and banks and markets are integrated. China's capital market development is far behind that of developed countries and even that of countries with

Y. Jianfeng (✉)
Institute of Finance & Banking, Chinese Academy of Social Sciences, Beijing, China



X. Zhang (ed.), *Exploration on China's Economic System Reform under New Normal of Development*, https://doi.org/10.1007/978-981-95-2461-7_7

a per capita GDP lower than China's (e.g. India). Therefore, China should accelerate the development of its stock, bond and derivatives markets during the 13th Five-Year Plan period (2016–2020). Third, with the goal of making the RMB a key reserve currency, we should build an open financial system that plays a supporting role in the international financial system.

Although the three financial reforms mentioned above are interdependent, we still need to determine the reform order: Financial liberalization is a precondition for the formation of a market-oriented system, which in turn is the basis for building an open financial system. Apart from the internal order of financial reforms, we also need to determine the order of financial reforms and other reforms in the overall economic system reforms. Financial reforms must not become a drag on other reforms.

Both the internal order of financial reforms and the order in which financial reforms are located in the overall economic system reforms are crucial. According to the experience and lessons of other countries, the violation of these two orders can lead to the failure of reforms and even to serious economic and financial crises. As for China, we can see from the various financial chaos that has occurred in China in recent years (e.g. higher leverage ratio, "money shortages" and "stock market crashes") that financial reforms should not be carried out ahead of time until the relationship between the government and the market in the real economy has been rationalized and other major reforms, especially fiscal system reforms, have been substantially initiated. As for the financial reforms, the fundamental way to eradicate financial chaos, reduce systemic risks and improve the efficiency of financial resource allocation is to substantially initiate financial liberalization reforms that allow the market to play a decisive role.

Compared with the third plenary session of the 18th CPC Central Committee, which proposed to "improve the financial market system," the fifth plenary session of the 18th CPC Central Committee adopted the *CPC Central Committee's Proposals for Formulating the 13th Five-Year Plan (2016–2020) for National Economic and Social Development* (hereinafter referred to as the "Proposals"), with more emphasis on financial reforms and more specific reform measures. The Proposals not only made clear that "we should accelerate the financial system reforms," but also pointed out in a special section that "we should expand the two-way opening of the financial sector to the outside world." It can be expected that the 13th Five-Year Plan period (2016–2020) will see significant progress in the financial reforms and opening-up, with fundamental changes in the entire financial system, and a new financial system that is aligned with the development concepts of "innovation, coordination, green, openness and sharing" will be a fundamental guarantee for transforming the entire economic system and doubling the GDP and per capita income of urban and rural residents by 2020 from the level in 2010.

## 7.1 Main Characteristics of China's Current Economic and Financial Development Model

The economic system is a huge complex network composed of institutions, norms and behaviors, while the financial system is a subsystem of this network. The institutions, norms and behaviors of the financial system are intertwined and interact with the institutions, norms and behaviors of other subsystems of the economic system. Therefore, we must be aware of the basic characteristics of the overall economic development model before defining the direction and focus of the financial system reforms and understanding thc importancc of thc financial system reforms for economic transition.

### *7.1.1 Main Characteristics of China's Economic Development Model*

For now, China's economic development model has two major characteristics: (1) The model is driven by factor inputs and especially investment, which means that the economic growth relies mainly on factor accumulation and especially high investment; (2) The model is dominated by the government, which means that the government plays a dominant role in the resource allocation process. For these two characteristics, it is worth comparing China with the US, which is the next target for us to catch up.

As shown in Table 7.1, consumption accounts for more than 80% of the US GDP, with household consumption accounting for nearly 70%. Therefore, the US is a typical consumption-driven, especially household consumption-driven economy. In contrast, consumption accounts for only about 51% of China's GDP, with household consumption accounting for less than 38%. Another difference from the US is that investment accounts for nearly 46% of China's GDP. Therefore, China is a typical investment-driven economy. When it comes to investment, we can see the significant share of government and state-owned enterprise investment in China, which together account for about 17% of its GDP, much higher than the share of government investment in the US GDP. When government investment (including state-owned enterprise investment) and government consumption are combined, the share of government economic activities in GDP is about 30% in China, which is roughly 12 percentage points higher than that in the US. Therefore, unlike the US, China is also an economy where the economic activities are dominated by the government. Given the fact that China's land, minerals, and financial resources are all under the government's administrative control, the intervention of the Chinese government in its economy is far greater than the calculation result, i.e. 30% (Fig. 7.1).

Thanks to this economic development model, China became the world's second-largest economy during the 12th Five-Year Plan (2011–2015), but we must transform this model during the 13th Five-Year Plan (2016–2020) in order to achieve the goal of doubling the GDP and per capita income from the level in 2010 and to come close

**Table 7.1** Comparison of GDP expenditure structure between China and the US (with each component as a percentage of GDP) (Unit: %)

| | Year | Consumption | Including: household consumption | Including: government consumption | Investment | Including: private sector investment | Including: government investment | Net exports |
|---|---|---|---|---|---|---|---|---|
| US | 2012 | 84.15 | 68.40 | 15.75 | 19.35 | 15.55 | 3.80 | -3.50 |
| | 2013 | 83.50 | 68.37 | 15.13 | 19.55 | 15.99 | 3.56 | -3.05 |
| | 2014 | 83.13 | 68.40 | 14.73 | 19.92 | 16.49 | 3.43 | -3.06 |
| China | 2012 | 50.81 | 37.13 | 13.68 | 46.45 | 29.26 | 17.19 | 2.74 |
| | 2013 | 51.04 | 37.26 | 13.78 | 46.49 | 29.29 | 17.20 | 2.47 |
| | 2014 | 51.42 | 37.92 | 13.50 | 45.85 | 28.89 | 16.96 | 2.73 |

*Note* "Government investment" in China includes state-owned enterprise investment and government investment, where state-owned enterprise investment is estimated based on the share of fixed assets completed by state-owned enterprises in previous years, and government investment is estimated based on the share of capital formed by the government in the capital flow statement; "Government investment" in the US includes investment by the federal government as well as state and local governments

*Data source* CEIC

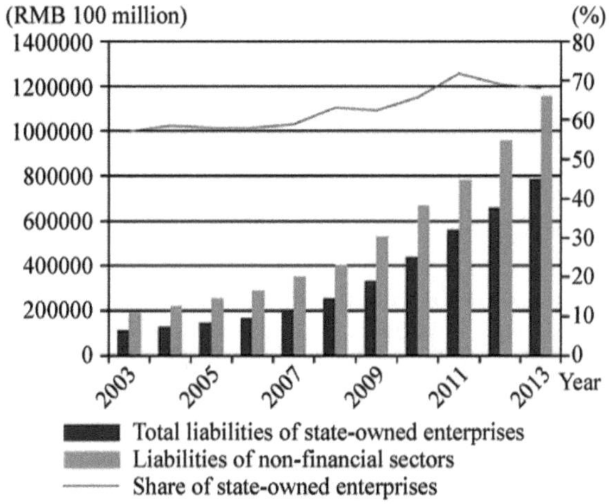


**Fig. 7.1** Total liabilities of non-financial sectors and state-owned enterprises and share of state-owned enterprises. *Data source* CEIC; Wealth Management Center, Institute of Finance & Banking, Chinese Academy of Social Sciences

to or even catch up with the world's largest economy. It is clear that during the 13th Five-Year Plan period (2016–2020), the global economic pattern will see further profound changes, while China's success in achieving faster growth and doubling the GDP and per capita income by 2020 will depend on whether we can speed up the economic restructuring in three aspects: aggregate supply, aggregate demand and development model. In terms of aggregate supply, the economic restructuring that China faces in the next five to ten years is a shift from relying on factor inputs to relying on technological progress. In terms of aggregate demand, the economic restructuring is a shift from relying on investment to relying on consumption. In terms of the economic development model, economic restructuring is a shift from the government-dominated model to a market-dominated model in which the market plays a decisive role.

In the above three aspects, the economic restructuring in terms of the economic development model is more important, which determines the economic restructuring in terms of aggregate supply and aggregate demand. Over the past three decades, the factor input-driven growth model has mainly based on direct and indirect capital inputs from the government under the government-dominated model. Meanwhile, the primary distribution income and disposable income of the household sector as a share of national income have been declining under the government-dominated model, and the declining income share of the household sector and the increasing share of investment in aggregate demand have made it difficult for consumption to become a driving force of economic growth. Even in terms of consumption, the share of consumption in the household sector has been declining, while the share of consumption in the government sector has been increasing.

The change from a government-dominated model to a market-dominated model will ultimately resort to economic system reforms. In this regard, the third plenary session of the 18th CPC Central Committee pointed out that the market should be allowed to play a decisive role and the government should play a better role. The fifth plenary session of the 18th CPC Central Committee noted in the Proposals that "we should play the fundamental role of consumption on growth," "we should play the key role of investment on growth," and "we should play the facilitating role of exports on growth." Obviously, the transition from the investment-driven model to a model in which consumption plays a fundamental role requires us to "base our development on innovation," as "innovation is the first driving force of development." Consumption growth without the support of technological progress is unsustainable, and investment without the support of technological progress is inefficient, while the essence of motivating the whole society's enthusiasm for innovation is giving play to the strong impetus of reforms and "improving the institutional system that enables the market to play a decisive role in resource allocation and the government to play its role better."

### *7.1.2 Main Characteristics of China's Financial Development Model*

The financial system is a complex network composed of financial institutions, financial products and financial markets. As a subsystem of the economic system, the financial system has the basic function of inter-temporal allocation of resources through the transformation of savings to investment in an uncertain environment. Financial systems in all countries vary greatly and are in a dynamic process of constant evolution. However, upon cross-comparison and cross-reference, we can define three essential characteristics of the financial system: (1) the structure of the financial system, i.e. whether the transformation of savings to investment is mainly achieved through the traditional deposit and loan operations of banks or through the investment and financing activities of the capital market.[1] In the former case, the system has a bank-oriented structure, while in the latter case, the system has a (capital) market-oriented structure. (2) The financial system's mechanism for inter-temporal allocation of resources. According to the roles of the market and the government in the resource allocation process, all financial systems can be divided into three categories: liberalized financial system in which the market plays a decisive role, constrained financial system in which the government plays a dominant role, and suppressed financial system in which the government fully curbs the market. (3) Opening-up of the financial system. In the era of financial globalization, there is no totally closed financial system. However, based on stability concerns, countries have varying degrees of control over the cross-border movement of funds, so there is no completely open system either.

Since 1978, China's financial system has been in a dynamic process of constant evolution. In fact, we can also notice significant changes when comparing our financial system before and after 2009. However, based on the above three essential characteristics of the financial system, we can still define China's financial system

[1] ①For more details, see Yin Jianfeng (2006), "Financial Structure and Economic Development."

as a (relatively) closed bank-dominated system with constrained financial institutions. Given that these three characteristics are concluded on a comparative basis, we present the following analysis by comparing China's financial system with those of other countries.

First, in terms of the mechanism for financial resource allocation, China's financial system is aligned with the government-dominated economic development model, and thus the government, rather than the market, plays the dominant role in the financial system. In addition to price controls (e.g. interest rate controls), the government's dominant role includes administrative controls on the entry and exit of financial institutions, administrative controls on financial operations and financial products, and implicit preferences or restrictions on the entities that have access to financial resources. Therefore, the PBOC's efforts in liberalizing the deposit rate cap and promoting the reform of market-oriented interest rate only imply a loosening of price controls, without any change in other administrative controls. For example, there is an issuance approval system in the stock market, and there remains a need for unified and market-oriented reforms of the bond issuance and trading system. More importantly, there is a huge difference in the availability of financial resources for enterprises with different ownership: the state-owned enterprises have dominated more than half of the stock market, but also occupied more resources in various debt financing, including bank loans. In terms of debt financing in the non-financial sector, the share of state-owned enterprises rose from 60% before the financial crisis in 2008 to 70% in 2013 (Table 7.2).

Second, in terms of savings channels and investment channels, China's financial system is aligned with the investment-driven economic development model and is a bank-oriented system in which the (traditional) banking sector plays a major role, instead of a market-oriented system in which the capital market plays a major role. From the households' financial assets structure, we can see the differences

**Table 7.2** Comparison of the financial assets structure of the household sector in China and the US (Unit: %)

| China | Deposits | Securities | Including: stocks | Insurance reserves | Non-corporate equity | Others |
|---|---|---|---|---|---|---|
| 2004 | 81.72 | 8.42 | 4.93 | 7.82 | | 2.04 |
| 2009 | 73.17 | 12.17 | 11.53 | 11.25 | | 3.41 |
| 2013 | 69.67 | 9.61 | 8.47 | 11.95 | | 8.77 |
| US | Deposits | Securities | Including: stocks | Insurance reserves | Non-corporate equity | Others |
| 2004 | 13.93 | 25.48 | 17.66 | 40.33 | 17.42 | 2.83 |
| 2009 | 16.66 | 24.87 | 14.92 | 42.51 | 12.87 | 3.09 |
| 2013 | 14.69 | 25.03 | 19.13 | 43.07 | 14.54 | 2.66 |
| 2014 | 14.85 | 24.41 | 19.56 | 43.57 | 14.53 | 2.65 |

*Data source* CEIC

between these two systems. When comparing the households' financial assets structure in China and the US, we found that China's household sector mainly focused on deposits, which accounted for about 70% of its households' financial assets in 2013. In contrast, in the US households' financial assets, deposits accounted for only about 15%, while securities and various funds accounted for nearly 70%. The bank-oriented system helps mobilize savings and promote large-scale investment in housing and infrastructure, but it has difficulties in adapting to the innovation-driven requirements and in playing the fundamental role of consumption on growth. It can be seen that one of the key reasons for the low consumption in China is that the household disposable income as a share of the national disposable income is low, which is mainly due to the low property income obtained through the capital market. Moreover, the bank-oriented financial system allocates most of the financial resources to the business sector instead of the household sector, so the system mainly benefits producers rather than consumers.

Third, in terms of the opening-up of the financial system, China's financial system remains a highly closed system, which is completely out of step with China's position as the world's largest trading nation. By comparing the capital account of China and the US in 2014, the following results can be seen: (1) Among the three major components of the capital account, China's securities investment had the lowest level of opening-up, with its securities investment assets and liabilities accounting for only 2.53% and 4.96% of its GDP, respectively, far below the level of the US In fact, the opening-up level of China's securities investment is even lower than that of India, whose economy lags behind China's. (2) In terms of direct investment, China's direct investment size remained lower than that of the US, despite the fact that China has been the world's largest recipient of direct investment for many years. More importantly, the development of China's foreign direct investment lagged far behind its speed of receiving direct investment, with China's direct investment assets amounting to only 7% of its GDP in 2014 (Table 7.3).

**Table 7.3** Balance of three major components of capital account as a percentage of GDP in 2014 (Unit: %)

| | Direct investment (assets) | Direct investment (debts) | Other investment (assets) | Other investment (debts) | Securities investment (assets) | Securities investment (debts) |
|---|---|---|---|---|---|---|
| China | 7.18 | 25.84 | 14.50 | 9.29 | 2.53 | 4.96 |
| US | 48.15 | 42.10 | 28.66 | 35.94 | 64.69 | 114.33 |

*Data source* CEIC

## 7.2 Current Financial Risks in China

China's government-dominated, bank-oriented and relatively-closed financial system is aligned with its government-dominated and investment-driven economic development model. Thanks to this economic and financial development model, China went through the century-long development process of other countries in just over thirty years. However, this economic and financial development model is now giving rise to potential systemic risks that cannot be ignored.

### *7.2.1 Excessive Leverage of the Real Economy*

The systemic risks are firstly reflected in the excessive leverage of the real economy. The leverage ratio of China's real economy continued climbing during the 12th Five-Year Plan period (2011–2015), which increased the pressure on debt servicing.

According to Table 7.4, the leverage ratio of China's real economy was 211% in 2014, which equaled or even exceeded the leverage ratios of some eurozone countries during the European debt crisis. This high leverage ratio resulted in a huge pressure of debt servicing: The principal and interest paid on debt by the real economy amounted to 138% of its GDP increase in 2014. Therefore, the third plenary session of the 18th CPC Central Committee pointed out the urgency of preventing regional and systemic financial risks, and the proposals of the fifth plenary session of the CPC Central Committee also emphasized that "we should prevent the occurrence of systemic and regional financial risks."

### *7.2.2 Increased Risks in the Banking Sector*

As China's financial system is still dominated by the (traditional) banking sector, systemic risks mainly come from the banking sector. According to the *Report on China's Banking Operations* released by the CBRC, as of the end of 2014, the balance of non-performing loans of commercial banks (excluding rural credit cooperatives) was RMB 842.6 billion, representing an increase of RMB 250.6 billion or 42.33% from the end of 2013; the non-performing loan ratio was 1.25%, up 0.25 percentage points from the end of 2013. As of the end of 2014, the balance of normal loans of commercial banks was RMB 64.5 trillion, accounting for 95.6%, and the balance of special-mentioned loans was RMB 2.1 trillion, accounting for 3.1%. The non-performing loan ratio was 1.25%, which was at a moderate and controllable level, but further analysis provided us with a clear picture of the severity of the situation.

From a dynamic point of view, the credit risks in the banking sector are increasing, with signs of acceleration. From the end of September 2011 to the end of 2014, both the non-performing loan ratio and the non-performing loan balance in the banking

**Table 7.4** China's real economy leverage ratio and M2/GDP (Unit: %)

| Year | Credit/ GDP | Bonds/ GDP | Inter-bank/ GDP | Non-banking financial/GDP | Total leverage ratio | Debt service/ GDP increase | M2/ GDP |
|---|---|---|---|---|---|---|---|
| 2010 | 127 | 26 | 8 | 5 | 167 | 80 | 181 |
| 2011 | 125 | 27 | 8 | 6 | 165 | 89 | 180 |
| 2012 | 134 | 29 | 11 | 10 | 184 | 108 | 188 |
| 2013 | 143 | 32 | 13 | 16 | 203 | 133 | 195 |
| 2014 | 148 | 33 | 13 | 18 | 211 | 138 | 193 |

*Note* "Total leverage ratio" refers to the ratio of all debts of the real economy (the government, non-financial enterprises and households) to GDP. "Credit" refers to domestic and overseas credit balance, including short-term, medium-term and long-term loan balance, bill financing balance, entrusted loans, financial leasing balance, other loan balance and overseas loans, etc. "Bonds" include national bonds, local government bonds, corporate bonds, company bonds, short-term financing bonds, medium-term notes, etc. "Inter-bank" refers to the net credit balance provided to the real economy through inter-bank business. "Non-bank financial" refers to credit balance provided by non-bank financial institutions to the real economy, including balance of trust companies' investment in underlying assets, housing and industrial and commercial enterprises, balance of securities companies' passageway business as well as balance of insurance companies' plans for investment in claims and real property. "Debt service" refers to the principal and interest paid on a quarterly basis under the assumptions of an interest rate and a debt maturity
*Data source* National Institution for Finance & Development

sector have risen for 14 consecutive quarters, with the non-performing loan ratio rising from 0.9% to 1.25% and the non-performing loan balance rising from RMB 407.8 billion to RMB 842.6 billion. If the increased efforts in writing off bad debts in the banking sector in 2014 are taken into account (according to incomplete statistics, the listed banks wrote off and transferred out a total of about RMB 200.317 billion of non-performing loans in 2014, twice as much as in 2013), and if this amount is included, the adjusted growth rate of non-performing loan balance in 2014 may be 100% or even higher.

From a static point of view, the data on non-performing loans may be underestimated. Given the strict control of risks by regulatory authorities and the reality that performance assessment is highly linked to asset quality, banks are likely to embellish their asset quality. Due to the ambiguity of the five-category loan classification, some defective loans that have risks (e.g. with a 90-day delinquency rate) are not included in non-performing loans in practice, but are temporarily classified as special-mentioned loans. According to the available data, the share of special-mentioned loans in the banking sector rose rapidly from 2.5% at the end of the first quarter of 2014 to 3.1% at the end of the fourth quarter of 2014. Moreover, there are cases in practice where risks that might have occurred are temporarily masked by postponing them through rollovers. It should also be noted that the statistics released by the CBRC only cover commercial banks and exclude over 2,000 credit cooperatives that remain unreconstructed and have generally lower asset quality than commercial banks. Combining the above factors, we surmised that the current data on the non-performing rate might be significantly underestimated.

From a structural point of view, some regions and sectors have more prominent risks. In terms of sectors, the non-performing loan balance in sectors such as photovoltaic, steel, shipping and flat glass increased rapidly. Under the impact of decreased growth of domestic investment and exports, increased pressure of excess capacity, decreased market demand and other factors, electrical machinery, textiles and other sectors have greater operating pressure, and coal, photovoltaic, steel, cement, shipbuilding and other related sectors are at the risk of a liquidity squeeze, which makes it more likely that the risks of these sectors are transmitted to the financial sector. In terms of regions, new non-performing loans are mainly distributed in the Yangtze River Delta and other regions, but there is a sign that they will gradually extend to other regions. Affected by the weak domestic and foreign demand, the export-oriented regional micro and small-sized enterprises are generally suffering from declining orders, rising costs, declining profits and other problems, private enterprises, especially small and medium-sized private enterprises are at risk of capital shortage, and the enterprises' credit risks are relatively concentrated in the coastal areas where the private economy is well developed. What is more worrying is that, with the dramatic increase in risk costs, the relationship between banks and enterprises in some areas is continuously deteriorating, thus resulting in greater difficulty and higher costs for enterprises to obtain financing. In the short term, there is no fundamental solution to this problem.

From an overall point of view, the overall credit risks of the banking sector remain in a tolerable range, but the trend of continuous increase in credit risks will not be reversed in the short term as the economic restructuring is far from over. The reports for the first quarter of 2015 released by the listed banks also confirmed that both the non-performing loan ratio and non-performing loan balance are going up slightly. According to our forecast, this trend will hardly be fundamentally reversed in the coming year.

### 7.2.3 *Risk of Asset Price Bubbles*

The risk of asset price bubbles is first reflected in the housing market. Although China's housing market has not yet seen the same crash as Japan's in 1990, a profound adjustment is underway and deflationary pressures are being generated through two channels: (1) The excess capacity in the housing market is putting long-term downward pressure on housing prices and the prices of related sectors. In 2014, China's housing sector saw negative year-over-year growth in terms of both sales value and square footage, which was recorded only once in the past decade when the global financial crisis erupted in 2008. The decline in both sales value and square footage was accompanied by an overall glut in the housing market. As shown in Fig. 7.2, new commercial housing units exceeded the new urban households in China in 2012. If the affordable housing units are also taken into account, the number of housing units

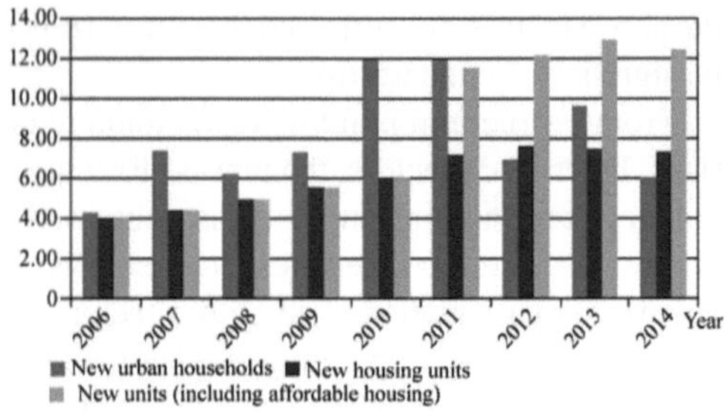


**Fig. 7.2** Measurement of housing market supply and demand in China. *Note* "New urban households" is calculated based on the new urban population and the average size of urban households. *Data source* CEIC

supplied will be more than twice the number of housing units demanded (new urban households). The future de-stocking in the housing market will not only lead to a long-term decline in housing prices, but will also put downward pressure on prices of the sectors that are forward linked (such as the steel and cement sectors) and backward linked (such as the building materials and textile sectors) with the housing market. (2) The declining value of housing collateral will cause a slow balance sheet recession, which is particularly evident in local governments and local financing platforms. In 2014, we saw not only a 30% negative growth in industrial, mining and storage land, but also a 26% year-on-year negative growth in housing land. The decline in land supply will directly affect the asset value and cash flow of the main debtor (i.e. local financing platforms) and raise the pressure on debt servicing.

The risk of asset price bubbles is also reflected in the stock market. Although the stock market has digested the previous bubble factors and entered a relatively healthy trajectory following the adjustments after July 2015, it is still necessary to recap the stock market spike before July 2015. As we can see, the stock price boom from 2014 to July 2015 was justified by investors' positive expectations for sector structure upgrading and various reforms (the so-called "reformed bull market"), but the stock prices rose at an abnormally fast pace. As an example, the Growth Enterprises Market saw its stock price boom from the end of 2012, at which time the Growth Enterprises Index was 600 points, while after more than 2 years, it was close to 4,000 points in early June 2015, representing a nearly sixfold increase. Moreover, with an accelerated upward trend, the Growth Enterprises Index increased by 165% in less than six months from early January to early June 2015. As of June 17, 2015, the Growth Enterprises Market had 475 stocks, with an average P/E ratio of 137.62x, and the Shenzhen Stock Exchange's small and medium-sized enterprise board had 759 stocks, with an average P/E ratio of 81.77x. The valuation levels of the Growth Enterprises Market and the Shenzhen Stock Exchange's small and medium-sized enterprise board were above the highest valuation level of previous bull markets in China (around 60x) and also above the valuation level of foreign technology stock markets when they reached the maximum level of bubbles.

Another major factor that led to the stock market spike was stock speculation with borrowed money (i.e. "leveraged bull market"). Basically, stock speculation with borrowed money is based on three methods: (1) investing the funds that are obtained by placing a mortgage on investors' housing or other assets to a bank; (2)

financing through stock pledges, or the so-called "securities margin trading," which is a relatively regulated financing method with higher transparency; and (3) stock financing based on a certain percentage of investors original funds, which is a private financing transaction in a gray area between stockbrokers and investors without the constraints of laws and regulations. Many bank funds enter the stock market through this channel. The so-called "umbrella trust" is one of the typical ways of operation, which opens the channel for bank funds to enter the stock market and removes the firewall of funds between banks and the securities market.

Only the data for the second method of financing are available. The financing balance was RMB 300 billion at the beginning of 2014 and increased to RMB 1 trillion by the end of 2014. The financing balance doubled in the first five months of 2015, putting the cumulative balance at over RMB 2.2 trillion. In addition, the scale of pledging business of securities companies reached RMB 700 billion, a considerable part of which entered the stock market. As of the stock market crash, the total scale of stock speculation with financing was RMB 3–4 trillion (of which, the scale of regulated financing business was RMB 2.2 trillion, the scale of financing through stock pledges was RMB 700 billion, and the scale of stock financing based on a certain percentage of investors original funds was about RMB 500 billion to 1,500 billion). In China, the number of stocks financed exceeded 10% of the actual market value of stocks in circulation, but in major stock markets in Europe and the US, the number of stocks financed as a percentage of the market value of stocks in circulation generally does not exceed 3%.

Apart from the excessive leverage that boosted the stock market, there are three more lessons worth thinking about: (1) At the policy level, China allowed the so-called "national bull market" by acquiescing to or even by actively boosting the stock market through media. (2) At the regulatory level, China did not monitor leveraged stock speculation in real time and did not provide timely regulation. (3) Most critically, the issuing and delisting system in China's stock market was not reformed, resulting in the supply in the primary market failing to keep up with the inflow of funds in the secondary market, and many junk stocks being included in the secondary market.

### *7.2.4 Long-Term Deflation*

The current systemic risks are mainly reflected in deflation. Japan witnessed a decade-long deflationary period after the early 1990s, typically characterized by negative PPI growth, and this period was also known as "Japan's Lost Decade." This was partly caused by the lack of new sources of economic growth due to the weak economic system reforms in Japan after the bursting of asset price bubbles, and also partly by the aging of the population. Since 2012, China has witnessed negative PPI growth for almost four years. Looking ahead to the next 5–10 years, the factors that will cause long-term deflation in China include not only the weak restructuring of the economy but also the rapid aging of the population (Fig. 7.3).

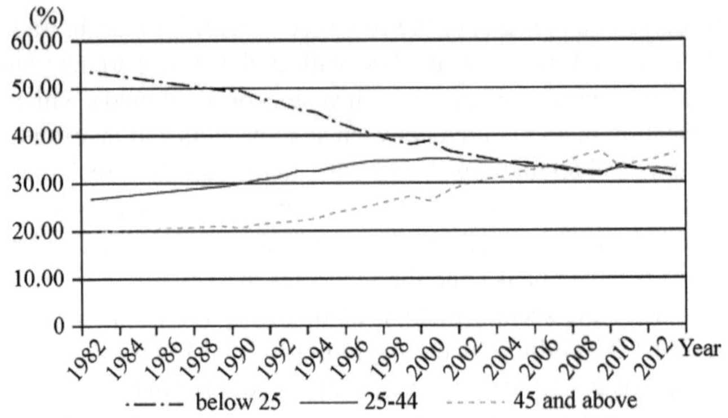


**Fig. 7.3** Evolution of China's population age structure, 1982–2013. *Note* Calculated based on data from the population sample survey of the National Bureau of Statistics. *Data source* CEIC

In China, population aging occurs not only at periods of low per capita income, which means that "people get old before getting rich," but also is reflected in the faster pace of aging. The growth rate of China's working-age population declined from 1.58% in 1985–2007 to 0.61% in 2008–2015 and will further decline to -0.4% in 2016–2020 based on the age-moving method. The population aging and the declining growth rate of the labor force participation directly resulted in a change in labor supply: the growth rate of labor inputs declined from 1.5% in 1985–2007 to 0.36% in 2008–2015 and is estimated to be -0.9% in 2016–2020.

Why does population aging cause the occurrence of deflation? The first reason is that it lowers the asset prices through three channels, thus leading to long-term asset price declines, debt accumulation and deflationary effects: (1) With the population aging, the demand in the housing market declines and the prices of housing drops; (2) In addition to the housing market, the demand for capital goods such as transportation and communication equipment, as well as education required for human capital accumulation, also declines. (3) As the size and share of the working-age population decline, the marginal returns on capital also decline. The second reason is that population aging brings about an output gap, which means that the aggregate demand is smaller than the potential outputs. There are two types of factors that contribute to the output gap: (1) Aggregate factors. While private sector investment declines, fiscal pressures from the population aging require the implementation of fiscal policies that increase taxes and reduce spending, which usually results from the Ricardo-Hayek effect of excessive fiscal spending prior to the demographic pressure. (2) Supply–demand structure factors. Given the low supply elasticity of the economy, it is difficult for the supply structure to keep up with changes in the demand structure. With the population aging, the weight of the aggregate demand structure gradually shifts from the traditional manufacturing sector to the service sector such as elderly care and medical care, which causes excess capacity and falling prices in the traditional manufacturing sector and drives down the overall prices of commodities. The third reason is that the aging population leads to deflationary expectations. The depressed asset prices and the continuous output gap will reverse the inflationary expectations of economic parties to deflationary expectations, thus further contributing to the maintenance of the deflationary status.

Currently, China has seen the asset price effects and supply–demand structure gap effects resulting from population aging. First, in terms of the potential impact of the population aging on the housing market: Based on the characteristics of home buyers, it can be found that people aged below 25 generally neither have the ability to purchase homes and nor have the demand for housing; first-time home buyers are mainly aged 25–44, and this age group is the main source of new demand for housing; people aged 45 and above also do purchase homes, but their demand is mainly for improving housing conditions, which means that the market demand will not be increased, as the purchase of a unit increases the demand and the sale or rental of a unit increases the supply. It is worth noting that China's population aged 45 and above has outnumbered the population aged 25–44 since 2007. This change in population structure, combined with the aforementioned excess capacity in the housing market, will put long-term downward pressure on the housing market.

Second, in terms of the imbalanced supply–demand structure caused by population aging: Different price levels are diverging as the elasticity of supply does not keep up with the structure changes in aggregate demand: (1) Divergence of CPI and PPI. The CPI includes the prices of the service sector excluding the manufacturing sector, while the PPI is mainly related to the manufacturing sector. Therefore, despite years of continuous decline in PPI, China's CPI growth remains positive. It is interesting to compare this divergence with the situation after the Asian financial crisis, when China still had its demographic dividend and, as a result, the deflation manifested itself in the simultaneous negative growth of both PPI and CPI. (2) Divergence of CPI components. It is observed that in the decade since 2006, the growth rate of the services CPI has consistently outpaced the growth rate of the non-food CPI and the core CPI.

### *7.2.5 External Financial Shocks*

External financial shocks are evident in the significant impact of large capital outflows and, in particular, large capital outflows on the macroeconomic and financial systems. In fact, similar to the aftermath of the Asian financial crisis, we have also seen a reversal from capital inflows to capital outflows after this global financial crisis, as evidenced by the rapid expansion of the item "errors and omissions" in the balance of payments statistics. During the Asian financial crisis, the item "errors and omissions" remained negative due to capital flight, and in 1998–2000, a period of severe deflation, the item "errors and omissions" was as high as 1–3 times the scale of reserve assets. From 2009, the item "errors and omissions" changed again from positive to negative, and its scale gradually expanded, hitting the record of USD -140 billion in 2014. However, such items in the capital and financial accounts as "capital account," "direct investment," and "securities investment" all showed a net increase, with the exception

**Table 7.5** China's international reserve assets, 2014–2015 (Unit: USD 100 million)

| Item | 2014Q1 | 2014Q2 | 2014Q3 | 2014Q4 | 2015Q1 | 2015Q2 |
|---|---|---|---|---|---|---|
| International reserve assets | 1255 | 224 | -1 | -300 | -802 | 131 |
| Monetary gold | 0 | 0 | 0 | 0 | 0 | 0 |
| Special drawing rights | 1 | -1 | 0 | 0 | 0 | 4 |
| Reserve positions in the IMF | -4 | -2 | 4 | -7 | -7 | -2 |
| Foreign exchange reserves | 1258 | 228 | -4 | -293 | -795 | 130 |
| Other reserve assets | 0 | 0 | 0 | 0 | 0 | 0 |

*Data source* SAFE

that "other investments," an item for measuring domestic and foreign borrowings, showed a net decrease.

In addition to the item "errors and omissions," another item "foreign exchange reserves" also began to decline after multi-years of increase. According to the data published by the State Administration of Foreign Exchange (SAFE),[2] after excluding the impact of non-trading value changes such as exchange rates and prices (the same as below), the international reserve assets decreased by USD 80.2 billion, the foreign exchange reserve assets decreased by USD 79.5 billion, and the special drawing rights and the reserve position in the IMF decreased by USD 0.7 billion in the first quarter of 2015; the international reserve assets increased by USD 13.1 billion, the foreign exchange reserve assets increased by USD 13 billion, and the special drawing rights and the reserve position in the IMF increased by USD 0.2 billion in the second quarter of 2015 (see Table 7.5). China's foreign exchange reserve assets decreased by USD 66.5 billion in the first half of 2015, compared to an increase of USD 148.6 billion in the same period in 2014.

Over the next 5–10 years, global capital flows will become more unstable due to the differences in the speed of economic recovery and the differences in macroeconomic policies across countries. In addition to the changes in the external environment that may lead to greater external financial shocks, China also faces a greater risk from the premature opening of the capital account. The reason why Japan experienced the crisis caused by the bursting of the asset price bubbles in the late 1980s and the subsequent "Lost Decade" is that it did not follow the basic order of reforms and opening-up: the reform of the real economic system, the deregulation of capital markets, the liberalization of interest rates and exchange rates, and the opening of the capital account. In contrast to that order, the first step Japan made in the 1980s when its real economy was not restructured and its capital markets were not developed, was to open its capital account, which resulted in massive capital currency arbitrage between the offshore yen market and the onshore yen market.

Currently, China has been struggling to reform its economic system which involves both size adjustment and interest adjustment, while the opening of the

[2] ②From 2015, the SAFE prepares and publishes the Balance of Payments Statement in accordance with the latest international standard *Balance of Payments and International Investment Position Manual* (Sixth Edition) issued by the IMF.

capital account becomes an area that all parties are interested in promoting as it seems to be an incremental reform with no conflict of interest. However, based on the lessons learned from Japan, the premature opening of the capital account under the circumstances of stagnant economic system reform, tough restructuring of the real economy and numerous shortcomings in the domestic capital market will definitely pose a major risk to China in the future.

## 7.3 Promoting Economic Transition with Financial Reforms and Opening-Up

To be in line with the reforms of the economic system in which the market plays a decisive role and the government plays a better role, China's financial system needs to be reformed in three aspects: (1) A shift should be made from government-dominated allocation of financial resources to the allocation of financial resources where the market plays a decisive role. (2) A shift should be made from the bank-oriented system to the (capital) market-oriented system in which the capital market plays a major role in the conversion of savings into investment and banks and markets are integrated with each other. China's capital market development is far behind that of developed countries and even countries whose GDP per capita is lower than China's (e.g. India), so China should accelerate the development of its stock market, bond market and derivatives market during the 13th Five-Year Plan period (2016–2020). (3) An open financial system that aims to make the RMB a key reserve currency and play a supporting role in the international financial system should be built. Since financial reforms and opening-up are usually accompanied by an increase in financial risks, it is crucial to strengthen regulation. The current "One Bank–Three Commissions Regulatory Structure," under which the PBOC, the CBRC, the CSRC and the CIRC regulate different parts of the financial sector, requires major reforms.

### *7.3.1 Contents Related to Financial Reforms Proposed by the Third Plenary Session of the 18th CPC Central Committee*

In the *Decision of the Third Plenary Session of the 18th CPC Central Committee on Major Issues Concerning Comprehensively Deepening Reform* (hereinafter referred to as the "Decision"), only 380 Chinese words in Article 12 are directly related to financial reforms, and such contents as the construction of a multi-tiered capital market, the reform of interest rate market and the convertibility of Renminbi under the capital account are not new concepts. It seems that financial reforms are not the focus of the Decision and are not innovative, but the opposite is true. The financial system is a part of the whole political and economic system, so the reforms of other parts of the superstructure must have a profound impact on it, and the reforms of other parts also depend directly or indirectly on the reforms of the financial system. The financial system is also a part of the whole economic system, so the restructuring in other areas of the economic system will inevitably lead to the restructuring of the financial system, and the restructuring of the financial system, as the "core of the modern economy," will inevitably promote the restructuring of the whole economic system. In fact, the Decision outlines the financial reforms embedded in the economic system reforms from three major aspects: financial resource allocation mechanism, financial system structure and financial investment opportunities.

The first aspect is the shift in financial resource allocation. China's current financial resource allocation model was formed at the third plenary session of the 14th CPC Central Committee and fully took shape at the Second National Financial Work Conference in 2002. The model can effectively mobilize savings and allocate them to large-scale investments in mature technologies, and it is a relatively stable and orderly resource allocation model. However, it has the disadvantage that when the economy reaches a considerable stage of development, it tends to result in excessive savings and insufficient consumption, and it allocates very few financial resources to venture capital that contains new inventions and technologies. In addition, in the context of the global financial landscape, it also greatly constrains China's financial soft power, thus putting China in a dominant and subordinate position in the international monetary and financial system and the international political and economic system as a whole. In this regard, it has been proposed in every CPC document and five-year development plan since 2002 that financial reforms should be carried out, but none of them have tackled the core issue of resource allocation.

In the Decision, the first part of the opening section immediately points to this core issue, stating that "the economic system reform is the focus of comprehensively deepening reform, and the core is to properly handle the relationship between the government and the market, so that the market plays a decisive role and the government plays a better role in the allocation of resources." In my opinion, the key to properly handling the relationship between the market and the government is that "the government plays a better role." Given that many market rules and market systems have not yet been established at the current stage, the government should mainly play a better role by actively reducing inappropriate intervention (or "cutting its own wrist"); promoting the establishment of market rules and systems; and strengthening market regulation and macro-control. The transition of the government's functions means that the constrained financial system will be shifted to a liberalized financial system while strengthening market regulation and macro-control means that we need to learn from the lessons of the global financial crisis and establish a modern financial regulatory system that prevents systemic and regional risks.

The second aspect is the restructuring of the financial system. China's bank-dominated financial system structure was also formed at the third plenary session of the 14th CPC Central Committee, whose document clearly underlined the importance of "developing and perfecting the financial market dominated by bank financing." The bank-dominated financial system structure is aligned with the constrained financial system and also serves the purpose of mobilizing savings and promoting large-scale investment at the early stage of economic development. However, when compared to the (capital) market-dominated financial system in financially developed countries, this structure cannot provide diversified investment channels for savings, cannot allocate savings to new inventions and technologies, and leaves a high concentration of credit and liquidity risk in the vulnerable banking sector. From a global perspective, a (capital) market-dominated financial system structure instead of a bank-dominated one has always been a characteristic of leading countries across the globe, so China's current bank-dominated system is by no means a vehicle for realizing the rejuvenation of the Chinese nation.

As far as the restructuring of the financial system is concerned, the second part of the Decision elaborates on the establishment and improvement of the basic economic system and points out the need to shift from a bank-dominated to a (capital) market-dominated system. It means that in the second decade of the twenty-first century, a long-lasting bull market will be seen in the capital market. Based on the clear proposal to protect the property rights of both state-owned and non-state-owned economies, the second part of the Decision also calls for the development of mixed ownership, employee stock ownership, and the conversion of non-state-owned enterprises into mixed-ownership enterprises when conditions permit. Many people probably do not understand what it means for the capital market, but in fact it implies the advent of the era of "capital popularization." More state-owned enterprises that are seemingly owned by the public but actually benefit a few people, and more privately-owned and privately-operated enterprises that grow slowly under the closed control of families will become public companies owned by the public and managed by professional managers, while more and more laborers will become capital owners instead of merely bank depositors. The US, for example, saw a large number of privately-owned and private-operated companies become public companies owned by the public and managed by professional managers during the period from the economic liberalization reforms introduced by President Reagan in the 1980s to 1999. Due to the 401K plan and the development of non-bank financial institutions, the US residents' asset portfolios became increasingly made up of direct or indirect holdings in corporate stocks; the US also saw a 20-year run-up in the stock market from 1981 to 1999. Along with the long-term bull market, the US economy has also developed a consumer-led and technological progress-driven development pattern. Apart from the establishment and improvement of the basic economic system, the reforms in other areas (such as land system, government functions, and fiscal system) will also boost the great development of the capital market. For example, as we look ahead to the next few years, we can expect that China's bond market will be dominated by general local government bonds and project-specific local government bonds issued directly or indirectly through platforms by local governments.

The third aspect is the development of new areas for financial investment. China's financial resources have been mainly allocated to the manufacturing sector, and to land finance based on land mortgages in the past decade, with little investment in the modern service sector. Insufficient financial investment in the service sector is one of the root causes of China's underdeveloped service sector, but this is not entirely the fault of finance. Actually, it is the result of excessive government controls and administrative intervention in the real economy. Therefore, the key premise for pushing the allocation of financial resources to the modern service sector is the reforms of the real economy, but not the financial reforms.

The Decision points out the importance of releasing the control in the main areas related to the modern service sector, thus creating huge opportunities for the entry of financial resources. For example, in terms of sci-tech system reform, it is clearly stated that we should "develop a technology transfer mechanism, improve the financing conditions for technology-based SMEs, improve the risk investment mechanism, create innovative business models, and boost the capitalization and commercialization of sci-tech achievements"; in terms of urban–rural integration and urbanization construction, we should "allow social capital to participate in urban infrastructure investment and operation through franchising and other means"; in terms of cultural system construction, we should "establish and perfect the modern cultural market system…to establish a multi-tiered market for cultural products and factors, and encourage the combination of financial capital, social capital and cultural resources"; In terms of health care, "social funds should be allowed to invest directly in the service fields with scarce resources and diversified needs, and to participate in the restructuring and reorganization of public hospitals through various forms." In addition, the reforms of the rural collective construction land, arable land and rural homestead system will also greatly promote the development of rural finance, because the root cause of the long-term sluggishness of rural finance actually lies in the lack of land for farmers, rural areas and agriculture to attract financial resources and use as collateral.

### *7.3.2 Proposals of the Fifth Plenary Session of the 18th CPC Central Committee on the Financial System Reforms*

The *Proposals for Formulating the 13th Five-Year Plan (2016–2020) for National Economic and Social Development* (hereinafter refer to as the " Proposals") adopted at the fifth plenary session of the 18th CPC Central Committee stated that "development is the fundamental principle," "reforms are the powerful driving force of development" and "innovation is the first driving force of development." The shift from an investment-dominated economic development mode to an economic development mode where consumption plays a fundamental role and investment plays a key role is predicated on innovation, while system reforms (namely a shift from a government-led resource allocation mechanism to a mechanism where the market plays a decisive role and the government plays a better role) are the basis of innovation. In contrast to the financial system's main task of mobilizing savings and promoting large-scale investment during the 12th Five-Year Plan (2011–2015), the financial system's primary task during the 13th Five-Year Plan (2016–2020) is to promote innovation, but the shift in the task of the financial system requires fundamental reforms of the financial system.

Different from the Decision of the third Plenary Session of the 18th CPC Central Committee, in which only "the improvement of the financial market system" is mentioned, the Proposals clearly states that we should "accelerate the reforms of the financial system." The essence of the financial system reforms lies in the shift from the government-dominated financial resource allocation mechanism to a mechanism that allows the market to play a decisive role. For this reason, the Proposals not only continues to emphasize the importance of "promoting the marketization of exchange rates and interest rates," but also specifically points out that we should "promote the reforms of the stock and bond issuance and trading systems." As we know, the Decision of the third plenary session of the 18th CPC Central Committee only concerns the stock registration system reform, but the Proposals of the fifth plenary session of the 18th CPC Central Committee mentions both stocks and bonds, which means that the reforms of two major capital markets (i.e. stock market and bond market) will be simultaneously on the agenda, and in particular, the bond market, where the issuance and trading have long been divided, will be unified.

The shift in the financial resource allocation mechanism not only involves the financial system reforms, but also depends on the reforms of other areas of the economic system, especially the reforms of state-owned enterprises and local governments, which are the main recipients of financial resources. The transition economics tells us that if borrowers have a soft budget constraint, the financial resource allocation efficiency will not be improved by the financial system reform such as interest rate marketization alone, which will even worsen the problem of soft budget constraint. The Proposals calls for "improving the mechanism for managing all types of state-owned assets and strengthening the supervision of state-owned assets with capital management as the main focus." It can be expected that during the 13th Five-Year Plan period (2016–2020), the state-owned enterprises will gradually change the status where there is no clear line between the functions of the government and enterprises, and become the real entities of the market economy. As far as local governments are concerned, the Proposals calls for "establishing a standardized debt financing mechanism for local governments" on the basis of deepening the reforms of the fiscal and taxation system.

The financial resource allocation mechanism in which the market plays a decisive role will lay a solid foundation for the shift from the traditional bank-dominated financial system to a capital market-dominated financial system. The Proposals points out that it is necessary to "improve the financial institution system with a reasonable division of work and mutual complementarity among commercial financial institutions, development-oriented financial institutions, policy-based financial institutions and cooperative financial institutions," to "actively foster an open, transparent and healthy capital market," and to "increase the proportion of direct financing." A clean and upright stock market will attract more people. It can be expected that during the 13th Five-Year Plan period (2016–2020), Chinese residents will transfer more deposits in their asset portfolios to the stock market. Currently, among RMB 34 trillion of market value of stocks in circulation, only about RMB 10 trillion is held by the household sector. With the adjustment of residents' asset portfolios, especially the increasing share of the household sector's income in the national income under the concept of coordination and sharing, the household sector's stock holdings may further increase by RMB 10 trillion during the 13th Five-Year Plan period (2016–2020). With the implementation of the stock market registration system, the adjustment of residents' asset portfolios, and the establishment and improvement of retirement pension systems including occupational pension, corporate pension, commercial pension insurance and other supporting systems, the increase in the supply and demand of stocks will push up China's stock market value and the number of listed companies. As shown in Table 7.6, during the 12th Five-Year Plan period (2011–2015), the number of listed companies in China was only half of that in the US, and China's stock market value was only more than 20% of that in the US In light with the goal of doubling income by 2020, China is likely to double the number of listed companies and stock market value during the 13th Five-Year Plan (2016–2020).

In addition to the stock market, the bond market is also a focus of reforms. Similar to the relative backwardness of the stock market, the gap between China's bond market and that of developed countries is more than multiple times. In 2014, China's bond market size was USD 4.8 trillion, equivalent to less than one-half of Japan's, more than one-third of the UK's and one-fifth of Europe's. However, we can observe in Table 7.7 the surprising fact that China's bond market is growing rapidly. China's bond size expanded from about one-fifth of the UK's in 2009 to one-third of the UK's in 2014, and from about one-tenth of Europe's in 2009 to about one-fifth of Europe's in 2014. Combined with the elaboration on public investment and financing mechanism, local government debt financing system and high-income bonds and equity-bond financing methods in the Proposals, it is expected that China's bond market value will double during the 13th Five-Year Plan period (2016–2020) and the rate of bond deepening (currently around 43 percent) is expected to approach the global average level (around 110 percent), which will completely change the pattern dominated by the traditional banking sector.

While the market plays a decisive role, the government should play a better role. Guided by the idea of combining decentralization and regulation, the Proposals clearly puts forward the need to strengthen the financial macro-prudential management system, and reform and improve the financial regulatory framework. The contents related to this area are increased and relatively specific based on the contents

**Table 7.6** Comparison of the stock markets in China and the US

| | Year | 2010 | 2011 | 2012 | 2013 | 2014 |
|---|---|---|---|---|---|---|
| Stock market value (RMB 1 billion) | US | 17,283.45 | 15,640.71 | 18,668.33 | 24,034.85 | 26,330.59 |
| | Chinese Mainland | 4027.84 | 3412.11 | 3697.38 | 3949.14 | 6004.95 |
| Number of listed companies | US | 4279 | 4171 | 4102 | 4180 | 4369 |
| | Chinese Mainland | 2063 | 2342 | 2494 | 2489 | 2613 |

*Data source* CEIC

**Table 7.7** Comparison of the bond sizes in China and developed countries (regions) (Unit: USD 100 million)

| Reporting Year | US | Europe | UK | Japan | China |
|---|---|---|---|---|---|
| 2014 | 234,899.85 | 232,094.95 | 137,800.27 | 102,548.82 | 48,509.89 |
| 2013 | 230,729.93 | 230,849.44 | 148,854.45 | 99,817.16 | 47,669.07 |
| 2012 | 216,175.53 | 223,668.50 | 170,633.92 | 117,143.75 | 40,722.78 |
| 2011 | 198,089.91 | 216,905.68 | 180,354.66 | 125,998.61 | 34,624.50 |
| 2010 | 179,249.85 | 215,339.94 | 149,993.57 | 116,623.45 | 30,629.612 |
| 2009 | 156,265.11 | 227,400.42 | 135,410.74 | 97,136.04 | 26,231.89 |

*Data source* CEIC and Tong Hua Shun (software for online stock trading and analysis)

regarding risk disposal in the Decision of the third plenary session of the 18th CPC Central Committee. For the purpose of controlling systemic risks, it is expected that during the 13th Five-Year Plan period (2016–2020), China's current pattern characterized by universal banking and "One Bank–Three Commissions Regulatory Structure" will be broken, and the mechanism for monitoring, supervising and disposing of systemic risks with the leadership of the State Council and the leading responsibility of the PBOC may be established.

As a final point, the opening-up of the financial sector should keep pace with the opening-up of the whole economy, and the opening-up of the financial sector means not only "bringing in foreign capital" but also "going global." In order to "expand the two-way opening-up of the financial sector," the Proposals sets out the requirements for opening-up on three levels: (1) To be aligned with the requirement of actively participating in global governance and "promoting the reforms of the international monetary system and international financial supervision," the financial opening-up means to make the RMB "a convertible and freely usable currency" by orderly promoting the capital account convertibility and including the RMB in the special drawing rights basket. Combined with the financial system reforms and the capital market development, it means that the RMB will become a global reserve currency during the 13th Five-Year Plan period (2016–2020). (2) The basic measure of opening-up is to allow the market to play a decisive role, including the negative list management mode for foreign exchange management and use, the liberalization of foreign investment exchange and capital application, and the two-way opening-up of domestic and foreign capital market investment. As a result, the three major components of China's capital account will increase significantly during the 13th Five-Year Plan period (2016–2020), and especially the sluggish foreign direct investment and two-way securities investment are likely to see explosive growth. (3) The government should play a better role, which means that it should strengthen the balance of payments monitoring with the goal of a basic balance of payments. It should be noted that the balance of payments is the balance after combining the current account and the capital account. If China's current account remains in surplus during the 13th Five-Year Plan period (2016–2020), it will be necessary to create a capital account deficit through capital export. In other words, capital export will be a priority in the 13th Five-Year Plan period (2016–2020). However, we should never ignore the global financial risks during the 13th Five-Year Plan period (2016–2020). Since the differences in the pace of economic recovery and macroeconomic policies among countries will lead to more fluctuations in global capital flows and exchange rates of major currencies, the two-way opening-up of the financial sector must be on an orderly basis.

### 7.3.3 Major Tasks to Be Strengthened in 2016

Given that the current pressure and exposures are related to financial risks, China should maintain a moderately loose macroeconomic policy while accelerating system reforms, and especially strengthen financial regulation while reforming fiscal policy.

First, a moderately loose macroeconomic policy should be maintained. The macro policy (especially monetary policy) needs to find a balance between de-leveraging and risk prevention, while keeping the stability and continuity of the policy. Moderate and orderly risk exposures should be allowed to gradually dissipate the normal losses in the economic cycle as well as the problems left over from the previous periods. However, it is important to prevent the deterioration and escalation of financial risks in this process. The adoption of timely and appropriate measures for stabilizing growth is crucial to prevent the spread of risks and reverse market expectations. Currently, the focus of the task for stabilizing growth is not on maintaining a given GDP growth rate or a given employment level, but on preventing the escalation and spread of potential financial risks.

Second, the financial regulatory policies should be optimized. In particular, there is a need for counter-cyclical regulatory innovation. When credit risk increases, it is of utmost importance to strengthen the risk regulation, but excessively strict regulation may cause an increase in banks' risk aversion, so it will be difficult for the real economy to obtain financing and the costs of financing will be increased. The enterprises' financing difficulties will amplify the extent of the real economy's decline, which in turn will lead to higher credit risks faced by banks, which is also known as the pro-cyclical effect of financial regulation. In the current practice, the regulatory policies and the overemphasis on credit risk in the banks' internal assessment have in fact led to a tightening of bank credit, which has had some negative impact on the real economy. In this regard, we advise the regulators to make attempts and innovations in the counter-cyclical regulation by drawing on the relatively mature international experience and taking China's reality into account, and to maintain a certain degree of flexibility and make dynamic adjustments in some policies that have a significant impact on the behaviors of banks (e.g. deposit-to-loan ratio, consensus loan size, risk tolerance, etc.) according to the operational needs of the real economy.

Third, the risk-sharing mechanism should be improved. The government should consider how it can innovate within a moderate scope to participate directly or indirectly in the sharing and disposal of risk losses. Currently, some local governments have set up revolving loan funds and risk funds to facilitate loan extensions for enterprises or directly share part of the credit losses, which has to some extent optimized the financing environment for enterprises (especially micro and small-sized enterprises). In addition, the governments in some areas with relatively prominent risks have actively intervened in the collection and disposal of non-performing credits, thus playing an active role in resolving regional financial risks and maintaining financial stability. In the future, we should continue to strengthen the work in related areas.

Fourth, securities brokers should tighten their risk control on clients' securities margin trading, and strictly prohibit bank funds from entering the stock market. The "umbrella trust" is one of the typical modes that opens up the channel for bank funds to enter the stock market and removes the firewall between the banks and the securities market. Since the reform and opening-up, China has never seen any systemic financial risks, thanks to the most important experience of sticking to the bottom line that "bank funds are not allowed to enter the stock market."

Fifth, the supply of new shares should be increased, the registration system for stock issuance should be rolled out more quickly, and various kinds of stock price manipulation should be cracked down. The current issuance frequency of new shares should also be changed, for which we advise changing the frequency to every trading day in the future. By increasing the supply of new shares, the overheated atmosphere in the stock market will be moderated. While increasing the supply of new shares, we should also gradually reduce the administrative controls in the process of new shares issuance, accelerate the roll-out of the registration system reform plan and realize a natural transition to the new shares issuance system.

# Chapter 8
# Reforms for External Opening-Up of the Financial Sector and Their Prioritization

**Zhang Bin**

**Abstract** Currently, the RMB exchange rate formation mechanism reform, the foreign exchange reserve management system reform, the capital account reform and the promotion of RMB internationalization are the key tasks in China's financial sector external opening-up strategy. This chapter mainly discusses the specific manner and order in which the above reforms should be implemented, with the conclusions as follows: In terms of the reasonable reform order, priority should be given to the RMB exchange rate formation mechanism reform, and a wide-range fluctuating RMB exchange rate formation mechanism is advisable in the near-term future. The foreign exchange reserve management system reform should also be promoted as soon as possible, with a focus on setting up the sovereign pension funds with parts of the foreign exchange reserves, so as to increase the foreign exchange reserves investment income and return the foreign exchange to the people. The RMB internationalization and the further opening-up of capital account should be placed in the latter stage of the reform process. The opening-up of capital account should be promoted in a gradual and pilot manner, and the RMB internationalization should be focused on the construction of market infrastructure.

Currently, the RMB exchange rate formation mechanism reform, the foreign exchange reserve management system reform, the capital account reform and the promotion of the RMB internationalization are the key tasks in China's financial sector external opening-up strategy. The reforms are aimed at unlocking the government's control over the market and allowing the market to play a greater role in the trading, pricing and resource allocation of foreign financial activities. Based on many painful lessons in history, market-oriented reforms do not mean the complete removal of government controls, so the approach and step-by-step arrangement of the reforms are crucial. If the reforms are carried out in the right direction but in the wrong manner, or are not properly ordered, they may seriously disrupt the market order in the short term, causing serious market turmoil and ending up in failure.

Z. Bin (✉)
Institute of World Economics and Politics, Chinese Academy of Social Sciences, Beijing, China

 
X. Zhang (ed.), *Exploration on China's Economic System Reform under New Normal of Development*, https://doi.org/10.1007/978-981-95-2461-7_8

This chapter mainly discusses the following issues: (1) RMB exchange rate formation mechanism system reform; (2) foreign exchange reserve management system reform; (3) RMB internationalization and capital account liberalization; (4) reform order. The main conclusions are as follows: In terms of the reasonable reform order, priority should be given to the RMB exchange rate formation mechanism reform, and a wide-range fluctuating or free-floating RMB exchange rate formation mechanism is advisable in the near-term future. The foreign exchange reserve management system reform should also be promoted as soon as possible, with the focus on setting up the sovereign pension reserve funds with parts of the foreign exchange reserves, so as to raise the investment returns of the foreign exchange reserves and return the foreign exchange to the people. The RMB internationalization and the further opening-up of capital account should be placed in the latter stage of the reform process. The opening-up of capital account should be promoted in a gradual and pilot manner, and the RMB internationalization should be focused on the construction of market infrastructure.

## 8.1 RMB Exchange Rate Formation Mechanism Reform

After the PBOC announced the RMB exchange rate formation mechanism reform on July 21, 2005, we witnessed three stages of changes in the RMB exchange rate formation mechanism, leading to a shift from de facto official pricing to partial market pricing. The first stage of the RMB exchange rate formation mechanism reform was from July 2005 to April 2012, when the RMB had a gradual and continuous appreciation against the USD for most of the time and was basically pegged to the USD during the market turmoil after the global financial crisis. In terms of the exchange rate formation mechanism, the difference between the exchange rate systems controlled by the monetary authority for appreciation or pegged to the USD was not significant. The monetary authority had full control over the pricing of the RMB exchange rate, but the market had no direct role in determining the exchange rate price.

The second stage of the RMB exchange rate formation mechanism reform was from April 2012 to August 11, 2015. During this period, the pricing of the RMB exchange rate was partially determined by the market. The milestone was that in April 2012, the daily floating range of the RMB/USD trading price in the spot foreign exchange market was expanded from 0.5% to 1%; in March 2014, the daily floating range was further expanded from 1 to 2%. Following the expansion of the daily fluctuations of the RMB exchange rate, the market's role in the formation of the RMB exchange rate began to emerge, but the monetary authority still had a dominant role. The RMB exchange rate formation mechanism during this period was unique in that it appeared to float within a range, but differed significantly from the typical range fluctuations. A typical range fluctuation has two elements: (1) a well-defined and fixed central parity rate; and (2) a fixed range of upward and downward fluctuations around the central parity rate. The RMB exchange rate differed from typical range fluctuations in that, on the one hand, there was no fixed, well-defined central parity rate, and the central parity rate of the RMB was not fixed; and, on the other hand, there was only a daily fluctuation limit on the central parity rate of the RMB, without longer-term fluctuation limits. The RMB spot exchange rate was more fluctuating than the central parity rate, but the trajectory of the spot exchange rate was within the limited range of fluctuations and followed the central parity rate. Through the management of the central parity rate, the monetary authority locked in the trend of the spot RMB exchange rate, which meant that it was still dominating the exchange rate.

The third stage of the RMB exchange rate formation mechanism reform is from August 11, 2015 to the present. On August 11, 2015, the PBOC announced the improvement of the RMB exchange rate central parity rate quotation mechanism, which marked a major step in the RMB exchange rate formation mechanism reform. The central parity rate quotation mechanism reform was a milestone for the monetary authority to cede pricing power over the exchange rate to the market, but in response to the huge pressure of RMB devaluation and the great turmoil in the offshore RMB market, the monetary authority adopted a larger-scale quantitative intervention measure after the central parity rate quotation mechanism reform on August 11, in an effort to maintain the stability of the RMB exchange rate. Under the RMB exchange rate mechanism after August 11, the monetary authority still appears to intervene heavily in the RMB exchange rate and has a dominant influence on the RMB exchange rate. However, after the abandonment of the RMB central parity rate management, the difficulty of its intervention in the foreign exchange market has increased sharply. The recent stability of the RMB exchange rate is only a short-term phenomenon, as a transition to a new mechanism is underway for the RMB exchange rate formation mechanism.

If the fixed exchange rate under the full control of the monetary authority is taken as the left end and the floating exchange rate under the full control of the market as the right end, the inclusion of rules for varying degrees of intervention by the monetary authority will lead to various intermediate options corresponding to the left and right ends. The left end brings short-term stability but will accumulate instability and deteriorate resource allocation efficiency in the future. The right end brings long-term stability and optimizes resource allocation efficiency, but results in unknown transition costs. In the process of reforming from the left end to the right end, we will see different intermediate options and correspondingly different levels of transition costs. By combining the specific domestic and international economic background that China is facing, we have analyzed the pros and cons of different intermediate options as a reference for the next step of exchange rate reform.

The different reform options are evaluated against the backdrop of the USD rate hike cycle, the downward pressure in the domestic economy and the monetary authority's high intervention in the foreign exchange market. The evaluation is mainly based on the perspective of macroeconomic management, with three dimensions: (1) macroeconomic stability; (2) resource allocation efficiency (economic growth sustainability); and (3) market-oriented reforms and opening-up in other fields, such as the opening-up of the capital market, the RMB internationalization and the three-pronged construction for the international financial center.

**Option 1: Free floating**

**Description:** There are no interventions in the central parity rate, with interventions in the market only in extreme cases.

**Pros:** No expectations of unidirectional currency changes, autonomous balance of payments, high independence of monetary policy; improved competitiveness of export and import substitution sectors; full use of the exchange rate as a price leverage function for cross-sectoral resource allocation; an institutional foundation for further opening-up of the capital market, RMB internationalization and international financial center construction.

**Cons:** The transition phase may be accompanied by a significant adjustment in the exchange rate, which will greatly increase the enterprises' foreign debt burden and price hike pressure.

**Overall Evaluation:** It is the goal of the reform, but is not appropriate to introduce it in a situation where the enterprises are facing serious currency mismatch and high foreign debt burden, as well as macroeconomic instability.

**Option 2: Wide-range floating**

**Description:** A wide range of annual fluctuations is set (e.g. 7.5% up or down in the RMB/USD exchange rate for a given trading day, or 7.5% up or down based on the basket exchange rate index for a given trading day, or both), and the monetary authority uses the central parity management tool and intervention tool only when the upper and lower limits are reached.

If the monetary authority has sufficient market credibility and the exchange rate level does not deviate to a significant extent, the market exchange rate will fluctuate within the range; even in the event of a large depreciation/appreciation pressure, the exchange rate will fluctuate slightly near the upper and lower limits as it is guaranteed by the credibility of the monetary authority.

It is discretionary to choose an annual fluctuation range that is 7.5% up or down based on the basket exchange rate index, and 7% or 8% also can be chosen. We have chosen 7.5% mainly based on the consideration of the following three aspects: (1) If the fluctuation range is too small, it leaves too little room for the market to play a really decisive role; (2) If the fluctuation range is too large, it may bring about serious exchange rate overshooting and excessive impact on the real economy; (3) China has witnessed several shocks due to that the annual fluctuation range of the RMB against the basket exchange rate index exceeded 7.5% (with cumulative annual appreciation exceeding 7.5% for a total of 16 months in the years 2008, 2009, 2010, 2012 and 2013), but the impact was within acceptable limits.

**Pros:** Autonomous balance of payments,[1] relatively high independence of monetary policy; full use of the exchange rate as a price leverage function for cross-sectoral resource allocation; an institutional foundation for further opening-up of the capital market, RMB internationalization and international financial center construction.

**Cons:** The transition phase may be accompanied by a moderate (devaluation) adjustment in the exchange rate, thus increasing enterprises' foreign debt burden.

**Overall Evaluation:** It is similar to a floating exchange rate and has the pros of a floating exchange rate while taking into account short-term macroeconomic stability.

**Option 3:Small-range fluctuation under frequent interventions, and shift to Option 2 or Option 1 (crawling peg) when the time is right**

**Option 3.1 Non-transparent rules**

**Description:** Based on non-transparent rules, the monetary authority frequently intervenes in the foreign exchange market to dominate the trend of exchange rate. When the time is right, it shifts to Option 2 or Option 1.

Although the rules are not transparent to the external world, the intervention of the monetary authority in the foreign exchange market requires grounds and rules. Based on the RMB exchange rate formation mechanism reform in 2005 and the past regulatory experience, the intervention methods are: (1) The cumulative annual depreciation/appreciation does not exceed 3%; (2) Weights are assigned to the basket exchange rate and fundamental market supply and demand factors (such as the trade surplus), and the exchange rate is regularly adjusted based on the changes in these factors.[2] Other possible methods include taking both the annual cumulative fluctuation limit and the peg to the basket exchange rate into account, or simply considering a discounted basket exchange rate (e.g. the RMB would need to depreciate by 1% against the USD under the stability of the RMB against a basket of currencies, but would only appreciate by 0.5% in operation).

After the introduction of the central parity rate quotation reform, it is difficult for the monetary authority to adjust the central parity rate according to the rules as frequently (daily) as it did in the past. It requires the monetary authority to fix the exchange rate closing price at a point determined according to the above rules and to guide the formation of the market maker's central parity rate on a daily basis, which increases the difficulty of intervention by the monetary authority.

**Timing definition:** The size of foreign debt, the ratio of foreign debt to income, and the currency matching in the business sector and the household sector are relatively reasonable, the pressure of capital outflow from the US Federal Reserve's interest rate hike is within acceptable limits, and the market believes that the PBOC's

[1] ①The main reasons are as follows: a. The current exchange rate level is not too far from the equilibrium exchange rate, and the 7.5 percent fluctuation range leaves the market with relatively sufficient space for pressure release; b. The clear commitment and strong intervention ability of the monetary authorities can effectively break the vicious circle of devaluation expectations and capital flight under the sheep-flock effect of the market.

[2] ②See Zhang Bin, Li Yuanfang, and Xiao Lisheng, Guessing the RMB Central Parity Rate, cn.reuters.com.

withdrawal from intervention in the foreign exchange market will not bring about drastic exchange rate turbulence.

**Pros:** Under the design of reasonable rules, it tends to a reasonable and equilibrium exchange rate; the enterprises have less pressure on short-term foreign debt.

**Cons:** Expectations of continued unilateral small-range depreciation,[3] capital outflows + currency arbitrage transactions, autonomous balance of payments disequilibrium, and serious impairment of the independence of monetary authority; potential currency mismatch in the medium and long term; delay in cross-sectoral resource allocation; delay in capital account, currency internationalization and international financial center construction, etc.

**Overall Evaluation:** If it does not point clearly to an equilibrium exchange rate, there will be little gain at a great cost.

**Option 3.2 Transparent rules**

The main difference from Option 3.1 is that the monetary authorities disclose the intervention rules. Due to the central parity rate quotation mechanism reform, it is more difficult to implement high-frequency adjustments to the exchange rate based on the indicators such as a basket of currencies and fundamental market factors.

In terms of results, the difference from Option 3.1 is that it reduces the market's uncertain expectations of future exchange rate movements and helps curb the vicious cycle between capital outflows and devaluation expectations.

**Option 4: Peg the USD or quasi-peg the USD and shift to Option 2 or Option 1 when the time is right**

**Description:** The main difference from Option 3 is a smaller fluctuation range under the intervention of the monetary authority.

**Pros:** No continued depreciation pressure and limited capital outflows; enterprises have less pressure on short-term foreign debt.

**Cons:** Autonomous balance of payments disequilibrium, and limited impairment of the independence of monetary authority; delay in cross-sectoral resource allocation; delay in capital account, currency internationalization and international financial center construction, etc.

**Overall Evaluation:** It is stable in the short term, but will accumulate instability in the future, with uncorrected resource allocation distortions.

By comparing the above exchange rate formation mechanism options, we argue that with the wide floating range of RMB, the relatively prudent pace of capital account liberalization, and the monetary authority's powerful influence in the market,

---

[3] ③Unilateral depreciation expectations can either be broken by the appreciation mechanism embedded in the rules or reversed by spontaneous supply and demand forces in the market.Against the background of the USD interest rate hike, it is difficult for the spontaneous supply and demand forces in the market to appreciate spontaneously before releasing the depreciation pressure through sufficient exchange rate adjustment, and the RMB is also depreciating against the USD according to the basket exchange rate rules. In the rules, the RMB can be allowed to appreciate based on the trade surplus, but the RMB appreciation space under the recessionary trade surplus will be questioned by the market, and it is difficult to reverse the devaluation expectations.

the RMB exchange rate expected and priced by the market is highly likely to fall within a wide range. It is a relatively suitable intermediate option for breaking out of the current exchange rate reform impasse. If the macroeconomic management authority is bold enough to completely abandon intervention and simply adopt a floating exchange rate system, it will probably be a better choice.

## 8.2 Foreign Exchange Reserve Management System Reform

Since the entry into the twenty-first century, China's foreign exchange reserve assets have grown rapidly and become an important part of national wealth. China's foreign exchange reserve assets have increased from USD 165.5 billion in 2000 to USD 3.6 trillion at present, putting China at the top of the world in terms of the scale of foreign exchange reserves. Such a rapid expansion of assets means a huge challenge for any assets management authority, and it is also true for China's foreign reserves management authority. Over the past decade or so, China has made a number of small attempts to reform the existing framework for foreign exchange reserve management. However, for the portion of foreign exchange reserve assets in excess of those needed for meeting the traditional functions of foreign exchange reserve assets, there is no foreign exchange asset management framework that meets the national conditions to scientifically manage foreign exchange assets and benefit the people from the perspective of institutional construction.

Currently, the obvious shortcomings in the understanding and practical operations of China's foreign exchange reserve management include: (1) Failure to meticulously study and define the attributes of foreign exchange reserve assets, and the resulting series of specious discussions that have impeded the promotion of further foreign exchange reserve management system reform at the cognitive level; (2) The lack of reasonable planning for the redistribution of foreign exchange reserve principal and its investment income between the government and residents, and the lack of corresponding reform of the management body, and the failure to make full use of foreign exchange reserve resources to improve national welfare; (3) Vague goals of foreign exchange reserve assets management, and significant deficiencies in the settings of the management authority. In response to these three shortcomings, a discussion is made as follows:

### *8.2.1 Whether Foreign Exchange Reserve Assets Can Be Separated?*

The question of whether China's huge foreign exchange reserve assets can be separated from the central bank has attracted widespread attention and discussion among academic circles and policy-making bodies in China. However, no consensus has been reached so far in these discussions. At the research level, the failure to reach a consensus is attributed to the conflation of discussions on the asset nature of foreign reserve assets, as well as the liability constraints on foreign reserve assets and the functional constraints on foreign reserve assets. If these concepts are broken down and discussed one by one in the context of China's national conditions, it will help to clarify the issues and reach a consensus.

Foreign exchange reserves are public assets. Foreign exchange reserves are assets held by the government's relevant functional department in foreign currencies. Similar to other assets held by the government, foreign reserve assets are also public assets. In the US, Japan and the UK, foreign reserve assets are held by their Treasury, while in most other countries, foreign reserve assets are held by their central banks. Although foreign reserve assets are public assets, it does not mean that the government is allowed to allocate foreign reserve assets among government departments or government-dominated enterprises at will, because foreign reserve assets are also subject to specific liability constraints, functional constraints, or other constraints. As an analogy, police cars are public assets, but the vast majority of them are used only by police departments and cannot be randomly assigned to other government departments because there are specific functional constraints on their use.

The management and use of foreign exchange reserve assets are subject to varying degrees of liability constraints, while China's foreign exchange reserve assets are subject to less strong liability constraints. According to international experience, there are usually two methods to acquire foreign exchange reserves: (1) by issuing foreign currency bonds and currency swaps or by borrowing funds from international organizations or private financial institutions; (2) by using domestic currency to purchase foreign exchange directly in the foreign exchange market. In the first method, the foreign reserve assets management authority has a well-defined pressure to repay the principal and interest, which constitutes relatively strong constraints on the management and use of foreign reserve assets. In the second method, the foreign reserve assets management authority has no explicit pressure to repay the principal and interest and has more freedom in the management and use of foreign reserve assets. As China's foreign exchange reserves are mainly acquired from the second method, China's foreign exchange reserve assets management authority has a higher degree of freedom in the management and use of foreign exchange reserve assets.

The accumulation of foreign currency assets by the monetary authorities is accompanied by an increase in local currency liabilities. However, the local currency liabilities of the monetary authorities are not equivalent to the liabilities on the balance sheets of commercial organizations, nor do they constitute a constraint on the management and use of foreign reserve assets. For modem central banks, the liabilities arising from the channel of monetary issuance are recorded on the liabilities of the monetary authorities' balance sheets, but they do not truly constitute liabilities, as the money issued by the monetary authorities is not redeemable.

China's situation is slightly unique. Over the past decade, China's monetary authority has released large amounts of currency through intervention in the foreign exchange market, which has put China under enormous pressure to maintain stable prices and asset prices. As such, while issuing currency, China's monetary authorities have also withdrawn a significant portion of the currency by raising the required reserve ratio and issuing central bank bills as a means of easing the pressure. For the required reserves, excess reserves and central bank bills held by commercial banks, the monetary authority pays varying degrees of interest. These interest payments can be considered as liabilities of the monetary authority. However, these liabilities will be covered mostly through new monetary issuance in the future.[4] These liabilities can be treated as the costs associated with holding foreign reserves, but do not constitute an inflexible constraint on the management and use of foreign reserve assets.

The management and use of foreign exchange reserve assets are subject to functional constraints, while China's current size of foreign reserve assets is far beyond the level needed to meet its traditional functions. The traditional functions of foreign exchange reserves include: (1) intervening in the foreign exchange market to influence exchange prices or to keep the orderly functioning of the market; (2) providing payments for the country's imports of goods and services, particularly when the country has difficulties in obtaining external financing; (3) underpinning investors' confidence in a country's foreign exchange payment capacity, thus reducing the likelihood of financial crises, and possibly reducing the costs of external financing; and (4) providing emergency liquidity to relevant sectors of the national economy, such as banks (Zhang Zhichao, 2009). To meet the traditional functions of foreign exchange reserves, the foreign exchange reserve assets management authority tends to place more emphasis on the high liquidity and safety of foreign exchange reserve assets and less on the pursuit of yield.

Given that the capital account has not been completely liberalized, China's current foreign exchange reserves are in excess of the size required to meet the traditional functions of foreign exchange reserves. The current size of China's foreign exchange reserves is enough to cover the foreign exchange demand for imported goods and enough to service foreign debt, while the main challenge is the foreign exchange demand arising from the sudden request of the residential and corporate sectors to convert RMB assets (namely broad money or M2) into foreign currency assets. If the monetary authority promotes capital account liberalization in a gradual manner and maintains a certain degree of flexibility in the exchange rates, the demand for foreign reserve assets will be much lower than its current size of foreign exchange reserves.

[4] ④Currently, other depository corporations have RMB 19 trillion of reserves in the monetary authorities, with an interest rate of 1.62 percent on required reserves, an interest rate of 0.72 percent on excess reserves, and a weighted interest rate of roughly 1.5 percent. When calculated as a whole, the annual interest payments are RMB 285 billion. Meanwhile, the size of bonds issued by the PBOC is around RMB 1.5 trillion, and its interest payment based on an interest rate of 4 percent is RMB 60 billion per year. The combined interest on reserve deposits and bond issues is about RMB 345 billion per year. The new money issued by the monetary authorities in each of the past ten years was basically no less than RMB 400 billion, so the monetary authorities were able to cover the interest payments on non-monetary debt by relying on annual new money issuance alone.

The prominent challenge that China faces in the process of its foreign exchange reserve assets management is, on the one hand, the value preservation and appreciation of the portion of assets in excess of those needed for meeting the traditional functions of foreign exchange reserve assets; and on the other hand, the reasonable return of foreign exchange to the people. China's foreign exchange reserves are far larger in size than those needed for meeting the traditional functions of foreign exchange reserves and have no mandatory liability constraints, so the main challenges for China in managing its foreign exchange reserve assets are different from the challenges in the traditional sense. In particular, there are two most prominent challenges for the portion of foreign exchange assets in excess of those needed for meeting the traditional functions of foreign exchange reserves: (1) value preservation and appreciation, and (2) return of foreign exchange to the people. As an analogy, if the government's tax revenue far exceeds the government's expenditure needs, the government should, on the one hand, prevent the excess revenue from depreciating through scientific management, and on the other hand, return the excess revenue to the people in a reasonable way.

The central bank's holding of such a large scale of foreign exchange assets is not helpful to address the most prominent challenges in the process of foreign exchange reserve assets management. The income earned by the central bank from foreign exchange reserve assets ultimately results in nothing more than an increase in foreign exchange reserve assets, while it lacks a reasonable mechanism to return the foreign exchange reserve investment income or principal to the people. In addition, given its functions and staffing structure, the central bank mainly manages foreign exchange reserve assets according to the traditional function goals by emphasizing more on the safety and liquidity of assets and less on the profitability of foreign exchange reserve assets. After all, the central bank finds it difficult to rationalize its mechanism and achieve the goal of preserving and increasing the value of foreign exchange reserve assets and returning them to the people. According to international experience, other countries facing a similar problem have separated out that portion of their foreign exchange reserve assets beyond the traditional functions and managed this portion of assets separately by establishing a sovereign wealth fund or sovereign pension fund.

### 8.2.2 How to Allocate Foreign Exchange Reserve Assets?

Although the parts of the foreign exchange assets can be separated from the central bank for special management to better achieve the goals of preserving and increasing the value of foreign exchange assets and returning them to the people, there are also risks involved. An improper allocation would not only fail to improve the current foreign exchange reserve management system, but may make it worse. An improper distribution may result in greater inefficient investment, greater loss of public assets, and serious inequities and corruption. There are several basic principles for the allocation of foreign exchange reserve assets. First, public assets should serve the public interest and must not be shared by departmental interests. The process of separating foreign exchange reserve assets from the central bank is also a process of decentralizing public assets allocation power among different departments, with huge stakes involved. It is important to prevent the allocation of foreign exchange reserve assets from becoming a competition among departments for their own benefits and to ensure that the institutions receiving capital injections will try their best to stick to the country's overall objectives of foreign exchange assets management in a credible manner and to serve the public interest rather than the interests of individual departments in a credible manner.

Second, the process of allocating foreign exchange reserve assets between the central bank and other departments should be open and transparent, as the foreign exchange reserve assets are a huge amount of public assets. The use of foreign exchange funds for national military, diplomatic, foreign aid purposes or in other forms that may involve national security and require certain confidentiality measures should be managed separately by the Ministry of Finance by setting up a separate account and should not be mixed with foreign exchange reserve assets.

Third, the institutions receiving capital injections from foreign exchange reserve assets should have a mechanism designed to achieve higher expected returns on investment. The institutions receiving capital injection from foreign exchange reserve assets should have professional asset management teams, and their management objectives, institutional settings and investment styles should be significantly different from traditional foreign exchange reserve asset management and will help achieve higher expected returns on investment.

Fourth, the portion of foreign exchange assets in excess of those needed for meeting the functions of foreign exchange reserves should finally be returned to the people in a reasonable manner. The foreign exchange reserve assets are taken from the people and should ultimately be used for the people, while the portion of foreign exchange reserve assets in excess of those needed for meeting the public functions should be returned to the people. It is difficult to achieve the goal of returning the foreign exchange to the people in a short period of time, but it is possible to get closer to this goal step by step over a long period of time through reasonable design and planning.

Based on the above principles for the allocation of foreign exchange reserves, a specific plan for promoting the reform of China's foreign exchange reserve management is proposed below. The main contents include:

(1) The Ministry of Finance issues special treasury bonds to be used to replace USD 0.5 trillion of foreign exchange reserve assets with the central bank and uses these foreign exchange reserve assets to establish 2–3 sovereign pension funds.
(2) Based on the performance of the sovereign pension funds, the Ministry of Finance issued special treasury bonds again and increased capital injections to the sovereign pension funds with excellent performance. The central bank's holdings of foreign exchange reserve assets are always kept at about USD 1.5 trillion, with the remaining portion in the hands of several sovereign pension funds.

(3) Individual pension accounts are widely available and introduced across the country as soon as possible. The investment income of the sovereign pension funds will be directly credited to the individual pension accounts of those who meet the conditions (e.g. retirement age).
(4) The national foreign exchange assets investment management committee, consisting of the central bank, the Ministry of Finance, relevant experts and market participants, is established. The committee explains and clarifies the investment status of foreign exchange assets to the National People's Congress on behalf of the government. The foreign exchange assets investment management committee is the top authority for managing foreign exchange assets including foreign exchange reserve assets, sovereign pension fund assets, and foreign exchange assets held by other government departments. The committee is responsible for defining the objectives of foreign exchange assets investment and the overall planning and management of foreign exchange assets investment; evaluating the investment performance of major foreign exchange assets management organizations; allocating foreign exchange funds among different foreign exchange investment organizations. The committee should not be involved in any specific investment business.

**Question 1: Will it additionally increase the fiscal burden?**

The process of acquiring foreign exchange reserve assets through bond issuance by the Ministry of Finance and injecting them into the sovereign pension funds involves the transfer of creditor-debtor relationships between different public departments, but will not additionally increase the government's debt to the non-government departments.[5] For example, the Ministry of Finance issues special treasury bonds of RMB 3.2 trillion to acquire USD 0.5 trillion of assets from the monetary authority and injects these assets into the sovereign pension funds. The issuance and interest payment of special treasury bonds are different from those of ordinary treasury bonds. First, the issuance of special treasury bonds is not for the household sector, but only for the monetary authority, so there will be no additional impact on the domestic financial market. Second, the Ministry of Finance needs to pay interest on the special treasury bonds held by the monetary authority, but at the same time, all the interest income earned by the monetary authority has to be fully transferred to the Ministry of Finance, so the fiscal burden will not be increased.

When the sovereign pension funds inject investment income into the individual pension accounts, it will involve a transfer of income between the government sector and the household sector, but there will be no additional increase in government debt. Even if the government transfers the principal portion of the foreign reserve assets

[5] ⑤The government's debt can be divided into two parts: (1) the government's debt to sectors other than the government, such as the government's debt to the household sector or to other countries, which is debt that actually needs to be repaid with interest; and (2) the government department's debt to other government departments, which will not increase the government's overall debt if the balance sheets of all government departments are consolidated.

to the household sector, it will merely reduce the government's savings and will not increase the government's debt to the household sector.

**Question 2: Will it bring about secondary exchange settlement?**

The key to the existence of a secondary exchange settlement lies in whether the central bank will intervene in the foreign exchange market on a continuous basis and in the RMB exchange rate formation mechanism reform. The investment income of the sovereign pension funds is allocated to the individual pension accounts of those who meet the conditions on a long-term and continuous basis, which will increase the foreign exchange supply in the foreign exchange market. The allocation of foreign exchange assets to the household sector through sovereign pension funds will not only not bring about secondary exchange settlement pressure on the foreign exchange market, but also help to increase the supply of foreign currencies in the foreign exchange market and boost confidence in the RMB exchange rate, thus supporting the relative stability of the RMB exchange rates under the current devaluation expectations.

**Question 3: Will it affect monetary policy operations or will it worsen the central bank's balance sheet?**

The purchase of foreign exchange assets from the central bank by the Ministry of Finance through the issuance of bonds simply means for the central bank that the foreign exchange assets on the central bank's balance sheet are converted into special treasury bonds. It will not affect the central bank's routine monetary policy operations, nor will it worsen the central bank's balance sheet.

**Question 4: Why is it necessary to set up the national foreign exchange reserve assets management committee?**

The national foreign exchange reserve assets management committee has essential functions that are not replaceable by foreign exchange assets investment organizations. First, the national foreign exchange reserve assets management committee is the body that focuses on defining and setting investment goals for the country's foreign exchange assets, while other foreign exchange assets investment organizations aim to achieve these goals. For example, a state-level foreign exchange assets management body, when setting the investment goals, will refer to the nominal yield of the assets (denominated in USD) and should also consider the objective of maximizing the purchasing power of the foreign exchange assets for future imports of goods and services, or other objectives. These are not the issues considered by specific foreign exchange assets investment organizations. Second, the national foreign exchange reserve assets management committee is the body responsible for providing the necessary external incentives to and supervising the foreign exchange assets investment organizations. Third, the national foreign exchange reserve assets management committee is also the body that explains and clarifies the management status of foreign exchange reserve assets to the public on behalf of the government.

**Question 5: Why is it necessary to set up 2–3 sovereign pension funds instead of one? Why is it necessary to set up sovereign pension funds in batches rather than all at once?**

The advantages of setting up multiple sovereign pension funds are: (1) the introduction of a competitive mechanism will improve the efficiency of the use of foreign exchange funds; (2) the transformation of the whole into parts will avoid attracting unnecessary and excessive attention from the international community. The setting up in batches means the separation of foreign exchange assets from the central bank in batches, with the same aim of improving the efficiency of capital utilization and avoiding excessive attention.

## 8.3 RMB Internationalization and Capital Account Liberalization

China has always maintained differentiated regulatory policies on the capital account: basically liberalizing medium- and long-term capital flows such as direct investment, while strictly regulating short-term capital flows such as securities investment and foreign debt. The RMB internationalization process since 2010 has been a de facto capital account liberalization. Some of the policies involved in the RMB internationalization and the development of the offshore RMB market in Hong Kong have actually facilitated cross-border capital flows and the holding of RMB assets by offshore investors, thus resulting in more large-scale and more fluctuating capital flows under the capital account. Our following discussion on RMB internationalization and capital account liberalization mainly focuses on the measures related to RMB internationalization.

### *8.3.1 Policy Measures for Promoting RMB Internationalization*

In the wake of the financial crisis, the Chinese government made a series of actions on the international monetary system reform and the promotion of RMB internationalization. The specific actions included as follows:

(1) China signed the bilateral currency swap agreements with other countries and regions. Against the backdrop of the global financial crisis, some countries and regions faced balance of payments difficulties and needed access to liquidity of the USD and other foreign currencies. Moreover, China's monetary authorities planned to improve the RMB's international status, and especially to provide financial support for RMB cross-border settlements. As of February 22, 2012,

China signed bilateral currency swap agreements totaling RMB 1.3362 trillion with 16 countries and regions, including South Korea, Malaysia, Belarus, Indonesia and Argentina.

(2) China launched a pilot program for RMB settlement in cross-border trade and finally extended it to the entire current account. The cross-border payment arrangements between the Chinese mainland and Hong Kong officially took effect on March 16, 2009, which marked the formal establishment of a multi-currency and all-around cross-border payment and clearing cooperation mechanism between the Chinese mainland and Hong Kong. On April 8, 2009, the State Council decided to launch a pilot program for RMB settlement in cross-border trade in five cities: Shanghai, Guangzhou, Shenzhen, Zhuhai and Dongguan. On July 1, 2009, the PBOC and other five departments jointly issued the *Measures for the Administration of Pilot RMB Settlement in Cross-border Trade*, and China's pilot program for RMB settlement in cross-border trade was officially kicked off. On June 22, 2010, the *Notice on Issues Concerning the Expansion of the Pilot Program for RMB Settlement in Cross-Border Trade* was issued, in which the number of domestic pilot areas was expanded from 5 cities to 20 provinces, municipalities and autonomous regions, the overseas territories were no longer restricted, and more importantly, the business scope of the pilot program was extended from goods trade to other current account settlements. According to the PBOC's latest policy in 2011, the RMB cross-border settlements are currently no longer restricted by domestic geographical areas or enterprise lists. Domestic enterprises are allowed to use RMB as a medium of exchange as long as there is a direct demand for transactions outside of China.

(3) China facilitated the RMB cross-border business under the capital and financial account on a controlled basis. (a) Direct investment. From the second quarter of 2010, China began to pilot RMB cross-border investment and financing business through a case-by-case approval process. In October 2010, Xinjiang became the first province, city and autonomous region in China that launched a pilot program for RMB cross-border direct investment. On January 6, 2011, the PBOC issued the *Measures for the Administration of Pilot RMB Settlement for Outward Direct Investment* (related to ODI). On October 14, 2011, the PBOC issued the *Measures for the Administration of RMB Settlement of Foreign Direct Investment* (related to FDI). (b) Securities investment. On January 4, 2012, the PBOC issued the *Measures for the Pilot Program of Domestic Securities Investment by RMB Qualified Foreign Institutional Investors in Fund Management Companies and Securities Firms* (related to QFII), thus providing a legal channel for foreign institutions to use RMB to undertake securities investment in the onshore market.

(4) China issued RMB treasury bonds in Hong Kong to boost the development of Hong Kong's RMB bond market. On September 28, 2009, the central government issued RMB treasury bonds totaling RMB 6 billion in Hong Kong. First of all, it was the first time that China's monetary authorities issued treasury bonds in Hong Kong, as all previous RMB bonds were issued by financial institutions of the Chinese mainland. Second, it was the largest size of RMB bond issue in Hong Kong, as the largest size in the previous issue was RMB 5 billion issued

by China Development Bank in 2007. The issuance of treasury bonds in Hong Kong's offshore RMB market enhanced the attractiveness of RMB assets to foreign investors and played a supportive role in facilitating the use of RMB in cross-border trade settlements. Also, the yield of treasury bonds served as a benchmark to provide a reference for the construction of Hong Kong's offshore RMB market and brought about confidence and hope for the development of Hong Kong's offshore RMB market. Fueled by a series of measures, the size of RMB bond market in Hong Kong continued to expand from RMB 16 billion in 2009 to RMB 35.7 billion in 2010 and RMB 104 billion in 2011.

(5) China boosted the development of personal RMB business in foreign countries. On the basis of personal RMB business in Hong Kong, the Bank of China and Bangko Sentral ng Pilipinas signed the *Agreement on Sale, Purchase and Transit of RMB Cash* on July 31, 2009, which officially rolled out RMB cash business in the Philippines. As a result, Hong Kong ceased to be the only official channel for RMB to flow back from abroad, and the mechanism for RMB to flow back from abroad was further improved. According to that agreement, the Bank of China is allowed to conduct RMB cash trading, deposit/withdrawal, and cash transfer business in the Philippines, and provide local commercial banks and non-bank financial institutions with RMB account opening, RMB deposit/withdrawal, RMB trading and other business. The signing of that agreement marked the expansion of overseas personal RMB business from Hong Kong, China to other countries and regions.

(6) China promoted RMB internationalization through international monetary system cooperation. As a first step, the Chinese government agreed in early September 2009 that it would purchase IMF bonds of up to USD 50 billion and pay for them in RMB. Although this purchase was executed in accordance with the IMF's standard process, it proved that the RMB possessed some initial functions of an international currency, which brought about some demonstration effects. If the IMF allocates these RMB funds to its member countries through loans, it is possible that the member countries will use the RMB for international payments, thus indirectly boosting the use of the RMB in the international arena. As a second step, countries reached a consensus at the G20 summit, which concluded on September 25, 2009, with a commitment to increase the voting share of emerging markets and developing countries in the IMF by at least 5%. After that, the IMF made a voting share reform, in which China's voting share increased the most. All these steps will contribute indirectly to the improvement of the RMB's international status.

(7) China facilitated direct transactions between RMB and other non-USD currencies. In December 2011, China and Japan concluded an agreement on "strengthening cooperation in developing financial markets in both countries," with details as follows: (a) promoting the use of RMB and JPY in cross-border transactions between China and Japan; (b) supporting the development of direct exchange markets between RMB and JPY. This agreement was signed in the context of the inactive transactions between RMB and non-USD currencies in China's foreign exchange market, the lack of reasonable quotations between

these currencies, the need to use USD as an intermediary currency for most transactions, and the resulting increase in exchange rate risk and currency conversion costs for enterprises. After the development of direct transactions between RMB and non-USD currencies, the enterprises will have more choices to use RMB or other non-USD currencies as settlement and denomination currencies, which will help them avoid exchange rate risks and reduce currency conversion costs.

Under the influence of the above policies, we saw dramatic changes in the cross-border use of RMB. The most prominent changes included the massive use of RMB in cross-border transactions, the rapid increase in RMB deposits in Hong Kong's offshore market, as well as the surge in RMB investment vehicles and transactions in Hong Kong's offshore market.

### *8.3.2 Controversies Over RMB Internationalization*

According to Wang Qing (2011), the RMB deposits in Hong Kong can basically be regarded as hot money because of the following characteristics: (1) the main holders are not residents but corporations; (2) the holdings are based on speculative motivations such as appreciation expectations and interest margins; and (3) all the RMB in Hong Kong is waiting for an opportunity to return to the Chinese mainland. However, according to He Dong,[6] 60% of RMB deposits in Hong Kong are held by enterprises, but these enterprises are participants in cross-border settlements, which shows that the vast majority of RMB cross-border settlements are supported by real transaction background, and we can not completely regard these funds as hot money.

Garber (2011) analyzed the demand–supply factors in Hong Kong's RMB-denominated deposit, bond, and equity markets, revealing the currency arbitrage mechanism between the offshore and onshore markets. According to Garber, the RMB appreciation expectations are the core factor that boosts the RMB market development in Hong Kong. For example, the transaction logic in Hong Kong's RMB deposit market, according to Garber, is as follows: RMB appreciation expectations → increase of speculative demand in the CNH market (with a wider spread between onshore and offshore RMB exchange rates) → Chinese mainland importers' preference for RMB settlement in Hong Kong → increased supply of RMB deposits in Hong Kong → decline the exchange rate spread → exchange rate equilibrium. If the spread between CNH and CNY is reversed, the above equilibrium mechanism will also be reversed and there will be a decrease in RMB deposits in Hong Kong.[7] In Garber's view, the existence of long-term appreciation expectations for the RMB exchange rate and the spread between the offshore and onshore markets are factors that will distort the practices of RMB FDI and RMB trade settlements. In the context

[6] ⑥He Dong's speech at the Roundtable Conference on RMB Internationalization held by Hong Kong Monetary Authority on May 23, 2011.

[7] ⑦From October to December 2011, the exchange rate spread between the CNH and CNY markets reversed and the RMB deposits in Hong Kong declined.

of appreciation expectations, although Chinese mainland importers' RMB settlements are supported by real transactions, these transactions are actually designed to meet the need for currency arbitrage, and RMB FDI may also have similar motives for currency arbitrage transactions. In addition to Garber's (2011) currency arbitrage transaction mechanism, Yu Yongding (2012) pointed out that the interest arbitrage transaction mechanism should also be taken into account. He examined the transaction behaviors in Hong Kong's RMB offshore market from the perspective of interest rate parity and explained why the onshore foreign exchange market saw a decline in foreign exchange holdings by domestic financial institutions and a shift from a surplus to a deficit in the sales and purchases of foreign exchange by banks on behalf of their clients from October 2011 to December 2012.

With the RMB trade settlements and the offshore RMB market development, the size of foreign exchange reserves increased. For most of the time since the introduction of the RMB trade settlement policy and the establishment of the CNH market, the imports settled in RMB have been far more than the exports settled in RMB. As the reduction in demand for foreign exchange in the Chinese mainland market brought about by the settlement of imports in RMB was much greater than the reduction in the supply of foreign exchange brought about by the settlement of exports in RMB, the net supply in the foreign exchange market increased. For the purpose of keeping the established exchange rate level, the monetary authorities had to purchase more foreign exchange assets, leading to an increase in foreign exchange reserves. Despite the absence of disagreement in the above understandings, the academic controversy lies in to what extent the foreign exchange reserves are increased under the above mechanism as different data sources and assumptions are used. In addition, there is another view that the increase in foreign exchange reserves cannot be attributed entirely to the liberalization of RMB trade settlements and the establishment of the CNH market, as overseas investors have replaced their original channels for acquiring RMB assets with RMB trade settlements and the CNH market. Up to now, there are no standardized empirical studies to answer this question.

The monetary authorities bear the pressure of money supply and suffer financial losses. As mentioned above, the liberalization of RMB trade settlements and the development of the CNH market caused the monetary authorities to purchase more foreign exchange and supply more RMB at the same time. The additional money supply can be withdrawn with the help of measures such as raising the bank reserve ratio and issuing central bank bills. Therefore, although the monetary authorities face money supply pressure, they do not necessarily expand the monetary base. However, the existence of the above mechanism poses a potential threat to monetary policy. Zhang Ming (2011) argued that it would be a major threat to the independence of domestic monetary policy. Zhang Bin (2011a) emphasized the financial losses suffered by the monetary authorities. Given the trend of RMB appreciation and the fact that the yield on RMB liabilities may be higher than the yield on foreign exchange assets, the monetary authorities' practice of increasing foreign exchange assets and RMB liabilities can result in financial losses.

Although capital controls remain in effect, the liberalization of RMB trade settlements and the establishment of the offshore RMB market in Hong Kong are in effect easing capital controls. According to MaCauley (2011) and Ito (2011), there is not a completely free flow of capital between the Hong Kong offshore market and the domestic onshore market. It shows that some of the controls on the capital account are actually remaining in effect for now. According to Yu Yongding (2011), although the capital controls have not been lifted, the liberalization of RMB trade settlements and the development of Hong Kong's offshore RMB market have opened a door for capital flows and even further stimulated short-term capital flows, so the relevant policies are de facto capital deregulation policies. Murase (2010) described the current arrangements in China as Dual Exchange Rates and identified the exchange rate spread between the onshore and offshore markets in the context of RMB appreciation expectations as a Tobin tax, i.e. the cost of transferring capital from abroad to the domestic market. However, the Tobin tax refers only to the inflow of foreign capital into China, while the outflow of domestic RMB funds overseas is actually a subsidy. Therefore, such policy arrangements imply the redistribution of benefits.

## 8.4 Reform Order

There is a consensus among the academic community on this issue: the exchange rate formation mechanism reform should be prior to the capital account liberalization, while the capital account liberalization should be advanced in a gradual manner. The main reasons for prioritizing the exchange rate formation mechanism reform are as follows: (1) a resilient exchange rate formation mechanism is the first line of defense to reduce the impact of international capital flows on domestic macroeconomic stability; (2) a resilient exchange rate formation mechanism is an important price lever for industrial restructuring and resource allocation, and is essential for sustainable economic growth; (3) the benefits of free capital flows are controversial, and the benefits of free capital flows are only more readily available when the domestic economic system, and especially the financial markets, are well developed.

The academic consensus is also well supported by the domestic experience. There is also a domestic view that the impossible trinity of monetary independence, fixed exchange rates and free capital flows does not hold. Before the completion of market-oriented exchange rate reform, China may attempt to further liberalize the capital account and internationalize the RMB. However, the practice from the last decade or so shows that the costs will be very high if we do not reform based on a reasonable surplus. During the period from the beginning of RMB unilateral appreciation expectations in 2004 to the end of RMB unilateral appreciation expectations in 2014, there was an increase in both the capital account surplus and the current account surplus in order to maintain exchange rate stability. It brought about a major threat to China's economic restructuring and macroeconomic stability. In terms of economic structure, it was difficult for the exchange rate to give full play to the role of price leverage to regulate the rational allocation of resources between traded and non-traded goods, resulting in the excessive expansion of China's export and import substitution sectors, which was tightly linked to both internal and external imbalances in China's economy (Zhang Bin and He Fan, 2005). In terms of macroeconomic stability, the monetary authorities continued to intervene heavily in the foreign exchange market and also expanded the RMB monetary base, which seriously threatened macroeconomic stability. Under the continuous expectations of RMB unilateral appreciation, the enterprises were provided with a good opportunity of almost risk-free interest arbitrage. A large number of enterprises lowered their financing costs or engaged in interest arbitrage by denominating their liabilities in foreign currencies, which not only increased the pressure on the monetary authorities to intervene in the foreign exchange market, but also exacerbated the currency mismatch in the enterprises' balance sheets. Once the RMB appreciation expectations are reversed, the enterprises will face much higher exchange rate risks.

The RMB depreciation expectations appeared after August 11, 2015. The depreciation expectations arose from the fact that the monetary authorities were still intervening in the foreign exchange market so heavily that the market did not believe the clearing level of the current exchange rates was driven by market forces. As a result of the accumulation of foreign currency liabilities in the earlier period, coupled with the creation of new cross-border interest arbitrage patterns in the depreciation environment, the monetary authorities were under such severe pressure to intervene in the foreign exchange market that capital control measures had to be taken again as a means of reducing the pressure for intervention in the foreign exchange market. It can be seen that the premature liberalization of the capital account before the establishment of the market-based exchange rate formation mechanism will not only trigger the impact of interest arbitrage on capital and threaten macroeconomic stability, but will also eventually make the capital account liberalization measures unsustainable due to the monetary authorities' increasing pressure for intervention in the foreign exchange market.

# Chapter 9
# Comprehensively Building a New Pattern of China's Fiscal and Taxation System

**Gao Peiyong**

**Abstract** Based on the comprehensive deepening of reforms and the "new normal" of economic development, the ongoing reforms of the fiscal and taxation system have many new features and changes that are different from those in the past. We should thoroughly and accurately understand the new features and changes of this round of fiscal and taxation system reforms, make comprehensive and timely adjustments to the past concepts, thoughts and practices, and comprehensively build a new pattern of China's fiscal and taxation system with concepts, thoughts and practices that are quite different from those in the past. In terms of taxation system reform, we should target establishing a modern taxation system that is aligned with the modernization of the national governance system and governance capacity. In terms of budget management reform, we should target establishing a comprehensive, standardized, open and transparent modern budget management system. In terms of central-local fiscal relationship adjustment or fiscal management system reform, we should target bringing into play the enthusiasm of both the central and local governments.

## 9.1 New Stage of China's Fiscal and Taxation System Reforms

This round of fiscal and taxation system reforms that are currently in progress has two particularly important backgrounds that are very different from those of the past reforms: the comprehensive deepening of reforms and the "new normal" of economic development. Under these new backgrounds, this round of fiscal and taxation system reforms has many new features and changes that are quite different from those in the past.

G. Peiyong (✉)
National Academy of Economic Strategy, Chinese Academy of Social Sciences, Beijing, China



X. Zhang (ed.), *Exploration on China's Economic System Reform under New Normal of Development*, https://doi.org/10.1007/978-981-95-2461-7_9

### *9.1.1 Fiscal and Taxation System Reforms Aligned with the National Governance Modernization Process*

The previous fiscal and taxation system reforms, as a component of the economic system reforms, were mostly deployed on the basis of the economic system reforms. For example, the fiscal and taxation system reforms in 1994 were initiated based on the need to establish a socialist market economy. When it comes to the basic goals and evaluation criteria of that round of fiscal and taxation system reforms, we always use the expression "establishing a basic framework for the fiscal and taxation system that is aligned with the socialist market economy."

The biggest difference between the reforms that are comprehensively deepened and those in the past is that they do not refer to reforms in a certain field or in a few fields, but are comprehensive reforms in all fields. For this reason, the goals of comprehensively deepening reforms should be leading reforms in all fields based on national governance. In other words, the goals are to develop and improve the socialist system with Chinese characteristics and promote the modernization of the national governance system and governance capacity. Of course, the fiscal and taxation system reforms deployed based on the goals must go beyond the limitations of the previous reform goals set forth as a part of the economic system reforms and must serve the overall goals of comprehensively deepening reforms as a key component of the national governance system under the current background. It means that the goals of the fiscal and taxation system reforms should and must be defined within the overall goals of comprehensively deepening reforms: following the overall process of comprehensively deepening reforms and aligning with the overall goals of comprehensively deepening reforms. In other words, the sub-goals of the new round of fiscal and taxation system reforms are consistent and overlap with the overall goals of comprehensively deepening reforms.

Therefore, compared with the previous fiscal and taxation system reforms, this round of fiscal and taxation system reforms is firstly highlighted by the following major change and prominent feature: on the basis of the world-renowned achievements of economic system reforms, this round of fiscal and taxation system reforms should be integrated into the overall process of comprehensively deepening reforms, and be positioned with the goal of modernizing national governance, with a view to realizing the linked reforms and improvements in various fields such as economic system, political system, cultural system, social system, eco-civilization construction system and the Party's building system, and creating the overall effect of reforms.

In other words, we should not only regard the fiscal and taxation system reforms as a major part of the economic system reforms, but also treat them as an important part of the national governance system, so that we can plan the specific contents and action routes of the fiscal and taxation system reforms from the perspective of integrating parts into the whole picture, and promote the modernization of the national governance system and governance capacity. It can also be said that the new round of fiscal and taxation system reforms constitutes profound changes related to the modernization of the national governance system and governance capacity.

### 9.1.2 Fiscal and Taxation System Reforms Based on the Fundamental and Supportive Role of National Governance

The previous fiscal and taxation system reforms were mostly planned on the basis of treating finance as an economic category and the fiscal and taxation system as an economic system arrangement. For example, when we look at the fiscal and taxation system reforms in 1994, it can be found that although the scale and scope of the reforms were large and the actual impact was not limited to the economic sphere, the subjective intent of these reforms was not, on the whole, free from the limitations of considering the finance as an economic category and the fiscal and taxation system as an economic system arrangement.

By setting the overall goals of comprehensively deepening reforms as the modernization of the national governance system and governance capacity, it not only gives the finance a new position as "the foundation and important pillar of national governance," but also gives a new interpretation of the functions and roles of the fiscal and taxation system (i.e. "being an institutional guarantee for optimizing resource allocation, maintaining market unity, boosting social equity, and realizing long-term stability of the country"), so that the positions of the finance and the fiscal and taxation system are fundamentally corrected for the first time. As finance is the foundation and important pillar of national governance, it is more than just an economic category; it is a fundamental and supporting factor for the excellence of the national governance system and governance capacity. As the fiscal and taxation system has functions and roles that go beyond the economic sphere, it is more than just an economic institutional arrangement in the general sense, but a comprehensive institutional arrangement that involves all fields such as economy, politics, culture, society, eco-civilization and the Party's building.

Therefore, compared with the previous fiscal and taxation system reforms, this round of fiscal and taxation system reforms are secondly highlighted by the following major change and prominent feature: from the overall perspective of national governance and based on the large picture of promoting the modernization of the national governance system and governance capacity, the finance should be built as a fundamental and supporting factor of national governance, and the fiscal and taxation system should be constructed as a comprehensive institutional arrangement covering all fields of national governance.

Obviously, it is an important and revealing judgment.

First, the modernization of the national governance system and governance capacity, as an extremely ambitious project, should certainly start with the construction of its foundation and pillars. We may and should take the fiscal and taxation system reforms as the starting point for comprehensively deepening reforms. The fiscal and taxation system reforms should not only focus on the improvement of the fiscal and taxation system itself, but also pave the way for comprehensively deepening reforms, so as to implement a series of actions as the foundation and important pillar of national governance and form the national governance system and governance capacity that is more complete, more stable, more effective and more useful for the development of the Party and the state, for the happiness and well-being of the people, for the harmony and stability of society, and for the long-term peace and security of the country.

Second, the fiscal and taxation system reforms, as a junction point of economic system reforms, political system reforms, cultural system reforms, social system reforms and eco-civilization system reforms in the big picture of comprehensively deepening reforms, is indeed a major project that may and should be prioritized or pushed forward as a breaking point and a main direction. Fundamentally, these are the reasons why the fiscal and taxation system reforms are the first ones among all major reforms systematically deployed around comprehensively deepening reforms and why the fiscal and taxation system reforms are the focus of attention of the whole society in the process of comprehensively deepening reforms.

### *9.1.3 Fiscal and Taxation System Reforms Marked with the Establishment of a Modern Fiscal System*

The previous fiscal and taxation system reforms were mostly focused on the natural characteristics of the fiscal and taxation system and defined the basic reform direction from the standpoint of establishing a fiscal and taxation system aligned with the socialist market economy system. After 1998, for example, as the fiscal and taxation system reforms moved to the stage of constructing the overall systems and mechanisms, we marked the reform direction as "building the basic framework of public finance system" based on the fact that only a fiscal and taxation system of public finance nature could be compatible with the socialist market economy system.

During the long history of human development, this round of fiscal and taxation system reforms takes "establishing a modern fiscal system" as the basic reform direction for the first time from the perspective of building full awareness of modern fiscal civilization. Behind such a choice, there is obviously a series of careful considerations.

First, with more than 30 years of development, China has grown to be the second-largest economy in the world and is approaching the largest economy. After becoming an economic giant, China will certainly pursue a new development goal of making great progress in all aspects, including economy, politics, culture, society, eco-civilization and Party building, so as to stand in the modern world with the image and realm as a great power.

Second, with more than 30 years of fiscal and taxation system reforms, China has initially established the basic framework of its public finance system that is aligned with the socialist market economy system. After the breakthrough in the construction of public finance, China will certainly pursue a new reform goal of further strengthening its contemporary characteristics to keep up with the development process of human civilization and to create the general pattern of a modern fiscal system.

Third, when we look at China's official terminology about reforms, only the enterprise system has been prefixed with the word "modern" so far, with none of the other institutional arrangements in other fields prefixed with this word. The previous state-owned enterprise system reforms took the modern enterprise system as a reference system, and similarly, the current fiscal and taxation system reforms also need to take the modern fiscal system as a reference and need to draw on the general rules and basic practices of the fiscal and taxation systems of mature market economies. If we follow the reform thinking that was used in the previous state-owned enterprise system reforms and take the establishment of a modern fiscal system as the basic direction of deepening the fiscal and taxation system reforms, the significance of the fiscal and taxation system reforms will definitely be no less than that of the previous state-owned enterprise system reforms.

Fourth, the key measures of a country's civilization include not only the productivity development level, the people's moral quality and the state of social harmony and stability, but also the national governance system and governance capacity, including fiscal governance system and governance capacity. Therefore, it is necessary and even urgent to modernize the country's governance system and governance capacity by establishing a modern financial system that is aligned with the overall process of national modernization, so that China's image as a modern civilized country can be built and its international status can be enhanced.

Therefore, compared with the previous fiscal and taxation system reforms, this round of fiscal and taxation system reforms are thirdly highlighted by the following major change and prominent feature: the fiscal and taxation system reforms should be arranged from the perspective of modern fiscal civilization, and its contemporary characteristics should be further strengthened based on the focus on natural characteristics.

By connecting "the establishment of a modern financial system" with the overall goals of "modernizing the national governance system and governance capacity" and recognizing the inherent links between the "modern" financial system and "modern" national governance, we can find the following logic: The overall goals of comprehensively deepening reforms are the modernization of national governance; the modernization of national governance is built on a solid and strong fiscal foundation and fiscal pillar; the construction of a solid and strong fiscal foundation and fiscal pillar depends on a scientific fiscal and taxation system; and the scientific fiscal and taxation system is based on a modern fiscal system. Therefore, it is possible to outline a clear and explicit "roadmap" for this round of fiscal and taxation system reforms: establishing a modern fiscal system → a scientific fiscal and taxation system → a solid and strong fiscal foundation and fiscal pillar → modernizing national governance system and governance capacity.

It means that we should put the focus of this round of fiscal and taxation system reforms on the modernization of the fiscal system. Therefore, we should not only summarize the evolution laws of the fiscal systems in human societies, but also identify the general pattern of modern national fiscal systems, so as to build a modern fiscal system that responds to the laws of history, meets the trend of the times, represents the direction of development, and matches the national conditions of China by combining history and reality.

### *9.1.4 Fiscal and Taxation System Reforms Under the "New Normal" of Economic Development*

The previous fiscal and taxation system reforms were mostly paralleled with high-speed economic growth. Thanks to the huge room provided by the interaction between high-speed economic growth and high-speed fiscal revenue growth, the previous fiscal and taxation system reforms were rolled out under relatively relaxed conditions, and the reform goals were approached or achieved mainly through "incremental adjustments." The fiscal and taxation system reforms in 1994 and several other high-impact fiscal and taxation system reforms after that all coincided with periods of high-speed economic growth in China.

Unfortunately, this round of fiscal and taxation system reforms was launched against the backdrop of China's economic development entering a "new normal" after a turning point in economic growth. With the declining demographic dividend, the rising costs of labor, and the inevitable slowdown in the social productivity growth rate as well as the overall economic growth rate as a result of the adjustment toward the vigorous development of the service sector, the fiscal revenue growth rate has declined significantly. For this reason, this round of fiscal and taxation system reforms is accompanied by a series of new issues and challenges that are very different from those in the past.

First, the fiscal revenue growth rate is declining after the economic downturn on the one hand, and on the other, the pressure of fiscal expenditure is also increasing along with the "painful period" of economic restructuring. Therefore, this round of fiscal and taxation system reforms is rolled out under relatively severe conditions of fiscal revenue and expenditure, and the traditional reform path of "incremental adjustments" becomes less effective.

Second, when deciding on fiscal policy, we have to face numerous constraints arising from the previous stimulus policies on the one hand, and on the other hand, we must explore a new macro-regulation mechanism and method compatible with the "new normal" of economic development under the pressure of economic downturn. Therefore, this round of fiscal and taxation system reforms is rolled out under relatively tight macroeconomic conditions, and it has become increasingly difficult to break through the various reform barriers such as the pattern of vested interests.

Third, we have not fully understood the operation rules of the fiscal and taxation system in the context of the transitional changes in economic growth on the one hand, and on the other, a new reform dividend from the fiscal and taxation system reforms is urgently required for transforming the economic development mode and maintaining sustainable and healthy economic development. Therefore, this round of fiscal and taxation system reforms is rolled out under relatively high reform pressure, and it is difficult to reproduce the previous reform pattern where reform tasks were accomplished in a gradual manner and reform goals were achieved with ease.

The above is the fourth major change and prominent feature of this round of fiscal and taxation system reforms compared with the previous fiscal and taxation system reforms.

Indeed, it reminds us that as China's economic development enters into a "new normal," its fiscal revenue and expenditure will also undergo a process for returning to the normal track after a special period of development. The "tight budget" that we are talking about is actually the "normal budget" from now on. The construction of a new pattern of fiscal and taxation system adapted to these transitional changes in economic growth and based on an economic growth structure that is quite different from that of the past 30 years should be the key focus of this round of fiscal and taxation system reforms.

The above features and changes are the essence of this round of fiscal and taxation system reforms, and mark a new historical stage in China's fiscal and taxation system reforms. We should thoroughly and accurately understand the new features and changes of this round of fiscal and taxation system reforms, make comprehensive and timely adjustments to the past concepts, thoughts and practices, and comprehensively build a new pattern of China's fiscal and taxation system with concepts, thoughts and practices that are quite different from those in the past.

## 9.2 Taxation System Reforms: Establishing a Modern Taxation System

As one of the three aspects of this round of fiscal and taxation system reforms, the taxation system reforms are targeted at establishing a modern taxation system that is aligned with the modernization of the national governance system and governance capacity. This change marks a new stage of China's taxation system reforms. Abandoning the traditional taxation reform thinking and practices and constructing a modern taxation system are new challenges that we must address in this new stage.

Under the premise of "stabilizing tax burdens," the third plenary session of the 18th CPC Central Committee made the following systematic arrangements for taxation system reforms:

Deepen the taxation system reforms, improve the local tax system, and gradually increase the proportion of direct taxes. Promote the VAT reforms and appropriately simplify the tax rates. Adjust the scope, steps and rates of consumption tax, and include high energy-consuming and high-polluting products and some high-grade consumer goods into the scope of taxation. Gradually establish a comprehensive and classified personal income tax system. Accelerate the legislation of housing tax and promote reforms in due course, accelerate the resource tax reforms, and boost the conversion of environmental protection fees into taxes.

On that basis, the fifth plenary session of the 18th CPC Central Committee also proposed the following directions for taxation system reforms in the 13th Five-Year Plan period (2016–2020):

Establish a taxation system with scientific tax categories, optimized structure, robust laws, fair regulation and efficient collection and management.

By combining the above contents, we can summarize the basic directions of this round of taxation system reforms as follows:

### *9.2.1 Gradually Increase the Proportion of Direct Taxes*

China's current taxation system structure and the resulting tax revenue structure have two prominent features. (1) Indirect taxes are the mainstay. In 2014, the tax revenue from indirect taxes such as VAT, sales tax and consumption tax accounted for over 70% of the total tax revenue. (2) Tax revenue mainly comes from enterprises. In 2014, the tax revenue from tax payments by enterprises accounted for more than 90% of the total tax revenue.

The most prominent contradiction brought about by such a structure is the inequitable distribution of tax burdens. On the one hand, indirect taxes account for more than 70%, implying the reality that China's tax burdens are mainly distributed based on the consumption of goods and services; on the other hand, more than 90% of tax revenues come from tax payments by enterprises, implying the reality that China's tax burdens are mainly passed on to consumers through the channel of enterprises.

Since China has become the second largest economy in the world, its social development level has been upgraded to the extent that equity and justice must be taken into account in the design of the taxation system structure, and its contradictions in income distribution and rich-poor disparity have repeatedly challenged the overall stability of social development, it is clearly essential for China to optimize the current taxation structure by gradually increasing the proportion of direct taxes on the premise of stabilizing tax burdens.

In this regard, how should China gradually increase the proportion of direct taxes?

First, China should gradually establish a comprehensive and classified personal income tax system. The current taxation system in which different taxation measures are adopted for 11 taxable income items should be gradually changed to a comprehensive taxation system that adopts a unified taxation measure for most of the taxable income items. This will definitely have a tax-increasing effect rather than a tax-reducing effect on the scale of individual income tax revenue.

Second, China should accelerate the legislation of housing tax and promote reforms in due course. The current housing taxation system in which housing owned by resident individuals is basically not subject to taxes during their holding period should be gradually changed to a housing taxation system in which housing owned by resident individuals is subject to taxes during their holding period. Despite the accompanying measures to reduce housing taxation during the housing transaction and circulation periods, it will definitely increase the tax revenue.

Third, China should look for opportunities to start collecting estate and gift tax. As a type of property tax, the estate and gift tax is levied on the transfer of property by the taxpayer. From a long-term perspective, the estate and gift tax is definitely something important in the modern taxation system and must be incorporated into it sooner or later. It should be noted that the introduction of the estate and gift tax was also a start from scratch, which will naturally have the effect of increasing tax revenue.

As we all know, the housing tax, the personal income tax and the estate and gift tax are all direct taxes by nature and are all direct taxes with the natural persons as taxpayers. The increase in tax revenue from direct taxes as a result of the changes in these three taxes will undoubtedly lead to a gradual increase in the proportion of direct taxes.

### *9.2.2 Gradually Reduce the Proportion of Indirect Taxes*

The gradual increase of the proportion of direct taxes should be subject to the limitation of "stabilizing tax burdens." Therefore, the gradual increase of the proportion of direct taxes should and must be premised on the gradual reduction of the proportion of indirect taxes, and the two operations should be synchronized and correspond to each other.

Up to now, the most significant measure to gradually reduce the proportion of indirect taxes has been the "replacement of business tax with VAT." The effect of reducing indirect taxes brought about by the "replacement of business tax with VAT" consists of at least three parts:

First, both the "1 + 6 Program" (one transportation sector + six modern service sectors) initially launched in Shanghai and the "2 + 7 Program" (transportation and postal services + seven modern service and broadcasting, film and television sectors) currently being implemented nationwide have great tax reduction effects. In 2014, the tax reduction in a single year actually amounted to about RMB 200 billion.

Second, the plan of replacement of business tax with VAT will be further expanded on the basis of the "2 + 7 Program." After the "replacement of business tax with VAT" is rolled out to all sectors of the country, the scale of tax reduction can reach about RMB 500 billion per year.

Third, After the completion of the "replacement of business tax with VAT," China will further "promote the VAT reforms and appropriately simplify the tax rates." On the one hand, the simplification of tax rates will result in fewer grades and classes of tax rates and, more importantly, on the other hand, fewer grades and classes of tax rates will definitely mean a corresponding reduction in tax rates, thus further lowering the level of VAT tax burdens. A preliminary calculation based on statistical figures for 2012 shows that each percentage point reduction in the standard VAT rate will mean a tax reduction of RMB 200 billion. In addition, if the urban construction tax, the education surcharge and the local education surcharge that are attached to the VAT are taken into account, the tax reduction will be up to RMB 220 billion. If the standard VAT rate is reduced by 2 percentage points, the overall "replacement of business tax with VAT" and the VAT reforms will result in a tax reduction of about RMB 900 billion.

When the indirect taxes are reduced by about RMB 900 billion, there will be more room for increasing the proportion of direct taxes, thus paving the way for a series of operations aimed at increasing the proportion of direct taxes, such as the introduction of the housing tax and the establishment of a comprehensive and classified personal income tax system.

### *9.2.3 Gradually Improve the Local Tax System*

China has not yet built a proper local tax system because there are only a few taxes with local tax attributes, the scale of local tax revenue is small, and the business tax, which used to exist and operate as the only major local tax, has been included in the central and local shared tax framework (i.e. VAT) after the "replacement of business tax with VAT." To bring into play both central and local enthusiasm, it is imperative to improve the local tax system and achieve the goal of a sound local fiscal system.

Of course, the improvement of the local tax system should be started by recreating the major local taxes, and two options are available for the long term and the near term:

From a long-term perspective, the housing tax is the most suitable option as the major local tax. However, the introduction of housing tax on individual residents involves a series of vested interest adjustments and the accompanying revolutionary changes in the collection and management mechanisms of taxation authorities, and the legislation of housing tax should have a process of extensive discussion and consultation. Therefore, at least for the near future, the housing tax may not be a major local tax, but it can be promoted gradually as a long-term option.

From a near-term perspective, the option that can immediately serve as the major local tax is probably the reformed consumption tax. A series of operations such as "adjusting the scope, steps and rates of consumption tax, and including high energy-consuming and high-polluting products and some high-grade consumer goods into the scope of taxation" can not only expand the consumption tax base accordingly, thus increasing the consumption tax revenue but also can move the consumption tax collection forward to the retail stage, thus equalizing the distribution of consumption tax revenue among regions. Following these adjustments, the consumption tax that is currently a central tax will be changed to a local tax, which will roughly offset the shortfall in local tax revenue caused by the "replacement of business tax with VAT" and maintain a generally balanced pattern between central and local fiscal resources.

On the basis of recreating the major local tax, it is also possible to improve the local tax system through other reforms such as "accelerating the resource tax reforms and boosting the conversion of environmental protection fees into taxes."

### 9.2.4 Gradual Shift to a Modern Tax Collection and Management Mechanism

Along with the conversion from the current taxation system to a modern taxation system, China also faces the task of converting the current tax collection and management mechanism to a modern tax collection and management mechanism. The fundamental directions of the conversion are as follows:

First, it should expand from the dominant collection of indirect taxes to the collection of both indirect and direct taxes, and establish a tax collection and management mechanism that deals with both indirect and direct taxes.

Second, it should expand from the dominant collection of corporate taxes to the collection of both corporate taxes and natural person taxes, and establish a tax collection and management mechanism that deals with both corporate and natural person taxes.

Third, it should expand from the dominant collection of corporate cash circulation taxes to the collection of both circulation taxes and holding taxes, and establish a tax collection and management mechanism that deals with both circulation and holding taxes.

Among the above three directions of the conversion, we should pay the most attention to the construction of a tax collection and management system facing natural persons and a third-party tax-related information reporting system. The former is a long-standing weak spot in China and is definitely not an easy task. Only by focusing on this "weak spot," clarifying the requirements of natural persons as direct taxpayers, and truly converting the tax collection and management mechanism in terms of legal framework, institutional design and resource allocation, can we facilitate the inclusion of direct taxes on natural persons into the scope of the tax collection and management mechanism. The latter is a long-overdue goal for China and is certainly a task that requires the mobilization of resources from all quarters. Only by aiming at this goal, centering on the need to share information associated with tax collection and administration, and regulating the tax-related behaviors of relevant parties in terms of rights and responsibilities, laws and systems, and law enforcement and compliance, can we form a balanced pattern of tax collection and management between corporate entities and natural persons, and ensure that tax authorities effectively implement tax collection and management in accordance with the law.

On a brighter note, the *Plan for Deepening the Reform of National-Local Tax Collection and Management System* (hereinafter referred to as the "Plan") published at the end of 2015 highlighted that "China should respond to the trends of gradually increased proportion of direct taxes, a large number of natural person taxpayers and difficulties in tax management, and build a natural person tax collection and management system with a focus on high-income individuals from the perspectives of legal framework, system design, collection and management methods, technical supports and resource allocation." It signals that the process of conversion to a modern tax collection and management mechanism has officially begun in China.

## 9.3 Budget Reforms: Establishing a Modern Budget System

As one of the three aspects of this round of fiscal and taxation system reforms, the budget management system reforms are targeted at establishing a modern budget management system that is comprehensively regulated, open and transparent.

Under the concept of making it "comprehensively regulated, open and transparent," the third plenary session of the 18th CPC Central Committee made the following systematic arrangements for budget management system reforms:

Improve the budget management system. Implement a comprehensively regulated, open and transparent budget system. Expand the focus of budget review from balanced status and deficit to expenditure budgets and policies. Clean up and standardize the linkage between key expenditure and financial revenue and expenditure increase or GDP, and abandon the linkage method. Establish a multi-year budget balancing mechanism, an accrual-based government comprehensive financial reporting system, and a standardized and reasonable central and local government debt management and risk warning mechanism.

On that basis, the fifth plenary session of the 18th CPC Central Committee also proposed the directions for budget management system reforms for the 13th Five-Year Plan (2016–2020) period:

Establish a comprehensively regulated, open and transparent budget system, improve the government budget system, and implement a multi-year budget balancing mechanism and medium-term fiscal planning management.

By combining the above contents, we can summarize that the basic directions of this round of budget reforms are the comprehensive adjustment to the government revenue and expenditure budget pattern based on the direction of "openness and transparency."

### 9.3.1 *A Long-Standing Problem*

When it comes to the problems of China's budget management system, we have to face a rather difficult and long-standing problem: China's "fiscal revenue and expenditure" or "budgeted revenue and expenditure" are unequal to "government revenue and expenditure."

It is considered a "long-standing problem" because of its existence at least as far back as the mid to late 1990s. As many of you remember, in March 1998, Premier Zhu Rongji described the pattern of government revenue at that time as "more fees than taxes," i.e. more revenue from non-regulated fees than from regulated taxes.[1] He also criticized this pattern by saying that "the people are discontented and overburdened."

[1] ①According to the statistics in 1996, the total government revenue, including regulated and non-regulated revenue, could account for 30% of the GDP, with tax revenue accounting for slightly more than one-third of the total government revenue (Gao Peiyong 1997).

Under this background, China launched a massive reform that was initially called the "fee-to-tax reform" and later the "tax-for-fees reform."

As we all know, in October 2003 after the "fee-to-tax reform" and "tax-for-fees reform," the third plenary session of the 16th CPC Central Committee officially proposed the goal of "implementing full-covered budget management of government revenue and expenditure," in order to fundamentally solve the inequality between "fiscal revenue and expenditure" and "government revenue and expenditure," and to standardize the government's revenue and expenditure behaviors and related mechanisms. More than ten years after that, China has introduced a series of adjustment and integration measures, gradually forming a practical pattern consisting of four types of budgets: public finance budget, government fund budget, social insurance budget and state-owned capital management budget. Moreover, as one of the new fiscal achievements in 2011, China officially announced that it had achieved the goal of "fully eliminating extra-budgetary funds and integrating all government revenues into budget management" (Ministry of Finance's Press Office 2011).

However, we find the results frustrating when looking beyond the surface phenomenon to its substantive effects today: At present, China's fiscal revenue and expenditure are still unequal to government revenue and expenditure. When analyzing issues such as the scale of fiscal expenditure and the level of macro tax burdens, we still have to carefully distinguish between the two concepts: "fiscal revenue and expenditure" and "government revenue and expenditure." When communicating with foreign counterparts in academia, we still have to spend much time patiently explaining the difference in meaning between "fiscal revenue and expenditure" and "government revenue and expenditure."

### *9.3.2 Non-Regulated Reality Underneath the Glossy Surface*

In reality, the government revenue and expenditure pattern is mainly composed of four types of budgets: general public budget, government fund budget, social insurance budget and state-owned capital management budget. On the surface, at least after the implementation of the new budget law in 2015, almost all government revenue and expenditure have been brought under the scope of budget management, and extra-budgetary government revenue and expenditure basically do not exist. Therefore, it can be concluded that the reform goal of full-covered budget management of government revenue and expenditure has been achieved. However, when looking beyond the surface to the substance, we will immediately find that there are still a series of long-standing non-regulated problems behind the reality of the four-type government budget pattern:

First, although there are four types of budgets and all of them are reported to the people's congress, only the public budget revenue and expenditure are considered and approved by the people's congress. In addition, the governmental fund budget revenue and expenditure, the social insurance budget revenue and expenditure and the state-owned capital management budget revenue and expenditure are all not subject to the approval procedure of the people's congress, but only to the consideration for the purpose of filing. In 2014, the general public budget revenue and expenditure accounted for slightly more than 60% of all government revenue and expenditure, so we can imagine the extent to which the people's congress is effective in approving the government budget.

Second, although all four types of budget revenue and expenditure are public in nature and are obtained from and applied to enterprises and residents, three of them, except for the general public budget revenue and expenditure which can be coordinated at all levels of government, are controlled by different government departments in terms of budget preparation and budget execution, and are in fact the "private money" of relevant government departments. More specifically, if we exclude the social insurance budget revenue earmarked for specified purposes, the government fund budget revenue and the state-owned capital management budget revenue as a percentage of all government revenue also amounted to 23.97% and 0.89% respectively, or a total of 24.86% in 2014.

Third, as China has not included all types of government revenue and expenditure in a unified institutional framework, the people's congress approves the government budget in a differentiated manner. In the absence of a unified institutional framework for all types of government revenue and expenditure, the operations of all types of government revenue and expenditure of the same nature are dominated by multiple departments. In this process, it is not uncommon for the government revenue and expenditure that has become "private money" of relevant departments to be diverted for other purposes, or even used for projects of vested interest to the relevant government departments.

Fourth, even after deducting the revenue from the transfer of state-owned land-use rights, the total government revenue as a percentage of the GDP was still above 30% in 2014. Although the total amount of government revenue is not small and the nature of various types of budgets is the same, the different degrees of their regulation have led to the scattered use and waste of government revenue, thus providing a reason for the continuous expansion of government revenue under the surface of financial constraint, and even providing a "pretext" for the continuous expansion of local government debt.

As a result, once the pattern of the current budget management is examined according to the standards of a modern budget system, various long-standing non-regulated problems will come to the surface one by one. Even after the introduction of the new budget law, the inclusion of all types of government revenue into budget management is merely a formality, or to a large extent, a glossy surface.

### 9.3.3 *First Regulated, Second Transparent: Action Paths for Budget Management Reforms*

After recognizing that the key to budget management reforms is to break through the barriers arising mainly from vested interests of the government departments and noting that the only way to truly achieve full-covered budget management of government revenue and expenditure is to regulate the government revenue and expenditure and its mechanisms, we can take the "first regulated, second transparent" action paths for budget management reforms as our reform strategy. In other words, the basic task of the budget management reforms is to comprehensively regulate the government revenue and expenditure behaviors and the mechanisms with the basic goal of full-covered budget management and the focus on including all types of government revenue and expenditure into a unified institutional framework.

However, the reform strategy of "first regulated, second transparent" does not mean that we can put aside the goal of "transparent budget" and focus only on full-covered budget management, or let everything go until the government revenue and expenditure behaviors and their mechanisms are well regulated. In fact, regulated budget and transparent budget are interlinked and work in unison with each other. Without the premise of regulating budget, it is difficult to realize transparent budget. Without the pressure of transparent budget, it is also difficult to get enough motivation to regulate budget. Therefore, we can also make the budget regulated through transparent budget. Only through the linkage of the two can the goal of full-covered budget management be fully realized in the true sense.

A further problem is that the true realization of the full-covered budget management is clearly not the formalistic one that is currently in place. What can be regarded as full-covered budget management? What criteria should be followed to truly realize it?

By drawing on the general practices in typical market economies across the world, we can establish two interrelated "acceptance criteria" to put the full-covered budget management into practice:

First, the people's congresses at all levels have "full-covered" controls over all types of revenues and expenditure of the same level of government from the legislative perspective. In other words, all types of government revenue and expenditure should be approved by the legislative body. The government's activities and its corresponding revenue and expenditure are legitimate only with approval. All types of government revenue and expenditure must enter the "public" track and be reviewed and approved by the legislative body in accordance with unified institutional standards. It is the most important thing of the "full-covered budget management."

Second, the fiscal and taxation departments have "full-covered" management of all types of government revenue and expenditure from the administrative perspective. In other words, all types of government revenue and expenditure must be managed by the fiscal and taxation departments responsible for the management of government revenue and expenditure, and there should be no government revenue and expenditure outside the management of the fiscal and taxation departments. All types of government revenue and expenditure must be put on the "public" track and be managed and supervised by the fiscal and taxation departments in accordance with unified institutional standards. It is an important foundation for achieving "full-covered budget management" from the legislative perspective.

The above discussion tells us that achieving full-covered budget management is not an easy task, and China is destined to go through a tortuous and difficult path. It is only possible to truly approach and eventually achieve the reform goals with great determination and effort.

## 9.4 Central-Local Fiscal Relation Adjustments: Giving Full Play to Both Central and Local Enthusiasm

As one of the three aspects of this round of fiscal and taxation system reforms, the central-local fiscal relation adjustments or fiscal management system reforms are targeted at giving full play to both central and local enthusiasm.

Under the principle of "giving full play to both central and local enthusiasm," the third plenary session of the 18th CPC Central Committee made the following systematic arrangements for adjusting the central-local fiscal relations:

Establish a system that aligns powers with expenditure responsibilities. Appropriately strengthen the central government's powers and expenditure responsibilities, and define the national defense, foreign affairs, national security, rules and management of the national unified market as the central government's powers; define some social security and cross-regional major project construction and maintenance as the common powers of the central and local governments, and gradually rationalize the power relations; and define regional public services as local government's powers. Divide the central and local government's respective undertakings and shared expenditure responsibilities according to their powers. The central government may delegate parts of expenditure responsibilities under its powers to local governments through the arrangement of transfer payments. For cross-regional public services with a large impact on other regions, the central government assumes part of the expenditure responsibility under local powers through transfer payments. Maintain the overall stability of the existing pattern of central-local fiscal resources, and further rationalize the revenue division between central and local government by combining taxation system reforms and considering the attributes of tax categories.

On that basis, the fifth plenary session of the 18th CPC Central Committee further proposed the following directions for adjusting the central-local fiscal relations in the 13th Five-Year Plan period (2016–2020):

Establish a system that aligns powers with expenditure responsibilities, and appropriately strengthen the central government's powers and expenditure responsibilities. Mobilize the enthusiasm of all parties, consider the attributes of tax categories, and further rationalize the revenue division between central and local government.

By combining the above contents and comparing the three aspects of this round of fiscal and taxation system reforms (i.e. budget management system reforms, taxation system reforms and central-local fiscal relation adjustments), we can find that the most urgent aspect that needs to be tackled with precision and accuracy and to be put into practice is the central-local fiscal relation adjustments.

### *9.4.1 Fiscal and Taxation System Reforms Need to Be Promoted in a Coordinated Manner*

The reasons why the central-local fiscal relation adjustments are in most urgent need of precise efforts and accurate implementation are as follows: First, the process of fiscal and taxation system reforms so far has not been well balanced, and the adjustments of central-local fiscal relations are relatively lagging behind.

In the past two years or so from the date when the third plenary session of the 18th CPC Central Committee was held, the process of this round of fiscal and taxation system reforms can be summarized as follows, based on the statements made by the fiscal and taxation departments:

With the official implementation of the new budget law on January 1, 2015, the budget management system reforms made "substantial progress." With the comprehensive roll-out of the replacement of business tax with VAT as planned, the taxation system reforms made "significant progress." With the adjustments of central-local fiscal relations, the research on fiscal system reforms reached a "milestone."

In contrast to the concrete progress made in the implementation stage of budget reforms and taxation system reforms, the fiscal system reforms aimed at adjusting the central-local fiscal relations are still at the "research" stage. Moreover, the fiscal system reforms that are at the research stage have only reached a "milestone." Even the latest research issue about "exploring and proposing guidelines for rationalizing the division of powers and expenditure responsibilities between the central and local governments" is actually a "research plan" that has not yielded results after years of research.

Obviously, the three aspects of fiscal and taxation system reforms are promoted in an unbalanced manner. Particularly, the adjustments of central-local fiscal relations are relatively lagging behind, which is a basic fact that we must face.

Besides, it can be seen from further analysis that the adjustments of central-local fiscal relations are lagging behind in part because the design of reform contents on this topic is not sufficiently detailed, concrete and immediate.

When looking at the relevant statements of the third and fifth plenary sessions of the 18th CPC Central Committee, we can easily find that both the budget reforms and the taxation system reforms include not only top-level designs and overall plans, but also implementation paths and specific measures. In some cases, those contents are even detailed in the preparation methods of the budget and final accounts and the components of the tax categories. However, the contents of the central-local fiscal relation reforms are much less detailed. As two main directions for the adjustments of central-local fiscal relations (i.e. "further rationalizing the revenue division between central and local governments" and "rationalizing the division of powers and expenditure responsibilities among different levels of governments"), the contents are relatively abstract and vague, and basically remain at the level of top-level design and overall plan. However, the specific issues, such as which taxes are classified as central taxes with a larger share for the central government, which taxes are classified as local taxes with a larger share for the local governments, which public services are regional in nature and are defined as local powers, and which public services are cross-regional in nature and are defined as common powers for the central and local governments, are not further discussed. Apparently, from all perspectives, it is absolutely necessary to make these contents clear.

Since the reform contents of the central-local fiscal relation adjustments are not designed as deeply into the implementation paths and specific measures as the other two aspects, it is naturally unsurprising that they are relatively lagging behind.

What's more, it should be noted that the three aspects of this round of fiscal and taxation system reforms are not simply parallel, but are organically linked and mutually compatible. If any one aspect of the reforms fails to keep pace with the other two aspects, the overall effect of the reforms will be reduced, the overall pace of the reforms will inevitably be slowed down, and even the overall reforms will fall into an unbalanced state.

As a matter of fact, the overall process of this round of fiscal and taxation system reforms has already seen an obvious "bottleneck" effect as the current adjustments of central-local fiscal relations are lagging behind. As one of the main directions of the taxation system reforms, the "replacement of business tax with VAT" directly involves a major change in the fiscal source structure of the local government bodies. Of course, such a change must be predicated on the simultaneous adjustments of central-local fiscal relations, and must also be based on institutional arrangements rather than expediency. As a basic goal of the budget reforms, "being comprehensively regulated, open and transparent" directly involves a major change in the pattern of non-general public budgets, such as the government fund budget. Of course, such a change must lead to adjustments in central and local finance, especially the pattern of central-local fiscal relations. Such adjustments are significant benefit allocations and therefore must also be based on institutional arrangements rather than expediency. It should be recognized that the comprehensive roll-out of the "replacement of business tax with VAT" has been slowed down and the process of making the non-general public budget regulated and transparent has been delayed to a certain extent due to the constraints of various reasons, including the relatively backward adjustments of central -local fiscal relations.

### 9.4.2 Central and Local Enthusiasm Needs to Be Brought into Play

The adjustments of central-local fiscal relations are in urgent need of being put into practice because China's current development and reform situation requires the adjustments of central-local fiscal relations, which will be conducive to "giving full play to both central and local enthusiasm."

As mentioned earlier, this round of central-local fiscal relation adjustments is different from the previous reforms, and is targeted at "giving full play to both central and local enthusiasm." Obviously, this target is set from the reality that local enthusiasm is not sufficient and needs to be mobilized.

Given the domestic and international economic complexities and the growing downward pressure on the economy, the top priorities for China are to accelerate the implementation of policies and measures conducive to stabilizing growth and to promote sustainable and healthy economic development. According to historical experience, China has relied heavily on mutual competition among its local areas to sustain its high economic growth over the past 30 years. As economic development enters into a "new normal," China still needs to rely on local enthusiasm to maintain medium-to-high economic growth. We could even argue that China is more relying on local enthusiasm today than ever before.

However, the problem is that local enthusiasm must be mobilized and brought into play under relatively stable central-local fiscal relations, which is a prerequisite. By connecting the trajectories of changes in both the local enthusiasm and the central-local fiscal relations, we can clearly observe that the past local enthusiasm for economic development was largely based on the rational adjustments and relative stability of the central-local fiscal relations. If there were no rational adjustments of central-local fiscal relations that aimed to mobilize local enthusiasm, and if there were no relatively stable central-local fiscal relations that brought the local enthusiasm into play, it would be unimaginable that local enthusiasm could be mobilized effectively, and the scale and quality of China's economy would never reach the level it is today.

It is very important to recognize this fact. It reminds us that the relative backward adjustments of central-local fiscal relations are a key factor that is currently undermining the effectiveness of the policies and measures for stabilizing growth. We must follow the unified arrangements to show the details about the central-local fiscal relation adjustments to the local governments in a timely manner, and to set the local governments' minds at ease, so that the series of policies and measures for stabilizing growth can really be put in place and can really be accurate and effective.

When observing the process of comprehensively deepening reform, we can further notice that this round of fiscal and taxation system reforms is deployed as a key project and basic project for comprehensively deepening reform. The fiscal and taxation system reforms are defined as a key project and a basic project mainly because a linkage of reforms in various fields such as economy, politics, culture, society, ecological civilization and Party's building is what means comprehensively deepening reform. Specifically, as the foundation and important pillar of national governance, the arrangements of the fiscal and taxation system reflect and show the basic relations between the government and the market, the government and society, and the central and local governments, and profoundly affect the institutional patterns in the fields of economy, politics, culture, society, ecological civilization and Party's building. Therefore, the fiscal and taxation system is one of the most crucial elements in the big picture of national governance.

As we can see, the progress and actual effects of the fiscal and taxation system reforms depend not only on the taxation system reforms or budget reforms, but also on the overall reforms that include three aspects (i.e. taxation system reforms, budget reforms and central-local fiscal relation adjustments), especially on the reforms of fiscal distribution relations, which are the most basic and fundamental aspect of central-local relations. If we cannot speed up the adjustments of central-local fiscal relations, the crucial effect it should play will be turned into a "foot-dragging" effect. Furthermore, it will slow down not only this round of fiscal and taxation system reforms, but more seriously, it will slow down the overall progress of comprehensively deepening reform aimed at modernizing national governance.

In the overall context of China's development and reforms, it can be further concluded that the fulfillment of a series of development and reform goals, including stabilizing growth, adjusting structure, promoting reforms, preventing risks, securing employment and benefiting people's livelihood, depends on the enthusiasm of both the central and local governments, and is based on giving full play to the enthusiasm of both the central and local governments. It means that it is now urgent to put in place the adjustments of central-local fiscal relations in accordance with the requirements of the Plan.

### 9.4.3 Tax-Sharing System Should Be the Base of Consensus Building

The relatively backward adjustments of central-local fiscal relations are attributed to a number of reasons, but the most significant reason is obviously that a broad consensus has not been reached between the central and local governments on the specific action plan for the adjustments. Therefore, we should explore how to build a consensus before breaking through the fence of central-local fiscal relation adjustments.

Given that the target of this round of central-local fiscal relation adjustments is "giving full play to central and local enthusiasm," we should precisely focus on this target instead of just treating it as a slogan or label when we begin to discuss the problem.

Historically, China's pattern of central-local fiscal relations before 1994 had changed several times and was very complex, but the overall basis was the "money sharing system," including the "total amount sharing system" and the "revenue classification and sharing system" at the early stage, as well as the "all-around contract system" at the later stage. The essence of "sharing" or "contract" is about "money," i.e., fiscal revenue. After 1994, there was a fundamental change from "money sharing" to "tax sharing." After that, a series of new concepts such as central tax, local tax and central-local shared tax emerged. Thanks to the "tax-sharing system," a basis for the relatively stable central-local fiscal distribution relations, the enthusiasm of both the central and local governments was enhanced to an unprecedented degree. In view of the fact that the effective mobilization of the central and local enthusiasm began in 1994 with the tax-sharing fiscal system reform, it is undoubtedly our natural choice to continue along the path of the tax-sharing system and make it perfect, but not to deviate from this direction or even to create a new path.

However, an important point is that the tax-sharing system described above is the one originally designed at the beginning of the reform, but not the one distorted in its subsequent actual operations.

From the *Decision of the State Council on the Implementation of the Tax-Sharing Fiscal Management System* in 1993, it can be seen that the tax-sharing fiscal system designed at the beginning of the reform had at least four meanings: "Rationalize the expenditure scope of the fiscal departments at all levels in accordance with the division of powers between the central and local governments; divide various taxes into central taxes, local taxes and central-local shared taxes as per unified standards based on the principle of combining powers and fiscal resources, and establish a central taxation system and a local taxation system, with separate central and local taxation authorities for tax collection and management; approve the amount of local revenue and expenditure in a scientific manner, and gradually implement a relatively standardized system for tax returns and transfer payments from the central government to the local governments; establish and improve a tiered budget system and strengthen the budget constraints at all levels." Apparently, the central-local fiscal relations formed based on the above original meanings should have been in line with the target of "giving full play to both central and local enthusiasm."

Unfortunately, the subsequent practice of the tax-sharing system deviated from these reform arrangements because of various objective and subjective reasons: The division of powers and expenditure responsibilities between the central and local governments remained unclear and irrational; the fiscal resources were not available, and the principle of "combining fiscal resources with powers," as the soul of the tax-sharing system, was replaced by "aligning fiscal resources with powers"; the tax division scope was changed, and some local taxes and even local major taxes were converted into central-local shared taxes, which further weakened the unsound local tax system; the planning of the transfer payment system was slow and the phenomenon of "private application for money" were widespread; the revenue-expenditure management power and revenue-expenditure balancing power of local fiscal departments were absent, and the fiscal management departments at different levels did not do real work in reality.

A comparative analysis shows that the underlying cause of all the contradictions and problems in the current pattern of central-local fiscal relations is not the tax-sharing system itself, but the poor implementation of the tax-sharing system. In other words, the problems arise from the fact that the actual implementation of the tax-sharing system does not conform to what it was designed for. Therefore, if we can return from the distorted tax-sharing system to a tax-sharing system that meets the original design purposes, it will be the most favorable choice for central-local fiscal relations to mobilize both central and local enthusiasm. Furthermore, the tax-sharing system is the only rational and reasonable one that can provide relative stability and is the basis for consensus building between the central and local governments.

Therefore, the most important task we are facing now is to materialize and refine the top-level design and overall plan of the adjustments of central-local fiscal relations in the Plan and put them into practice under the tax-sharing fiscal system.

An extension of this conclusion is that the specific action plan for the adjustments of central-local fiscal relations should be extensively accepted and actively cooperated by local governments and should be formed in the effective interaction between the central and local governments; otherwise, the plan will not be promoted solidly even if it is produced; or the plan will be inevitably distorted again even if it is implemented.

Undoubtedly, the task is extremely challenging, but we have no choice but to complete it.

## References


CPC Central Committee (2013), Decision of the CPC Central Committee on Some Major Issues Concerning Comprehensively Deepening Reform, People's Publishing House, Edition 2013.

Gao Peiyong (2014), Understanding the "Roadmap" of Taxation System Reforms in the Third Plenary Session, Taxation Research, Issue 1.

Gao Peiyong (2015), Putting the Central-Local Fiscal Relation Adjustments into Practice, Guangming Daily, December 23, 2015.

Gao Peiyong (ed.) (2009), Implementing Full-Covered Budget Management of Government Revenue and Expenditure (China Fiscal Policy Report 2008/2009), China Financial & Economic Publishing House, Edition 2009.

General Office of CPC Central Committee and General Office of the State Council (2015), Plan for Deepening the Reform of National-Local Tax Collection and Management System, People's Daily, December 24, 2015.

Lou Jiwei (2013), Four Directions for Fiscal and Taxation Reforms—Fifth Round of China-US Strategic and Economic Dialogue China Taxation, China Taxation, Issue 9.

Ministry of Finance (2014), Report on the Implementation of the Central and Local Budget 2013 and the Draft of the Central and Local Budget 2014, Economic Daily, March 19, 2014.

Ministry of Finance's Press Office (2011), New Achievements in Finance in 2011, Ministry of Finance website, December 25.

OECD (2004), The Legal Framework for Budget Systems: An International comparison, a special issue of the OECD Journal on Budgeting, Vol. 4, No. 3.

State Council (1993), Decision of the State Council on the Implementation of Tax-Sharing Fiscal Management System, People's Daily, December 15, 1993.

# Chapter 10
# Strategic Adjustments of the State-Owned Economy

**Huang Qunhui**

**Abstract** In response to the "new normal" of economic slowdown, structural optimization and engine transformation, China must make major adjustments to the state-owned economy layout. Currently, the problems of the state-owned economy include a large volume with ambiguous functional positioning, excessive focus on heavy chemical industrial sectors, rapid expansion of local state-owned enterprises, failure to meet the requirements of an innovative country in terms of innovation direction and efficiency, the serious challenge of international "competitive neutrality," insufficient effective competition in naturally monopolistic sectors, and low industrial concentration in competitive sectors. Under the "new normal," the strategic adjustments to the layout and structure of the state-owned economy should focus on "quality" rather than "quantity." We should stop focusing on the "quantitative goal" of the specific proportion of the state-owned economy to the national economy as a whole, and pay more attention to the "qualitative goal" of optimizing the layout of the state-owned economy and promoting the state-owned economy to better achieve its functional positioning and mission requirements. Specifically, we should promote the strategic adjustments of the state-owned economy in a classified manner based on functional positioning, adjust the industrial layout of the state-owned economy on a selective basis based on national strategic criteria and public service criteria, and promote the merger and reorganization of state-owned enterprises in a coordinated manner based on the dual objectives of comprehensively deepening reform and optimizing market structure.

## 10.1 Problem Formulation

Since the reform and opening-up, China has witnessed tremendous development in the state-owned economy, which played an important role in maintaining its rapid economic growth, accelerating its industrialization process and improving the economy's international competitiveness. The state-owned enterprise reforms from

H. Qunhui (✉)
Institute of Industrial Economics, Chinese Academy of Social Sciences, Beijing, China



X. Zhang (ed.), *Exploration on China's Economic System Reform under New Normal of Development*, https://doi.org/10.1007/978-981-95-2461-7_10

1978 to 2013 can be divided into three stages: "decentralization and interest concessions," "institutional innovation" and "state-owned capital management" (Huang Qunhui and Yu Jing 2013). At each stage, a series of major reform measures were adopted, including the economic responsibility system, the replacement of profit delivery by taxes, the contract operation system, the establishment of the modern enterprise system, the strategic adjustments of the state-owned economy and the construction of a new state-owned assets management system with the State-owned Assets Supervision and Administration Commission (SASAC) as the core. Specifically, two major reforms, i.e., the strategic adjustments of the state-owned economy and the establishment of the modern enterprise system, contributed greatly to the achievement of today's development of the state-owned economy. Considering that China's state-owned enterprises have left much to be explored and improved so far in establishing the modern enterprise system, we can say that the strategic adjustments of the state-owned economy played a greater role. In the late 1990s, the strategic adjustments of the state-owned economy, with a focus on narrowing the scope of the state-owned economy, not only changed the situation of a large and extensive state-owned economy, but more importantly, solved the problem of how to get out of the predicament for all state-owned enterprises that were more concentrated in heavy chemical industrial sectors at the mid-industrialization stage.

At present, China's economy is entering a "new normal" with slower growth and a better structure, which means a major change in the stage of economic development from mid-industrialization to late industrialization. At this new stage, China's economy is facing both a series of new trends and a series of risks. The next direct question that needs to be addressed is how the layout and structure of the state-owned economy, which was strategically adjusted and adapted to the mid-industrialization stage, should be strategically adjusted again to adapt to the changing environment at the late industrialization stage, thus allowing China to respond to and lead the "new normal." This question is undoubtedly of great importance, not only for the future development of the state-owned economy, but also for the realization of China's future industrialization under the new economic normal. However, the current studies on the strategic adjustments of the state-owned economy at the new stage have only put forward some ideas and thoughts, but few of them are really of academic significance. In contrast to the low attention paid by the studies on the strategic adjustments of the state-owned economy, the merger of China's top two high-speed rail makers, China North Railway (CNR) and China South Railway (CSR) has ignited great enthusiasm for M&A and restructuring of state-owned enterprises in the capital market, with great expectations from the capital market for future state-owned enterprise restructuring. However, we should carry out an in-depth and systematic study on the guiding principles, basic directions and overall planning of the strategic adjustments of the state-owned economy under the new economic normal before promoting the restructuring of state-owned enterprises at the operational level. It is also the important practical significance of this chapter.

## 10.2 New Requirements for the State-Owned Economy Under the New Economic Normal

China's President Xi Jinping pointed out on November 10, 2014, that the new economic normal has three basic characteristics: a shift in economic growth rate from high growth rates to medium-to-high growth rates, a process of optimizing economic structure, and a transition in economic growth engines. On December 9, 2014, the Party's Central Economic Work Conference further summarized the basic characteristics of the new economic normal in nine aspects (i.e. consumer demand, investment demand, exports and balance of payments, production capacity and industrial organization methods, production factors, market competition, resource and environmental constraints, economic risks, resource allocation patterns and macro-control methods). All these characteristics show that the new economic normal is a new stage of economic development in China. According to our study and in terms of China's industrialization process, this new stage marks China's entry into the late industrialization stage, which means that the late industrialization stage is a step in the process of entering a "new normal" of economic growth. This process is accompanied by the emergence of some major trends, including the trends of economic slowdown in terms of economic growth rate, the trends of economic tertiarization in terms of economic structure, the trends of structural optimization in terms of internal sector structure, the trends of supply-side factor intensification and de-capacity in terms of economic growth engines, as well as the trends of deep integration between industrialization and informatization, as well as between manufacturing and service sector due to the overlap of this process with international re-industrialization and the Third Industrial Revolution (Huang Qunhui 2015). In other words, the economic environment that China was familiar with has changed dramatically. Meanwhile, as China launched new national development strategies such as the "Silk Road Economic Belt," "21st Century Maritime Silk Road" and "Made in China 2025," the state-owned enterprises are required to take on new missions. For the state-owned economy, these new trends under the new economic normal and these new national development strategies mean that on the one hand, environmental changes have posed new challenges to the state-owned enterprises and the state-owned enterprises must embrace the challenges and adapt to the new environmental changes for survival and development (i.e. "adapting to the "new normal"); on the other hand, the country will assign new missions to the state-owned enterprises at the new stage of economic development, which in turn will also pose new requirements for the state-owned enterprises (i.e. "leading the "new normal").

### 10.2.1 Adapting to the Economic Slowdown Under the "New Normal" and Actively Transforming the Development Mode of the State-Owned Economy

China's economic growth rate was 10.4% on average per year from 2001 to 2011, but declined to 7.7%, 7.7% and 7.4% in 2012, 2013 and 2014 respectively, and fell further to 7% in the first and second quarters of 2015. According to the Frontier Research Group on China's Economic Growth (2014), China's growth rate is expected to be 6.4% to 7.8% in 2016–2020; according to the Research Group on Medium and Long-term Growth of the Development Research Center of the State Council, China's average growth rate is expected to be 6.5% in 2015–2025; according to the Macroeconomic Operation and Policy Simulation Laboratory of the Chinese Academy of Social Sciences, China's potential economic growth rate is estimated to be 5.7% to 6.6% in 2016–2020 and 5.4% to 6.3% in 2021–2030 (Li Yang and Zhang Xiaojing 2015). It means that the economic slowdown since 2012 is a trend, but not a cyclical short-term decline that will rebound in a "V" shape in the future. The theoretical explanations provided by the academic community for this trend include the disappearance of the demographic dividend and the structural slowdown (Frontier Research Group on China's Economic Growth 2013). In our opinion, this trend is caused by the fact that China has stepped from mid-industrialization to late industrialization since 2011. The historical experience of other countries shows that a key change in the characteristics of economic development in the late industrialization period compared with the mid-industrialization period is that the investment-supported high growth rates and heavy chemical industrial sectors-dominant development mode in the mid-industrialization period will be unsustainable, and the economic growth rate will naturally decline in the late industrialization period due to the change of dominant sectors and the decline of potential economic growth rates.

As a response to China's rapid industrialization process, investment-driven high growth rates and extensive economic development mode, China's state-owned economy has been developed mainly through investment-driven scale expansion. Against the backdrop of rapid economic growth, enterprises are faced with numerous opportunities for growth, and the imitation-based and wave-like consumer demand and large-scale infrastructure investment demand make "leapfrog development" a strategic goal that most enterprises have pursued and can achieve. Different from the opportunity-driven leapfrog development approach of the private enterprises, the state-owned enterprises are more inclined to choose the investment-driven leapfrog development approach, due to objective and subjective reasons: First, the state-owned enterprises are assigned with the national missions for national security and economic catching-up, which requires the state-owned enterprises in the sectors related to national security, natural monopolies, important public goods and services, economic pillars and high technologies to expand rapidly in scale and to compete with large foreign multinational companies. Second, local governments require local state-owned enterprises to expand rapidly in scale for the purposes of improving tax revenue and local economic development performance. Third, state-owned enterprises' decision-makers have a stronger incentive to rely on investment for rapid expansion due to the tenure system of government officials and the organizational appointment system of state-owned enterprises' entrepreneurs. After a long period of practice, state-owned enterprises are more accustomed to this investment-driven leapfrog development approach. Fourth, after the strategic restructuring of the state-owned economy, and with China's rapid industrialization process, most state-owned enterprises are engaged in heavy chemical industrial sectors that require high investment. Fifth, in terms of financing systems and mechanisms, state-owned enterprises have more ease of access to large-scale investment.

As China's economy is gradually stepping into the new economic normal with the shift from high growth rates to medium-to-high growth rates, the end of the imitation-based and wave-like consumption stage, the low-cost comparative advantages becoming unsustainable, the market competition changing from low costs to differentiation, the driving force of factor scale weakening, and the economic growth relying more on high-quality human capital and technological progress, the previous investment-driven leapfrog development approach which the state-owned enterprises were familiar with will no longer adapt to the new changes in the environment. At this new stage of economic development, state-owned enterprises have to achieve profitable (but not highly profitable) and sustainable (but not leapfrog) development through continuous innovation under the premise of clear national missions and functional positioning. To this end, it is necessary to actively promote such major reforms and measures as the classification and functional positioning of the state-owned enterprises based on their missions, the strategic restructuring of the state-owned enterprises based on their positioning, as well as the establishment of a modern enterprise system and a modern governance mechanism conducive to innovation based on their classification, so that the state-owned economy can be transformed from the "investment-driven leapfrog development approach" to the "innovation-driven sustainable development approach."

### 10.2.2 Adapting to the New Requirements of Economic Structure Optimization and Upgrading, and Actively Promoting the Strategic Adjustments to the Layout and Structure of the State-Owned Economy

One of the important characteristics of the new economic normal is the optimization and upgrading of the economic structure. From the structure among primary, secondary and tertiary sectors, in 2013, the added value of the tertiary sector as a percentage of GDP reached 46.1%, while the added value of the secondary sector accounted for 43.9%, making it the first time that the tertiary sector exceeded the secondary sector and became the sector with the biggest proportion in GDP. From the perspectives of China's industrialization process and the trend of sector structure optimization, the proportion of tertiary sector output value exceeded the proportion of secondary sector output value for the first time in 2013, representing to a certain extent a symbolic turning point. In 2014, the proportion of the tertiary sector reached 48.2%, which was 5.6 percentage points higher than the proportion of the secondary sector. In the first half of 2015, the proportion of the tertiary sector further increased to 49.5%, showing a clear trend of tertiarization in China's economy. From the perspective of the internal structure of the secondary sector, the trends of high-processing degree and technology intensification are obvious, and technology-intensive sectors and strategically emerging sectors are developing rapidly. Under the background of the overall declining growth rate of the secondary sector, the equipment manufacturing sector among three major sectors (raw materials sector, equipment manufacturing sector and consumer goods sector) in the secondary sector grows at the fastest speed and ranks first. From the perspective of specific sectors, the growth rate of high-tech sectors has remained higher than the average growth rate of the secondary sector, with particularly rapid development in the energy saving and environmental protection sector, new-generation information technology sector, biopharmaceutical sector, new energy automobile sector, etc. High-tech sectors such as biomedicine and artificial intelligence have continued to grow at a high rate of 10% to 12% in the past two years, nearly five percentage points higher than the average growth rate of industrial enterprises above the designated size. Meanwhile, there are outstanding over-capacity problems in steel, electrolytic aluminum, cement, flat glass, shipbuilding and other sectors. The traditional economy and the emerging economy show very different growth patterns, which highlights the need to optimize and upgrade the structure of China's economy.

As China enters the twenty-first century, most of its state-owned capital is distributed in heavy chemical industrial sectors, which is in line with China's mid-industrialization stage. In 2012, China's industrial and construction sectors had 43.06% of national state-owned assets, while heavy chemical industrial sectors such as coal, oil and petrochemicals, metallurgy, building materials, electricity, and machinery had 78.44% of all state-owned assets. For China, a country in the mid-industrialization stage, these sectors are generally related to the national economy and the people's livelihood and are of strategic importance. However, it must be noted that such sectors as coal, metallurgy and building materials have relatively prominent over-capacity problems. In fact, as China enters the late industrialization stage and advances in the new technological revolution, the national strategic significance of some of these sectors has diminished on the one hand, and on the other hand, the annual peak demand of these sectors has been reached and the future demand will gradually decrease, so the excess capacity in these sectors is absolutely excess capacity. If the state-owned capital is further distributed mainly in these sectors, the national missions and strategic significance of the state-owned capital will become less prominent on the one hand, and on the other hand, the benefits of the state-owned enterprises will be affected, and the goals of preserving and increasing the value of state-owned assets and making the state-owned enterprises bigger, stronger and better will be difficult to achieve. Therefore, under the "new normal" of economic development at the late industrialization stage, it is necessary to adapt the state-owned economy to the new requirements of economic structure optimization, transformation and upgrading, and actively promote the strategic adjustments of the layout of the state-owned economy.

### *10.2.3 Adapting to the New Requirements of the Transformation of Economic Growth Engines, Comprehensively Deepening the State-Owned Enterprise Reforms and Promoting the Innovation-Driven Strategy*

As we enter the late industrialization stage, the supply-side factors that determine economic growth have all changed significantly. In terms of labor force, the "demographic dividend" brought about by the population's age structure gradually disappeared after 2010, with the working-age population aged 15–59 decreasing by 3.45 million and 2.44 million in 2012 and 2013, respectively, as compared to that in the previous year, and the labor force participation rate decreasing from 76% in 2005 to 70.8% in 2011. In terms of capital, the marginal product of capital in the secondary sector declined from 0.61 in 2002 to 0.28 in 2012. It means that the labor force, capital and other factors are weak in driving economic development at the late industrialization stage, and the more fundamental engine is innovation, as the original intention of the "innovation-driven strategy." This innovation includes both the general technological innovation, and the institutional innovation for deepening reform and opening-up. In terms of technological innovation, we need to adapt to the new trend of integrated development between industrialization and informatization through technological innovation, promote the continuous upgrading of traditional sectors and the cultivation and development of emerging sectors, deepen the industrialization process, realize the advanced sector structure and improve the total factor productivity. In terms of institutional innovation, we should, on the one hand, break down the institutional and mechanical barriers that hinder the full supply of China's current production factors through institutional innovation, promote the market-oriented process of factors, and boost the quantity and efficiency of supply factors; on the other hand, we should break down the institutional and mechanical constraints on China's technological innovation through institutional innovation, and enhance the efficiency of China's technological innovation, so that the industrialization process can be deepened and the role of a deepened industrialization process in promoting the economy can be brought into play. It means that the new engine of China's economic development under the "new normal" is largely institutional innovation.

Comprehensively deepening the reforms of state-owned enterprises is an important part of institutional innovation under the new economic normal, and a key engine of economic development under the "new normal." First, the third plenary session of the 18th CPC Central Committee required that the investment and operation of state-owned capital must serve the national strategic goals, including providing public services, developing important forward-looking strategic sectors, protecting the ecological environment, supporting scientific and technological progress, and ensuring national security. As a result, the state-owned enterprises must adjust their business strategies and directions accordingly and determine their future strategic directions based on these national mission requirements. Through business strategy adjustment and implementation, the state-owned enterprises achieve their missions of supporting scientific and technological progress and developing forward-looking strategic sectors. The state-owned enterprises serve as a key driver of economic development under the "new normal." Second, by comprehensively deepening the reforms of state-owned enterprises, it is not only conducive to vitalizing the state-owned enterprises, promoting technological innovation and market competitiveness of state-owned enterprises, making the state-owned economy bigger, stronger and better, and promoting the development of the whole economy, but also conducive to creating a fair competition environment, establishing an effective competition order, and benefiting the development of the non-public economy and the whole economy. For example, the mixed-ownership reform not only helps state-owned enterprises become real market players and stimulate market vitality, but also helps avoid the constraint of "competitive neutrality," promote the effective implementation of the "going-out strategy" and expand the growth space of private enterprises. Another example is that the reform of state-owned enterprises in natural monopolies is aimed at strategically restructuring their businesses and concentrating more state-owned capital on business steps that are natural monopolies rather than on the entire sector chain, thus promoting the level of competition and efficiency of the whole sector. The third example is that the state-owned enterprises in sectors with an excessive competition or excess capacity should actively promote the merger and reorganization strategy, which will help to establish a reasonable industrial organization structure, form an efficient industrial concentration and enhance the efficiency of the whole sector.

To sum up, along with the major changes in the economic environment such as the new economic normal, as well as the introduction of new national strategies such as BRI and "Made in China 2025," the development strategy of the state-owned economy is inevitably subject to major changes. It means that not only the internal business development strategy and organizational structure of the enterprises should be changed accordingly, but more critically, the strategic adjustments should be made at the macro level of the state-owned economy, which includes both the adjustments of the overall layout and the adjustment of the sector structure. If the strategic adjustments of the state-owned economy, with a focus on narrowing the scope of the state-owned economy from 1996, are called the first adjustments, the strategic adjustments of the state-owned economy under the "new normal" will be the second adjustments or readjustments. The most essential difference between the strategic adjustments of the state-owned economy under the "new normal" and the first strategic adjustments of the state-owned economy is that they are aimed at better serving the national economic development strategy under the "new normal," rather than at narrowing the scope of the state-owned economy. Therefore, the readjustments of the state-owned economy include not only the "subtraction" of state-owned capital, but also the "addition" of state-owned capital, with a view to realizing the effective flows of state-owned capital based on the national missions and national economic development goals under the "new normal."

## 10.3 Current Layout and Structure of the State-Owned Economy and Relevant Problems

Although the state-owned economy in a broad sense refers to all economic activities and processes based on the ownership of economic resources by the state, and can be understood as all administrative and operational assets owned by the state and the economic activities derived therefrom, the "state-owned economy" in the discussion of the strategic adjustments of the state-owned economy refers narrowly to the state-owned enterprises' operational assets and their activities.

### *10.3.1 The Total Size of the State-Owned Economy is Expanding, but the Functional Positioning of the State-Owned Economy is not Clear*

After the development of state-owned assets in 2003, China's state-owned economy has made considerable progress on the whole. According to estimated data from China's national balance sheet, China's state-owned operating assets (i.e. total state-owned assets of non-financial enterprises) (including liabilities) were RMB 70.3 trillion in 2011 (Li Yang et al. 2013). According to the data cited in the China Enterprise Development Report 2015 from the Ministry of Finance and the SASAC, the total assets in the consolidated statements of Chinese state-owned enterprises were RMB 85.38 trillion, RMB 100.23 trillion, and RMB 104.1 trillion in 2011, 2012, and 2013, respectively, of which the total state-owned capital (state-owned paid-in capital and its amount of equity attributable to them) were RMB 21.99 trillion, RMB 25.18 trillion, and RMB 29.60 trillion, respectively. Similarly, according to the data from the Ministry of Finance, the country's operating state-owned capital reached RMB 7.0 trillion in 2003, and increased to RMB 33.7 trillion in 2014, representing an average annual growth of more than 30%. For the same period, the number of state-owned enterprises rose from 146,446 to 160,515, representing an increase of 14,069. Based on the assets of RMB 104.1 trillion in the consolidated statements of state-owned enterprises in 2013, the ratio of state-owned enterprise assets to GDP in China was about 1.8:1, while that ratio in OECD countries was 0.25:1 in 2007, implying that the role of China's state-owned economy in the national economy is far more prominent than that of OECD countries. The rapid development of the state-owned economy benefits both from the establishment of the incentive and restraint mechanism to preserve and increase the value of state-owned assets after the establishment of the SASAC, and from the fact that most state-owned enterprises are involved in fast-growing sectors. However, the rapid expansion of state-owned capital has caused a series of criticisms, such as "the state advancing and the people retreating," the use of administrative resources by state-owned capital to obtain a monopoly position, and the damage to market equity and efficiency. It reflects that in practice, the assessment of the state-owned assets preservation and appreciation rate is not appropriate for all state-owned enterprises. The key is to clarify what the functional positioning of the state-owned capital is and to assess whether the state-owned capital has achieved its positioning requirements. For some state-owned enterprises that are positioned for public welfare or policy-based purposes, it is not necessary to assess their profitability or their state-owned capital preservation and appreciation rates. However, the reality in China is that since the state-owned enterprises are not classified and not assigned a specific mission, many state-owned enterprises are engaged in both market-oriented and policy-based businesses, and cover both competitive and naturally monopolistic sectors, resulting in the conflicts between "profit-oriented missions" and "public policy-based missions" for the state-owned enterprises. On the one hand, the state-owned enterprises have to ensure their continuous development and growth by pursuing profitability, which requires the assessment of the state-owned assets preservation and appreciation rates; on the other hand, the state-owned enterprises have to make up for the market defects and position themselves as public policy tools to serve public goals, which requires them to sacrifice profitability. Currently, these two positioning requirements have put state-owned enterprises in a dilemma between profitability and unprofitability. If they are unprofitable, they cannot accomplish the goals of preserving the value of state-owned assets and growing the state-owned economy, but if they are profitable, they are accused of compromising market equity and efficiency and sacrificing public service goals (Huang Qunhui and Yu Jing 2013). The overall layout of the state-owned economy covers competitive, naturally monopolistic and public policy-based fields, but the business goals of the state-owned enterprises in different fields are not clearly distinguished, and even a single state-owned enterprise's businesses cover all kinds of fields of different nature, and the leaders of the state-owned enterprises have the dual roles as both administrative officials and professional entrepreneurs. In other words, both the state-owned enterprises and the leaders of the state-owned enterprises have mixed or unclear positioning, which prevents the state-owned enterprises from becoming real enterprises. Therefore, we need to adjust the existing layout of the state-owned economy and classify the governance of state-owned enterprises in the future based on their functional positioning and mission requirements.

### *10.3.2 The State-Owned Economy is Mainly Distributed in the Secondary Sector, but There is a Clear Trend of Restructuring to the Tertiary Sector*

Looking at the central enterprises alone, we can find that in 2013, the primary sector accounted for 0.2% of the total assets of all central enterprises, the secondary sector accounted for 64.5%, and the tertiary sector accounted for 35.3% (Song Qun 2014). Looking at the national state-owned enterprises, we can find that among the 14 major sectors (i.e., farming, forestry, animal husbandry and fishery; industrial sectors; construction; geological exploration; transportation; post and telecom; wholesale and retail; housing; information technology services; social services; health and sports services; education and culture; scientific research and technology; organs, society and others), the state-owned industrial enterprises accounted for the largest share (26.6%) of the number of the state-owned enterprises across the country in 2014, and the capital of the state-owned industrial enterprises also accounted for the largest share (33.32%) of the capital of the state-owned enterprises across the country. If we simply treat the industrial and construction sectors as the secondary sector, about 40% of the state-owned capital was distributed in the secondary sector in 2014. It can be said that the sector structure of China's state-owned economy basically coincides with the sector structure of the overall national economy. Moreover, along with the structural trend of China's economic tertiarization, the share of China's state-owned industrial enterprise capital in the total state-owned enterprise capital has decreased by 17.35 percentage points in seven years from 50.67% in 2007, while in the same period, the state-owned capital in the social service sector has increased by 15.02 percentage points from 9.05% to 24.07%. As shown in Fig. 10.1, after simply dividing the above 14 sectors into the primary sector (farming, forestry, animal husbandry and fishery), secondary sector (including sector and construction), and tertiary sector (including transportation, post and telecom, wholesale and retail, housing, information technology services, social services, health and sports services, education and culture, research and technology, etc.), it can be seen that the shares of state-owned capital among these sectors have been changing in the decade from 2005 to 2014, with an overall trend that the share of the primary sector has been maintained at about 1%, the share of the secondary sector has been decreasing, and the share of the tertiary sector has been increasing.

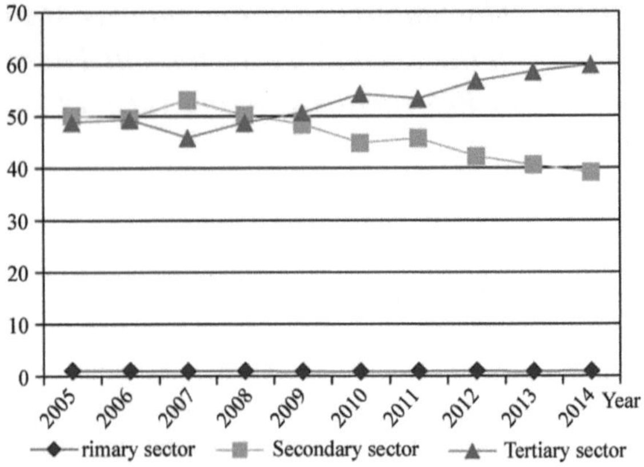


**Fig. 10.1** Changes in the shares of state-owned enterprise capital in primary, secondary and tertiary sectors, 2005–2014. *Data source* Calculated based on the data in the state-owned enterprises' final financial reports issued by the Ministry of Finance

### *10.3.3 Industrial State-Owned Capital is Mainly Distributed in Heavy Chemical Industrial Sectors, with Insufficient Distribution in Strategic Emerging Sectors*

If the industrial sectors are divided into 16 categories as per the Ministry of Finance's criteria, that are oil and petrochemicals, electric power, machinery (including automobile), metallurgy, coal, tobacco, chemicals, military, electronics, building materials, pharmaceuticals, textile food, forest, municipal utility, and other industrial sectors, it can be seen that since 2003, the industrial state-owned capital has been mainly distributed in 5 sectors, namely oil and petrochemicals, electric power, machinery, metallurgy and coal, and the sum of the state-owned capital in these five sectors accounted for 66.03%, 76.54%, 73.31% and 71.55% of the total state-owned capital in all industrial sectors in 2003, 2008, 2013 and 2014 respectively. Specifically, the oil and petrochemicals sector and the electric power sector have been the two sectors with the largest shares of state-owned capital, basically accounting for 45% to 50%; the metallurgy sector has been in the third place except for 2014 when it ranked fourth after the machinery sector; the coal sector slipped from the fourth place in 2008 to the sixth place in 2014, following the machinery sector and the municipal utility sector. The shares of state-owned capital in the machinery sector and the municipal utility sector have increased significantly in recent years, from 7.08% and 3.05% in 2008 to 9.98% and 7.54% in 2014 respectively, reflecting the trend of advanced sector structure and the functional positioning of the state-owned economy to serve people's livelihood. However, most of the state-owned capital is distributed in traditional sectors, and many of them are distributed in the middle and low end of the value chain. There are both the problem of excess capacity and the problem of insufficient distribution of strategic emerging sectors. On the one hand, the central enterprises have an excess capacity of 200 million tons of crude steel, about 20% of alumina and about 25% of cement; while on the other hand, the share of state-owned capital allocated in strategic emerging sectors such as energy saving and environmental protection, emerging information, biology, new energy, new energy automobile, high-end equipment manufacturing and new materials is low, with only 10.62% of such enterprises in central enterprises (Song Qun 2014). According to the *Report on the Development of China's Strategic Emerging Industries 2015* published by the Academy of Chinese Engineering S&T Strategy for Development, as of the first half of 2014, 63.5% of the listed enterprises engaged in strategic emerging sectors were private enterprises, 13.6% were central state-owned enterprises, and 13.2% were local state-owned enterprises. Therefore, in terms of the state-owned capital distribution among industrial sectors, the state-owned economy has not yet played a sufficient guiding role in reflecting the strategic directions of national economic development. In the past decade or so, China experienced the mid-industrialization stage with heavy chemical industrial sectors in a period of great development, so this strategic distribution of state-owned capital among industrial sectors was reasonable. The boom of heavy chemical industrial sectors and the economic growth model driven mainly by major investment projects over the past decade or so have led to considerable growth in the size of assets and revenue in the state-owned sectors of the economy. However, as China is stepping into the new economic normal, the state-owned economic development approach formed in the past decade or so, which focused on the distribution of capital in heavy chemical industrial sectors and was based on scale expansion, can no longer adapt to the requirements of the new economic normal at the late industrialization stage. In view of the increasingly prominent problems of excess capacity and poor economic efficiency, it is urgent for industrial state-owned capital to withdraw from the fields of excess capacity and move to strategic emerging sectors so that an industrial state-owned capital distribution structure appropriate for the new economic normal can be formed, as shown in Fig. 10.2.

### 10.3.4 The Total Assets of Local State-Owned Enterprises Are Increasing, but Their Efficiency is Lower Than that of Central Enterprises

From the perspective of affiliation and regional layout, the proportion of state-owned capital of local enterprises has been increasing in recent years and is larger than that of central enterprises. Specifically, the total state-owned capital in the eastern region accounts for more than half of the local state-owned capital, but the proportion of state-owned capital in the central and western regions has been on the rise. According to the Ministry of Finance, as of 2014, there were 106,373 local state-owned enterprises in China, much more than the number of central enterprises, accounting for 67.1% of the total number of state-owned enterprises; the total state-owned capital of local state-owned enterprises was RMB 19.89118 trillion, higher than the total state-owned capital of central enterprises, accounting for 54.8% of

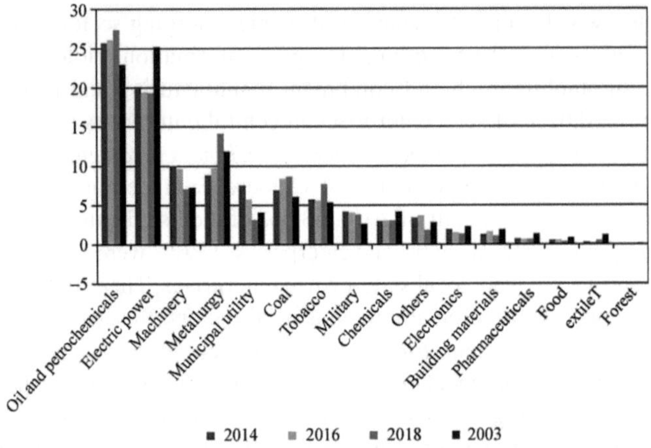


**Fig. 10.2** Structure of the distribution of state-owned capital in industrial sectors. *Data source* Calculated based on the data in the state-owned enterprises' final financial reports issued by the Ministry of Finance

the total state-owned capital of all state-owned enterprises. The proportion of state capital in local state-owned enterprises has been rising since 2008, from 41.3% in 2008 to 57.7% in 2013, but declined in 2014. In terms of the specific share by province, the size of state-owned assets and state-owned enterprises varies greatly from province to province and is related to their level of economic development. The top provinces in terms of state-owned assets in 2012 were Jiangsu, Shanghai, Guangdong, Beijing, Chongqing, Zhejiang, Tianjin, and Shandong, with each of these provinces having total state-owned assets of more than RMB 2 trillion (Ma Shuping and Yuan Dongming 2015). In 2014, both the number of state-owned enterprises and total state-owned capital in the eastern region accounted for 56%, while the number of state-owned enterprises in the central and western regions accounted for 20.1% and 23.4%, respectively, and their total state-owned capital accounted for 18.0% and 25.7%, respectively. In recent years, the shares of state-owned capital in the central and western regions have been on the rise. The shares of state-owned capital in the central and western regions were only 11.6% and 11.4% in 2005, which means that they have about doubled in recent years. In general, the local state-owned assets and the local state-owned enterprises mainly serve three functions: (1) public services such as water supply, gas supply, public transportation, etc. (2) Urban development and infrastructure construction as well as supply of factors such as land and capital. For example, 30% of the assets of state-owned enterprises in Chongqing are distributed in public infrastructure, and the assets of Hubei Communications Investment Group Co., Ltd. alone account for more than 50% of the total operating assets in Hubei Province. (3) Cultivating pillar sectors and promoting local economic development. For example, more than 80% of the operating assets of municipal-owned enterprises in Shanghai are distributed in key areas and local advantageous sectors such as strategic emerging sectors, advanced manufacturing sectors and modern service sectors; 71% of the assets of provincial-owned enterprises in Hunan Province are distributed in machinery manufacturing and metallurgy sectors; and the assets of state-owned enterprises in Shaanxi and Henan provinces are mainly distributed in energy & chemical, equipment manufacturing, and non-ferrous metals sectors (Huang Qunhui 2015). Compared to central enterprises, local state-owned assets are also characterized by lower overall returns. According to the data in the *Report on Final Financial Accounts of State-owned Enterprises 2013* by the Ministry of Finance, although the total amount of local state-owned assets was RMB 6.9 trillion more than the total amount of central state-owned assets, the net profit created by central state-owned enterprises in 2013 was RMB 1.2 trillion, about twice as much as the net profit of local state-owned enterprises. It reveals that the revenue level and profitability of local state-owned enterprises are not as good as those of central state-owned enterprises (Xiang Anbo and Shi Ning 2015). In addition, there are obvious differences in the revenue levels and profitability of state-owned enterprises across regions. According to the *China Statistical Yearbook 2014*, the total profits and the total assets contribution rate of the state-owned and state-controlled enterprises across the country were RMB 1,519.41 billion and 11.9% respectively in 2013, while the total profits and the total assets contribution rate of the state-owned and state-controlled enterprises in regions varied greatly. Specifically, in terms of total profits, the top three provinces were Shaanxi (RMB 137.11 billion), Shanghai (RMB 131.39 billion) and Shandong (RMB 121.40 billion), while the bottom three provinces were Tibet (RMB 91 million), Hainan (RMB 1.62 billion) and Qinghai (RMB 3.76 billion); in terms of total assets contribution rate, the top three provinces were Heilongjiang (20.4%), Shanghai (18.2%), Guangdong (17.3%), while the bottom three provinces were Tibet (1.1%), Beijing (6.2%), Shanxi (7.3%). From the affiliation and regional distribution, we observe the co-existence of rapid expansion and poor profitability of local state-owned capital, and it is more prominent in the central and western regions. The positive reason may be the development of urban infrastructure and the improvement of public service functions in recent years at the local level, especially in the central and western regions. However, it also reflects that the risk of over-indebtedness of local governments is expanding in recent years, as well as the fact that some late-developing regions have also started to distribute assets in the heavy chemical industrial sectors, which exacerbates the problem of excess capacity. From the perspective of the functional positioning of central and local state-owned capital, a more reasonable positioning for local state-owned capital should be the regional public service function, while the central state-owned capital should play a guiding role in the national economic development strategy. Therefore, we need to strategically adjust the existing affiliation and regional layout of state-owned capital in accordance with this positioning.

### 10.3.5 Central Enterprises Are Expanding Their Overseas Assets, but Face the Challenge of "Competitive Neutrality"

From the perspective of internationalization, the central enterprises, as part of the state-owned enterprises, play a key role, but in the future, they will face the mission requirements under the Belt and Road Initiative (BRI) and the serious challenge of "competitive neutrality" in the international arena. According to the *2013 Statistical Bulletin of China's Outward Foreign Direct Investment* jointly released by the Ministry of Commerce, the National Bureau of Statistics and the SAFE in September 2014, state-owned enterprises accounted for 59.8% and 55.2% of the non-financial outbound direct investment (ODI) stocks at the end of 2012 and 2013, respectively. In 2013, the non-financial ODI stocks reached USD 543.4 billion, and the non-financial ODI flows were USD 92.74 billion, of which the state-owned enterprises accounted for 43.9%, the limited liability companies accounted for 42.2%, the companies limited by shares accounted for 6.2%, the joint-stock cooperative enterprises accounted for 2.2%, the private enterprises accounted for 2%, the foreign-invested enterprises accounted for 1.3%, and the others accounted for 2.2%. It can be seen that state-owned enterprises are the main force for Chinese enterprises to go global. Among the state-owned enterprises, the central enterprises play a more crucial role. For example, the overseas M&A amounts of the central enterprises accounted for 83%, 86%, 80%, 91%, 76%, and 74% of the total M&A amounts of all enterprises from 2005 to 2010 (Yi Gang 2012). By the end of 2014, a total of 107 central enterprises had set up 8,515 branches in over 150 countries and regions around the world. From the beginning of the 12th Five-Year Plan (2011–2015), the central enterprises' overseas assets increased from RMB 2.7 trillion to RMB 4.9 trillion (based on the total assets of central enterprises of RMB 48.6 trillion in 2013, it can be calculated that the central enterprises' overseas assets accounted for about 10%), representing an average annual growth of 16.4%; the central enterprises' operating revenue increased from RMB 2.9 trillion to RMB 4.6 trillion, representing an average annual growth of 12.2%; the central enterprises' overseas investment accounted for about 70% of China's total non-financial ODI, and their turnover of overseas contracted projects accounted for about 60% of China's total turnover of overseas contracted projects (Zhang Yi 2015). Although the central enterprises have embarked on the internationalization process through overseas M&A and started to participate in the international division of labor and operations, they are still at the primary stage of "going global" and have not yet participated deeply in the international division of labor. Especially, the global pattern that actively utilizes international industrial transfer and accelerates the global layout of sectors has not really formed. When it comes to the future strategic adjustments in the overseas layout of state-owned capital, we need to pay attention to two aspects: (1) We should actively respond to the BRI and actively expand the layout in regions. Up to now, the overseas regions where Chinese state-owned enterprises have made deployments under the "going global" strategy are Hong Kong, the US, Australia, Singapore and the UK (excluding the Cayman

Islands and the British Virgin Islands). According to the *China Statistical Yearbook 2014*, Hong Kong, the US, Australia, Singapore and the UK accounted for 57%, 3.3%, 2.6%, 2.3% and 1.8% of China's ODI stocks in 2013, respectively. In terms of trade, the total imports and exports of BRI countries accounted for 25% of China's total imports and exports, and China's total imports and exports accounted for 11.5% of the total imports and exports of BRI countries in 2013 (Cheng Jun 2015). As the main force in implementing the BRI, state-owned enterprises have a long way to go. (2) In the process of going global, state-owned enterprises are increasingly restricted by the principle of "competitive neutrality" advocated by the US. As part of its efforts to promote a new trade and investment order with the Trans-Pacific Partnership (TPP) as the core, the US attempted to define the state-owned enterprises as "heavily influenced by the government" and "Government shareholding of 20% or above," and intended to restrict the international behaviors of these enterprises on the grounds of "competitive neutrality," including regulating the government's influence on the behaviors of state-owned enterprises through "domestic measures," ensuring full and timely disclosure of information through a strict reporting and enforcement system, and strengthening the enforcement of the principle of competitive neutrality through a review, questioning and sanction system. Looking ahead, China's state-owned enterprises should take precautions not only by influencing the TPP negotiation process through various means to facilitate the globalization of China's state-owned enterprises, but also by actively pushing forward the mixed-ownership reforms to avoid obstacles to "going global" (Feng Lei and Tang Jing 2015).

### *10.3.6 Despite the Increasing Innovation Resources and Achievements of State-Owned Enterprises, They Are Still Insufficient to Meet the Requirements Under the Strategy of an Innovation-oriented Country*

IN terms of innovation assets distribution, the state-owned enterprises and especially the central enterprises have a large number of high-quality innovation resources and a lot of high-level R&D achievements, but their innovation directions and efficiency are not fully satisfactory to meet the mission requirements under the strategies of "building an innovation-oriented country" and "innovation-driven development." In terms of innovation resources, as of the end of 2011, the central enterprises had 1.25 million sci-tech personnel and R&D personnel, including 226 academicians of the Chinese Academy of Sciences and the Chinese Academy of Engineering. The total R&D expenditure of central enterprises increased rapidly, from less than RMB 100 billion in 2007 to RMB 274.721 billion in 2011, with an average annual growth rate of 29.4%. All the 11 key areas identified as areas for breakthroughs in the *Outline of National Medium and Long-term Science and Technology Development Plan* are covered by the central enterprises. Among the 16 major national science and technology projects, the central enterprises take part in 15 of them. The central enterprises' participation rates are 29.5% in the "863 Project," 23.3% in the Science and Technology Support Program, and even 13.5% in the "973 Project" for basic research, respectively. In terms of innovation output, China's state-owned enterprises have 214,000 patents with independent intellectual property rights, including 137,000 patents owned by central enterprises. From 2005 to 2011, the central enterprises received 467 national science and technology awards, or 24.6% of the total number of national science and technology awards. In particular, the central enterprises received 3 National Science and Technology Progress Special Awards (100% of the total), 44 National Science and Technology Progress First-class Awards (57.9% of the total) and three National Technical Invention First-class Awards (37.5% of the total). Besides, a number of innovation results with independent intellectual property rights and advanced world standards have been achieved by the central enterprises in the fields and major engineering projects related to manned spaceflight, lunar orbiting exploration, extra-high voltage power grid, regional aircraft, 4G standard, 350 km/h high-speed trains, 3,000-m deepwater drilling platform, 12,000-m drilling machine, experimental fast reactor, high-grade cold-rolled oriented silicon steel, and 1-million-ton direct coal liquefaction (Li Zheng 2012). However, one empirical measurement research shows that as of 2009, 58.8% of China's industrial sectors have reached or approached the level of major OECD countries, but 11.8% are still far behind the level of major OECD countries. These sectors can be divided into two categories: (1) new industrial sectors relating to pharmaceuticals and optoelectronic device manufacturing with frequent innovation activities worldwide, including pharmaceutical manufacturing, electrical machinery and equipment manufacturing, communication equipment, computer and other electronic equipment manufacturing, instrumentation and cultural and office machinery manufacturing; (2) industrial sectors that can be easily monopolized, including petroleum processing, coke making and nuclear fuel processing, coal extraction, oil and gas extraction, tobacco production, electricity and heat production and supply, gas production and supply, and water production and supply (Lu Ming et al. 2014). It means that on the one hand, we should increase the distribution of innovation assets in sci-tech and high-tech research and development, boost the technological inputs for the development of key strategic emerging sectors, and strengthen the supporting sci-tech layout in related businesses; and on the other hand, we should deepen the reforms of state-owned enterprises, especially those in monopolistic sectors, stimulate the innovation vitality of state-owned enterprises, so that the innovation efficiency of state-owned enterprises can be improved, the technological gap between China and other countries can be narrowed as soon as possible, and we can contribute to building China into an innovation-oriented country and transforming its economic development mode.

### 10.3.7 The Scale of State-Owned Enterprises Continues to Expand, but the Sector Structure Needs to Be Further Optimized

From the perspective of sector structure, the average scale of state-owned capital per state-owned enterprise has been expanding, but there are problems of insufficient effective competition in naturally monopolistic sectors and low industrial concentration in competitive sectors. Since the establishment of the SASAC, the scale of state-owned enterprises has expanded rapidly. According to the data available in the Ministry of Finance's final financial reports of state-owned enterprises, the average state-owned capital per state-owned enterprise rose from RMB 48 million in 2003 to RMB 210 million in 2014. According to the calculations in the *China Statistical Yearbook 2014*, the total assets per state-owned and state-controlled industrial enterprise rose from RMB 276 million in 2003 to RMB 1.88 billion in 2013, while the total assets per private industrial enterprise rose from RMB 22 million to RMB 90 million in the same period. Both in terms of scale and scale growth rate, state-owned enterprises have far surpassed private enterprises. In 2014, the percentages of state-owned capital in large state-owned enterprises, medium-sized enterprises and small enterprises were 44.5%, 22.5% and 33%, respectively, with state-owned capital mainly concentrated in large enterprises. Despite the increasing scale of state-owned enterprises, the overall concentration of competitive sectors in China is still not high compared to the international level, which affects the efficiency level of enterprises. For example, the US, Japan, and South Korea, three countries that boast the highest level of steel production in the world, have high degrees of concentration in their steel sectors. In 2007, the market share of the top four steel companies in the US, Japan and South Korea was 68.7%, 73.9% and 88.87% respectively, while the market share of the top four steel companies in China was only 35%. For another example, in the coal sector, the current market concentration rate of the top four companies in China is only 20%, and the market concentration rate of the top eight is only 28%, while the relatively reasonable rates should be 40% and 60%, respectively (Li Rongrong 2013). For example, compared with the US, China's manufacturing market structure is still highly fragmented as shown in the data in 2007. Among 480 four-digit manufacturing sectors in China, there are only 60 oligopolistic sectors ($H \geq 1000$), accounting for 12.50%, while among 435 manufacturing sectors in the US, there are 134 oligopolistic sectors, accounting for 30.8%. In contrast, in China's manufacturing market structure, there are 116 extremely fragmented sectors ($H < 100$), accounting for 24.17%, and 106 highly fragmented sectors ($100 \leq H < 200$), accounting for 22.08%, while the shares of these two market structure types in the US are only 7.58% and 6.67%, respectively (Guo Shulong and Li Qihang 2014). In addition, from the perspective of the Fortune 500 companies, there is still a large gap between the market concentration level of the Fortune Global 500 companies in China and that in the US, Europe and Japan. According to the revenue of each country's Fortune Global 500 companies in 2010 as a proportion of the global total output value of relevant sectors, the US and the EU have an obvious global monopoly position in the refinery & petrochemicals, pharmaceuticals, and automobile sectors, with their Fortune Global 500 companies accounting for as much as one-fourth to one-third of the global total output value of relevant sectors, while China exceeded 10% of the global total output value of the refinery & petrochemical sector only in 2010, and there is still a large gap with Europe and the US (Hu Angang et al. 2013). After years of strategic adjustments of the state-owned economy, the state-owned enterprises dominate in the naturally monopolistic sectors such as electric power, telecom, civil aviation, oil & gas, postal services, railroads and municipal public utilities. It can be said that it is generally consistent with the functional positioning of the state-owned economy. However, not all segments of these sectors are naturally monopolistic, as it is generally considered that the transmission and distribution networks of the electric power sector, the road and rail networks of the railroad sector, the oil pipelines of the oil sector, the gas pipelines of the natural gas sector, and the telecom, telephone and broadband networks of the telecom sector are network segments that are naturally monopolistic, while the electricity generation and sales business of the electric power sector, the transportation business of the railroad sector, the exploration and sales business of oil and natural gas sector, and the mobile telephone, internet, television networks and value-added services of the telecom sector are segments that are not naturally monopolistic and allows for competition. Currently, the business scope of state-owned enterprises covers both network and non-network segments of the entire sector, which curbs effective competition to a certain extent and affects the efficiency of social services. As a result, there is a flood of social opposition to the state-owned enterprises in these sectors, and the problem of corruption seems to be concentrated in these sectors. In fact, the reforms of state-owned enterprises in these sectors have become the focus of China's state-owned enterprises and state-owned capital reforms.

## 10.4 Directions and Measures for Strategic Adjustments of the State-Owned Economy Under the "New Normal"

The CPC Central Committee's proposals for formulating the 13th Five-Year Plan (2016–2020) for National Economic and Social Development proposed that: "we should improve the mechanism of reasonable flows of state-owned capital, promote the strategic adjustments of the layout of state-owned capital, lead more state-owned capital to be invested in key sectors and critical areas that are related to national security and the lifeline of the national economy, and firmly make state-owned enterprises stronger, better and larger to better serve the national strategic goals." This means that, following the strategic adjustments of state-owned capital at the end of the Ninth Five-Year Plan period (1996–2000), which focused on the goal of "getting state-owned enterprises out of difficulties," China will implement a new round of strategic adjustments to the layout of state-owned capital in the Thirteenth Five-Year Plan period (2016–2020) for "better serving the national strategic goals."

During the 13th Five-Year Plan period (2016–2020), the strategic adjustments to the layout and structure of the state-owned economy should focus on "quality" rather than "quantity," which means that we should no longer focus on the "quantitative goal" of the specific proportion of the state-owned economy to the national economy,[1] but should pay more attention to the "qualitative goal" of optimizing the layout of the state-owned economy and promoting the state-owned economy to better achieve its functional positioning and mission requirements. Through the strategic adjustments, the state-owned economy under the "new normal" should be more clearly positioned to better serve the national strategies and the people's livelihood, and play a key role in such national strategies as building an innovation-oriented country, BRI and "Made in China 2025." The sector layout should be more reasonable, with state-owned capital mostly concentrated in key fields that are truly related to national security and the lifeblood of the national economy, such as the provision of public services, the development of important forward-looking and strategic sectors, the protection of the ecological environment, the support for scientific and technological progress, and the safeguarding of national security, as well as in dominant enterprises in public welfare sectors, and with further enhanced dominance and influence of state-owned enterprises in these fields. The difference in functional positioning between various types of state-owned enterprises and between central and local state-owned enterprises should be clarified to make the hierarchical layout and structure relationship among enterprises more scientific. The scale and distribution of state-owned enterprises should be rationalized to form a market structure with both economies of scale and competitive efficiency. The shareholding structure of the state-owned economy should be optimized, the mixed-ownership economy should be developed vigorously, the vitality of the state-owned economy should be revealed, and the advantages of the state-owned economy and the private economy should be complemented and integrated.

### *10.4.1 Actively Promote the Strategic Adjustments of the State-Owned Economy Based on the Classified Functional Positioning of State-Owned Enterprises*

The third plenary session of the 18th CPC Central Committee proposed four major tasks for deepening the reforms of the state-owned economy, including promoting the functional positioning and strategic reorganization of the state-owned economy, deepening the mixed-ownership reforms, establishing a new state-owned capital

[1] ①For example, a research paper on the strategic adjustments of the state-owned economy made the specific plans as follows: the state-owned economic activities as a percentage of GDP should be gradually reduced from less than or equal to 40 percent in 2012 to less than or equal to 30 percent in 2020 and less than or equal to 20 percent in 2030 (Chen Dongqi et al., 2015).

management system with a focus on capital management, and improving the modern enterprise system. In our view, these reform tasks are premised on the state-owned enterprise classification reform (Research Group of the Institute of Industrial Economics, Chinese Academy of Social Sciences 2013). In the face of the huge state-owned economy, we should define its functional positioning and mission requirements, and on that basis, classify the state-owned enterprises into three categories: public policy-based, specific functional and general commercial.[2] Currently, most of the state-owned enterprises are a mixture of the above three categories, or do not have a clear definition of their specific positioning. Therefore, after the definition of their functional positioning, we need to classify them through strategic adjustments in the short term and achieve reasonable and effective flows of state-owned capital that meet the requirements of their functional positioning by establishing a management system that focuses on "capital management" and making use of two types of platforms (i.e. state-owned capital investment companies and state-owned capital operation companies) in the long term. The specific classification of these three categories of enterprises and the corresponding directions of strategic adjustments of the state-owned economy can be found in Table 10.1.

### *10.4.2 Scientifically Adjust the Sector Layout of the State-Owned Economy Based on National Strategies and Public Service-Related Criteria*

Based on the consensus that the basic functional positioning of the state-owned economy is to serve the national strategies and the public livelihood, the strategic adjustments to the sector layout and structure of China's state-owned economy under the "new normal" will focus on developing sectors that are strategically important to the country and highly beneficial to the people's livelihood. With the introduction of the national strategies such as BRI and "Made in China 2025" under the "new normal," and the promotion of the modernization process, China's public livelihood services have become more demanding. Therefore, the state-owned capital previously distributed in the heavy chemical industrial sectors that have excess capacities should be adjusted to the high-end and emerging manufacturing sector related to "Made in China 2025," the sectors related to the national strategy "The Belt and Road", and the sectors related to the improvement of the service functions of the central cities. It forms key contents of the future strategic adjustments of China's state-owned economy. Based on the two criteria (i.e. national strategies and public services),

[2] ②According to the *Guidance Opinions of the CPC Central Committee and State Council on Deepening the Reforms of State-owned Enterprises* released on August 24, 2015, the three categories of enterprises (i.e. public policy-based, specific functional and general commercial) can correspond to the public welfare enterprises, commercial class II enterprises and commercial class I enterprises, respectively.

**Table 10.1** Strategic adjustments of the state-owned economy based on functional positioning and enterprise missions

| Category | Functional positioning and enterprise missions | Governance features | Directions of strategic adjustments of the state-owned economy |
|---|---|---|---|
| Public policy-based (public welfare enterprises) | These enterprises serve as a tool of state policy to make up for the shortcomings of the market economy and undertake the missions imposed on them by China's status as a market economy | In terms of ownership structure, these enterprises are generally wholly state-owned enterprises. In the new management system with a focus on "capital management," the representative state-owned equity holder is usually a state-owned capital investment company. The regulatory emphasis is on the achievement of their public welfare goals, rather than on profitability | The short-term adjustment directions include divesting the enterprises' existing profit-making businesses, exiting the profit-making market fields and focusing their business activities on the achievement of public policy goals. The long-term adjustment directions include increasing the state-owned capital or establishing new enterprises of this category according to the needs of national policies, as well as withdrawing the state-owned capital or revoking the corresponding enterprises according to policies |
| General commercial (commercial class I enterprises) | These enterprises, as competitive players in the market economy, actively respond to the fierce competition in the market, realize the preservation and appreciation of state-owned assets through the pursuit of profits in the competition, and undertake the missions of "fostering market players" in a country that has transformed into a market economy | In terms of ownership structure, these enterprises are mixed-ownership enterprises with state-owned equity participation. The representative state-owned equity holder is generally a state-owned capital operation company. Their operations are in full accordance with the requirements of the *Company Law*. The regulatory emphasis is on the achievement of their profitability and the assessment of the state-owned capital preservation and appreciation | The short-term adjustment directions include completely divesting businesses that are naturally monopolistic and investing the withdrawn state-owned capital in enterprises that are more aligned with the goals of public services and national strategies. The long-term adjustment directions include establishing a state-owned capital flexible flow mechanism based on the platform of the state-owned capital operation company, enhancing the vitality and improving the efficiency of enterprises through market-oriented means, and fully relying on market competition to achieve the state-owned capital preservation and appreciation |

(continued)

**Table 10.1** (continued)

| Category | Functional positioning and enterprise missions | Governance features | Directions of strategic adjustments of the state-owned economy |
|---|---|---|---|
| Specific functional (commercial class II enterprises) | These enterprises are related to the national economy and people's livelihood, the infrastructure, the implementation of the national economic development strategies, the guarantee of national economic security and other functions, and undertake the missions of economic catching-up pursued by a catching-up country | In terms of ownership structure, these enterprises are mixed-ownership enterprises controlled by state-owned capital. The representative state-owned equity holder is generally a state-owned capital investment company. Their overall operations are in accordance with the requirements of the *Company Law*, but are governed by separate sector regulations. The regulatory emphasis is on profitability and growth | The short-term adjustment directions include splitting the businesses that are clearly public policy-based and the competitive businesses that are generally non-strategic, and focusing on the businesses in specific functional areas. The long-term adjustment directions include actively exiting those sectors and segments where the competition pattern tends to mature and the strategic importance tends to decline and continuously making efforts to play a greater functional role in various emerging sectors and fields that provide public services, safeguard national security and satisfy national strategic requirements |

*Data source* Prepared by the author

Table 10.2 specifically analyzes the changes in the status of each sector under the "new normal," presents the corresponding changes in the layout of state-owned capital in these fields, and shows the directions of the strategic adjustments to the sector layout of the state-owned economy.

In addition, there are four points worth noting: First, along with the tertiarization trend, the proportion of industrial sectors in the national economy will gradually decline in the future, and the overall adjustment direction of state-owned capital will be a decrease in the proportion, but the strategic significance of industrial sectors to the country will not be lowered, which will mainly be reflected in the construction of an innovation-oriented country. Similarly, we expect that the forward-looking and strategic guiding role played by state-owned capital will also be mainly reflected in innovation. We look forward to seeing the state-owned capital play an innovation-driven role no matter it is invested in the strategic emerging sectors or the ten manufacturing sectors of "Made in China 2025." Although there is debate about the role of state-owned enterprises, the current distribution of innovation resources in China shows that only state-owned enterprises, especially large central enterprises, are truly able to shoulder the responsibilities as core enterprises for building a major independent innovation ecosystem in the national innovation system. The key to the problem is to form a scientific innovation strategy for state-owned enterprises. The state-owned enterprises should focus more innovation resources on the

**Table 10.2** Directions of strategic adjustments to the sector layout of the state-owned economy under the "new normal"

| Sectors | | Changes in the significance of national strategies | Changes in the significance of livelihood services | State-owned capital adjustment directions |
|---|---|---|---|---|
| Farming, forestry, animal husbandry and fishery | | → | → | ↓ |
| Industrial sectors | | → | → | ↓ |
| | Traditional industrial sectors (coal, oil extraction and petrochemicals, metallurgy, building materials, electric power, chemicals, machinery, forests, food, textiles, pharmaceuticals, electronics, tobacco, etc.) mainly dominated by heavy chemical industrial sectors | ↓ | → | ↓ |
| | Strategic emerging sectors (energy saving and environmental protection, new-generation information technology, biology, high-end equipment manufacturing, new energy, new materials and new energy vehicles, etc.) | ↑ | → | ↑ |
| | Ten manufacturing sectors of "Made in China 2025" (new-generation information, high-grade CNC machine tools and robots, marine engineering equipment and high-tech ships, advanced rail transit, energy saving and new energy vehicles, electric power equipment, agricultural equipment, new materials, bio-pharmaceuticals and high-performance medical devices, etc.) | ↑ | → | ↑ |
| | Military-industrial sector | ↑ | → | ↑ |

(continued)

**Table 10.2** (continued)

| Sectors | | Changes in the significance of national strategies | Changes in the significance of livelihood services | State-owned capital adjustment directions |
|---|---|---|---|---|
| | Municipal utility industrial sector | → | ↑ | ↑ |
| Construction | | ↓ | → | ↑ |
| Geological survey and water conservation | | ↑ | → | ↑ |
| Transportation | | → | → | ↓ |
| Warehousing | | → | → | ↓ |
| Post and telecom | | → | → | ↓ |
| Wholesale and retail, catering | | → | → | ↓ |
| Housing | | ↓ | → | ↓ |
| Information technology services | | ↑ | → | ↑ |
| Social services | | → | ↑ | ↑ |
| Health, sports and welfare | | → | ↑ | ↑ |
| Education, culture and broadcasting | | ↑ | ↑ | ↑ |
| Scientific research and technology | | ↑ | ↑ | ↑ |
| Others | | → | → | ↓ |

*Note* "↓" indicates that its significance for national strategies has declined, or its significance for livelihood services has declined, or the state-owned capital can be gradually reduced; " → " indicates that its significance for national strategies has not changed, or its significance for livelihood services has not changed, or the state-owned capital remains basically unchanged; "↑" indicates that its significance for national strategies has increased, or its significance for people's livelihood services has increased, or the state-owned capital can be gradually increased

construction of a major independent innovation ecosystem, lead the innovation directions by integrating innovation resources, form innovation radiation sources, cultivate major common technology platforms with forward-looking features, and seek breakthroughs in major core and cutting-edge technologies as well as pioneering technologies in strategic emerging sectors, so that the state-owned enterprises can effectively play a leading role in the economic restructuring and sector transformation. From the perspective of the national innovation strategy, the state-owned enterprises should play a dominant role in building the following three types of major common technology platforms: (1) strategic common technologies. These common technologies emerged at the pre-competition stage, have wide application fields and prospects, and are likely to be widely applied in one or more sectors, such as those formed from basic research and applied basic research in such fields as information, biology and new materials. (2) Key common technologies. These common technologies are related to the technological development and technological upgrading of a certain sector. (3) Basic common technologies. These common technologies can support technology development or competitive technology development in a certain field, such as those for measurement, testing and certification (Huang Qunhui 2013). Second, the central and local enterprises should put different emphases on the layout of state-owned capital. For the central enterprises, the layout of state-owned capital should focus on realizing the intention of national strategies and building a national public service network; for the local enterprises, the layout of state-owned capital should focus mainly on local urban public services, urban infrastructure construction and other fields. Since the total scale of local state-owned capital is larger than the total scale of central state-owned capital, the future reforms of local state-owned capital are of great strategic significance, and especially, the reforms of local state-owned capital platform companies are important for preventing China's economic risks and promoting China's healthy economic development. Third, the state-owned capital in the sectors and fields that are not highlighted in both national strategies and public livelihood services should, in principle, be adjusted in the direction of gradual contraction. Even for the sectors and fields where the state-owned capital increases, the state-owned capital should also be invested in a mixed-ownership manner. For example, public utility projects should adopt the PPP approach as much as possible and should avoid being exclusively state-funded. Fourth, different from the layout of state-owned capital listed in Table 10.2, the BRI strategy requires adjustments to the regional layout of the state-owned enterprises' overseas business. Given the large number of BRI countries, the state-owned enterprises need to seek technical cooperation, capacity cooperation and resource cooperation according to the differentiated situation in each country, and these cooperation sectors and fields are not limited to those listed in Table 10.2 where state-owned capital is increased. Under the BRI strategy, the major adjustments to the strategic layout of the state-owned economy are the strategic adjustments to the overseas regional layout, and state-owned enterprises are required to shift the focus of their "going global" strategy to BRI countries.

### 10.4.3 Promote M&A and Restructuring of State-Owned Enterprises in a Coordinated Manner Based on the Dual Goals of Comprehensively Deepening Reforms and Optimizing Market Structure

The M&A and restructuring are important means to implement the strategic adjustments of the state-owned economy. Under the BRI national strategy, CRRC Corporation Limited was established at the end of 2014 through the merger of two major railroad equipment manufacturing companies, China North Railway (CNR) and China South Railway (CSR), and State Power Investment Corporation Limited was established in May 2015 through the merger of China Power Investment Corporation and State Nuclear Power Technology Corporation. In the new period after the third plenary session of the 18th CPC Central Committee, the curtain of large-scale M&A and restructuring of central enterprises was lifted. Although these two M&A cases have attracted great attention in the capital market, it is not uncommon to see the M&A and restructuring of central enterprises after the establishment of SASAC in 2003. Through M&A and restructuring, the previous 196 central enterprises have been reduced to the current 111 center enterprises, and there have been reports of a reform goal to reduce the number of central enterprises to 30–50 after the establishment of SASAC, but so far this goal has not been achieved. We believe that this goal conforms to the reality of efficient operations and regulation of central enterprises under the "new normal" in the future, and that China should actively promote M&A and restructuring of central enterprises. However, we also argue that the adjustments to the layout of the state-owned economy through M&A and restructuring of state-owned enterprises need to take into account the need of comprehensively deepening reforms and the need to establish an effective market structure, so China should promote M&A and restructuring of state-owned enterprises in a coordinated manner based on these two needs. From the perspective of the need to comprehensively deepen reform of the state-owned economy in the new period, we should not only solve the problem of natural monopolies in some sectors through restructuring, with the aim of optimizing the relevant business allocation, curbing monopolies and forming a business pattern with prominent main businesses, open networks and effective competition in the naturally monopolistic sectors, but also establish a state-owned economic management system that focuses on "capital management" and set up state-owned capital investment companies and state-owned capital operation companies through M&A and restructuring in accordance with the requirements of the third plenary session of the 18th CPC Central Committee. From the perspective of the need of optimizing market structure, the number of state-owned enterprises in a specific sector should neither be too few nor too many, otherwise it will result in monopolies or excessive competition among state-owned enterprises. The M&A and restructuring of state-owned enterprises should be conducive to forming a market structure with both economies of scale and competitive efficiency, and to the solution of the problem of overcapacity. Based on these considerations, we think that China should promote the M&A and restructuring of state-owned enterprises in the following aspects:

First, we should select the sectors with high market competition, low concentration level and obvious overcapacity problem, including resource sectors, iron and steel, automobile, equipment manufacturing, and overseas project contracting. Through M&A and restructuring of state-owned enterprises in such sectors, it is possible to reduce the number of enterprises, expand their scale, break through the market fragmentation caused by local or sector forces, promote the formation of a national unified market, effectively improve the concentration level of these sectors, optimize the capacity allocation and promote the digestion of excess capacity. It should be emphasized that, due to the obvious overcapacity problem and poor economic efficiency in these sectors, it should be a priority and urgent task to promote the M&A and restructuring of these sectors among the current strategic adjustments of the state-owned economy.

Second, we should divide the naturally monopolistic sectors into network segments that are naturally monopolistic and non-network segments that allow for competition, and carry out overall planning and step-by-step implementation according to the characteristics of the sectors. Through a number of policy measures such as enterprise restructuring, splitting of competitive businesses and increasing controls on sectors, we can promote the construction of a competitive market structure and the building of a fair competition system, so that the state-owned economy in monopolistic sectors can become a more dynamic component of the socialist market economy system and the reform and development results can better benefit other sectors of the national economy and the people. The previous strategic adjustments of the state-owned economy prompted the state-owned enterprises to focus their businesses on naturally monopolistic sectors, while the readjustments under the "new normal" should prompt the state-owned enterprises to focus their businesses on naturally monopolistic segments. Specifically, we should explore the feasibility of peeling off such businesses as telecom infrastructure, long-distance oil and gas pipeline networks, and power grids from enterprises and forming independent network operators. Based on the feasibility, we can consider the following measures: (1) In the oil sector, we should merge China National Offshore Oil Corporation and Sinochem Group into a new national oil company through merger, restructuring and capital injection policies on the one hand, and on the other hand, we should deepen the internal reorganization of China National Petroleum Corporation and China Petroleum and Chemical Corporation, and set up several specialized companies for such fields as oil extraction, pipeline transmission, refining, equipment installation, manufacturing and sales, etc. so that the three companies will have exclusive ownership or controls over the fields of oil extraction and pipeline transmission and private funds will be introduced into the other fields to form mixed-ownership companies. (2) In the power grid sector, we should separate the network segments and non-network segments and merge the network segments of State Grid Corporation of China and China Southern Power Grid Company Limited. After the separation of power transmission and distribution, State Grid Corporation of China and regional power grid companies will operate the transmission networks, and provincial power grid companies will be in charge of power distribution, so that the electricity sales and equipment manufacturing businesses can be liberalized and a mixed-ownership economy can be developed. (3) In the civil aviation transportation sector, we should focus on cultivating several regional air transportation enterprises and solving the problem of high monopoly in feeder airlines, and transforming three enterprises. China National Aviation Fuel Group, China Aviation Supplies Holding Company, and China TravelSky Holding Company should be transformed into joint-stock companies with diversified equity participation by various air transport enterprises. Meanwhile, in the railroad sector, we should also set up several railroad operation companies by region. (4) In the telecom sector, we should set up specialized companies according to the basic telecom businesses (base stations and fixed networks) and value-added service businesses. Specifically, the basic telecom business should be controlled by three major companies, including China Mobile Communications Group Co., Ltd., China Telecommunications Corporation and China United Network Communication Group Co., Ltd., while the value-added service businesses should be liberalized to develop mixed-ownership enterprises.

Third, we should actively promote the construction of a state-owned capital management system that focuses on "capital management." By combining administrative reorganization measures and capital market-based M&A and restructuring, we should transform or establish new state-owned capital investment and operation companies, so that the ownership of state-owned assets scattered in numerous sectors and enterprises will be held by these state-owned capital investment and operation companies. We suggest that the M&A and restructuring of state-owned enterprises in both competitive and monopolistic sectors should be done in combination with the setting up of state-owned capital investment and operation companies. The restructuring of state-owned enterprises in competitive sectors should be promoted through the establishment of state-owned capital operation companies, with the assets of the restructured state-owned enterprises held by the state-owned capital operation companies; the restructuring of state-owned enterprises in monopolistic sectors should be promoted through the transformation of state-owned capital investment companies, with the assets of the restructured state-owned enterprises held by the state-owned capital investment companies. The current restructuring of central enterprises is one-sided, as it is not combined with the requirement of "establishing state-owned capital investment and operation companies" as proposed by the third plenary session of the 18th CPC Central Committee, which means that further restructuring may be required in the future. It should be noted that when setting up state-owned capital investment and operation companies at the local level, we should pay special attention to cutting off the connection between the former local financing platform companies and the governments' financing functions, so that the platform companies can transform into market-oriented entities.

Fourth, we should also consider the restructuring of central enterprises that are not under the regulatory scope of SASAC. Apart from over 100 enterprises regulated by SASAC and over 20 enterprises regulated by the Ministry of Finance and Central Huijin Investment Ltd., there are still nearly 10,000 state-owned enterprises affiliated with nearly 100 central departments, and these enterprises should also be included in the unified state-owned capital regulation in the future and be added as important targets for reforms and restructuring, so that we can establish a new three-tier, three-category and full-covered state-owned capital management system (Huang Qunhui et al. 2015).

## 10.5 Conclusions

The promotion of strategic adjustments of the state-owned economy under the new economic normal is a major and systematic reform project that requires scientific planning, orderly advancement and coordinated support. This chapter provides some suggestions regarding the directions and measures for strategic adjustments of the state-owned economy under the new economic normal. However, it is important to formulate specific strategic adjustment plans as well as corresponding policies and rules and propose specific supporting measures in the process of practical promotion.

In particular, the promotion of strategic adjustments to the state-owned economy may be followed by various risks, including loss of state-owned assets, damage to employees' rights and interests, social conflicts and group incidents, which need to be prevented in advance.

## References

Chen Dongqi, et al. (2015), Research on Directions and Reform Measures for Strategic Adjustments to the Layout of State-owned Economy, Macroeconomics, Issue 1.

Cheng Jun (2015), Constructing Great Lines of Financial Development and Boosting the Economic and Trade Development Along the Belt and Road, World Economic Research, Issue 14.

Chinese Academy of Science and Technology for Development (2015), Report on the Development of China's Strategic Emerging Industries 2015, Science Press, Edition 2015.

Feng Lei and Tang Jing (2015), Vigorous Development of Mixed Ownership in Response to the Principle of Competitive Neutrality, Globalization, Issue 4.

Guo Shulong and Li Qihang (2014), Research on the Dynamic Changes in China's Manufacturing Market Concentration Level and Its Influencing Factors, Economist, Issue 3.

Hu Angang, Wei Xing, and Gao Yuning (2013), Evaluation of the Competitiveness of China's State-owned Enterprises (2003–2011): From the Perspective of the Fortune Global 500, Journal of Tsinghua University (Philosophy and Social Science), Issue 1.

Huang Qunhui (2013), Research on the Functional Positioning of Central Enterprises in the National Independent Innovation System, Journal of Graduate School of Chinese Academy of Social Sciences, Issue 3.

Huang Qunhui (2015a), Progress, Problems and Directions of Local State-owned Enterprises and State-owned Assets Reforms, Academic Journal of Zhongzhou, Issue 5.

Huang Qunhui (2015b), Trends and Risks in China's Economy at the Late- Industrialization Stage, China Economist, Issue 1.

Huang Qunhui and Yu Jing (2013), New Thoughts in the New Era: State-owned Enterprise Classification Reform and Governance, China Industrial Economics, Issue 11.

Huang Qunhui, Yu Jing, and He Jun (2015), Preliminary Exploration on Building a New Management System for the State-Owned Economy, Tianjin Social Sciences, Issue 1.

Li Lei (2015), Scanning of Local State-owned Capital and State-owned Enterprise Reform Programs, Modern SOE Research, Issue 1.

Li Rongrong (2013), The Problem is Not Monopolies, but Low Concentration of Sectors, Market Observer, Issue 6.

Li Yang and Zhang Xiaojing (2015), The "New Normal": The Logic and Prospects of Economic Development, Economic Research Journal, Issue 5.

Li Yang et al. (2013), China's National Balance Sheet 2013, China Social Sciences Press, Edition 2013.

Li Zheng (2012), Report on Independent Innovation of Central State-owned Enterprises 2012, Economic Press China, Edition 2013.

Lu Ming, Liu Jianping, and Cheng Shixiong (2014), Dynamic Measurement of Technological Gaps in Industrial Sectors between China and Major OECD Countries, The Journal of World Economy, Issue 9.

Ma Shuping and Yuan Dongming (2015), Exploration and Insights on Local State-owned Capital Management, China Economic Times, February 13, 2015.

Research Group of the Institute of Industrial Economics (2013), Chinese Academy of Social Sciences, Discussion on the Major Tasks of Comprehensively Deepening the State-owned Economy Reforms in the New Era, China Industrial Economics, Issue 9.

Song Qun (2014), Research on Deepening the Adjustments to the Layout and Structure of Central Enterprises, Globalization, Issue 7.

Xiang Anbo and Shi Ning (2015), Encouraging Local Governments to Explore State-owned Capital Management Models Based on Local Conditions, China Economic Times, March 29, 2015.

Yi Gang (2012), Opportunities, Risks and Policy Supports for Chinese Enterprises to Go Global, China Market, Issue 12.

Zhang Yi (2015), Accelerating the Construction of The Belt and Road and Promoting International Capacity Cooperation, State-Owned Assets Report, Issue 7.

# Chapter 11
# Urban–Rural Integration Pattern and Promotion Strategies

**Wei Houkai**

**Abstract** As China's economy enters the "new normal" characterized by "growth deceleration, optimized structure, diversified engines and improved quality," there will be new trends in the urban–rural integration pattern in the future, including a decrease in the urbanization growth and citizenization willingness, a continuous narrowing of the urban–rural gap, a shift of factors from one-way flows to two-way interactions, and a shift of policies from urban-biased to rural-biased. As a "double-edged sword," the "new normal" will not only bring about good opportunities for the development of urban–rural integration, but will also put the promotion of urban–rural integration under severe challenges, including the increased difficulties in farmers' income increase and citizenization, the urgent need for comprehensive treatment of "rural diseases," the urgent need for balanced allocation of resources between urban and rural areas, and the urgent need for accelerating the integration of the urban–rural dual systems. Under the "new normal," the promotion of urban–rural integration requires a "package" of systematic and integrated solutions, rather than a piecemeal approach. The current priorities are to comprehensively deepen the urban–rural integration supporting reforms, build the unified urban–rural household registration system, land management system, employment management system, social security system, public service system and social governance system, facilitate the free flow and equal exchanges of urban and rural factors and the balanced allocation of public resources, and realize the equality of urban and rural residents' quality of life, so that urban and rural residents will be able to benefit from the equal standard of living and quality of life.

Currently, China's economic development has entered the "new normal." China's urban–rural integration pattern under the "new normal" will have new characteristics and trends, and face new opportunities and challenges. It can be said that China's urban–rural integration has currently entered a new stage of adapting to the "new normal." At this new stage of development, the promotion of urban–rural integration requires new ideas, new mechanisms and new measures. In particular, the key to

W. Houkai (✉)
Rural Development Institute, Chinese Academy of Social Sciences, Beijing, China



X. Zhang (ed.), *Exploration on China's Economic System Reform under New Normal of Development*, https://doi.org/10.1007/978-981-95-2461-7_11

promoting urban–rural integration at the new stage is how to facilitate the free flow, equal exchanges and balanced allocation of urban and rural factors, build a new urban–rural relationship that adapts to the "new normal" and a sustainable long-term mechanism for urban–rural integration, foster a new development pattern in which "urban areas lead and integrates with rural areas under positive interaction and common prosperity," so that both rural and urban residents can benefit from the fruits of modernization and the integration goals of equal rights, equal quality of life, equal benefits, equal ecological construction, equal environmental treatment, and equal prosperity of urban and rural areas can be achieved.

## 11.1 China's Urban–Rural Integration Pattern and Trends Under the "New Normal"

Since the reform and opening-up, we have witnessed China's high economic growth for more than 30 years, and created the "Chinese miracle" (Lin Yifu et al. 1999). China achieved an average annual GDP growth of 9.9% from 1979 to 2011, and an average annual growth of 10.4% from 1991 to 2011, demonstrating a trend of high growth. With the sustained high economic growth, China has seen a significant boost in its comprehensive economic strength, a significant increase in its development level and a significant improvement in the living conditions of its people. In terms of development level, China reached the threshold of an upper-middle-income economy as classified by the World Bank with a per capita GDP of USD 4434 in 2010 and steadily ranked among the upper middle-income economies with a per capita GDP of USD 7595 in 2014.[1] In terms of industrialization stage, China has generally entered the late-industrialization stage (Huang Qunhui 2014) according to the three-stage industrialization division (i.e. early, middle, and late industrialization) proposed by Hollis B. Chenery et al. (1989), so the future emphasis should be put on promoting the transformation and upgrading of various sectors and improving the overall quality of industrialization. In terms of urbanization stage, China's urbanization rate exceeded 50% in 2011 and reached 54.8% in 2014, marking that China has steadily entered the deceleration stage in the mid-stage of rapid urbanization, and the future focus of China's urbanization should be on improving the overall quality of urbanization (Wei Houkai 2011).

Along with the continuous expansion of the economic aggregate and the transformation of the development stage, China's economy entered a "new normal" characterized by "growth deceleration, optimized structure, diversified engines and improved quality" after 2012. The "new normal" is a natural result of the new stage of China's economic development, and it conforms to the general regularity of world economic

[1] ①According to the World Bank's criteria, the dividing line between lower-and-middle-income and upper and middle-income economies was USD 3975 in 2010 and USD 4086 in 2012 in terms of gross national income (GNI) per capita (World Bank 2011, 2013).

development. China's new economic normal is characterized by "a shift from high-speed growth to medium–high growth," "the continuous optimization and upgrading of the economic structure," and "a shift from the factor-driven and investment-driven models to the innovation-driven model" (Xi Jinping 2014). As the primary characteristic of the "new normal," the growth deceleration is mainly a structural slowdown (Li Yang 2015). Under the "new normal," China's average economic growth rate from 2012 to 2014 has dropped to 7.6% from more than 10% in the past. Urban–rural integration is not only the product of economic and social development to a certain stage, but also the fundamental solution to the "three rural issues" (i.e. agriculture, rural areas and farmers). As China's economy enters the "new normal," the promotion of urban–rural integration will be a strategic way to "stabilize growth, adjust structure, transform mode and improve quality." At the same time, China's urban–rural integration pattern will have new trends and characteristics under the "new normal." Specifically, the new pattern is reflected in the following aspects:

### 11.1.1 Decrease in Urbanization Growth and Citizenization Willingness

After the turning point in 2011 when its urbanization rate exceeded 50%, China's urbanization progress has been gradually slowing down and showing a trend of deceleration. The average annual growth of China's urbanization rate was 1.35% in 2001–2005, 1.39% in 2006–2010, but dropped to 1.21% in 2011–2014. In particular, the urbanization speed in the more economically developed eastern regions declined from 1.58% in 2006–2010 to 0.98% in 2011–2014. It is estimated that China's urbanization speed will further decline to 0.8% to 1.0% by 2030. According to the author, China's urbanization speed will be 1.04% in 2011–2020 and 0.81% in 2021–2030 (Wei Houkai 2014a), while according to the United Nations, China's urbanization speed will be 1.18% in 2011–2020 and 0.77% in 2021–2030 (United Nations 2014). Obviously, the "new normal" of China's urbanization in the future will be a decrease in the urbanization speed and an overall improvement in the urbanization quality. It is worth noting that the citizenization willingness of the agricultural transfer population has also begun to decline in recent years following the rapid promotion of urban–rural integration. According to a survey conducted by the relevant statistical departments, the citizenization willingness of agricultural transfer population in many regions excluding Changzhou and Zhengzhou has been as low as 30% to 50% since 2014. For example, among the surveyed migrant workers, only 41.5%, 40.8%, 41.1%, 34.5%, 51.6%, 45.6% and 46.2% in Zhongshan (Guangdong Province), Harbin (Heilongjiang Province), Yantai (Shandong Province), Fuling (Sichuan Province), Ordos (Inner Mongolia), Guang'an (Sichuan Province) and Shaanxi Province, respectively, desired to settle in urban areas (see Table 11.1). In the past, farmers were attracted by urban welfare that was much higher than rural welfare, and strongly desired to migrate to urban areas, but failed to do so as a result of the barriers of urban–rural dual household registration systems, social security systems and other institutions and policies. Nowadays, most parts of the country, except for a few mega-cities, have abolished the distinction between agricultural and non-agricultural accounts and implemented a unified urban–rural household registration system. In particular, most small and medium-sized cities have liberalized their household registration and are actively encouraging farmers to settle in cities, but farmers are reluctant to migrate to cities, with a low willingness for citizenization. This shift is largely due to the central government's explicit granting of more property rights to farmers and the improved level of public services in rural areas. As farmers have more choices, their perceptions are changing.

### 11.1.2 Continuous Narrowing of the Urban–Rural Gap

Along with economic development and urbanization, China will also see an inverted "U" shaped shift from the expansion to the narrowing of the urban–rural income gap (Dong Min and Guo Fei 2011; Yu Xiuyan 2013). For example, the urban–rural income ratio in the US expanded from 1.7 in the early nineteenth century to 3.0 in 1930, and then declined to 1.4 in 1970; the urban–rural income ratio in Japan expanded from 1.19 in 1950 to 1.44 in 1960, and then declined to 0.91 in 1975; and the urban–rural income ratio in South Korea expanded from 0.997 in 1960 to 1.49 in 1970, and then declined to 0.96 in 1980 (Yu Xiuyan 2013). After the reform and opening-up, China witnessed two major expansions in the urban–rural income gap in 1984–1994 and 1998–2003, respectively, but after a period of basic stability, the urban–rural income gap tended to narrow after 2009. From 2009 to 2014, the ratio of urban residents' per capita disposable income to farmers' per capita net income in China declined from 3.33 to 2.92, with an average decrease of 0.08 per year. The extent to which the urban–rural income gap narrowed this time was less than those in two declines in 1979–1983 and 1995–1997, respectively. It mainly resulted from the fact that with the increasing costs of agricultural production and the prices of agricultural products approaching the ceiling, the farmers could only increase their income by relying on the increase of wage income and transfer income, and it would be increasingly difficult to increase their income due to the accelerated urbanization and citizenization. Currently, the level of the urban–rural income gap in China is still high, much higher than the lowest level recorded in 1983 after the reform and opening-up, and well above the level of various developed countries. The income ratio between urban and rural residents was as high as 2.75 in 2014, even on the basis of per capita disposable income. However, it is certain that the entry of China's economy into the "new normal" will make the narrowing of the urban–rural income gap in recent years a long-term stable trend, rather than just a short-term fluctuation as in the previous two cases. In other words, China has entered a period of continuous reduction of the urban–rural gap, and the inflection point of the inverted U-shaped changes in the urban–rural gap has been crossed (Fig. 11.1).

**Table 11.1** Survey on citizenization willingness of migrant workers in different regions of China, 2014

| Survey units | Survey locations | Sample size (persons) | Citizenization willingness (%) |
|---|---|---|---|
| Zhongshan Survey Team, National Bureau of Statistics | Zhongshan City | 82 | 41.5 |
| Changzhou Survey Team, National Bureau of Statistics | Urban areas in Changzhou City | 152 | 82.9 |
| Harbin Survey Team, National Bureau of Statistics | Eight districts and six counties (cities) in Harbin City | 341 | 40.8 |
| Yantai Survey Team, National Bureau of Statistics | Five districts in Yantai City | 90 | 41.1 |
| Zhengzhou Survey Team, National Bureau of Statistics | Zhengzhou City | 120 | 75.0 |
| Fuling Survey Team, National Bureau of Statistics | New urban areas and 26 townships and neighborhoods in Fuling City | 84 | 34.5 |
| Ordos Survey Team, National Bureau of Statistics | One district and three banners in Ordos City | 186 | 51.6 |
| Shaanxi Provincial Bureau of Statistics | Huxian, Yaozhou, Longxian, Linwei, Huayin, Pucheng, Baota, Lueyang, Xixiang, Suide, Luonan and other counties and districts | 1100 | 46.2 |
| Urban–Rural Survey Team, Guang'an Bureau of Statistics | Six districts (cities and counties) in Guang'an City | 500 | 45.6 |

*Data source* Compiled based on the relevant data released by the statistical departments

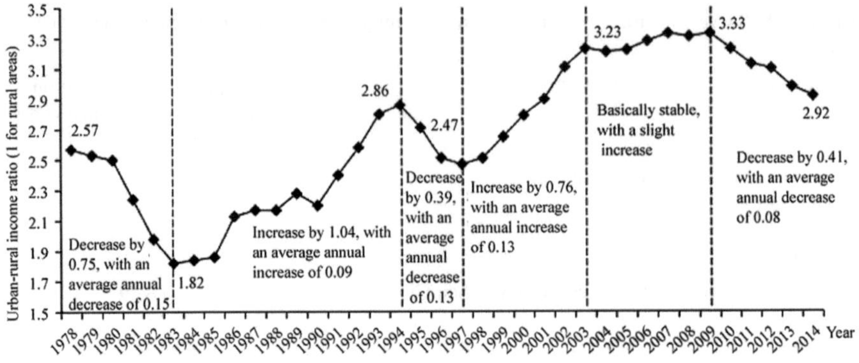


**Fig. 11.1** Changes in China's urban–rural income gap since reform and opening-up. *Data source* Compiled based on *China Statistical Abstract (2015)* and the National Statistical Bulletin 2013–2014

| | |
|---|---|
| 城乡居民收入比(农村为1) | Urban–rural income ratio (1 for rural areas) |
| 下降0.75,年均下降0.15 | Decrease by 0.75, with an average annual decrease of 0.15 |
| 提高1.04,年均提高0.09 | Increase by 1.04, with an average annual increase of 0.09 |
| 下降0.39,年均下降0.13 | Decrease by 0.39, with an average annual decrease of 0.13 |
| 提高0.76,年均提高0.13 | Increase by 0.76, with an average annual increase of 0.13 |
| 基本稳定,略有上升 | Basically stable, with a slight increase |
| 下降0.41,年均下降0.08 | Decrease by 0.41, with an average annual decrease of 0.08 |
| 年份 | Year |

### 11.1.3 A Shift of Factors from One-Way Flows to Two-Way Interactions

The shift of the urban–rural relationship from dual separation to integration is the natural result of economic and social development. Under the pattern of urban–rural integration, the development of both urban and rural areas needs to follow the concept of equality, openness, integration and sharing, so that the free flow, equal exchange and balanced allocation of urban and rural factors can be realized. Under the influence of the traditional dual systems and urban-biased policies, China's urban–rural factor flows have long been unidirectional. Under the influence of the traditional dual systems and urban-biased policies, China's urban–rural factor flows have long been unidirectional. In other words, the factors such as rural population, resources and capital are constantly flowing to cities, while urban population is prohibited from moving to rural areas, urban public resources are rarely extended to rural areas, and urban talents and capital rarely flow to rural areas. In recent years, as urban–rural integration has been promoted in practice across the country, the extension of urban public resources and public services to rural areas has accelerated significantly, and the flows of talents, capital and technology to rural areas have gained significant progress. In particular, developed cities and regions such as Beijing are currently at the early stage of two-way urban–rural integration as the flow of their capital, technology and talents to the rural areas have all reached a certain level (Luo Laijun et al. 2014). From the experience of Beijing and other places, we can see the future direction of urban–rural integration in China. In 2014, China's GDP per capita exceeded USD 7500, and the urbanization rate exceeded 50%. Specifically, Tianjin, Beijing and Shanghai have a per capita GRP of more than USD 15,000 and an urbanization rate of more than 80%; Jiangsu, Zhejiang, Liaoning, Fujian and Guangdong have a per capita GRP of more than USD 10,000 and an urbanization rate of more than 60%. It shows that China, especially the developed coastal areas, has the conditions to promote two-way urban–rural integration, and the two-way flows of urban and rural factors will become the "new normal" for the development of urban–rural integration in China. Under the "new normal," the migration of the population from rural to urban areas will tend to slow down, while the flows of urban capital, technology and talents to rural areas will accelerate. The biggest challenge will be to allow urban residents to migrate to live and live in rural areas according to their own choice under the premise of deepening the reforms of the rural property rights system.

### *11.1.4 A Shift of Policies from Urban-Biased to Rural-Biased*

In terms of industrialization strategy, most countries have undergone a shift from urban-biased policies such as "agriculture supporting industry and rural areas serving urban areas" to rural-biased policies such as "industry nurturing agriculture and urban areas supporting rural areas" as a result of the increase in industrialization level. According to the experience of representative countries or regions, when both the nominal rate of assistance to agriculture (NRA) and the relative rate of assistance to agriculture (RRA) are used, such a policy shift will be achieved at a GDP per capita of USD 1850 and USD 1958, respectively (Li Ming et al. 2014). Most countries have extended their social pension insurance systems from urban areas to rural areas during the transition from the mid-industrialization stage to the mature stage (Yang Cuiying, and Tuo Guozhu 1997). As early as 2004, the central government proposed that China has entered the development stage of "industry subsidizing agriculture and urban areas leading rural areas," and has increased the inputs to agriculture and rural areas year by year. However, in terms of equal opportunity and balanced allocation, China's public policies are still urban-biased, and rural residents still have far less access to opportunities and fewer public resources per capita than urban residents. This bias towards urban areas is both a bias towards big cities and a bias towards administrative centers (Wei Houkai 2014b). As a result, small towns and rural areas that are far away from big cities and high-ranking administrative centers are deprived and squeezed

**Table 11.2** Construction of public utilities, 2013

| | Water supply rate (%) | Gas supply rate (%) | Sewage treatment rate (%) | Domestic waste treatment rate (%) | Public facility investment per capita[c] | |
|---|---|---|---|---|---|---|
| | | | | | Amount (RMB) | Villages = 1 |
| Cities | 97.56 | 94.25 | 89.34 | 95.09 | 3774.4 | 16.1 |
| Counties | 88.14 | 70.91 | 78.47 | — | 2511.1 | 10.7 |
| Administrative town | 81.73 | 46.44 | 18.9[a] | — | 878.0 | 3.8 |
| Townships | 68.24 | 19.50 | 5.1[a] | — | 465.8 | 2.0 |
| Villages | 59.57 | 19.76 | 9.1[a] | 36.6[b] | 233.9 | 1.0 |

*Note a* refers to the proportion of Administrative towns, townships and administrative villages that treat domestic wastewater; *b* refers to the proportion of administrative villages that treat domestic waste; *c* is calculated based on the population in urban areas of cities, the population in counties, the household registration population in built-up areas of administrative towns and townships, as well as the household registration population and the population of temporary residents in villages
*Data source* Compiled based on *China Urban–Rural Construction Statistical Yearbook (2013)*

as they are provided with minimal development opportunities and public facility inputs, and their public services are seriously lagging behind. If the investment in the construction of public utilities per capita in villages in 2013 is regarded as 1, it will be 2.0 times for villages, 3.8 times for administrative towns, 10.7 times for counties, and 16.1 times for cities. This difference in investment has led to a huge difference in the level of municipal utilities between urban and rural residential locations. Currently, China's administrative towns, townships and villages have extremely low levels of gas supply rate, sewage treatment rate and domestic waste treatment rate, and their public utilities and public services are very backward. Under the "new normal," whether urban and rural residents can benefit from equalized basic public services and equal quality of life will be the key to structural optimization and quality improvement. For this balanced allocation of public resources, the government needs to change the long-standing urban-biased approach in terms of investment and policy support, and implement rural-biased policies to direct more public resources to the vast number of towns, villages and rural areas (Table 11.2).

## 11.2 Challenges in Promoting Urban–Rural Integration Under the "New Normal"

The "new normal" means a change in the development stage and is an inevitable stage of China's economic development. The development stage under the "new normal" will be the stage for comprehensively promoting urban–rural integration. Under the "new normal," both structural optimization and quality improvement require governments at all levels to coordinate urban and rural development, devote more opportunities and public resources to agriculture, farmers and rural areas, build a long-term mechanism for fundamentally solving the "three rural issues," and promote the formation of a new urban–rural relationship and integration pattern based on "urban areas leading rural areas and urban–rural integration." The pursuit of an innovation-driven model will boost the flows of talents, capital and technologies to the rural areas, thus enhancing the level of rural public services, strengthening the competitiveness of agriculture and the sustainable development of rural areas, and finally forming a new development pattern where agricultural efficiency is increased, farmers' income is raised, and rural areas are prosperous. However, it should be observed that the "new normal" is a "double-edged sword," which not only provides good opportunities for the development of urban–rural integration, but also will put the promotion of urban–rural integration under severe challenges. These challenges are integrated, complex, and multi-dimensional as they are intertwined with various problems and contradictions accumulated over time.

### *11.2.1 Increased Difficulties of Farmers' Income Increase and Citizenization*

Increasing the income of farmers is the key to narrowing the income gap between urban and rural areas. In China, the per capita net income of rural residents grew at an average annual rate of 10.6% in 2010–2013, and the per capita disposable income of rural residents grew by 9.2% in 2014 over the previous year, both of which were 2.4 percentage points higher than that of urban residents. However, in terms of the composition of farmers' income increase, the rural residents' per capita disposable income in 2014 included 39.6% of wage income, 17.9% of net transfer income and 40.4% of net operating income. As can be seen, farmers' income increase in recent years mainly relies on non-agricultural sectors, and the contribution of agriculture to farmers' income increase is decreasing. Under the "new normal," a larger portion of migrant workers that work in cities and towns will gradually become citizens as part of the urban population. In such a situation, the contribution of wage income and net transfer income to farmers' income will drop significantly, and farmers' income increase will rely more on operating income and property income. In terms of farmers' household operating income, the rising costs of factors such as wages, rents and agricultural materials, as well as the "ceiling" effect of agricultural prices in recent years, have resulted in limited room for price increases and profitability of agricultural products. Under such circumstances, it will be increasingly difficult for farmers to increase their income, while the increased potential is mainly reflected in two aspects: (1) the agricultural productivity and competitiveness can be improved by relying on the development of modern agriculture; (2) the property income of farmers can be continuously increased by accelerating the reforms of rural property rights system and granting more property rights to farmers.

Meanwhile, the difficulty of citizenization and integration of migrant workers into cities will gradually increase under the "new normal." First, the current scale of migrant workers who need to be citizenized is large, and the degree of citizenization is low, costly and difficult. According to the difference between the urbanization rate of the resident population and the urbanization rate of the household registration population, there are now about 234 million agricultural transfer populations residing permanently in cities and towns in China, and their citizenization rate is only about 40% (Wei Houkai and Su Hongjian 2013). It is estimated that the average public costs per capita for citizenization of the agricultural transfer population are about RMB 130,000, of which about RMB 26,000 needs to be invested intensively in the short term (Shan Jingjing 2013). Second, the slowdown of economic growth at the "new normal" development stage will increase the employment pressure and have a significant impact on the employment of migrant workers. Obviously, it will be a long and arduous process to solve the employment problems of migrant workers and to fully integrate them into the cities (Fig. 11.2).

| 增长速度(%) | Growth rate (%) |
|---|---|
| 城镇居民人均可支配收入 | Per capita disposable income of urban residents |
| 农村居民人均纯收入 | Per capita net income of rural residents |
| 年份 | Year |

**Fig. 11.2** Trends of income growth of urban and rural residents in China since the reform and opening-up. *Note* The data for rural residents in 2014 represents the per capita disposable income growth rate. *Data source* Compiled based on *China Statistical Abstract (2015)* and the National Statistical Bulletin 2013–2014

### *11.2.2 Urgent Need for Comprehensive Treatment of "Rural Diseases"*

In recent years, rapid urbanization has resulted in the aging of the rural population, the hollowing out of villages, the degradation of labor quality, the problems of "left-behind children, left-behind women, left-behind elderly" and environmental pollution in rural areas, thus forming the "rural diseases." (1) Aging of rural population. As a large number of young and strong laborers have been working and settling down in cities, some elderly people have been left behind in rural areas, resulting in serious aging of the rural population. In 2013, 17.1% of China's rural population was aged 60 or above, and 11.2% was aged 65 or above, which were 4.3 and 2.8 percentage points higher than those in urban areas. (2) Hollowing out of villages. With the rapid promotion of urbanization, a large number of rural people have migrated to cities and towns, leaving many "hollowed-out" villages. In Sichuan Province, the vacancy rate of rural houses in many places has approached 40% (Yang Suiquan et al. 2015). (3) Degradation of labor quality. With huge numbers of young and middle-aged laborers working and doing business in cities, most of the people left in the rural areas are the elderly, women and children, making the rural labor quality seriously degraded. China's agriculture is becoming "elderly agriculture." (4) Problems of "left-behind children, left-behind women, left-behind elderly." In the current rural areas of China, there are nearly 50 million left-behind elderly people, nearly 50 million left-behind women, and 61,025,500 left-behind children that account for 37.7% of all children in rural areas. The problems of "left-behind elderly, left-behind women and left-behind children" have emerged as prominent social problems in rural areas. For example, left-behind elderly people lack care, living support and spiritual comfort, and have no one to rely on when they become disabled; left-behind children are more vulnerable to discrimination and accidental injury, often feel irritable, lonely and sullen, and have more psychological problems than non-left-behind children. (5) Environmental pollution. The serious backwardness of sanitation facilities, the extremely low rate of domestic waste and sewage treatment, coupled with the excessive use of chemical fertilizers and pesticides and the massive use of agricultural mulch, have resulted in increasingly serious pollution of the rural environment. Therefore, how to strengthen the comprehensive treatment of "rural diseases" and promote the common prosperity of both urban and rural areas has become a serious challenge in the course of promoting urban–rural integration under the "new normal" (Table 11.3).

**Table 11.3** Proportion of the elderly population in urban and rural areas in China, 2013 (Unit:%)

| Elderly population | China | Cities | Towns | Rural areas |
|---|---|---|---|---|
| Aged 60 or above | 14.9 | 12.8 | 13.3 | 17.1 |
| Aged 65 or above | 9.7 | 8.4 | 8.5 | 11.2 |

*Data source* Compiled based on *China Population & Employment Statistics Yearbook 2014*

### 11.2.3 Urgent Need for Balanced Allocation of Resources Between Urban and Rural Areas

Realizing the balanced allocation of public resources between urban and rural areas is a core element of promoting urban–rural integration. With the rapid promotion of new rural construction and urban–rural integration in recent years, the fiscal authorities at all levels have increased investment in rural facilities and public services, and the growth rate of public investment in rural areas has been significantly higher than that in urban areas. However, in terms of per capita resource possession, the current per capita public investment in rural areas is still lower than that in urban areas due to the previous low base, and in some cases, the difference is even large. For example, in terms of medical and health, about 80% of China's medical and health resources are currently concentrated in cities, and in particular, advanced medical and health technologies, equipment and talents are highly concentrated in large hospitals in cities. In contrast, the rural areas have poor medical and health facilities, a lack of medical and technical personnel, and a common phenomenon of aging and low professional level. Since 2007, the rural health expenditure per capita has gained rapid growth and its ratio to the urban health expenditure per capita has increased significantly, but it was still only 39.4% in 2013. In terms of social security, the proportion of the resident population in rural areas is still close to half of the rural population, but the government's investment in rural social security is only one-eighth of that for urban areas, and the per capita share of national social security investment for rural residents is only one-thirtieth of that for urban residents (Liu Chang 2011). In 2010, the per capita transfer payment from rural social assistance was only RMB 452.92, which was only equivalent to 8.9% of that in urban areas, representing a difference of more than 11 times between the two (Zhu Changbai 2012). Therefore, looking ahead, China still has a long way to go to achieve a balanced allocation of public resources between urban and rural areas. Under the "new normal," it is necessary to continue allocating more public resources to the rural areas, and rely on incremental adjustments to promote the relative balance of the stock. The balanced allocation between urban and rural public resources mentioned here is only a relative balance rather than an absolute balance. On the one hand, rapid urbanization will lead to a gradual decrease in the resident population in rural areas, so the construction of rural infrastructure and public services needs to take into account the factor of population migration, and the layout of public service facilities should be adapted to the future urban and rural population distribution pattern; on the other hand, a significant portion of the rural population, although living in rural areas, consumes public services, especially public services in the fields of education, culture and health care, in cities (Fig. 11.3).

| 人均卫生费用(元) | Per capita health expenditure (RMB) |
|---|---|
| 全国 | China |
| 城市 | Urban |

(continued)

(continued)

| | |
|---|---|
| 农村 | Rural |
| 农村/城市 | Rural/Urban |
| 农村/城市(%) | Rural/Urban (%) |
| 年份 | Year |

### 11.2.4 Urgent Need for Accelerating the Integration of the Urban–Rural Dual Systems

The urban–rural dual structure is the main barrier to urban–rural integration. Despite the great efforts made by governments at all levels in recent years to break the dual structure between urban and rural areas, it is still deeply rooted in many areas such as land, public services, social security and social governance. In terms of land management, the urban land is owned by the country and managed on a centralized and unified basis by the country or the cities, while the rural land is collectively owned, with farmers owning the right to use and operate it, and the collective economic organizations or villagers' committees operating and managing it. The dual land management systems in urban and rural areas have led to the division of urban and rural land markets and the separation of land administration, thus seriously affecting the process of urban–rural integration. In particular, rural collective construction land cannot be directly traded in the market, and needs to be expropriated by the government before it can be used for urban construction, so it is easy to cause social conflicts. In terms of social security, the urban and rural residents' social security systems are running on a dual track with large gaps, and it is still a very difficult task to integrate the urban and rural social security systems for inter-regional transfer and connection. For example, as far as the minimum living allowance is concerned, the standard, level and funding of social assistance in rural areas are generally lower than those in urban areas and are not institutionalized due to the different social assistance systems and policies in urban and rural areas. In 2013, the average standard of minimum living allowance in urban areas was still 1.41 times that in rural areas, and the average expenditure level in urban areas was 1.75 times that in rural areas (see Table 11.4). Under the "new normal," the promotion of urban–rural integration requires not only the full integration of urban and rural systems to change the urban–rural dualism and division to urban–rural integration and co-governance; but also solving the problems of inter-regional transfer and connection, increasing the efforts of national coordination, and promoting the process of national equalization of basic public services and social security integration. Obviously, given the large development disparities among regions, the central government needs to increase transfer payments to rural and less-developed regions in order to achieve nationwide urban–rural integration. However, as China's economy changes from high growth rates to medium-to-high growth rates, its fiscal revenue growth rates

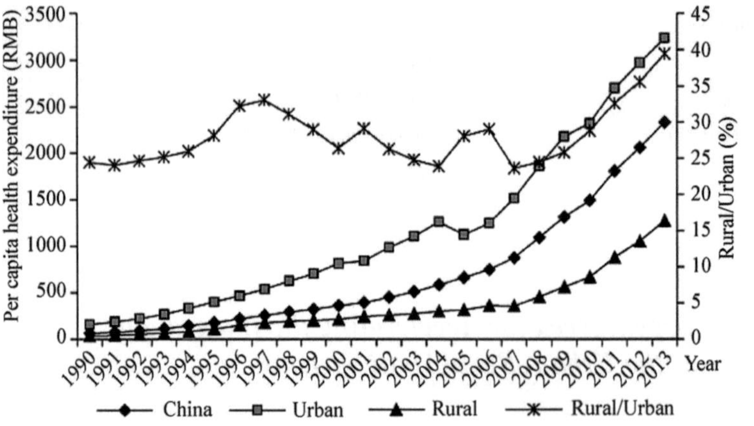


**Fig. 11.3** Comparison of per capita health expenditure in urban and rural areas in China. *Data source* Prepared based on *China Health and Family Planning Statistical Yearbook 2013*

will also gradually decline. Under such circumstances, the central government and less-developed regions will face relatively large fiscal pressure.

**Table 11.4** Average standard of minimum living allowance and average expenditure level in urban and rural areas in China (Unit: RMB/person/month)

| | | Year | | | | | | | |
|---|---|---|---|---|---|---|---|---|---|
| Index | | 2006 | 2007 | 2008 | 2009 | 2010 | 2011 | 2012 | 2013 |
| Average standard of minimum living allowance | Urban | 169.6 | 182.4 | 205.3 | 227.8 | 251.2 | 287.6 | 330.1 | 373.3 |
| | Rural | 70.9 | 70.0 | 82.3 | 100.8 | 117.0 | 143.2 | 172.3 | 264.2 |
| | Urban–rural ratio | 2.39 | 2.61 | 2.49 | 2.26 | 2.15 | 2.01 | 1.92 | 1.41 |
| Average expenditure level of minimum living allowance | Urban | 83.6 | 102.7 | 143.7 | 172.0 | 189.0 | 240.3 | 239.1 | 2433.9 |
| | Rural | 34.5 | 38.8 | 50.4 | 68.0 | 74.0 | 106.1 | 104.0 | 1393.5 |
| | Urban–rural ratio | 2.42 | 2.65 | 2.85 | 2.53 | 2.55 | 2.26 | 2.30 | 1.75 |

*Data source* Compiled based on *China Civil Affairs Statistical Yearbook 2014*

## 11.3 Overall Strategy for Promoting Urban–Rural Integration Under the "New Normal"

The urban–rural integration is a complex issue that involves a wide range of elements. Under the "new normal," the promotion of urban–rural integration requires a "package" of systematic and integrated solutions, rather than a piecemeal approach. The current priorities are to comprehensively deepen the urban–rural comprehensive supporting reforms, establish a unified urban–rural household registration system, land management system, employment management system, social security system, public service system and social governance system, facilitate the free flow and equal exchanges of urban and rural factors and the balanced allocation of public resources, and realize the equality of urban and rural residents' quality of life, so that urban and rural residents will be able to benefit from the equal standard of living and quality of life. It can be said that the establishment of four institutions and two systems that are unified in urban and rural areas is the fundamental guarantee to promote urban–rural integration.

### *11.3.1 Build the Unified Urban–Rural Household Registration System*

The urban–rural dual household registration systems are an important institutional basis for the urban–rural dual structure. In recent years, all regions of China have accelerated the pace of household registration system reforms under the unified deployment of the central government and the State Council, abolished the division between agricultural and non-agricultural households, and relaxed the policy for rural residents to settle in cities and towns to varying degrees. The vast majority of provinces have established a residence permit system and a unified urban–rural household registration system. However, the overall situation is that the current household registration system reforms are still limited to the level of liberalizing household registration, and have not gone deeply into the social welfare system reforms. The supporting system reforms are seriously lagging behind. Under the "new normal," it is vital to further deepen the household registration system reforms, and establish and improve the unified urban–rural household registration system, so as to provide institutional guarantee for eliminating the urban–rural dual structure and promoting urban–rural integration.

#### 11.3.1.1 Define the Ultimate Goals of the Household Registration System Reforms

The promotion of the household registration system reforms not only means breaking the division between urban and rural areas, registering households according to the place of permanent residence, and implementing a unified household registration system for urban and rural areas, but also means stripping away the various benefits embedded in the household registration and restoring the essence of the household registration. The key to the household registration system reforms is the comprehensive and supporting reforms of the various right and benefits embedded in household registration. The household registration system reforms are only the "symptoms," while the reforms of various rights and benefits embedded therein are the "diseases." Both the symptoms and the root causes must be treated, and both long-term and short-term goals must be combined. The goals of the household registration system reforms are not about eliminating the household registration system, but about stripping away the various rights and benefits embedded in the household registration, eliminating the status difference between urban and rural residents, establishing the unified urban–rural household registration system, and achieving equal citizen status and rights.

China has made it clear that "by 2020, we should basically establish a new household registration system that is aligned with the building of a moderately prosperous society, effectively supports social management and public services, protects the rights of citizens according to the law, and is people-oriented, scientific, efficient, standardized and orderly." It points out the direction for the promotion of the household registration system reforms during the 13th Five-Year Plan. However, the existing household registration system reform programs still focus on the adjustments of the household migration policies and the implementation of differentiated settlement policies. From administrative towns, small cities, medium-sized cities, large cities to mega-cities, the settlement policies are more and more strict. Although this new type of household registration system adopts the basic form of registering households according to the place of permanent residence, legal and stable residence and occupation are still regarded as the basic conditions for household migration. Obviously, this practice follows the existing idea of "relaxing the conditions for settlement," so it is not the ultimate goal of the household registration system reforms, but can only be regarded as short- to medium-term transitional goals. From a long-term perspective, the ultimate goals of the household registration system reforms can only be based on the sole criterion of registering households according to the place of permanent residence, so that urban and rural areas can implement a unified household registration system.

#### 11.3.1.2 Promote the Household Registration Reforms in a Steady and Phased Manner

Under the current circumstances, China's household registration system reforms should adopt a dual-track approach. The so-called dual-track approach means that, on the one hand, we should follow the existing idea of "relaxing the conditions for settlement," prioritize the stock and promote the classification, and gradually solve the problem of the settlement of agricultural transfer population that lives in cities and towns and meets the conditions (such as having a legal and stable residence and occupation); on the other hand, we should strip away the various benefits embedded in the existing household registration, and gradually establish the equalized basic public service system as well as the unified social security, employment management, land management system and social governance system in urban and rural areas, so as to achieve full coverage of basic public services for the resident population based on the registration of the resident population. In essence, the former is the adjustments of the household registration policies, while the latter is the true sense of the household registration system reforms. Therefore, the ultimate success of the household registration system reforms depends on the establishment of an equalized basic public service system and an institutional mechanism that integrates urban and rural areas. Once this institutional mechanism that integrates urban and rural areas is formed, the reform idea of "relaxing the conditions for settlement" will lose its significance. In that case, the two reform tracks will finally converge.

Given that the promotion of the household registration system reforms is a long-term arduous task, we must combine long-term and short-term goals, define the goals, tasks and specific measures for each phase, formulate practical implementation plans, and make steady progress in a phased manner. At the national level, China should strive to gradually establish the unified urban–rural household registration system, the urban–rural integrated institutional mechanism and the equalized basic public service system based on the registration of the resident population and realize the integration of urban and rural development by 2025.

For the near term, we should sort out and strip away the various benefits embedded in the existing household registration system, implement the nationwide residence permit system, issue unified residence permits to the urban migrants who reside in cities and towns, and provide the holders with access to basic local public services and some public benefits, such as political rights, labor rights, employment training opportunities, compulsory education and basic social security, so as to effectively protect the basic rights and interests of the agricultural transfer population and basically realize the full coverage of basic public services for the urban resident population. Meanwhile, the agricultural transfer population that meets certain conditions, such as people who have a fixed residence and a stable source of income, or who have been employed or have lived there for a certain number of years, should be allowed to settle down on a priority basis.

For the medium term, we should strengthen the urban–rural comprehensive supporting reforms, completely strip away the various rights and benefits embedded in household registration, and gradually establish the unified urban–rural household registration system, social security system and equalized basic public service system, so as to achieve full coverage of basic public services for the urban and rural residents by 2020. Both urban and rural residents shall be allowed to exercise the basic rights of citizens and receive public services and benefits, including the right to vote, the right to stand for election and the right to public welfare, in accordance with local standards, in their place of permanent residence.

For the long term, we should further deepen the comprehensive supporting reforms, strive to form a unified social security system and equalized basic public service system on a national scale after 10–15 years of efforts, realize the integrated social security and full coverage of basic public services for the resident population a national scale, and ensure the full integration of the agricultural transfer population into the cities in political, economic, social and cultural fields, their equal sharing of the fruits of reforms and development, as well as their equal participation in democratic politics.

### *11.3.2 Establish the Unified Urban–Rural Land Management System*

China has adopted urban–rural dual land management systems for a long time. For accelerating urban–rural integration, we must get rid of the dual management systems, eliminate the fundamental barriers of the land systems, establish a unified urban–rural land management system, and strictly standardize the land management rules.

#### 11.3.2.1 Improve the Unified Land Registration System

The implementation of the unified land ownership registration system and the legal clarification of the holders of land use rights and the purposes of land use are the basis for the establishment of the unified urban–rural land management system. Currently, we should amend the *Land Administration Law of the PRC* and other relevant laws as soon as possible to address the problems of land classification and overlapping management, and establish and improve the unified urban–rural land registration system. First of all, it should be made clear that the land administration department is the only land ownership registration body that confirms, registers and issues certificates for urban and rural land rights in a unified manner. Second, the standards for land registration should be unified. All types of land, including urban state-owned land, rural collective land, arable land, forest land, grassland, and non-agricultural construction land, should be included in the unified land registration system, be recorded in the unified land register and be issued with certificates of rights, so that we can establish the unified urban–rural land registration information system. Third, we should take land as the core and coordinate all types of real estate, such as land, houses, grasslands, forest land and sea areas, which are currently scattered in various sectors, in order to establish a unified real estate registration system.

#### 11.3.2.2 Implement the Unified Urban–Rural Land Administration

In terms of land administration, different approaches and methods are currently adopted for urban and rural land in China, with separate administration for urban and rural areas. Therefore, it is imperative to break the urban–rural separate administration and implement the unified urban–rural land administration. First, we should strengthen the cadastral survey. By combining it with land survey, and based on the principles of "legal ownership, clear boundary, and accurate area," we should put efforts into rural cadastral survey, especially the cadastral survey of rural collective land ownership and construction land use rights, so as to fully map out the details of each parcel of land in urban and rural areas, such as its use type, area, ownership and boundary. Second, we should establish a unified cadastral information center. On the basis of the cadastral survey and by integrating relevant resources from various departments as well as the graphic data and attribute data about urban and rural land, we should establish a cadastral information center that is unified in urban and rural areas, networked across the country, and opened to the whole society for resource sharing. Third, we should establish a unified land statistics system. The land administration department and the statistics department should be responsible for establishing the land classification standards, land statistics calibers and index systems that are unified for both urban and rural areas, and then release the land data in a unified manner, so as to change the current situation of untrue and inaccurate statistics. Fourth, we should implement a unified land administration for both urban and rural areas. We should neither decentralize the authority of land administration, nor take the urban–rural difference, the different ownership and the different attachments on the land as the basis of "separate administration." The urban and rural land administration business shall be under the unified authority of the land administration department according to the law. For state-owned forest, grassland and agricultural land, the land use certificates can only be issued by the competent land administration department on behalf of the State Council, while the types of land use can be different.

#### 11.3.2.3 Establish the Unified Urban–Rural Land Market

First, the urban and rural construction land systems should be unified. By revising the *Land Administration Law of the PRC*, the *Real Right Law of the PRC*, the *Guaranty Law of the PRC*, the *Law of the PRC on the Administration of Urban Real Estate* and other related laws as soon as possible, we should amend the provisions that hinder the equal access to the market for rural collective operating construction land and accelerate the establishment of a unified and standardized construction land system. Article 10 of the *Constitution of the PRC*, which stipulates that "urban land is owned by the state," should also be revised according to the new context. Second, the principles of "equal access to the market, equal rights and equal prices" should be upheld. The rural collective operating construction land should be allowed to enter the market with the same status as the state-owned construction land under the premise of its compliance with the planning and use controls, and have the same rights and functions as the state-owned construction land, so that it can be sold, leased, and pooled as shares in the primary market, and can be leased, transferred, and mortgaged in the secondary market (Jiang Daming 2013). The houses on rural collective land, which are also known as "small property rights houses," are currently unprotected by laws for their construction, sales and purchase because they do not conform to the planning and use controls. For this reason, we should study and formulate the classified policies and measures as soon as possible, and bring forward the specific methods for disposing of these "small property rights houses." Third, the circulation of rural collective operating construction land should be standardized. Based on the experience of Guangdong, Zhejiang and other regions, we should formulate and introduce the Regulations on the Circulation of Rural Collective Operating Construction Land as soon as possible, so that the pre-conditions, transaction methods and procedures, land proceeds, and legal responsibilities for the circulation of rural collective operating construction land can be regulated in a unified manner. The rural collective operating construction land should be traded in a unified transaction platform through bidding, auction and listing. Fourth, the usufruct rights of farmers' homesteads should be effectively protected. As non-operating construction land, homesteads are currently not included in the scope of "equal access to the market." However, on a long-term basis, we should accumulate experience through pilot projects to gradually include farmers' homesteads in the unified urban–rural construction land market. Fifth, a unified urban–rural land trading platform should be established. On the basis of rights confirmation, registration and certificate issuance, farmers' contracted land, collective construction land, homesteads and forest land use rights should be incorporated into the unified land trading platform, and the trading procedures should be standardized, so that the reasonable and orderly circulation of rural collective land can be promoted.

### *11.3.3 Establish the Unified Urban–Rural Employment Management System*

The establishment of a unified urban–rural labor market and employment management system is an important guarantee for promoting urban–rural integration. Thanks to the central government's unified deployment in recent years, various regions have seen remarkable results in urban–rural employment integration, and the employment discrimination suffered by migrant workers has been initially alleviated. However, the urban–rural segmentation of the labor markets has not yet been fundamentally eliminated, and the inequality between urban and rural employment is still prominent. Therefore, we must deepen the reforms of the labor and employment systems, promote the free flow of labor force between urban and rural areas, and completely eliminate all kinds of employment restrictions and discrimination suffered by migrant workers. Based on the goal of promoting the equality and full employment of urban and rural workers, we should establish a unified urban–rural employment and unemployment registration system and a public employment and entrepreneurship service system that is equal in urban and rural areas, so as to promote the establishment of a labor market characterized by equal competition, standardization and order, and urban–rural integration.

#### 11.3.3.1 Eliminate All Barriers to Equal Employment of Urban and Rural Workers

The dual household registration systems and labor markets have separated urban and rural areas for a long time and have resulted in serious urban–rural employment discrimination. The most prominent discrimination is the employment discrimination suffered by migrant workers, which is mainly reflected in two aspects: (1) Unequal employment opportunities. Even today, there are restrictions on the sectors and types of jobs available to migrant workers in some places, and some job postings include a household registration requirement. (2) Unequal pay and benefits. For example, migrant workers have unequal access to labor remuneration, rest and leave, labor protection, and association benefits, are often subject to illegal forced labor, suffer from disparities in their employment subsidies, and are provided with a low level of social security. Compared with the employees of state-owned entities in urban areas, migrant workers have longer working hours, lower wages, no welfare protection and no guarantee of their rights, which are the common problems faced by migrant workers. Therefore, we should further deepen the institutional reforms and completely eliminate all barriers to equal employment of urban and rural workers, especially the various employment restrictions faced by migrant workers. All units should conduct unified recruitment for urban and rural workers, prohibit all forms of employment discrimination against migrant workers, grant and protect equal employment rights and benefits to migrant workers, guarantee equal pay for equal work and equal benefits for migrant workers in accordance with the law, and establish and improve the integrated employment policies and systems that are equal in urban and rural areas, including the policies on employment opportunities, entrepreneurship support, vocational training, labor protection and employment management.

#### 11.3.3.2 Establish the Unified Urban–Rural Employment and Unemployment Registration System

In China, only urban employment and unemployment registration systems have been in place since the early 1980s, without including rural laborers in the scope of employment and unemployment registration. The policies related to employment assistance and employment services introduced by governments at all levels are also mainly targeted at urban workers. This dual urban–rural employment management system, which excludes rural workers who are employment-ready and meet employment requirements but are not employed, is not only a kind of discrimination against rural workers, but also causes the employment and unemployment situation of the whole society not to be truly reflected, which is not conducive to macro-control and social stability. Even today, the relevant departments only release data on the number of new urban jobs and the urban registered unemployment rate. As the rural labor force working in urban areas is not included and not all urban unemployed people are willing to register themselves, the urban registered unemployment rates are often lower than the reality and fail to effectively reflect the overall unemployment status of our society (Yang Yiyong and Gu Yan 2011). Therefore, we should draw on the experience of such regions as Jiangsu, Qingdao, Shandong and Chengdu, Sichuan, promote and establish a unified urban–rural employment and unemployment registration system across the country as soon as possible, include rural laborers in the scope of employment and unemployment registration, issue the unified employment and unemployment registration certificates for them, and regularly publish the unified urban–rural registered unemployment rate. When conditions are ripe, we should replace the registered unemployment rate with the surveyed unemployment rate.

#### 11.3.3.3 Improve the Public Employment and Entrepreneurship Service System that is Equal in Urban and Rural Areas

Currently, we should adhere to the principles of urban–rural integration and equality, put the focus on rural areas, take the construction of public service platforms as a breakthrough, coordinate urban and rural employment and entrepreneurship, and establish a public employment and entrepreneurship service system that is equal in urban and rural areas. First, we should integrate all kinds of labor markets such as labor service markets and talent markets, unify the labor markets that are separated between urban and rural areas and among various industries and sectors, and build a public employment service system that is unified in urban and rural areas, equal, open, standardized and orderly. Second, we should break the boundaries between urban and rural areas, and treat urban and rural workers equally in terms of public employment and entrepreneurship services such as job seeker registration, job referral, employment guidance, employment training, and entrepreneurship support, and apply uniform standards. We should also increase the financial inputs to strengthen the vocational training for the agricultural transfer population and integrate them into the national education and training system. Third, we should include landless farmers as well as the people who are unemployed and have difficulties in finding jobs in the scope of employment support and employment assistance, and achieve full coverage and seamless transfer and connection between urban and rural areas in terms of various employment assistance policies such as social insurance subsidies, unemployment insurance benefits, business start-up subsidies and the identification of those who have difficulties in finding jobs.

### *11.3.4 Establish the Unified Urban–Rural Social Security System*

In recent years, China has generally achieved full coverage of basic pension insurance and basic medical insurance for urban and rural residents, and has basically built the framework of basic social security system with an emphasis on pension insurance, medical insurance and minimum living allowances (Hu Xiaoyi 2012), but many problems still exist, such as low-level coordination, unbalanced development in urban and rural areas, imperfect transfer and connection mechanism and low-level insurance protection in rural areas, resulting in that the long-established urban–rural separation in terms of social security has not been fundamentally changed. At present, we should adhere to the guidelines of "broad coverage, basic protection, multiple levels, and sustainability," focus on enhancing equality and adjusting to mobility, put efforts into improving mechanisms, expanding coverage, raising the level of protection and the level of coordination, gradually establish a basic social security system with "nationwide coverage, inclusive sharing, urban–rural integration, and equal services," and eventually realize the goal of basic social security for all.

#### 11.3.4.1 Establish the Unified Urban–Rural Basic Medical Insurance System

Currently, China has seen full coverage of the social medical insurance systems, but this does not mean that all urban and rural residents have signed in medical insurance. The current systems are dual between urban and rural areas, separated by groups, and "fragmented." The three basic medical insurance systems are quite different in terms of population insured, management bodies, financing methods, protection levels, operation modes and reimbursement rates, and there is no connection between urban and rural areas. The basic medical insurance for urban employees and the basic medical insurance for urban residents are managed by the human resources and social security departments, while the new rural cooperative medical insurance is managed by the health and family planning departments. This "fragmentation" not only brings inequality between urban and rural residents and among different groups, but also results in duplication of insurance coverage, duplication of fiscal inputs, and mutual constraints in management. Therefore, we must strengthen the integration of resources, coordinate urban and rural medical insurance, and establish a basic medical insurance system that is unified in urban and rural areas, so that urban and rural residents can enjoy equal basic medical insurance services. General speaking, we can take three steps: First, we should gradually abolish publicly funded medical insurance for employees of government agencies and institutions at all levels, include employees of government agencies and institutions and migrant workers in the unified basic medical insurance for employees, and establish a unified basic medical insurance system for urban workers. Second, we should integrate the basic medical insurance system for urban residents and the new rural cooperative medical insurance system to establish a unified basic medical insurance system for urban and rural residents. Third, we should integrate the basic medical insurance system for urban and rural residents and the basic medical insurance system for urban employees, and establish a unified basic medical insurance system for urban and rural residents, so as to achieve institutional equality and the sharing of public resources between urban and rural residents.

#### 11.3.4.2 Establish the Unified Urban–Rural Basic Pension Insurance System

Currently, China's basic pension insurance systems suffer from urban–rural separation, huge differences in insurance benefits for different groups, large differences in the levels of coordination of various insurance, heavy fiscal burden on the government, and increased risk of being unsustainable. In particular, there is a huge gap between urban and rural pension insurance systems in terms of participation methods, funding and contribution modes, funding sources, coordination levels, payment levels, and eligibility conditions (Shao Wenjuan and Liu Xiaomei 2013). From the perspective of equality, the integration of various pension insurance programs and the establishment of a unified basic pension insurance system for urban and rural residents will be the general direction of future reforms. In 2013, China integrated the new rural social pension insurance and urban residents' social pension insurance and made it clear that an equal, unified and standardized basic pension insurance system for urban and rural residents would be fully established by 2020. In the basic pension insurance for urban and rural residents after the integration, the funds are raised in the form of "individual contributions, collective assistance, government subsidies." The central government gives full subsidies to the central and western regions and 50% subsidies to the eastern regions according to the basic pension standards. From a long-term perspective, we must also break the occupational boundaries, change the dual pension system, speed up the reforms of the basic pension insurance system for government agencies and institutions, and build a basic pension insurance system consisting of three insurance systems for government agencies and institutions, urban workers and urban and rural residents. On that basis, we should also properly integrate the three insurance systems, and eventually establish a basic pension insurance system that is nationally coordinated and unified in urban and rural areas, so that all people can equally enjoy basic pension protection.

#### 11.3.4.3 Improve the Unified Urban–Rural Social Assistance System

For the purpose of accelerating the equalization of basic social security services, we must break the boundaries and institutional barriers between urban and rural areas in accordance with the requirements of equalization, and establish and improve the unified urban–rural social assistance system as soon as possible. First, the urban and rural social assistance policies should be unified. Except for some assistance programs that are unique to urban and rural areas, such as "rural five-guarantee support" (i.e. the system for providing food, clothing, medical care, housing and burial expenses for childless and infirm rural residents) and urban vagrants and beggars assistance, we should adopt a unified system framework for urban and rural areas, implement unified standards and policies, establish a social assistance system that covers basic living, medical, education, housing, employment, legal and other assistance, and provide equalized social assistance services for urban and rural people in need. In particular, we should accelerate the establishment of a unified urban–rural minimum living allowance system and medical assistance system. Second, the targets of urban and rural social assistance should be unified. We should determine the targets of urban and rural social assistance in a unified manner in accordance with the unified standards and take into account the special characteristics of urban and rural areas. We should further improve the temporary assistance system to include non-household residents, migrant workers and other flowing populations into the scope of social assistance in a unified manner. Third, the support for rural areas should be increased. The central government and local governments at all levels should increase the fiscal inputs for rural social assistance, further promote the implementation and improvement of medical assistance, education assistance, employment assistance, housing assistance and legal assistance in rural areas, continuously upgrade the standards and levels of social assistance in rural areas, and promote the balanced allocation of social assistance resources in urban and rural areas.

### 11.3.5 Establish the Unified Urban–Rural Public Service System

The integration of urban and rural public services is an inherent requirement for balancing urban and rural development, and an important guarantee for promoting urban–rural coordinated development. At the current stage, the key to promoting the integration of urban and rural public services is to accelerate the construction of rural public service systems, promote the extension of urban public services to rural areas, realize the equalization of basic public services in urban and rural areas, and gradually narrow the gap between urban and rural public service levels. Currently, we must promote the equalization of basic public services in urban and rural areas by taking the balanced allocation of urban and rural public service resources as the direction, and gradually developing an urban–rural integrated, sustainable and equal public service system.

#### 11.3.5.1 Accelerate the Extension of Urban Infrastructure to Rural Areas

When accelerating urban–rural infrastructure integration, we should focus on solving the challenges in rural areas. Promoting the extension of urban infrastructure to rural areas and establishing and improving the long-term mechanism for rural infrastructure construction and investment are the key links in boosting urban–rural infrastructure integration. In the process of coordinating urban and rural development, we must organically combine the new urbanization with the construction of new rural areas, follow the idea of networking and connection between urban and rural infrastructures as well as co-construction and co-sharing, accelerate the extension and coverage of urban transportation, information, power supply, water supply and drainage, gas supply, heat supply, sanitation, fire protection and other infrastructure in rural areas, strengthen the seamless connection of roads and municipal public infrastructure among cities, towns and villages, and gradually form an integrated urban and rural infrastructure network.

In terms of transport, we should follow the idea of "integrated roads, stations and transport lines," vigorously strengthen the construction of rural roads and passenger transport stations, improve the three-level passenger transport network that connects central urban areas to counties, counties to townships, and townships to administrative villages in a phased and batch manner, adopt unified stations, unified scheduling, unified fares, unified vehicle identification, and unified settlement, and build a road network that connects rural areas and villages with trunk lines, as well as a perfect and convenient passenger transport network that integrates urban and rural areas. Meanwhile, we should continuously increase the coverage of urban public transport, optimize the layout of lines and stations, gradually extend public transport to the suburbs and surrounding towns and villages, and promote urban–rural public transport integration.

In terms of information, we should put the focus on promoting the integration of postal, communication and information service facilities in urban and rural areas. We should adjust and optimize the layout of postal outlets in rural areas, promote the full coverage of universal postal services in townships, steadily push forward the construction of "village postal stations" with unified standards, unified logos and unified facilities, accelerate the urban–rural postal integration, and build a public system of universal postal services that covers urban and rural areas, benefits all people, reaches moderate levels and achieves sustainable development. We should incorporate telecommunication infrastructure into urban and rural construction planning, accelerate the construction of telecommunication pipelines, networks, base stations and other facilities, extend fiber optic communication and wireless communication networks to rural areas, achieve seamless and full coverage of both urban and rural areas, and improve the quality and level of communication. We should accelerate the construction of information service facilities in rural areas, improve township and village websites and information service centers, extend various urban information resources and information services to rural areas, and build an urban–rural integrated information service system.

In terms of public utilities, we should focus on promoting the integration of power supply, water supply, gas supply, heat supply and sanitation in urban and rural areas. In terms of power supply, we should coordinate the planning of urban and rural power grids, speed up the transformation and upgrading of rural power grids, actively promote the standardization of rural power grids, continuously improve the power supply capacity and power supply quality of rural power grids, and realize the power supply integration and undifferentiated services in urban and rural areas. In terms of water supply, we should follow the idea of "unified allocation, unified supply, unified calculation, unified pricing, and coordinated profits/losses," rely on the central cities and counties, accelerate the construction of water supply pipelines and networks in townships, realize the connectivity of networks, supply, operations and management between urban and rural areas, and promote the formation of an urban–rural integrated water supply pattern based on the same sources, the same networks, the same quality and the same prices. In the areas where conditions permit, we should also actively promote the integration of gas and heat supply in urban and rural areas. In addition, we should also extend urban sanitation, firefighting and other infrastructure and public services to rural areas in accordance with the concept of integration.

#### 11.3.5.2 Build an Urban–Rural Integrated Public Service System

The equalization of basic public services in urban and rural areas is the core of building an urban–rural integrated public service system. The equalization of basic public services means that all citizens have equitable and available access to basic public services that are roughly equal, while the core is the equalization of opportunities. The equalization mentioned here consists of three main aspects: equalization between urban and rural areas; equalization among regions, and equalization among residents. Among them, the equalization of basic public services between urban and rural areas is the most important component. Currently, China has set the goal of "achieving overall equalization of basic public services by 2020." According to international experience, the equalization of basic public services between urban and rural areas is a long-term process (Fan Liming and Guo Jian 2012). Based on China's actual realities, we can broadly follow three steps to achieve the goal of high-level and sustainable equalization of basic public services: as a first step, we should basically achieve the equalization of basic public services in urban areas by 2015, and cover the agricultural transfer population residing in urban areas; as a second step, we should basically achieve the equalization of basic public services in urban and rural areas by 2020, and cover the entire rural population; as the third step, we should achieve high-level and sustainable equalization of basic public services across the country by 2030.

The specific measures for building an urban–rural integrated public service system with the equalization of basic public services in urban and rural areas as the core are as follows: (1) The governments should increase their inputs. Governments at all levels should not only increase the fiscal inputs to public services, but also direct public financial resources to the rural areas. The role of the fiscal funds in direction and leverage should be given full play, and private capital should be actively encouraged to participate in the construction of public services in urban and rural areas. (2) The past practice of GDP-based assessment should be changed, and the construction of public service system should be fully incorporated into the government assessment index system as soon as possible. We should set up a comprehensive assessment index system to strengthen the monitoring and evaluation of the level and process of basic public services in each region, and propose improvement measures based on the evaluation results. (3) Urban public services should be extended to rural areas, and the connection and integration of public services between urban and rural areas should be promoted. In particular, we should accelerate the extension and coverage of urban public services related to culture, sports, education, health care and sanitation in rural areas, and boost the full integration of social security policies and systems between urban and rural areas. (4) The public service resources in urban and rural areas should be integrated. In light of the trend of the urban and rural population, we should effectively integrate urban and rural resources, adjust and optimize the layout of facilities, combine scattered single services into centralized integrated services, scale up the supply of public services, and improve the supply efficiency and level of urban and rural public services.

### *11.3.6 Establish a Unified Urban–Rural Social Governance System*

There has long been an urban–rural dual governance system in China. The urban–rural dual governance refers to the implementation of dual governance measures in terms of population registration and management, planning and construction, public services, social security, fiscal system, and administrative governance according to the demographic or geographical criteria in urban and rural areas. This urban–rural dual governance is not only an important cause of the current "three rural issues" in China, but also a key obstacle to China's sustainable and healthy economic and social development and urban–rural integration. For promoting urban–rural development integration, we must break this dual governance system, remove all kinds of institutional obstacles, set up a unified urban–rural administrative governance system, change from urban–rural dual governance to urban–rural co-governance, and boost the formation of a new governance pattern that is equitable and fair, standardized and orderly, efficient and convenient, and urban–rural integrated.

#### 11.3.6.1 Change from Urban–Rural Dual Governance to Urban–Rural Co-Governance

In recent years, many regions have set up urban–rural coordinated development offices, in an effort to effectively boost urban–rural coordination and harmonize the relations among various departments. However, urban–rural coordinated development involves many aspects and cannot be achieved by a single department. For long-term development, we should put the concept of urban–rural coordination into all areas and the whole process of economic and social development, incorporate the function of urban–rural coordination into the regular functions of the departments at all levels, form a long-term mechanism that governs both urban and rural areas, realize the full-area planning, service and governance that covers both urban and rural areas, and promote the change from urban–rural dual governance to urban–rural co-governance. We should change the traditional concept of "valuing urban areas and neglecting rural areas," break the institutional obstacles of "urban–rural dual governance" and "separate governance in towns and villages," and extend the management functions of the departments at all levels to rural areas in accordance with the idea of "whole-area planning, whole-area management and urban–rural co-governance." In particular, we should extend the economic and social management and public service functions related to planning, land, transport, communication, scientific education, culture, sanitation, epidemic prevention, urban management, water utilities, security and fire fighting from urban to rural areas, implement the unified planning, construction, protection and management, formulate the unified policies that cover both urban and rural areas, and boost the formation of an urban–rural integrated administrative governance system with consistent powers and responsibilities, reasonable division of duties, scientific decision-making, smooth implementation and strong supervision. In the process of promoting the urban–rural development integration, all new policies to be introduced in the future, except those directly related to land contracting, collective economy, agricultural production and urban construction, should eliminate the distinction between urban and rural areas and should be based on unified standards, unified policies, unified management and unified services.

#### 11.3.6.2 Establish an Urban–Rural Integrated Community Governance System

As primary self-governance organizations, urban and rural communities have played a fundamental role in the social governance system. Under the long-term influence of urban-biased policies, China has seen remarkable results in the construction of urban communities, while the construction of rural communities has seriously lagged behind. Currently, rural communities are generally suffering from insufficient funding and inputs, outdated public facilities, lack of professional staff, and poor management system. In the process of promoting the urban–rural development integration, we must abandon the traditional idea of "valuing urban and neglecting rural areas," adjust the urban-biased community policies, focus on the integration of community development in urban and rural areas, establish an urban–rural integrated community governance system, and accelerate the integration of urban and rural community management and services. At this stage, we should focus on strengthening the construction of new rural communities and promoting rural community management. In the process of promoting the construction of rural communities, we should respect the will of farmers and should not forcibly demolish rural houses for the sake of community construction. For areas where conditions are favorable, we should follow the principle of "geographical proximity, moderate scale, and facilitating the integration of public resources," actively and steadily promote the demolition of villages and construction of residential buildings in accordance with local conditions, and establish new rural communities on a classified and batch basis, and gradually push forward the shift from a street, town and village-based system into a community system. We should learn from the management modes and service concepts in urban communities, strengthen the planning and construction of rural communities, increase the investment in public services and facilities, set up and improve community service centers and one-stop service halls, continuously enhance community service functions, gradually extend community services to natural villages, and effectively boost the comprehensive service capacity and level of rural communities. We should fully implement the matrix management of urban and rural community services, promote the decentralization of social management powers to rural areas, the allocation of funds to rural areas, transfer of personnel to rural areas, and the provision of services to rural areas, and realize the sophisticated management with "dedicated personnel in specific positions and in charge of concrete duties at defined times."

## References


Chenery, Robinson and Syrquin (1989), Industrialization and Growth: A Comparative Study, Shanghai Sanlian Bookstore, 1989 Edition.

Dong Min and Guo Fei (2011), The Inverted U-shaped Trend of Urban-Rural Income Gap in the Urbanization Process and the Countermeasures, Contemporary Economic Research, Issue 8.

Fan Liming and Guo Jian (2012), International Comparison on Equalization of Basic Public Services in Urban and Rural Areas: Process and Experience, Journal of Central University of Finance & Economics, Issue 7.

Hu Xiaoyi (2012), Accelerating the Urban-Rural Coordination in Social Security, Social Security Studies, Issue 1.

Huang Qunhui (2014), The "New Normal," Late Industrialization and New Dynamics of Industrial Growth, China Industrial Economics, Issue 10.

Jiang Daming (2013), Establishing a Unified Construction Land Market for Urban and Rural Areas, People's Daily, December 19, 2013.

Li Ming, Shao Ting, and Liu Shouying (2014), The International Experience of Urban-Rural Integration and Its Implications for China, Chinese Rural Economy, Issue 6.

Li Yang (2015), China's "New Normal" of Economy is Different from the World's "New Normal" of Economy, People's Daily, March 12, 2015, p. 7.

Lin Yifu, Cai Fang, and Li Zhou (1999), China's Miracle: Development Strategies and Economic Reforms, Shanghai People's Publishing House, 1999 Edition.

Liu Chang (2011), Social Security System with Urban-Rural Integration in the Perspective of Income Distribution, Macroeconomic Management, Issue 2.
Luo Laijun, Luo Yuzhe, and Luo Tao (2014), Confirmatory Study on Two-way Urban-Rural Integration in China—Based on Survey Data from Huairou District, Beijing, Management World, Issue 11.
Shan Jingjing (2013), The Costs of Citizenization of Migrant Workers and Their Sharing Mechanisms, published in China Urban Development Report No. 6—Citizenization of Agricultural Transferred Population edited by Pan Jiahua and Wei Houkai, Social Sciences Academic Press (China), 2013 Edition.
Shao Wenjuan and Liu Xiaomei (2013), Research on the Integration of the Social Pension Insurance Systems for Urban and Rural Residents in China, Journal of Changchun University, Issue 11.
United Nations (2014), World Urbanization Prospects: The 2014 Revision, New York.
Wei Houkai (2011), Ideas for Strategic Adjustments in China's Urbanization, China Economic & Trade Herald, Issue 7.
Wei Houkai (2014), A New Road to Urbanization with Chinese Characteristics, Social Sciences Academic Press (China), 2014 Edition.
Wei Houkai (2014), Administrative Hierarchy and Scale Growth in Cities of China, Urban and Environmental Studies, Issue 1.
Wei Houkai and Su Hongjian (2013), Research on the Citizenization Process of China's Agricultural Transfer Population, Chinese Journal of Population Science, Issue 5.
World Bank (2011), World Development Report 2012: Gender Equality and Development. Washington, DC: World Bank.
World Bank (2013), World Development Report 2014: Risk and Opportunity-Managing Risk for Development. Washington, DC: World Bank.
Xi Jinping (2014), Seek Sustained Development and Fulfill the Asia-Pacific Dream, People's Daily, November 10, 2014, p. 2.
Yang Cuiying and Tuo Guozhu (1997), The Empirical Analysis of Economic and Social Conditions for Establishing a Social Pension Annuity Insurance Scheme for Farmers, China Rural Survey, Issue 5.
Yang Suiquan, Zhang Menglin, and Qian Li (2015), The Solution for Unused Rural Houses in the Context of Urban-Rural Integration, Rural Economy, Issue 1.
Yang Yiyong and Gu Yan (2011), Suggestions for Adopting the Surveyed Urban Unemployment Rate as a Binding Indicator in the Outline of the 12th Five-Year Plan, China Development Observation, Issue 3.
Yu Xiuyan (2013), The Relationship between Urbanization and Urban-Rural Income Gap: The Inverted-U Law and Its Applicability to China, Social Scientist, Issue 10.
Zhu Changbai (2012), The Integration of Urban-Rural Dual Characteristics of Inclusive Growth and Social Assistance—From the Perspective of Equal Opportunities, Seeking, Issue 12.

# Chapter 12
# Challenges and Measures for Deepening Service Sector Reforms

**Xia Jiechang**

**Abstract** Systems and mechanisms are among the most important factors affecting the development of the service sector. In China, the reforms of systems and mechanisms in the service sector have long lagged behind those in the agricultural and industrial sectors. The inflexibility of service sector systems and mechanisms directly hinders the rapid, healthy and orderly development of China's service sector. By comprehensively deepening the reforms of the service sector systems and mechanisms, it will be of great significance to promoting the great development of the service sector, providing a strong endogenous impetus for the sustainable development of the service sector, and forming a "new normal" led by the service economy. The reforms of the service sector systems are considered as a systematic project that requires breakthroughs in key areas and overall advancement, and will create supporting conditions for deepening service sector reforms.

## 12.1 Accelerate the Formation of an Economic Structure Led by the Service Sector Under the "New Normal"

At present, China is seeing a shift in economic growth rates, structural adjustments and the entry of reform and opening-up into a tough phase. At this particular stage, we will say goodbye to the high growth rates of at least 10% that we are used to in the past, and will also take a fresh look at the growth rates, economic structure and growth engines. In this context, General Secretary Xi Jinping put forward the concept of the "new normal," and stressed that we should accelerate the development of the service sector and cultivate it as a key pillar of the modern sector system. The "new normal" represents the scientific judgment and understanding of China's current stage of development, and also stands for new trends in macro-economic controls. Accelerating the formation of a service sector-led economic structure and cultivating the service sector as China's pillar sector are the major strategic measures currently adopted by China to actively adapt to the "new normal."

X. Jiechang (✉)
National Academy of Economic Strategy, Chinese Academy of Social Sciences, Beijing, China

 
X. Zhang (ed.), *Exploration on China's Economic System Reform under New Normal of Development*, https://doi.org/10.1007/978-981-95-2461-7_12

### *12.1.1 Service Sector Under the "New Normal" of China's Economy*

According to the industrialization experience of developed countries, a country will see a booming period of the service sector after its economic structure crosses the intersection of secondary and tertiary sectors. This trend is becoming increasingly evident in China after it crossed the intersection of the secondary and tertiary sectors in 2013. The service sector is becoming the backbone of China's national economy.

#### 12.1.1.1 Service Sector Becomes a New Economic Growth Engine Under the "New Normal"

According to the data in the *Statistical Communiqué of the People's Republic of China on the 2014 National Economic and Social Development*, the growth rate of the added value of China's tertiary sector was 8.1% in 2014, higher than that of the secondary sector (7.3%) and that of the primary sector (4.1%), making the tertiary sector the only one among the three sectors 0.7 percentage points higher than the GDP growth rate of 7.4%. In terms of the contribution rates of the three sectors, the contribution rate of the tertiary sector was 52.81% in 2014, higher than that of the secondary sector (42.11%) and that of the primary sector (5.08%). The tertiary sector contributed 3.9 percentage points to GDP, higher than the 3.1 percentage points of the secondary sector and the 0.4 percentage points of the primary sector. China is accelerating its shift from an industry-led economy to a service-led economy.

#### 12.1.1.2 The Proportion of the Added Value of the Service Sector Increases Rapidly

According to the preliminary calculations of the National Bureau of Statistics of China, the value added of the service sector in 2014 was RMB 30.7 trillion, representing a year-on-year increase of 8.1%. Based on the calculation at current prices, the added value of the service sector took 48.2% of GDP, 1.3 percentage points higher than that in 2013, and 5.6 percentage points higher than that of the secondary sector. This marked China's completion of the expected target of 47% set in the 12th Five-Year Plan (2011–2015) ahead of schedule. In the first quarter of 2015, the proportion of the added value of the service sector hit a record of 51%, making the service sector "half of the national economy."

#### 12.1.1.3 The Investment in Service Sector Fixed Assets is Expanding Rapidly

In 2014, the investment in fixed assets (excluding agricultural households) reached RMB 50.2005 trillion, with a nominal increase of 15.7% from that in 2013 (with a real increase of 15.1% after deducting price factors). Specifically by sector, the investment in primary sector fixed assets was RMB 1.1983 trillion, up 33.9% from that in 2013; the investment in secondary sector fixed assets was RMB 20.8107 trillion, up 13.2%; the investment in tertiary sector fixed assets was RMB 28.1915 trillion, up 16.8%. Among the three sectors, the service sector witnessed the fastest growth in fixed asset investment, reflecting investors' preference for the service sector.

#### 12.1.1.4 Foreign Capital Brings China into a True "Service Economy Era"

In 2014, the foreign capital actually used in the manufacturing sector was RMB 245.25 billion (USD 39.94 billion), representing a year-on-year decrease of 12.3% and accounting for 33.4% of the total foreign capital in the country; the foreign capital actually used in the service sector was RMB 406.81 billion (USD 64.52 billion), representing a year-on-year increase of 12.5% and accounting for 53.9% of the total foreign capital in the country. There were 23,778 non-financial foreign-invested enterprises established in China, with an increase of 4.4% compared to 2013. Specifically, 13,925 non-financial foreign-invested enterprises in the service sector were established, representing a growth rate of 11.12% and accounting for 58.56% of all non-financial foreign-invested enterprises that were established. It means that China's manufacturing-based foreign capital attraction pattern is changing to a service-based foreign capital attraction pattern. With foreign investment, China is entering a true "service economy era."

#### 12.1.1.5 The Trade in Services Expands Rapidly, and the Globalization Process Quickens Significantly

In 2014, China's total imports and exports was USD 4.3 trillion, with an annual growth of 6.1% after excluding non-comparable factors, including an 8.7% increase in exports and a 3.3% increase in imports. In 2014, the total imports and exports of trade in services exceeded USD 604.3 billion, up more than 12.6%, including exports of USD 222.2 billion, up 7.6%, and imports of USD 382.1 billion, up 15.8%; the trade deficit in services further expanded to USD 159.9 billion, up 35%. During the 12th Five-Year Plan (2011–2015) period, the trade in services as a percentage of foreign trade continued climbing and reached 10.3%, 10.8%, 11.5% and 12.3% in 2011, 2012, 2013 and 2014, respectively. Service outsourcing remained at high growth rates. In 2014, the contract amount and execution amount of international service outsourcing projects undertaken by China were USD 71.83 billion and USD

55.92 billion respectively, up 15.1% and 23.1% year-on-year respectively. For the first time, China's foreign direct investment exceeded USD 100 billion and reached USD 102.9 billion, up 14.1%, of which, the investment in the service sector increased by 27.1% and accounted for 64.6%.

#### 12.1.1.6 The Employment Absorption Capacity of the Service Sector Further Improves

In 2011, the number of people employed in the service sector as a percentage of all employed people in China surpassed that of agriculture, making the service sector the most employment-absorbing sector in China. In that year, there were 760 million people employed nationwide, including 35.7% in the service sector and 34.8% in agriculture. For the first time, the service sector overtook agriculture as the leading source of employment in China. Despite the gradual decline of China's economic growth rates in recent years, the registered unemployment rate in urban areas has not gone up, thanks in large part to the rapid growth of the service sector. The employment elasticity coefficient of the service sector is much higher than that of industry. Due to the rapid growth of the service sector, the labor force transferred from industry and agriculture as well as the new labor force has been mainly absorbed by the service sector. In 2014, employment in the service sector continued its good status, and the proportion of employment in the service sector reached 40.6%, implying that the target of the 12th Five-Year Plan (2011–2015) was completed ahead of schedule.

#### 12.1.1.7 New Forms and Models of the Service Sector Continue Emerging

Driven by technological progress and consumption demonstration effect, new forms and models of the service sector have been continuously emerging in China. For example, there is an increasing number of service applications and innovations based on big data, cloud computing, and the Internet of Things. The rapid development of new forms such as creative design, system process services, remote diagnosis and equipment lifecycle management services has provided a strong support for the transformation and upgrading of the manufacturing sector. The new service models such as eco-tourism, distance education, leisure-based elderly care, digital home and smart community are developing rapidly, the consumption channels are further broadening, and the consumption of services is increasing and becoming popular among ordinary people, which strongly drives up consumer demand and plays a positive role in expanding domestic demand.

### *12.1.2 The "New Normal" Led by the Service Sector Is a Natural Result of Economic and Social Development*

As China's economy enters a new stage of transformation and development, it is neither accidental nor temporary for the service sector to dominate the national economy. It is a natural result of globalization, marketization, urbanization and informatization.

#### 12.1.2.1 The Gradient Transfer and Capital Flows Triggered by Economic Globalization Create New Opportunities for the Development of the Service Sector

Globalization provides a platform for both developed and developing countries to pursue development in accordance with their own comparative advantages and is a dividend for the economic growth of the world. As a developing country that had taken over the transfer of manufacturing, China had certainly focused on the secondary sector for the past period of time. However, along with the industrialization process, the global gradient transfer and the changes in the pattern of capital flows, China has now ushered in new opportunities for the development of its service sector. With the demographic dividend fading and the costs of labor and enterprises rising, China's advantage in manufacturing as an international OEM is weakening, and foreign capital is more interested in the huge market potential of China's service sector. As China's service sector opens up to the world, it is becoming increasingly convenient for foreign capital and service factors to enter the Chinese market. Against this backdrop, it is a natural result that the opening-up will lead to great development and efficiency improvement in the service sector.

#### 12.1.2.2 The Direction of Reforms Toward a Market Economy Stimulates the Growth and Efficiency Improvement of the Service Sector

The intangibility of the service sector and the increasing online transactions of services determine that service transactions are more likely to suffer from "information asymmetry" and "moral hazard." How to create an effective institutional environment is particularly important for the service sector. A good institutional environment, including an integrity system, an effective intellectual property protection system, adequate market competition, and fair and transparent transactions, is a basic prerequisite for the great development of the service sector. After the 18th CPC National Congress clearly put forward the reform direction of giving play to the decisive role of market mechanisms, China has continuously developed and improved the market economy systems. As the market economy systems and mechanisms become more mature, the monopolies and controls in the service sector are being gradually cracked, and the service sector is becoming more and more liberalized. It greatly stimulates the vitality and motivation of service enterprises, promotes effective competition among service sector players, and enhances the service sector productivity and effective supply.

#### 12.1.2.3 New Type of Urbanization Creates a Huge Space for the Development of the Service Sector

As ideal spaces for the service sector to grow, cities not only embrace the agglomeration of population and various factors, as well as the resulting massive demand for services and scale effects but also improve the efficiency and quality of the service sector through the agglomeration of population and factors. China is actively and orderly promoting a new type of urbanization, which means that various factors will be more spatially agglomerated, the scale and density of the population will be significantly increased, various industrial parks will be clustered in cities or towns, and as a result, the demand for living services, public services and production services will increase significantly. It will create a market space for the great development of the service sector. In addition, urban residents will have higher income levels, higher quality of life and more modern lifestyles, and their human capital will be significantly higher than that of rural residents. Whether in terms of service demand or the ability in service supply, urban residents will be significantly stronger than rural residents and become the main driver for service sector development.

#### 12.1.2.4 New-Generation Information Technologies Create "Infinite Possibilities" of Services

In this information era, how the new-generation information technologies such as mobile internet, cloud computing, big data and the IoT are integrated with and deeply applied in various economic and social fields and sectors has become the core content of the new round of global sci-tech revolution and sector changes. As an infrastructure of economic and social development and an innovation factor, the internet is constantly releasing chemical reactions and amplifying effects through integrated innovation, which, like the electricity revolution a hundred years ago, is profoundly changing the traditional patterns of consumption, business models and trading modes. For example, it changes the forms of traditional sectors, resulting in the production, processing, storage and transmission of information gradually taking center stage in economic activities. As these economic activities are usually a part of the service sector, it makes services "ubiquitous" and "unlimited." For another example, information technologies allow many products or services that were previously non-tradable to become tradable, so that the possibility of service transactions is increased and the development of service trade is accelerated.

## 12.2 Major Challenges for China's Service Sector Reforms

### 12.2.1 *Inflexible Systems and Mechanisms, and Low-Level Marketization*

According to the most common definition, an institution means a generally accepted rule of the game in a society and a "contract" established to determine and bind people in their relations with each other. Through the research on economic growth phenomenon and the empirical analysis of the US economic growth, Douglass C. North, a well-known US institutional economist, proposed that institutional factors would have a great influence on economic growth. He also argued that productivity could be improved and economic growth could be achieved through institutional innovation, even without technological changes. In this sense, institutions are the most important factor affecting economic growth, transaction costs and economic efficiency. Sound market mechanisms and standardized market order are the basic conditions for the development of the modern service sector. Unlike agriculture and manufacturing sectors, which provide tangible products, the service sector is usually about the transactions of rights rather than physical objects, and it relies more on advanced production factors and intangible assets such as knowledge, innovation, human capital, reputation and brand. Therefore, the service sector development requires more-improved market mechanisms and systems. Except for traditional service fields such as catering, trade, wholesale and retail, tourism, etc., China's institutions, mechanisms and policy arrangements in many modern service fields, including access mechanisms, service standards, administrative regulation and pricing mechanisms, still have the strong shadow of a planned economy, so that the decisive role of market mechanisms is far from being played.

There are many reasons behind the inflexible systems and mechanisms and the low-level marketization in China's service sector, but the bureaucratic administrative approval and the overlapping management are among the most important ones. For example, there are various kinds of laws and regulations enacted in various places for pre-approval projects in the service sector. If these laws, rules, regulations and documents can not be revised or repealed in time with the changes of the new forms, new problems and new patterns of the modern service sector, it will become a major obstacle to the development and reforms of the modern service sector. In addition, the poor communication among the superior and subordinate departments, the conflict of interests among different departments, the mismatches and inconsistencies among policies, regulations and management methods adopted by government departments, greatly disrupt the normal operations of the service enterprises. The onerous and complex administrative approval, as well as the inflexible and inefficient management, are the biggest obstacles to the development and reforms of the service sector. How to streamline administration, decentralize powers and allow the market to play its role, will be an important topic for the next steps of service sector reforms.

### 12.2.2 The Serious "Service Internalization" Phenomenon in Industrial Enterprises and the Low Degree of Social Specialization Limit the Demand for Services

The emphasis on specialization and transactions is one of the key features of a market economy. Technological progress, efficiency gains and economic growth cannot be achieved without specialization. Influenced by the ideology of planned economy, most of China's industrial enterprises have either large-scale but wide business scope, or small-scale but wide business scope. A large number of services or service links are internalized in industrial enterprises. Many industrial enterprises are still in the stage of self-enclosure, self-service and self-circulation, and still adopt the traditional production modes, which means the internal service production and provision of service products required by industrial enterprises. Industrial enterprises adopt few and limited outsourcing services, which are mainly related to the production of products, mostly a single function or a certain part of their production and operations. However, the producer services related to product manufacturing, such as logistics, planning and consulting, R&D and design, financial leasing, business services, procurement and marketing, and human resources, account for a small proportion of their total expenditure. In this way, a large number of producer services that should have been marketized, industrialized and socialized become services provided internally by industrial enterprises. It not only severely inhibits the market demand for producer services, but also lowers the service efficiency and supply quality, because the industrial enterprises are not professional service providers after all, and they do not specialize in the service sector.

### 12.2.3 The Government Fails to Provide Adequate Regulation to the Service Sector

When it comes to government regulation, the existing literature generally argues that the government should provide an effective and comprehensive policy assurance so as to promote the development of the service sector, while Western economists generally tend to deregulate the service sector. Through simulation studies and cross-country comparisons, Nicoletti and Scarpetta (2003) pointed out the huge influence of government regulation on the service sector. In particular, the regulation of ICT service fields such as wholesale, finance, insurance and business services may harm the externalities of the new economy and create negative externalities on productivity growth. According to Brant (2003), inappropriate restrictive regulation undermines the incentives of enterprises and particularly limits the growth of the service sector, so governments should consider the issue in the framework of economic growth when developing service sector regulation. For example, financial, communication, and transportation services are the main input factors in the production of goods and account for the majority of product costs; the efficiency of service inputs is an important factor in the competitiveness of firms; and education, training, and health services are key contributors to the overall economic growth rate. Specific service policy orientation will directly affect the productivity level of these fields. Therefore, the government departments of various countries should take into account the realities of their countries when formulating sector policies.

Since the service sector provides intangible products and there is a serious information asymmetry between supply and demand parties, effective and reasonable regulation is especially important for the development of the service sector. The vast majority of fields of industry requiring micro-regulation, such as public transportation and telecom services, are parts of the service sector. Moreover, there is a serious information asymmetry in the products offered in some service fields, such as medical services and education services. These fields also require regulation by government departments. However, when we look at the current policy structure, we can find that the government lacks a basic concept and a clear policy direction in the process of regulating the service sector, and the targets and methods of regulation are wrong, which results in many fields of the service sector that need government regulation not only failing to develop healthily, but also suffering from serious shortage, rapid price increase and low service quality.

### 12.2.4 The Service Sector Has an Unreasonable Organizational Structure and an Imperfect Corporate Governance Structure

In terms of the organizational structure of China's service sector, some fields have low entry barriers and serious government intervention, resulting in disorderly competition and chaotic operations, and other fields are exclusively monopolistic, leading to inefficiency. For example, in the field of accounting services, the latest data from the professional management information system of the Chinese Institute of Certified Public Accountants showed that as of 2012, there were 8,128 accounting firms, 99,085 certified public accountants and 98,089 non-practicing members in China. Currently, there are nearly 200,000 individual members of the Chinese Institute of Certified Public Accountants and more than 250,000 people with CPA qualifications in China, but only a few of them have an income of more than RMB 10 million. Meanwhile, there are as many as 20 types of qualifications in China's certified public accountant professional services market, making it difficult to provide comprehensive services. In addition, the government's excessive intervention disturbs the normal order of competition in the market, so that China's accounting services market is unable to form a mechanism of "survival of the fittest," the service quality is low, the market competition is disorderly, and the business chaos is everywhere. As all players want to gain market share, it is difficult to form self-regulation, and scandals emerge one after another. Similar problems also exist in other fields such as law services and advertising services. In addition, there are a number of professional service providers that are nominally separated from the government, but are actually remaining dependent on government departments. They lack effective internal governance structures, are weak in competitiveness, and are at a disadvantage in the increasingly fierce international competition for professional services. For example, there are 24 large-scale exhibition enterprises in Shanghai, but most of them have not established modern enterprise systems, and have such problems as inflexible mechanisms, unclear division of responsibilities, powers and benefits, less internationalized and specialized exhibition, and imperfect corporate governance structures, which leads to the lack of vitality in the development of the service sector.

## 12.3 Measures and Suggestions for Deepening the Service Sector Reforms

During the 12th Five-Year Plan period (2011–2015), the Chinese government attached great importance to the development of the service sector, introduced a large number of policies and measures to support the development of the service sector, and issued a series of guiding opinions, management measures and other policy documents. For example, the policy system and statistical system for the development of high-tech service sector were further improved. In December 2011, the General Office of the State Council issued the *Guiding Opinions on Accelerating the Development of High-Tech Service Sector*, which further defined the policies and measures for the development of high-tech services. The development of sci-tech service sector was also given high priority. In October 2014, the State Council issued *Several Opinions on Accelerating the Development of Sci-Tech Service Sector* (hereinafter referred to as "Opinions"), which pointed out that we should deploy, cultivate and grow the market players of sci-tech services, innovate the modes of sci-tech services, extend the service chain of sci-tech innovation, promote the professional, networked, large-scale and international development of sci-tech services, and provide an important guarantee for building China into an innovative country and upgrading China's economy. For the first time, the State Council made a comprehensive deployment on the development of sci-tech services. In addition, the State Council issued a series of documents and policies on the development of the service sector, such as the *Guiding Opinions of the State Council on Accelerating the Development of producer service Sector and Promoting the Adjustment and Upgrading of Sector Structure*, the *Opinions of the State Council on Accelerating the Development of Sports Sector and Promoting Sports Consumption*, as well as the *Opinions of the State Council on Accelerating the Development of Elderly Service Sector*. These policies and measures on promoting the development and reforms of the service sector have indeed played an important role. However, we should clearly see that the overall development level of China's service sector is still not high, and there are still many fields that need urgent reforms. For the 13th Five-Year Plan period, we propose to deepen the reforms of the service sector from the following aspects, so as to realize the sound and rapid development of China's service sector:

### *12.3.1 Break Monopolies and Actively Promote Free Competition in the Service Sector*

The service sector encompasses numerous fields, which vary widely in nature. Some service fields (e.g. telecom services) are naturally monopolistic, while others (e.g. education services) have externalities. However, as far as the overall trend is concerned, we should gradually eliminate entry barriers and basically achieve the liberalization of entry and exit. In some fields where serious administrative monopolies currently exist, such as telecom, finance, insurance, railroad transportation, air transportation, radio and television, and publishing and media, reforms must be vigorously carried out, except for a few fields that involve national security and must be monopolistic and operated by the state. The current reform measures are mainly aimed at allowing competition among the new enterprises formed after the spin-off of the original state-owned enterprises. These are obviously shallow reforms. We should focus our reforms on liberalizing the market access of the service sector, introducing competition mechanisms, allowing the coexistence of entry and competition, and especially permitting the entry of new market players. Stimulating private enterprise investment and allowing the entry of non-state market players are key steps for the government to break the administrative monopolies. Only when private capital is extensively involved in market competition, the efficiency can be improved, the services can be enhanced, and the national benefits can be increased. For some fields that cannot be fully opened in the short term, we should also take practical measures to realize the "separation of government and enterprises, separation of government and capital, separation of government and affairs" as far as possible. For fields that are not naturally monopolistic, we should actively introduce market mechanisms, lift excessive and cumbersome administrative regulation, allow fair competition, and improve service efficiency. Even for fields that are now at a low level of administrative monopolies, we should never set excessive entry barriers so that the incumbent enterprises can boost their efficiency.

The report to the 18th CPC National Congress made a major breakthrough in the ownership theory by proposing the theory of fair competition for different market players with the core content of guaranteeing equality in the use of production factors, equality in market competition, and equality in legal protection (referred to as "three equalities") for different ownership entities in accordance with the law. In terms of service sector development policies, the core elements of this theory include:

First, the market access should be relaxed. With regard to the service sector, the 12th Five-Year Plan (2011–2015) clearly underlines that "all fields of the service sector that are not explicitly prohibited by national laws and regulations are open to foreign capital and social capital, domestic and foreign capital and domestic and foreign enterprises are treated equally, and all types of investors can enter such areas in the form of a sole proprietorship, joint ventures, cooperation, etc. Except for the provisions of national laws and regulations, all departments shall not set pre-approval procedures for the registration of various types of service enterprises in various forms." Therefore, we should actively boost the establishment of an open and effective market entry system for the service economy, gradually reduce the administrative monopolies in the market access system, and promote healthy competition and development of the service economy. This principle should be the basic guideline for the reforms of China's service sector access mechanisms and must be robustly implemented. China has long placed various barriers to market access in the service sector, mainly due to the lack of in-depth research and even some misunderstanding of the basic theory of market access. The existing high access thresholds or administrative monopolies in the service sector are theoretically based on "national economic security" or "national security." However, it has been proven that the government does not have a basic definition of "national economic security" or "national security" in the process of policymaking, and their connotations and extensions are very vague, which has resulted in the abuse of these concepts and the unlimited magnification of monopolies in the service sector. Therefore, in the process of liberalizing the service sector, we need to strengthen the research on basic theories, clearly define the key and core concepts such as "national security" and "national economic security," determine their connotations and extensions, and modify them dynamically with economic development.

Second, the ownership restrictions should be lifted as much as possible. Currently, state-owned capital generally accounts for large shares in many monopolistic service fields, while non-state-owned capital accounts for very small shares. This severe asymmetry leads to an overwhelmingly competitive advantage of state-owned capital over non-state economic enterprises in market competition. However, this competitive advantage is not a result of the difference in their capabilities, but a result of their high degree of monopolies. Therefore, we should break the monopolies in the non-basic public service fields as much as possible, and lift the ownership restrictions. Apart from introducing foreign capital, we should also create a competitive environment and provide equal opportunities for private enterprises and other market players, form a diversified investment and financing mechanism that includes government investment, private investment and foreign investment, and gradually increase the shares of the non-public economy in the service sector.

Third, the non-basic public service fields should be gradually liberalized and the market should be given full play to allocate resources. We should clearly define the basic public services and the industrialized and socialized services, and change the pattern where public institutions provide industrialized and socialized services, so that the market demand of the service sector will be expanded. In addition, we should strengthen the research on market management methods that are suitable for the development of new service modes and new service fields, in order to comply with the basic requirements of the great development of the new service sector.

Fourth, effective incentive mechanisms should be adopted. Currently, China's hospitals, schools, and service fields such as finance, communications, and transportation are generally "overstaffed and inefficient." However, if the incentive mechanisms are rationalized, these service providers will be motivated. There is a huge room for productivity improvement and a great potential for service provision.

### 12.3.2 Promote Integrated Development Between the Service Sector and Manufacturing and Agriculture, and Boost Sector Upgrades Through Integration and Interaction

China's manufacturing sector is now under double pressure, as high-end manufacturing fields are flowing back to developed countries, and labor-intensive manufacturing fields are transferring to developing countries where labor costs and business costs are lower. The problems of low efficiency, low added value, and backward production and management methods in the agricultural sector have not been fundamentally changed. How to upgrade the manufacturing sector, modernize the agriculture sector, improve the overall competitiveness of the sectors and climb up to the global value chain is a challenging and long-term task for China. As the boundaries of modern sectors become increasingly blurred, their development is characterized by and follows the trend of "industry tertiarization, service productization and sector integration." As we move toward the "Made in China 2025" strategy and the ambitious goal of agricultural modernization, we must break the traditional production methods, create a good development environment for sector integration, and develop modern manufacturing and modern agriculture with the concept of cross-sector integration. In other words, we should embed the knowledge-rich producer services into manufacturing and agriculture, so as to realize the interactive integration between the producer service sector and manufacturing sector, and the organic integration of the producer service sector and agriculture.

First, we should promote the interactive integration between the producer service sector and manufacturing sector, and give play the role of the producer service sector in upgrading and transforming the manufacturing sector. It is recommended to focus on the following four aspects: (1) We should encourage the separation and development of producer services from manufacturing. According to international and domestic experience, the promotion of specialized and socialized development of producer services is closely related to the enhancement and specialization of the manufacturing sector. This will not only release the service market demand and cultivate specialized service providers, but also allow manufacturing enterprises to focus on their main business activities. It is a "double-purpose" choice. (2) We should extend the manufacturing chain, add more service factors to the final products and realize service-based operations, with a view to increasing the profitability of the manufacturing sector and changing the trend of continuous decline in manufacturing profitability. (3) We should change the traditional practice of "valuing material factor inputs and neglecting service factor inputs" in the manufacturing sector. We should pay more attention to the knowledge-intensive service factors such as R&D and design, software information, quality control, modern logistics, supply chain management, inspection and testing, financing and leasing, energy-saving and environmental protection solutions. Only when the manufacturing sector is equipped with a "smart brain," we can push China's manufacturing sector towards intelligent manufacturing. (4) We should reform the ways in which industrialization and informatization are integrated. In the past, China placed more emphasis on the use of information technologies in industrial manufacturing, but obviously, it has limitations. We should not only pay attention to the informatization and intelligence of the manufacturing production process, but also penetrate the informatization in the whole production value chain, and realize the network-based three-dimensional deep integration, which means that the R&D and design before production, the processing and manufacturing during production, and the marketing and services after production are integrated into the common networked information platform. On that basis, a number of intelligent manufacturing clusters will be created. With this platform, we will promote the deep integration between services and the whole manufacturing value chain, so that the producer service sector will serve as a key driver for supporting "Industry 4.0" and implementing the "Made in China 2025" strategy.

Second, we should promote the integration between modern services and agriculture. It is recommended to focus on the following five aspects: (1) We should boost the development of sci-tech information services in agriculture. The deep integration between sci-tech information services and agriculture is the fundamental path for turning traditional agriculture into modern agriculture. We should encourage colleges and universities, scientific research institutions and leading agricultural industrialization enterprises to establish an agricultural sci-tech alliance and actively build a cloud-based platform for agricultural sci-tech services. The efficient and full-coverage information services in agriculture are important for the modernization of agriculture. By virtue of the modern internet, mobile internet, IoT and other technologies, and based on the whole-process closed-loop operations, we should initially establish the food safety grading standards, focus on "food safety testing" including safety food testing, green food testing, organic food testing and functional food testing, and create a global benchmark and a brand image in the field of food safety. The combination of the internet and traditional agriculture will give rise to huge possibilities that have never been seen before, and will enable farmers and agriculture to improve their ability to develop markets through the widespread application of the internet. (2) We should innovate the agricultural products circulation system. Rural e-commerce has become an important tool for revitalizing rural resources, smoothing the agricultural products circulation, serving agriculture, rural areas and farmers, and improving the level of rural income, so we should pay great attention to the development of rural e-commerce. Given that the logistics of fresh agricultural products is an aspect to be improved in the current agricultural products circulation system, we should put efforts into developing the logistics of fresh agricultural products, speeding up the standardization of cold chain logistics and gradually solving the bottleneck of "last mile problem" of fresh agricultural products. (3) We should popularize agricultural machinery and technologies and improve the socialized service system. We should establish an agricultural machinery information service platform, set up an agricultural machinery information service network featuring "up and down connection and resource sharing," provide specialized and socialized services in multiple fields such as demonstration promotion, agricultural machinery operations, technical training, sales and maintenance, information consultation and intermediary, and gradually form a new and diversified agricultural machinery service mechanism that is market-oriented and service-based and integrates demonstration, promotion and services. (4) We should improve the agricultural standardized service system. We should stick to the core principle of ensuring product quality and safety, and guide the whole process of production, processing and circulation with standardized concepts, protocols and norms. The focus should be on building a service network platform for standardized information and agricultural quality and safety information and achieving the transparency and sharing of standard information resources. It is necessary to establish a grade marking system that includes "standards-based production," "standards-based circulation" and "indication of origin, quality and standard of finished products." Through the establishment and improvement of the local agricultural quality and safety inspection and testing stations, we should completely establish an agricultural quality and safety testing system and traceability system. (5) We should perfect various public service platforms. The rural service sector is highly public and not-for-profit, and serves the vast number of farmers and agricultural enterprises that are in a relatively disadvantaged position in the market. By building public service platforms such as talent service network platform, sci-tech information platform, information service platform and equipment service platform, integrating and consolidating resources, it is possible to reduce the cost of farmers or agricultural enterprises to obtain and use these resources and enhance their willingness to use modern service factors, thus boosting the shift from traditional agriculture to modern agriculture.

### *12.3.3 Expand the Scope of Liberalized Service Fields and Improve the Liberalization Level of the Service Sector*

Upon its accession to the WTO, China made nine commitments in 12 fields of trade in services and 104 commitments in more than 160 sub-fields, which was close to the average level of developed countries (108). As China's service sector keeps opening-up to the outside world, the level of foreign capital utilization in the service sector is also improving, and the service sector becomes the sector with the largest amount of foreign capital utilization. In the second quarter of 2015, 67% of the foreign capital attracted by China was invested in the service sector, showing the preference of foreign investors for the service sector.

In terms of reform strategy, we should choose the approach of "leading the reforms of domestic modern producer service sector by opening-up." In China's first round of opening-up, the focus was mainly put on commodity markets and the manufacturing sector, and the achievements of the approach of "leading reform by opening-up" are mainly reflected in the fact that China became a global manufacturing center. As a next step, we should increase the opening-up degree of the service sector, so as to realize the strategic goal of transforming from a manufacturing power to a service power. It should be pointed out that the service sector should be opened up internally and externally at the same time, and we should not "pay attention to the external opening-up and ignore the internal opening-up." When we look at the history of China's service sector development, reforms and opening-up, we can find that all local governments have actively promoted the external opening-up of the service sector, and the results of the attraction of foreign capital have become one of the measures of the political performance of local leaders, but they have not paid enough attention to the internal opening-up of the service sector. The low degree of internal opening-up is mainly attributed to the fact that major service fields are largely monopolized by the state-owned economy and service factors cannot move freely among different ownership systems. The root of the monopolies in terms of ownership lies in the policy discrimination against private capital. Many high-margin service enterprises basically do not allow the entry of private capital, and even if they do, high thresholds are set.

Regional monopolies are another reason for the insufficient internal opening-up. China's current central-local fiscal relationship has not been well rationalized. Local protectionism triggered by the established fiscal system is relatively serious. Since only local service factors and resources are allowed to enter local service fields, there is naturally no free flow of service factors among regions. As the important and indispensable part of the next service sector reforms and opening-up, we should break the geographical restrictions, encourage the free flow of service factors among regions, optimize the allocation of service factor resources within broader regions, improve the efficiency of service factors, enhance inter-regional competition, and encourage each region to find its own comparative advantage in the flow of service factors and form its own characteristic service field.

### 12.3.4 Reform the Service Sector Investment System, Optimize the Service Sector Investment Structure and Improve Investment Efficiency

In 1993, the proportion of investment in the service sector exceeded 50% of all investment, much higher than the proportion of added value of the service sector in the same period. The service sector as a whole failed to show the characteristics of "low inputs, high outputs and fast results." In the 1980s, an increase of RMB 1 in the added value of services required a capital investment of about RMB 3. However, from the 1990s, the required capital investment increased to more than

RMB 5. It indicates that from a dynamic point of view, the service sector is increasingly capital-intensive. In terms of the internal structure of service sector investment, such fields as transportation, warehousing, postal services and real estate absorb a high proportion of investment, accounting for more than 60% of all service sector investment. In terms of the investor, investment in the service sector is still mainly dominated by state-owned investment. The service sector covers 14 fields. Except for five fields (wholesale and retail, accommodation and catering, real estate, rental and business services, residential services and other services), the other nine fields are observed to have more than 50% of state-owned investment. More specifically, three fields – transportation, warehousing and postal services, water, environment and public facilities management, and education - have more than 80% of state-owned investment.

First, we should reform the existing investment approval system. China's current investment approval system still places many restrictions on the service sector. For example, the governments still require cumbersome approvals for investments in many service fields such as railroads, highways, express delivery and real estate. The current investment approval system is a distortion of the market investment decisions because the investment approvers are not accountable for the outcome of the investment and the criteria, principles, and procedures for approval are not transparent enough. It is also an important cause of inefficient investment in the service sector. Looking ahead to future development, we should fully remove the existing investment approval system. With the exception of government-invested projects, the approval of private investment projects should be completely abolished.

Second, we should vigorously encourage private investment in the service sector. While breaking the monopolies, we should use various financial, land and fiscal policies and tools to actively guide private capital to invest in the service sector.

Third, we should diversify the investment methods through policies in various aspects such as taxation. In addition to direct investment from the construction unit for capital construction and technological transformation, we should encourage the adoption of project financing, equity investment, project mergers and acquisitions, leasing investment, BOT and other investment methods that are widely accepted in the world. In particular, we should coordinate the tax policies of these new investment methods, so that the tax burden of these different investment methods will be roughly balanced.

Fourth, we should actively push forward and improve the pilot program for the "replacement of business tax with value added tax" in the fields of the modern service sector, and encourage more social capital to invest in the modern service sector. In 2012, Shanghai, Beijing and other cities rolled out the pilot program for the "replacement of business tax with value added tax" in some fields of modern services. Generally speaking, this reform promoted specialization and boosted the development of the modern service sector, and according to the pilot results, it helped to reduce the tax burden of modern service enterprises. However, this reform also led to a higher tax burden for some service enterprises. It was caused by specific reasons, as the current VAT regulations leave the vast majority of service enterprises with less input VAT that can be deducted. For manufacturing enterprises, their production process requires a large number of material resources, but for service enterprises, their business activities rely heavily on non-material "knowledge" and "labor" resources rather than material resources. In other words, they rely mainly on human capital and intangible assets as intermediate inputs. Therefore, we should include intangible assets, human capital and other non-material inputs into the scope of input VAT deduction as soon as possible, so as to effectively reduce the tax burden of modern service enterprises and attract more social capital to invest in the modern service sector.

Fifth, we should increase the public and basic investment in the service sector and implement fiscal and taxation policies that are conducive to the development of the service sector. The governments should not increase investment in the competitive fields of the service sector, but should focus on supporting the construction of public infrastructure, market integrity systems, standard systems as well as the development of public service platforms and other underdeveloped fields of the service sector. Through reasonable tax policies, we should encourage the high-level division of professional works between manufacturing and service sectors, and seek a "win–win" situation between manufacturing and service sectors based on specialization and cooperation. For technology-based, innovative producer service enterprises engaged in R&D and design, inspection and testing certification, energy saving and environmental protection, we should implement a tax incentive policy that allows them to enjoy a preferential corporate income tax rate of 15% by treating them as high-tech enterprises.

Sixth, we should establish a multi-level and diversified financing service system and improve the financial policy system that supports the development of the service sector. We should encourage the development of angel investment and venture capital, and support the development of financial guarantee institutions. A multi-level capital market system should be built to meet the financing needs in different fields of the service sector. We should increase the support of financial innovation for the productive service sector by broadening the types and scope of mortgages, pledges and guarantees to be provided by institutions to modern service enterprises. Based on the experience of some developed countries, we can set up a special fund for the service sector, so that the development of small and micro service enterprises that meet the national policies can be financially supported and their financing bottlenecks can be solved.

### *12.3.5 Break the Land Monopolies and Reduce the Cost of Investment in the Service Sector*

It is a well-established fact that the cost of land in the service sector is high. The service sector encompasses many different fields, but it would be unfair to treat all the land used by the service sector as commercial land and charge high land prices. For example, the producer service enterprises engaged in logistics, R&D, and other fields, although pursuing profitability, serve as public platforms to a certain extent and provide typical quasi-public goods. If a land discrimination policy is adopted, these service enterprises will find it difficult to pay the high cost of land and will have to operate with very little profit. In addition, influenced by the traditional philosophy of "valuing industry and neglecting services," a number of regional governments often give priority to the land needs of industry when allocating land, thus making it impossible to meet the land needs of services. In China, all construction land is currently supplied by the state, and there is a huge difference in the price between land for industrial use and land for service use, so the cost of investment in the service sector is raised and the development of service sector investment is limited. In this regard, the specific measures that we should adopt include: piloting innovative land development models and reducing the investment cost. We should pilot the annual rental system for parts of service sector land. We should allow the original owners of collective land or allocated land to hold the properties under cooperative development, and securitize land assets, etc. Subject to urban planning and overall land use planning, we should make full use of the collective construction land circulation policies and encourage modern service sector projects to use collective construction land. We should allow the units that have acquired land through allocation to use factory buildings, warehousing space, traditional commercial street properties and land resources for modern services such as information services, R&D and design, and cultural creativity, without any change in the land use and the holder of the right to use the land.

### *12.3.6 Promote Service Consumption Through Market Liberalization and Enhanced Regulation*

Expanding the residents' demand for service consumption and spurring the domestic demand is a requirement for the medium and long-term strategic adjustment of China's economic structure, an important measure to respond to the international financial crisis and achieve steady and rapid economic growth, as well as an inevitable choice to improve people's livelihood and raise their living standards. Service consumption is a kind of instant consumption based on experience. From the perspective of supply and demand, if the supply of corresponding services is insufficient, the demand for service consumption will be difficult to be met and the service consumption will be suppressed. From the perspective of quality evaluation, consumers lack sufficient information about the quality and the specific effects of the services before they are provided with them. Therefore, it is important to create a social environment suitable for service consumption.

First, we should open up the market, improve the supply level, and meet the service demand of the people. For example, in the fields of civil aviation, publishing and media, financial services, health care, education and culture, we should provide service products tailored to people's demand by introducing new competitors, so that the level of service consumption will be enhanced, which is of great significance and importance.

Second, we should establish a systematic market regulation system. Considering the information asymmetry in the e-commerce market, housekeeping service, hourly worker market, healthcare market, and beauty market, we should strengthen market regulation and achieve information symmetry between suppliers and consumers as much as possible, so that we can provide credibility assurance for service consumption and cultivate potential markets for service consumption.

### 12.3.7 Improve the Level of Micro Regulation of the Service Sector

In a market economy, it is vital to encourage free competition and strengthen market regulation. The marketization of the service sector does not mean that the government leaves the micro market of the service sector unchecked. On the contrary, the marketization of services will bring more responsibilities to the government. In particular, more systematic support from the government will be needed in market regulation.

First, we should distinguish between the government's regulatory responsibility and its provision responsibility. In the context of a market economy, the government is the most important provider of public services. However, not all public services are provided by the government or state-owned enterprises. The key issue here is to distinguish between the government's regulatory responsibility and its provision responsibility. For national defense and governmental services, the government is obligated to provide these services. However, for other public services, such as postal services, compulsory education, scientific research, and public cultural services, the government is duty-bound but can provide these services in two ways: (1) The government sets up public institutions with direct investment, and these institutions provide public services directly to society. Compulsory education is a typical example of this model. Compulsory education in China means that the government sets up schools with investment and provides funds for their operations, and the schools provide free and compulsory education services directly to society. (2) The government provides the services to society after purchasing the corresponding services from non-profit or for-profit organizations. In terms of the direction of future reforms, the government should adopt the second model for service provision.

Second, we should establish a correct regulatory concept. In the process of micro-regulation of the service sector, the government should distinguish between the basic concepts of market regulation, administrative monopolies and nationalization. For service fields with severe information asymmetry, natural monopolies and other special circumstances, the government needs to strengthen regulation. However, such regulation means neither simple administrative monopolies nor pure nationalization, but rather a market-based approach to regulating service quality, service delivery methods and other aspects. Even for service fields that are administratively monopolized for avoiding resource waste, the government should help to maintain competitive status and, in particular, provide private capital with equal access to these fields.

Third, we should establish a fair and transparent regulatory system. The government has regulatory responsibility for the majority of fields of the service sector. In other words, the government not only needs to directly regulate the qualifications of service providers, service provision quality, service prices, and service delivery times, but also needs to regulate market access issues. The purposes of such regulation are, on the one hand, to prevent service providers from taking advantage of information asymmetry or monopoly status to raise service prices, lower service quality, and exclude other service providers from entering the market, and, on the other hand, to avoid resource waste. The regulatory system should meet the following criteria: Under the transparent and lawful regulation, all enterprises are treated equally and the same standards are applied, without special treatment of some enterprises or discrimination against others because of their special status. All market players should have access to the market. For service fields with serious information asymmetry, uniform quality standards should be established. For service fields that require government pricing, the pricing process should be more competitive (e.g. determine prices through bidding mechanisms) and more transparent.

Fourth, we should vigorously combat unfair competition, strengthen the enterprises' awareness of establishing brands and improve service quality. In this regard, another key task is to put a clear line between the functions of the government and enterprises in some fields. For example, in some service fields that play a market intermediary function, the government should completely cut off any affiliation and association between government departments and economic verification intermediaries, or other interest transfer relationships, so as to ensure that economic verification intermediaries truly become independent and impartial market players for verification services. For example, in the financial sector, the government should aim at financial security, the establishment of a sound financial services market and the prevention of systemic financial risks by effectively strengthening its regulation of financial institutions, rather than simply punishing financial irregularities.

Fifth, we should ensure the fairness of services. The services provided in many service fields are deemed essential to achieve social fairness in modern society. In other words, all members of society should have access to these services, regardless of their ability to pay, as required by social ethics and values. The typical examples of these services include basic education and basic medical and health services. Some people even argue that basic telecom services and basic transportation services should also be provided for public welfare. When these services (e.g. postal services, basic telecom services, and public transportation services) are operated by state-owned enterprises, the government can achieve universal coverage of these services by means of administrative orders. In a market economy, the government should establish a sound universal service mechanism to make these services fairly accessible to the people. The specific measures include: regulating the exit of enterprises (i.e. requiring incumbent enterprises not to abandon the operations in some of their loss-making areas in order to meet the needs of universal service); establishing a universal service fund; and guaranteeing the provision of universal service through fiscal and taxation means.

### *12.3.8 Cultivate Service Sector Innovation Teams and Provide Talent Support for Service Sector Development*

Talents, especially innovative talents, are the key to service sector development. The most important "inputs" in the service sector are human capital. It is the duty of the government to cultivate and introduce high-quality talent in the modern service sector. By providing financial support and reforming the talent cultivation modes, we should support the cultivation of service sector innovation teams, encourage service innovation and tolerate innovation failures. We should follow the principle of "seeking not all, but useful," actively promote new distribution methods such as technology invested as capital stock, management shareholding and stock option incentives, establish a flexible flow mechanism for innovative talents, encourage more high-end talents to gather in the service sector, so as to provide strong intellectual support for the development of the service sector.

## References


Douglass C. North (2011), Institutions, Institutional Change and Economic Performance (Chinese translation), Truth & Wisdom Press, Shanghai People's Publishing House, 2011 Edition.

Li Yongjian and Xia Jiechang (2011), Does the Service Sector Save Investment? - A Study Based on Aggregate and ICOR, Journal of Graduate School of Chinese Academy of Social Sciences, Issue 5.

Liu Zhibiao (2014), The Pulling Effect of Comprehensively Deepening Reforms on the Development of Service Sector, Journal of Beijing Technology and Business University, Issue 2.

Xia Jiechang (2013), Breaking Monopoly and Improving Regulations: The Key to Deepening the Modern Service Sector Reforms, Journal of Beijing Technology and Business University, Issue 5.

Xia Jiechang (2015), Entering the Era of Service Economy with Foreign Investment, Economic Information Daily, May 4, 2015.

Xia Jiechang and Guan Yonghao (2013), How to Escape from the Dilemma after the Replacement of Business Tax with VAT and the Next Steps, Reform, Issue 6.

Xia Jiechang and Shang Tieli (2006), Overview of the Studies on Modern Western Service Economy, Social Sciences Abroad, Issue 3.

Zhou Zhenhua (Ed.) (2011), Service Economy Development and Institutional Environment, Truth & Wisdom Press, Shanghai People's Publishing House, 2011 Edition.

# Chapter 13
# Promoting the Construction of Labor Market Institutions

**Wang Meiyan, Jia Peng, and Cai Fang**

**Abstract** With the economic and social transformation, the benefits appeals of labor market participants are increasingly diversified, and various conflicts are increasingly prominent and frequent. It should be observed that there is a new trend in labor-capital relations, but it is not a worsening of the situation, but a result of people raising their expectations of income. In response to this trend, the government has the responsibility to speed up the construction of labor market institutions. According to international experience, the developed countries alleviated conflicts in labor-capital relations, not by changing the opposition between labor and capital, but by strengthening the construction of labor market institutions and forming effective mechanisms for coordinating labor-capital relations (including the accelerated introduction of labor laws, the establishment of a minimum wage system, the enhancement of the role of labor unions, and the formation of a tripartite consultation mechanism) when they developed to a stage where the labor supply–demand relations had undergone fundamental changes. However, the countries and regions that escaped the middle-income trap established relatively complete labor market institutions and developed an institutional framework for resolving disputes and confrontations in labor-capital relations under pain or even compulsion when faced with increased labor-capital frictions. Currently, China's efforts should shift from direct intervention in the economy to providing better public services and improving social security mechanisms. The current stage of development has provided an opportunity to form a relatively complete social security mechanism. In other words, the government and society should take the lead in developing an efficient labor market, reducing the employment risks faced by people, improving the residents' ability to secure their income and living standards, and further reducing the incidence of poverty and vulnerability.

W. Meiyan (✉) · J. Peng · C. Fang
Institute of Population and Labor Economics, Chinese Academy of Social Sciences, Beijing, China



X. Zhang (ed.), *Exploration on China's Economic System Reform under New Normal of Development*, https://doi.org/10.1007/978-981-95-2461-7_13

Currently, China's economic development has entered a "new normal." With the economic and social transformation, the benefits appeals of labor market participants are increasingly diversified, and various conflicts are increasingly prominent and frequent (Zhou Xiaoguang and Wang Meiyan 2015). Sound labor market institutions are not only conducive to harmonious labor relations, but also contribute to the sustained and stable economic growth and continuous expansion of employment.

However, a well-functioning and mature labor market cannot be created overnight, and the labor market mechanisms, which consist of a series of institutions, systems and rules, are not fixed. Therefore, the labor market will never stop growing, transforming and developing. In all countries that have transitioned from a formerly planned economy to a market economy, the main mechanisms that allow the labor market to play its role have yet to be reconstructed through reforms.

Choosing labor market regulations that fit the national condition is important. When transitioning to a market economy, all countries are usually faced with the question of how to choose different labor market regulation tools. Whether employment can be expanded is a key criterion for the choice and evaluation of the institutions. Many European countries have implemented a series of regulatory measures since the 1970s that are prone to labor market inflexibility, leaving their employment growth much slower than that of the US.

Meanwhile, as many economists pointed out, there is no single institutional principle in labor market regulation, and the market economy allows and creates diversity (Freeman 1998). Currently, China is faced with both the task of cultivating the labor market to a higher level from scratch in the process of the dual economy development, and the task of transforming the allocation of labor resources to the track of market mechanisms in the process of transitioning from a planned economy to a market economy. Therefore, labor market cultivation is an extraordinarily challenging institutional reform and development task in China. In the process of establishing the labor market institutions from scratch, China should fully draw on international experience and choose regulatory measures that are suitable for its national conditions to ensure effective management of its labor market, without reducing the flexibility and competitiveness of the labor market.

The CPC Central Committee and the State Council released the *Opinions on Building Harmonious Labor Relations* on March 21, 2015, putting forward new requirements for the construction of China's labor market institutions. This chapter outlines China's labor market institutions and points out the possible reform directions.

## 13.1 Labor Market Regulations and Legislation

With the gradual disappearance of the infinite supply of labor, the so-called "law of supply and demand" in labor relations will gradually replace the "quantity paradox" in urban–rural relations. In other words, labor supply–demand relations will determine the bargaining position between employees and employers, and will have a relative influence on government legislation and policy decisions (Olson 1985; Anderson 1995). Regardless of whether or not governments or enterprises have good intentions about treating workers well, it was from the beginning of the changes in labor supply–demand relations in Western countries that the governments enacted laws that tended to protect workers' rights and interests, the trade unions took a higher position to play a greater role in employment relations and wage decisions, the employers began to improve employment conditions for hiring stable and highly-qualified employees, and the workers were given more choice and were less subject to "hunger chains." In view of this, China is now facing a great opportunity for the formation and improvement of labor market institutions.

However, the changes in labor supply–demand relations do not mean that labor relations can be naturally improved through bargaining by workers in the labor market. Undoubtedly, the changes in supply–demand relations in the labor market represent a good opportunity for the development of trade unions' organizations and collective wage bargaining mechanisms. As the overall bargaining position of the workers gradually improves, the employees working in large enterprises and monopolistic sectors have greater incentives and motivations to form a counter-weight to employers and gain their own position in the labor market because of the strong presence of their enterprises in the market (John Kenneth Galbraith 2006). However, small and medium-sized enterprises are unable to share the fruits of enterprise growth with their workers and are unable to satisfy the benefits appeals of their workers because they lack market strength or because they are not self-sustaining (Lin Yifu 2004). In such cases, the government's labor market regulations will become an irreplaceable arrangement that is extraordinarily necessary and urgent.

When labor is abundant and labor supply exceeds labor demand, workers are often disadvantaged in employment relations and are vulnerable to unequal treatment. It is common for employers to violate labor legislation and infringe on workers' interests, resulting in unsatisfactory working conditions and treatment for workers. Although employers may gain economic benefits to a certain extent by infringing on workers' interests at the micro level, the workers who are subjected to long-term unequal treatment will not only suffer from interest losses and affect the economic development, but also trigger discontent against employers and even against society, thus endangering the stability of the whole society.

China's labor market has long been in a state where supply exceeds demand, and accordingly, workers are disadvantaged in the labor-capital game. As a result, the interests and rights of workers are continuously unprotected, which is a major cause of social discord. As we see a fundamental change in the state of labor supply and demand, workers have a much bigger say in labor-capital negotiations. Meanwhile, if the wages of workers are not raised or their interests are not better protected, the labor force required for economic development will not be adequately supplied. The workers' wage increase mainly relies on the labor market, while the protection of workers' interests requires greater efforts from the government.

As a public policymaker, the government should advocate and implement policies that protect the interests of workers. At present, China is shifting from the long-term stage of unlimited labor supply to a new stage of labor shortage, which means it is a great time for the government and society to increase protection for workers. At the turning point of the new development stage, the government should actively protect the interests and rights of ordinary workers through legislation and various regulations. A labor market that provides good protection for workers will contribute to the maintenance and enhancement of social harmony.

One of the successful lessons learned by China from its labor market transformation and cultivation is the combination of deregulation and regulation. During the shift from planned allocation of labor resources to market allocation, China has carried out profound reforms of the employment systems and related regulations that were formed under the conditions of a planned economy, and it has been expressed as a process of deregulation. The whole process of China's economic reforms has been accompanied by the reforms of various policies that restricted the movement of rural labor and the reforms of breaking the "iron rice bowls" in cities, so that labor resources have been increasingly allocated based on market mechanisms and the level of urban–rural labor market integration has been continuously improved.

Such deregulation reforms include breaking the permanent worker system and abolishing "iron rice bowls" in enterprises, reforming the urban ticket system and housing and other welfare systems, improving policies on urban living, employment and social security for migrant workers, and gradually relaxing the household registration system. During its participation in economic globalization, China has gained a comparative advantage in labor-intensive sectors in international competition by virtue of the active roles fully played by its labor market. China's labor market is characterized by sufficient flexibility, which has been followed by many other developing and transition countries (Ministry of Finance of India 2006).

In parallel with the deregulation of the labor market institutions, China has never stopped regulating the legislation and rules of the labor market. For example, the Standing Committee of the National People's Congress adopted the *Labor Law* in 1994, with specific provisions on employment promotion, labor contracts, collective contracts, working hours, leaves, labor remuneration, labor safety and health, special protection for female workers and minor workers, vocational training, social insurance and welfare, labor disputes, labor supervision and inspection, and legal liabilities. In the late 1990s, the Chinese government introduced a wage level guidance system. In 2004, China promulgated the *Minimum Wage Regulations*, which promoted the full implementation of the minimum wage system in China. Over the past decade or so, the collective wage negotiation system and the collective contract system have been developed to a certain extent. In 2008, China introduced a series of new labor market laws, including the *Labor Contract Law*, the *Employment Promotion Law* and the *Law on Labor Dispute Mediation and Arbitration*. In 2012, the Standing Committee of the National People's Congress amended the *Labor Contract Law* and further regulated labor dispatch.

## 13.2 Wage Level Guidance System and Minimum Wage System

As China's labor market gets developed, the connection between the level of labor wages and the labor supply and demand status becomes increasingly close. Meanwhile, a number of systems and regulations concerning wages have been implemented. In 1999, the Ministry of Labor and Social Security issued the *Notice on the Establishment of the Wage Level Guidance System in Labor Market*, which marked the initial establishment of the wage level guidance system in China's labor market. The *Labor Law*, which came into effect in 1994, clarified the implementation of the minimum wage system in China, marking the legal establishment of the system. In 2004, the Ministry of Labor and Social Security promulgated the *Minimum Wage Regulations*, which promoted the full implementation of the minimum wage system in China.

### *13.2.1 Wage Level Guidance System*

In 1999, the Ministry of Labor and Social Security issued the *Notice on the Establishment of the Wage Level Guidance System in Labor Market*, which marked the initial establishment of the wage level guidance system in China's labor market. Through the establishment of a wage level guidance system in the labor market, the government's labor and wage administration departments can make full use of the labor market price signals to guide enterprises to reasonably allocate wages, the market mechanism is brought into the internal allocation of enterprises, and the enterprises are provided with an important basis for reasonably determining wage levels and wage relationships among various categories of personnel and for carrying out collective wage negotiations. The wage level guidance system is conducive to promoting the formation of reasonable price levels in the labor market, providing both employers and workers with objective market standards for reference in negotiating wage levels, reducing the blindness of both parties, and improving the success rate of workers in seeking employment and the overall efficiency of labor market operations. In addition, the system facilitates the reasonable and orderly movement of workforce, adjusts the employment structure across regions and sectors, closely connects the labor price mechanism with the labor supply and demand mechanism, and makes the labor market systems complete.

According to the *Notice on the Establishment of the Wage Level Guidance System in Labor Market*, the labor protection administrative departments shall investigate, analyze, summarize and evaluate the wage levels of different occupations (jobs) in various types of enterprises on a regular basis in accordance with the national unified norms and system requirements, so as to form the wage levels of various occupations (jobs) and publish them to the society, which can be used to guide enterprises to reasonably determine the employee wage levels and wage relationships and regulate labor market prices.

According to the *Notice on the Establishment of the Wage Level Guidance System in Labor Market*, the wage levels for guidance in the labor market should be based on the scientific investigation and analysis of relevant data and information, and the high, median and low levels must be determined in accordance with the methods described in the *Wage Level Investigation Methodology*, so that the wage levels for guidance can be comparable among different regions. The wage levels for guidance should be released once a year by the end of June. The wage levels for guidance should be specially announced in public employment agencies and should be entered into computers and released through the labor market information networks in cities where conditions permit, so as to make them available to enterprises, workers and others. In recent years, great progress has been made in the construction of the wage level guidance system in the labor market. The system was initially introduced in large and medium-sized cities such as Beijing and Shanghai and has been gradually extended to small and medium-sized cities. The number of cities that have adopted the wage level guidance system, as well as the number of jobs with wage levels for guidance, has increased year by year.

During the 13th Five-Year Plan (2016–2020) period, we should further improve the wage level guidance system and accelerate the formation of a unified and standardized enterprise salary investigation and information release system in order to provide a standard that can be referred to for collective wage negotiations.

## 13.2.2 Minimum Wage System

The minimum wage refers to the minimum labor compensation payable by the employer in accordance with the law, provided that the worker has performed normal labor during the legal working hours or the working hours agreed upon in the labor contract between the worker and the employer in accordance with the law. The minimum wage system is an important institutional arrangement to guarantee fair employment. Proper minimum wage rates, proper basis for rate adjustments and proper frequency of adjustments are the core of the design and implementation of the minimum wage system. In recent years, we have seen frequent and dramatic increases in minimum wage rates across China. According to international experience, the harmony between fair employment and stable development of the labor market can be achieved only if the minimum wage rates and the adjustment methods are reasonably determined.

### 13.2.2.1 China's Labor Costs Are Rapidly Increasing

As a country with abundant human resources, China had a comparative advantage in labor-intensive sectors in the early stages of development. However, the change in labor costs has a direct impact on China's competitive advantage in labor-intensive sectors. In recent years, China's labor costs have been rapidly increasing. For example, from 2008 to 2014, the real wage level of migrant workers, net of price factors, increased by 10.8% per year, faster than the growth rate of GDP per capita during the same period. Based on international comparisons, there are some characteristics of labor cost changes in China at the current stage:

First, demographic factors have played an important role in driving up wages. As a result, wage increases will be the trend in the medium to long term. With demographic changes, China has seen an acceleration of population aging, with the total working-age population declining for the second year in a row. In 2014, the total working-age population aged 16 to 60 (excluding 60) was 915.83 million, decreasing by 3.71 million from the end of 2013. The changes in labor supply have led to frequent labor shortages and higher wages. The relative stability of demographic factors determines the stability of labor supply and demand trends.

Second, labor costs have been increasing faster than the growth of labor productivity. The unit labor costs refer to the ratio of workers' labor costs to labor productivity, and an increase in unit labor costs implies that the labor costs are increasing faster than the growth of labor productivity. According to our calculations, from 2004 to 2012, the unit labor costs in China's manufacturing sector increased from 0.189 to 0.265 and increased from 31% to 40% compared to the average level of the US manufacturing sector during the same period. However, the unit labor costs of major manufacturing countries such as Japan and South Korea were on a downward trend during the same period.

Third, the increase in labor costs drives economic transformation and upgrading, but the excessively rapid increase is not conducive to economic restructuring. According to international experience, economic restructuring and upgrading is a step-by-step process. If the labor cost increases are excessively rapid, China will lose its competitive advantage in traditional sectors before the formation of emerging sectors, thus putting itself in a period of vacuum of comparative advantage and stagnation of economic growth.

From now to 2020, China will strive to move from a middle-income country to a high-income country. During this period, we should focus on maintaining the flexibility of the labor market institutions. It is important to give full play to the positive role of minimum wage in ensuring fair employment, but also to avoid excessively high rates and excessively rapid increase, thus contributing to the increase of labor costs.

#### 13.2.2.2 Minimum Wage Rates and Actual Wage Changes

There is a consensus among major developed countries that appropriate minimum wage rates can raise the wages of low-income workers without reducing the number of jobs. As a general rule, when the minimum wage rates are lower than 30% of the average wage levels, the changes in the minimum wage rates will have no impact on the average wage levels and employment. However, if the minimum wage rates are higher than 40% of the average wage levels, the changes in the minimum wage rates may have a negative effect on the average wage levels as well as on employment.

After thoroughly analyzing the wage levels of workers in all forms of employment, especially informal employment, we found that the minimum wage rates have now reached 42% of the average wage levels in society and have reached 48% of the median wage levels. When it comes to the international level, the minimum wage rates in OECD countries in 2013 were about 39% of the average wage levels in society. Therefore, the current minimum wage rates in China are already at a high level.

Under such circumstances, if we continue to rapidly increase the minimum wage rates, the average wage levels in society may be driven up. The minimum wage increases will usually raise the reservation wages of the labor force, and the spillover effects of the minimum wage and the social security expenditures linked to the minimum wage will further bring some negative effects on the labor market, especially on the low-income groups and young workers. These negative effects have become evident in some developed countries. France, for example, has a minimum wage rate that is about 67% of its median wage level, while its unemployment rate among workers aged 15 to 24 is as high as 24%.

The dramatic and continuous increase of the minimum wage rates may be detrimental to long-term human capital accumulation. The relatively high minimum wage rates are also prone to false labor market signals, which can lead young people to abandon their studies and enter the labor market prematurely. Obviously, it is not conducive to the long-term human capital accumulation required for upgrading the sector structure.

#### 13.2.2.3 The Minimum Wage Rates Are Adjusted Frequently and Dramatically

The *Minimum Wage Regulations* released in 2004 stipulate that the minimum wage rates should be adjusted once every 2 years. The years from 1995 to 2014 are divided into three periods: from 1995 to 2004, from 2005 to 2010, and from 2011 to 2014, as the year 1995 was the year when most municipalities and provinces started to implement the minimum wage system, the year 2005 was the first year after the implementation of the new *Minimum Wage Regulations*, and the year 2011 was the first year after the financial crisis. By calculating the average frequency of the adjustments of the minimum wage rates by municipalities and provinces in each period, we found that the minimum wage rates were adjusted on average once every 1.79 years in the period from 1995 to 2004, once every 1.75 years in the period from 2005 to 2010, and once every 1.20 years in the period from 2010 to 2014. Therefore, it can be seen that the interval for adjusting the minimum wage rates is shortening.

However, among the countries across the world that have established a minimum wage system, 66% have not defined the frequency for adjustments of the minimum wage rates, 19% define the frequency as once a year, and 15% define the frequency as once every two years or more. A clear definition of the frequency of adjustments

**Table 13.1** Adjustments of minimum wage rates since 2010

| Year | Number of municipalities and provinces that made adjustments | Adjustment interval (years) | Growth rate (%) |
|---|---|---|---|
| 2010 | 30 | 2.33 | 24.34 |
| 2011 | 24 | 1.09 | 22.29 |
| 2012 | 24 | 1.30 | 19.54 |
| 2013 | 26 | 1.25 | 16.37 |
| 2014 | 18 | 1.22 | 13.92 |

*Data source* China's Minimum Wage Database, http://www.chinaminimumwage.org

of the minimum wage rates is likely to solidify wage adjustment expectations, while frequent adjustments of the minimum wage rates are not conducive to the establishment of stable labor relations, especially in economies dominated by labor-intensive enterprises.

In terms of the adjustment magnitude, all municipalities and provinces have made dramatic and continuous adjustments to the minimum wage rates after the financial crisis in 2010. Both the nominal minimum wage and the real minimum wage are continuously increasing. Although the growth of the minimum wage has decelerated, it is still much higher than the growth of the economy over the same period (Table 13.1).

#### 13.2.2.4 Policy Recommendations for Improving the Minimum Wage System

The 13th Five-Year Plan period (2016–2020) is a decisive stage in building a moderately prosperous society. The minimum wage system, as a typical labor market system, is of great importance in improving the income level of low-income people. During the 13th Five-Year Plan period (2016–2020), we recommend that China should further improve the minimum wage system from the following aspects:

(1) We should properly understand the functions of the minimum wage system. The local governments have continuously and dramatically raised the minimum wage rates since 2010, and seemingly have used it as a means of regulating income distribution. However, according to a large number of empirical studies, the minimum wage system is not an effective means of regulating income distribution and fighting poverty. The minimum wage system was initially designed to achieve relatively fair employment and to eliminate the extreme phenomena of employers' illegal employment and wage undercutting in the labor market due to information asymmetry, rather than as a means of regulating income distribution. In this regard, we should adhere to the principle of "holding the bottom line" when setting the minimum wage rates.

(2) We should set reasonable minimum wage rates. The experience of various countries proves that the adjustments of minimum wage rates are usually based on

two factors: the living demand of workers and the overall economic situation. The living demand mainly includes the average wages in society, the living costs, social insurance, and the living standards of other members of our society, while the overall economic situation includes economic development, productivity, and employment. Over the past few years, local governments have placed too much emphasis on aligning minimum wage adjustments with the changes in average wages in society and living costs, and have given less consideration to the changes in the economic development stage as well as productivity. This approach should be changed to reasonable adjustments of the minimum wage rates in line with economic development. Meanwhile, we should improve the basic database for minimum wage rates, including basic information on employment and wages of various forms and groups, etc. In particular, we should scientifically calculate the average wage levels in society and improve rationality in setting the rates.

(3) We should improve the frequency of minimum wage adjustments. Given the obvious changes in economic development and the fact that China's minimum wage rates are already at a high level after several dramatic adjustments, it is not appropriate for China to set mandatory rules on the intervals for adjusting the minimum wage rates. Before adjusting the minimum wage rates, we should thoroughly analyze its various impacts on the labor market and economic development, and anticipate the possible negative effects.

(4) We should adopt the hourly minimum wage system and abandon the current practice of combining the monthly minimum wage and the hourly minimum wage. According to international experience, most developed countries, such as the US, the UK and Canada, have defined only hourly minimum wage rates and have not set monthly minimum wage rates. China's *Minimum Wage Regulations* provide that "the minimum wage rates shall usually take the form of monthly minimum wage rates and hourly minimum wage rates. The monthly minimum wage rates are applicable to workers in full-time employment, and the hourly minimum wage rates are applicable to workers in part-time employment." Despite the clear explanation of the conversion between the monthly minimum rates and the hourly minimum wage rates in the *Minimum Wage Regulations*, there are still some difficulties in the practical implementation of the minimum wage system. After the implementation of the monthly minimum wage rates, enterprises become more motivated to abuse the minimum wage system. As the minimum wage rates are raised, enterprises may require workers to extend their working hours in order to reduce the increased costs associated with the increased minimum wage rates. Meanwhile, when implementing the hourly minimum wage rates, the governments need to distinguish between forms of employment such as full-time and part-time employment, which increases the difficulty and complexity of regulation and raises administrative costs.

(5) We should establish a special committee on minimum wage, and the determination, adjustments and evaluation of minimum wage rates should be undertaken by third-party institutions with professional research capabilities. We recommend that the government should establish a special committee on minimum

wage to complete the technical tasks related to the minimum wage system. The national unified minimum wage rates should be defined, and the local minimum wage rates should be reviewed by the special committee on minimum wage.

(6) We should make efforts in the implementation of the minimum wage system. We have found from the actual implementation of the minimum wage system in recent years that local governments have actively adjusted the rates but neglected the implementation. After the gradual increase of the rates, the ineffective implementation will not only undermine the authoritativeness of the system, but also hinder the realization of the original intention of fair employment.

## 13.3 Collective Wage Negotiation System and Collective Contract System

The collective wage negotiation system and the collective contract system are crucial to the adjustments of labor relations. The *Labor Law* promulgated in 1994 has provisions for collective contracts. After that, a series of laws, regulations and documents concerning the collective wage negotiation system and the collective contract system were promulgated and implemented one after another, providing the policy basis for the work of collective wage negotiations and collective contracts. The *Labor Contract Law* came into force in 2008, with some "special provisions" on collective contracts, labor dispatch, part-time employment and other aspects. Compared with the *Labor Law*, the *Labor Contract Law* has more detailed and operational provisions for collective contracts. This section will describe the government's efforts in promoting the collective wage negotiation system and the collective contract system, and will analyze the collective contract signing progress, as well as the useful explorations on promoting collective wage negotiation in all regions.

### *13.3.1 The Government's Efforts in Promoting Collective Contracts*

In the past few years, the government, enterprises and workers have complemented each other's strengths and coordinated their efforts in promoting collective wage negotiations under the tripartite mechanism for coordinating labor relations, and have played an important role in promoting collective wage negotiations. After over a decade of efforts, the collective wage negotiation system and the collective contract system have been developed to a certain extent. The coverage of the collective wage negotiation system continues to expand, and the collective contract signing rate continues to increase.

The *Labor Law* promulgated in 1994 stipulated that "a collective contract may be signed between an enterprise and its employees on matters such as labor remuneration, working hours, rest and leave, labor safety and health, and insurance and welfare." After that, the labor departments at all levels carried out the pilot project of signing collective contracts actively. There were 57 enterprises in Beijing, Guangdong, Fujian and other places selected for the pilot project. In 1995, a pilot project for collective negotiation and collective contract system was rolled out in more than 800 enterprises in eight municipalities and provinces, including Beijing, Guangdong and Fujian.

In 1997, the General Office of the Ministry of Labor issued *Several Opinions on Collective Wage Negotiation in Foreign-Invested Enterprises*, which provided guidance for foreign-invested enterprises to carry out collective wage negotiations. In 1997, the collective negotiation and collective contract system was gradually established across the country. In April 1998, the All-China Federation of Trade Unions (ACFTU) formulated and issued the *Guiding Opinions on Trade Unions' Participation in Collective Wage Negotiations*, which clarified the basic requirements for trade unions to carry out collective wage negotiations and prompted the continued implementation of the collective negotiation and collective contract system throughout the country.

In 2000, the *Trial Measures for Collective Wage Negotiations* were promulgated and implemented, which provided comprehensive regulations on collective wage negotiations and collective wage agreements, and clarified the basic rules for collective wage negotiations between enterprises and employees. In 2001, the *Trade Union Law* was amended to provide that "trade unions shall coordinate labor relations and safeguard the labor rights and interests of enterprise workers through equal negotiations and based on the collective contract system. Trade unions shall represent the workers to equally negotiate and sign collective contracts with enterprises and public institutions that are managed as enterprises."

In 2001, five ministries and associations, including the Ministry of Labor and Social Security, issued the *Notice on Further Implementation of Equal Negotiation and Collective Contract System* in order to further promote the equal negotiation and collective contract system and accelerate the cultivation of autonomous coordination mechanisms between the two parties in labor relations. This was followed by a steady progress of collective negotiation mechanisms in enterprises. As of 2002, the tripartite mechanism for coordinating labor relations was put in place in 30 provinces, autonomous regions and municipalities directly under the central government. As of 2003, more than 290,000 enterprises had established a collective wage negotiation system.

In 2004, the *Collective Contract Regulations* were implemented to further regulate the behaviors of collective negotiations and signing collective contracts. In 2005, the Ministry of Labor and Social Security, the ACFTU, the China Enterprise Confederation and the China Enterprise Directors Association jointly issued the *Notice on Further Promoting Collective Wage Negotiations*, underlining that the collective contract system should be further improved, and that for areas where foreign-invested enterprises, private enterprises and township enterprises, especially small enterprises, are relatively concentrated, the trade unions should represent the workers to equally negotiate and sign collective contracts with the enterprises or their representatives. In 2005, the tripartite mechanism for coordinating labor relations was generally established in all cities above the prefecture level in China. By the end of 2005, more than 6600 tripartite coordination organizations had been established nationwide, and 340,000 enterprises had set up collective wage negotiation systems. There were 8030 and 10,702 tripartite coordination organizations established nationwide in 2006 and 2007 respectively.

In 2008, the *Labor Contract Law* was put into effect, with more detailed provisions on collective contracts. For example, according to the *Labor Contract Law*, "the employees of an enterprise and the employer may, through equal negotiations, conclude a collective contract on matters such as labor remuneration, working hours, rest and leave, labor safety and health, and insurance and welfare. The draft collective contract shall be submitted to the workers' congress or all workers for discussion and adoption." For another example, according to the *Labor Contract Law*, "in regions below the county level, the trade unions may enter into collective contracts for specific sectors such as construction, mining and catering services with the enterprise representatives, or enter into regional collective contracts."

In the *Report on the Work of the Government* at the 1st Session of the 11th National People's Congress, Wen Jiabao pointed out that "we should promote the establishment of a collective wage negotiation system in enterprises, improve the wage level guidance system, and improve and put into practice the minimum wage system." This was the first time that the collective wage negotiation system was included in the government's work report, which highlighted the importance of the collective wage negotiation system in the new labor market conditions. The ACFTU issued the *Opinions on the Establishment of Collective Negotiation Instructors* and the *Opinions on Collective Negotiation Offer Actions* in June 2008, and also issued the *Guiding Opinions on the Active Implementation of Sector-based Collective Wage Negotiations* in July 2009.

In April 2008, the Ministry of Human Resources and Social Security held a national symposium on labor relations and proposed the "Rainbow Plan." This plan was designed to fully promote the collective wage negotiation system and the collective contract system. The symposium set the development goals for the next five years: the universal establishment of the collective negotiation and collective contract system in enterprises above the designated size in the eastern region by 2008 and 2009; the universal establishment of the collective negotiation and collective contract system in enterprises above the designated size in the central region by the end of 2010; and the universal establishment of the collective negotiation and collective contract system in enterprises above the designated size across the country by the end of 2012. Meanwhile, the symposium also called for the active promotion of regional and sector-based collective consultations, and gradually extending the collective contract system to all types of small and medium-sized enterprises, and striving to establish a collective negotiation and collective contract system in all types of enterprises within five years.

In May 2010, the Ministry of Human Resources and Social Security, the ACFTU, the China Enterprise Confederation, and the China Enterprise Directors Association jointly issued the *Rainbow Plan on Deepening the Implementation of the Collective Contract System*. The plan set the goal of striving to implement the collective contract system in all types of enterprises where trade unions have been established in the three years from 2010 to 2012. In 2010 and 2011, the coverage rate of the collective contract system reached more than 60% and 80% respectively. For small enterprises without trade unions, efforts were made to increase the coverage ratio by signing regional and sector-based collective contracts. The collective negotiation mechanism was gradually improved, and the effectiveness of the collective contracts was significantly enhanced.

In 2010, the National Trade Union Grassroots Organization Construction Conference was held, and it was proposed that enterprises should be vigorously promoted to universally establish trade union organizations and universally carry out collective wage negotiations in accordance with the law. The conference set the following goals: over 60%, 75% and 90% of the enterprises as legal entities across the country should establish trade unions in 2010, 2011 and 2012, respectively; more than 82%, 87% and 92% of their employees should join the trade unions in 2010, 2011 and 2012, respectively; and the goal of universal establishment of trade unions in enterprises according to the law should be basically achieved.

In terms of the establishment and development of trade unions, the number of trade union grassroots organizations across the country remained basically stable in the 1990s and declined in the late 1990s. From 2000 to 2002, there was a significant increase in the number of trade union grassroots organizations. After 2003, the number of trade union grassroots organizations showed a trend of steady growth, reaching 2,767,000 in 2013. The number of trade union members remained largely stable throughout the 1990s, at about 100 million. As we entered the twenty-first century, the number of trade union members began to grow rapidly, reaching 299 million in 2013 (Fig. 13.1).

| | |
|---|---|
| (万个) | (Unit: 10,000 organizations) |
| (亿人) | (Unit: 100 million members) |
| 年份 | Year |
| 工会基层组织数 | Number of trade union grassroots organizations |
| 工会会员人数 | Number of trade union members |

In early 2011, the ACFTU issued the *Plan for the Further Promotion of Collective Wage Negotiations from 2011 to 2013*. The plan proposed to establish a collective wage negotiation system in more than 80% of the enterprises that have established trade union organizations, to basically implement collective wage negotiation in the enterprises that have established trade unions, and to realize the establishment of a collective wage negotiation system in all of the Fortune Global 500 enterprises in China from 2011 to the end of 2013. The plan also detailed the annual planning goals for each year from 2011 to 2013 and proposed work priorities and major measures.

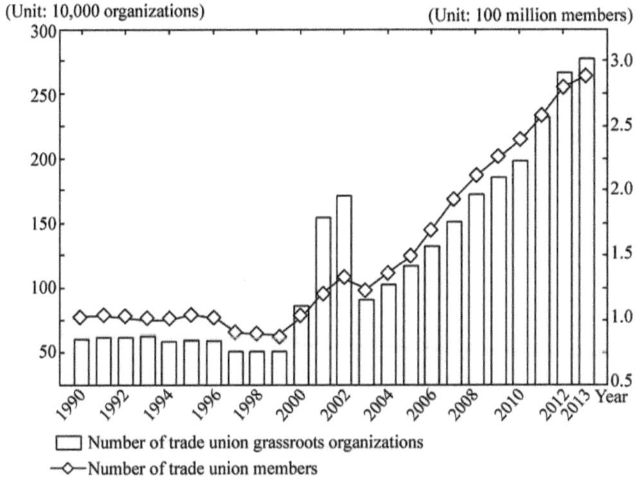


**Fig. 13.1** Number of trade union grassroots organizations and number of trade union members in China. *Note* The number of trade union grassroots organizations before 2003 includes the number of units partially covered by the trade unions due to the adjusted interpretation of the indicator. *Data source* National Bureau of Statistics (2015)

### *13.3.2 Collective Contract Signing Progress*

With the promotion of the collective wage negotiation system and collective contract system, both the number of collective contracts submitted to the labor security departments for review and approval and the number of employees involved across the country have been increasing. In 1998, there were 150,000 collective contracts involving 50 million workers; in 2001, there were 270,000 collective contracts involving more than 70 million workers. In 2002, the number of collective contracts increased dramatically to 635,000, involving more than 80 million workers. After the implementation of the *Labor Contract Law* in 2008, there are 703,000 collective contracts in 2009, covering more than 94 million workers. In 2014, there were 1.7 million collective contracts, covering 160 million workers (Fig. 13.2).

| | |
|---|---|
| (万份) | (Unit: 10,000 contracts) |
| (亿人) | (Unit: 100 million employees) |
| 年份 | Year |
| 集体合同数 | Number of collective contracts |
| 涉及职工数 | Number of employees involved |

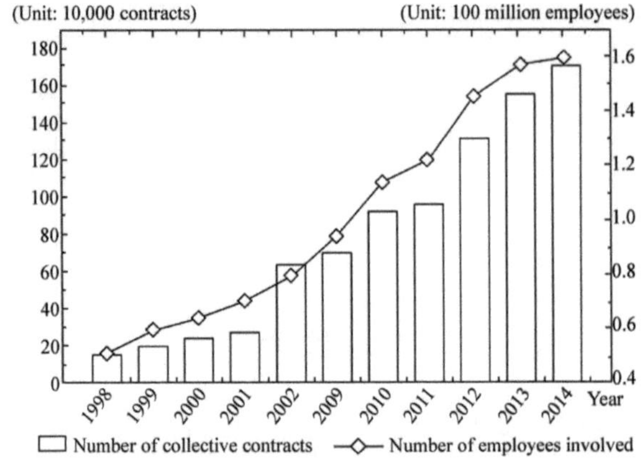


**Fig. 13.2** Number of collective contracts submitted to the labor security departments for review and approval and the number of employees involved. *Note* The *Statistical Bulletin on Human Resources and Social Security Development* from 2003 to 2008 did not publish the number of collective contracts and the number of employees involved. *Data source* Ministry of Human Resources and Social Security (previous years), the *Statistical Bulletin on Human Resources and Social Security Development,* http://www.mohrss.gov.cn/

### *13.3.3 Useful Explorations on Promoting Collective Wage Negotiation in All Regions*

All parts of China have actively explored the possibility of promoting collective wage negotiations. For example, Hangzhou issued the *Opinions on Further Promoting Collective Wage Negotiations*, according to which the enterprises that have established the collective wage negotiation system shall be promptly issued a rectification proposal if they refuse to negotiate wage increases with employee representatives; if the enterprise refuses to rectify the situation, the labor security departments will order it to rectify the situation within a specified period. In Hangzhou, more than 90% of the enterprises that have established trade unions have adopted the collective wage negotiation system.

The *Three-Year Action Plan of Beijing Trade Unions on Further Promoting Collective Wage Negotiations* was released in December 2010. According to the plan, Beijing promoted enterprises above the designated size to carry out collective wage negotiations independently, and enterprises below the designated size to establish negotiation mechanisms by signing regional and sector-specific wage agreements.

In recent years, the Qingdao Federation of Trade Unions vigorously promoted collective wage negotiations with the goal of establishing a collective negotiation and wage co-determination mechanism, continuously explored the forms, methods and means of collective wage negotiations, and made collective contracts and collective wage negotiations an important means for trade unions to coordinate labor relations. A series of documents were issued to clearly stipulate that enterprises should establish a collective negotiation system and have the right to offer, and that enterprises should establish a mechanism for annual average wage increases for employees through collective wage negotiations. In Qingdao, the content of wage negotiations was further enriched, including negotiations on wage level and wage distribution system, as well as negotiations on wage adjustments and payment methods. The forms of wage negotiations were diversified and developed gradually from intra-enterprise negotiations to regional and sector-based negotiations. In addition, Qingdao also explored the collective wage negotiations for contingent workers in public institutions. If an enterprise or unit refuses to sign a collective wage agreement without cause, the human resources and social security departments shall order it to correct the situation; if the enterprise or unit refuses to correct the situation, it shall be recorded in the list of "poor reputation units," which shall be made public to society.

In the process of promoting wage negotiations, Luohe City, Henan Province, insisted on the principle of "one enterprise and one policy" in order to tackle the problems regarding collective wage negotiations in a targeted manner. For enterprises with good production and operation efficiency, the focus was on negotiating wage levels, bonus distribution, subsidies and benefits; for enterprises with poor production and operation efficiency, the focus was on solving problems such as wage payment methods and living expenses of employees who have left their jobs; for non-public-owned enterprises, the focus was on solving the problems of increasing the total wages of enterprise employees correspondingly with the increase in enterprise efficiency by referring to the local wage levels for guidance, consumption index and other factors.

### *13.3.4 Main Conclusions*

The collective wage negotiation system and the collective contract system are crucial to the adjustments of labor relations. Over the past decade or so, a series of laws, regulations and documents concerning the collective wage negotiation system and the collective contract system were promulgated and implemented one after another, providing the policy basis for the work of collective wage negotiations and collective contracts. The tripartite mechanism for coordinating labor relations plays a key role in promoting collective wage negotiations by allowing the three parties to play their respective functions so that they have complementary advantages and coordinate with each other. With the promotion of the collective wage negotiation system and collective contract system, both the number of collective contracts submitted to the labor security departments for review and approval and the number of employees involved across the country have been increasing. The coverage of the collective wage negotiation system continues to expand, and the collective contract signing rate continues to increase. All parts of China have actively explored the possibility of promoting collective wage negotiations.

During the 13th Five-Year Plan period (2016–2020), we should pay attention to non-public-owned enterprises, promote collective wage negotiations in accordance with the law, continuously expand the coverage, enhance the effectiveness, and form a wage determination mechanism and a normal increase mechanism that reflects the supply and demand relationship in the human resources market and the economic efficiency of enterprises. We should urge enterprises to conduct collective negotiations with workers on working conditions, labor quotas, special protection for female workers, etc. and conclude collective contracts. We should strengthen the capabilities of collective negotiation representatives and improve the level of negotiations. We should provide more guidance on the collective negotiation process and urge both enterprises and employees to fulfill the collective contracts in earnest.

## 13.4 Implementation of the Labor Contract Law and Other Regulations

China's labor market has long been in a state of unlimited supply, as a result of which workers are in a disadvantaged position in the labor-capital game and their rights and interests are not well-protected. The phenomenon of labor shortage surfaced in some regions such as the Pearl River Delta in early 2004, and gradually spread to other regions (Cai Fang and Wang Meiyan 2005; Liu Zuanshi 2008; Cui Chuanyi 2008; Wang Cheng 2005). Given the changes in the age structure of the population, we can see that China's labor market will no longer be characterized by unlimited supply. In China's labor market, there is a transition from a state of unlimited supply to a state of limited surplus.

In terms of the labor market conditions, we should pay particular attention to two facts: First, China has seen a trend of employment informalization in recent years (Cai Fang and Wang Meiyan 2004; Knight and Song 2005). Compared to the formal sectors, the informal sectors are characterized by more employment irregularities and more conflicts between employers and workers. Second, the labor wages in China have increased in recent years, but the wage growth is still much lower than the labor productivity growth, which means that workers are only sharing a small part of the benefits of labor productivity gains (Cai Fang et al. 2009).

With the increase of informal jobs in cities and the new changes in the labor market, China has continuously enhanced the regulation the labor market after entering the twenty-first century, and a number of laws, regulations and ordinances related to labor, employment and wages have been introduced one after another, including the *Employment Promotion Law*, the *Labor Contract Law* and the *Law on Labor Dispute Mediation and Arbitration.* Among them, the *Employment Promotion Law* and the *Labor Contract Law* are relatively important laws for promoting workers' employment and protecting their legitimate rights and interests. They summarize the experience of previous labor legislation and meet the new regulatory requirements after the new changes in the labor market. Therefore, it is important to have an accurate understanding and knowledge of them.

### 13.4.1 Employment Promotion Law

In 1994, the Labor Law was enacted, with contents on employment promotion, including the creation of employment conditions and the expansion of employment opportunities by the state; the development of employment agencies and the provision of employment services by local governments at all levels; non-discrimination against workers on the grounds such as ethnicity, race, gender and religious beliefs; the equal employment rights between women and men and the prohibition of recruitment of minors. In general, the provisions were non-specific. In the late 1990s, when a large number of urban workers were laid off and unemployed and the urban unemployment rate went up, the government released a series of active employment policies, including active fiscal policies to restructure the economy and improve the role of economic growth in boosting employment; establishing the public and social employment service system; establishing and improving the "three guarantees"; strengthening employment and re-employment training; and providing re-employment supports and assistance. These active employment policies played an important role in promoting employment.

However, the employment problem is still a major and long-term problem in China. China has a huge workforce with a high percentage of the working population in the total population, which makes employment a major component of people's livelihood problems in China and gives rise to effective demand at the institutional level. In this context, the *Law of the People's Republic of China on Promotion of Employment* (hereinafter referred to as "*Employment Promotion Law*") was adopted at the 29th meeting of the Standing Committee of the 10th National People's Congress on August 30, 2007, and came into effect on January 1, 2008, including the provisions on fair employment, employment services and management, vocational education and training, employment assistance, supervision and inspection, and legal liabilities. It was enacted for the purposes of promoting employment, coordinating economic development and employment expansion, and contributing to social harmony and stability. By analyzing the contents of the law, we can easily find that the active employment policies adopted by the government are all reflected in the law one by one. In other words, the government has defined the contents of the active employment policies by means of legislation.

For example, according to the *Employment Promotion Law*, "the state should implement fiscal policies conducive to employment promotion, increase capital investment, improve the employment environment, and expand employment," which reflects the active fiscal policy. The law contains specific provisions on employment services and management, which mirror the establishment of the public and social employment service system. The law also underlines that "the state should establish a sound unemployment insurance system to ensure the basic livelihood of the unemployed and promote their employment in accordance with the law," which echoes the establishment and improvement of the "three guarantees." In addition, the law contains clear provisions on strengthening employment and re-employment training, vocational education and training, and providing re-employment support and assistance.

Apart from reflecting the government's active employment policies, the *Employment Promotion Law* talks about and defines fair employment in large part. Pursuant to this law, "the people's governments at all levels should create an environment of fair employment, eliminate discrimination in employment, and formulate policies and take measures to provide support and assistance to people with employment difficulties." This law also contains special provisions that no discrimination should be made against women, ethnic minority workers, persons with disabilities, carriers of infectious diseases, and rural workers who migrate to cities for employment. Undoubtedly, this law will have a positive effect on promoting employment.

According to previous studies, the main factors leading to urban unemployment in China are not cyclical factors, but rather frictional and structural factors (Cai Fang et al. 2004). In other words, the main component of China's unemployment rate is the natural unemployment rate. Frictional unemployment occurs in the period of transition between two jobs and is directly influenced by the labor market and government service information, while structural unemployment is determined by the extent to which the labor skills are matched with jobs. If we identify these two types of unemployment as the main contradictions that need to be solved, it is an urgent task to cultivate a better labor market and form a favorable employment environment. Since the natural unemployment rate can be reduced by improving the labor market functions, the strengthening of the government's service functions in the labor market will have a major effect on reducing the unemployment rate in China. Obviously, the implementation of the *Employment Promotion Law* will facilitate employment expansion and reduce natural unemployment.

### 13.4.2 Labor Contract Law

The *Labor Contract Law of the People's Republic of China* (hereinafter referred to as "*Labor Contract Law*") was adopted by the Standing Committee of the National People's Congress and came into effect on January 1, 2008, for the main purposes of improving the labor contract system, clarifying the rights and obligations of the parties to the labor contracts, protecting the legitimate rights and interests of workers, and building and creating harmonious and stable labor relations. While adhering to the basic framework of the labor contract system defined in the *Labor Law* of 1994, the *Labor Contract Law* has made significant modifications.

The main contents of the *Labor Contract Law* of 2008 are reflected as follows: for the provisions in the *Labor Law* of 1994, it provides more detailed and operable provisions, and in some parts, it makes some substantial amendments to address the main problems in the existing labor contract system in a targeted manner. Before the promulgation of the Labor Contract Law in 2008, labor contracts had a significant tendency to be short-term, which affected the harmony and stability of labor relations. For better protection of workers' right to employment stability, the *Labor*

*Contract Law* has set higher requirements for employers to enter into indefinite-term employment contracts with workers. The law also includes new provisions on labor dispatch and part-time employment, and new content about protecting the legal rights and interests of employers according to actual needs.

The enactment of the *Labor Contract Law* has sparked a heated debate, and people hold different views. Among them, two dominant and opposing views are misconceptions that prevent us from accurately understanding the importance and necessity of this law. One view is that the premature introduction of this law may push up China's labor costs and lead to a premature loss of comparative advantage in labor-intensive sectors. The other view is that this law should be firmly embraced in order to end the era of low labor prices as soon as possible. Although these two views are opposing, they both hold that the original purpose of the *Labor Contract Law* is to raise labor costs, so that all the arguments are focused on the question of whether the labor compensation should be raised, without considering the original purpose of the law in protecting the legitimate rights and interests of workers. Therefore, these two views are both misconceptions. In this regard, we would like to eliminate the potential misinformation generated by these two representative views.

It should be noted that it is normal to have different opinions on the promulgation and implementation of the *Labor Contract Law*, and it is not worth making a fuss about it at all. The reasons are as follows:

First, we should look at the traditions in labor economics. The debate on whether and how to regulate the labor market has been longstanding in labor economics. There is even far from a consensus in academia on some of the well-established labor market regulations that are commonly adopted across countries. For example, no consensus has been reached on whether the minimum wage system, the equal pay for equal work between men and women, and the mandatory leave system are protecting workers' income or undermining their employment opportunities. Since the new law has a strong focus on protecting workers' rights and interests, it is natural and not necessarily just for the sake of opposing the law that the liberal economists have expressed their concerns that over-protection of workers may produce lazy workers and that higher employment costs of enterprises may hurt employers' willingness to hire and lead to job losses.

Second, we should look at the conflicting interests in the labor market. Given the obvious interest bias in employment relations, the market economy countries have set up a tripartite negotiation mechanism that covers workers and their representatives (i.e., trade union organizations), employers and their representatives (e.g., trade associations), and the government for handling such relations. In employment relations, workers and employers are often pitted against each other, because higher wages mean higher labor costs and lower profits. As a result, employers always complain about the regulations that protect workers' rights and the possibility of raising labor costs.

In this regard, the government plays a role in coordinating and balancing the interests of the two parties. There has long been insufficient protection for workers in the labor market. With the current expansion of employment in both urban and rural areas, we have seen a turning point for policy adjustments and there is an urgency to provide greater protection for workers' rights and interests. The *Labor Contract Law* is an important pronouncement and a milestone in this regard.

Third, we should look at the direction of labor market policy reforms in various countries. The labor market has the requirements of both security and flexibility, which leads to a difficult equilibrium relationship in real labor market policies. It is considered as a dilemma of policy choice. Different countries have a certain bias between these two requirements. For example, the US labor market was described as "large amounts but less-secure employment opportunities and relatively low incomes," while the European labor market was characterized by "secure but few employment opportunities and relatively high incomes."

However, labor market policies are continuously adjusting, with flexible labor markets gradually increasing their security and stable labor markets gradually increasing their flexibility. Therefore, a new term "flexisecurity" has been created in Western countries. They have combined flexibility and security in their policy goals, in an attempt to find a balance between the two. Specifically, they are encouraging a flexible form of employment that is simultaneously compatible with their social security. When it comes down to it, the divergent views on the *Employment Contract Law* have reflected the different emphasis on stability or flexibility.

Specifically, the prevailing but misleading views on the timing of China's enactment of the *Labor Contract Law* hold that the original intent of this law is to raise labor compensation, tip the scales of labor-capital relations in favor of workers, and the inevitable result is higher labor costs. These views are incorrect, as the implementation of the *Labor Contract Law* will indeed lead to higher labor costs, but it is not at its core. In this regard, we must first clarify and make a distinction between two types of labor cost increase factors related to the *Labor Contract Law*: One is penalties for illegal employment practices, and the other is additional regulatory constraints imposed by the law.

The former type is mainly targeted at the illegal employment of enterprises in labor relations. The new provisions on illegal employment in the *Labor Contract Law* are about the basic rights of workers that must be protected under all conditions and at all stages of economic development. These factors include the provisions on probationary periods and liquidated damages, the application of minimum wage rates, and the guarantee of basic labor conditions. The resulting cost increase is obligatory and necessary for enterprises.

The latter type is mainly targeted at irregularity in previous employment. The new law restricts some unfair employment and unregulated labor relations. In other words, the new law aims to protect the legitimate rights and interests of both employees and employers by standardizing the hiring and firing practices that were previously unregulated, inconsistent, and often decided in one-on-one bargaining. Due to the asymmetries in labor relations, there is a long history of practices that are not favorable to workers. After such practices are regulated by the new law, enterprises may suffer from the impact of increased costs. This type of factors include the provisions on employment termination conditions, the provisions on social security, the requirements on compensation payments, and the constraints on labor dispatch firms, etc.

Due to the different labor intensities of enterprises and the degree of standardization of their labor relations, the above factors may lead to different levels of increase in labor costs for different categories of enterprises. Based on our observations, and with the exception of the extreme cases where money is earned solely through a sweatshop system, it is reasonable to assume that the implementation of the Labor Contract Law may indeed lead to a certain degree of wage cost increases for enterprises within the context of legal employment relations. How should we interpret these labor cost increases?

In fact, the labor cost increases, even as a result of legislative factors, have not exceeded the general trend of average wage growth. Besides, the wage increases caused by legislative factors also have a substitution relationship with the general trend. When it comes down to it, the acceleration of wage growth in recent years is a reflection of the changes in labor demand and supply relationships. Wage increases are what attract labor, regardless of the factors that lead to the increases. In other words, the *Labor Contract Law* sets standards for the scope, items and scale of the labor costs that enterprises are bound to increase. Therefore, the labor cost increases that may result from legislative factors will not be fully superimposed on the current wage increases.

Will the trend of labor cost increases weaken China's comparative advantages in labor-intensive sectors as well as its competitive advantages in international specialization? As discussed in the preceding sections, China's manufacturing wage levels have remained relatively low for a considerable period of time. More importantly, the acceleration of wage growth in recent years is underpinned by rapid increases in labor productivity. According to economic theories, the long-term trend of average wage increases should be consistent with the trend of labor productivity growth (Harper 1957). If the labor productivity growth rate is higher than the wage growth rate, the competitive advantages will not be lost. Therefore, there is huge room for wage growth in China's manufacturing sector as long as the comparative advantage of abundant labor supply is not lost.

As we have already observed, China's labor supply is becoming non-infinite and China is making gains in the long-term task of transforming its dual economic structure. Clearly, the trend of wage increases observed in recent years is a result of this turning point in economic development. Meanwhile, the further wage increases that we expect will be largely a result of this change. The labor market regulation factors are the necessary changes required to maintain harmonious labor relations. However, the *Labor Contract Law* does not interfere with the basic allocation mechanism that wages are determined by market supply and demand relations.

Frankly speaking, the *Labor Contract Law* does have a clear orientation of protecting workers' rights and interests. If we have to answer the question of which side the scales in labor-capital relations should be tilted toward, we can set a reference point for development stages: when the infinite labor supply gradually shifts to labor shortages, there should be a gradual shift from the employer-dominated unbalanced labor-capital relations to a balanced market position of workers and employers.

In terms of timing, the experience of developed countries showed that such changes as the government's adoption of legislation to protect workers' rights and the trade unions' greater role in collective negotiations on matters like wage decisions all took place at such a turning point when there was a systemic shortage of labor. In terms of pertinence, the trend of employment informalization that has developed in China in recent years expanded urban and rural employment but also weakened the protection for workers and reduced social security coverage.

In addition, despite some increases in wages in recent years, its growth rate remains significantly below the growth rate of labor productivity. Workers share only a small part of the fruits from the increased labor productivity. Therefore, we can say that the enactment and implementation of the *Labor Contract Law* is well-timed, and its provisions are effective in regulating the functioning of the labor market and are conducive to safeguarding the legitimate rights and interests that the workers could not benefit from for a long time. We must allow workers to effectively share the fruits of economic growth before we can truly ensure the long-term, rapid, sound and healthy development of the economy, which is consistent with the goal of building a harmonious socialist society.

However, what cannot be denied is that there are many practical problems that need to be solved in the implementation of the *Labor Contract Law*. The first type of problem is the possibility of excessive regulations. For example, the labor dispatch system, which was formed in the government's active employment policies, played a role in facilitating the matching between supply and demand in the labor market, promoted flexible employment, contributed to solving the severe layoffs and unemployment that emerged in the late 1990s, and helped people survive from employment shocks. Nowadays, frictional and structural unemployment arising from matching problems is the dominant phenomenon among the unemployment problems that still exist in China, and we cannot exclude that we will not experience another labor market shock in the future. Therefore, it is necessary to protect this efficient form in the labor market, but it does not mean that we should not regulate it as necessary.

The second type of problem is the connection that needs to be made with other systems in the implementation of this law. For example, enterprises are currently under heavy burdens, such as the burden of taxation and the burden of paying various social insurance contributions. If the policies are strictly followed, the social insurance contributions of enterprises will take up about 30% of the total payroll. As a result of the heavy burdens, many enterprises are avoiding the burden of social insurance contributions by hiring part of their new employees on a temporary basis, making their employment relationships short-term and informal. Since these practical burdens are huge, they will also be a real obstacle to the implementation of the *Labor Contract Law*. Although this fact should not be used as an excuse for the non-regular employment treatment of workers, it is indeed necessary to consider the different systems in a coordinated manner and make them interconnected.

In addition, migrant workers face difficulties in accessing social security when systems are not well connected. Migrant workers are not yet included in the urban social security system due to their high mobility, nor the urban social security system due to their high mobility. More importantly, migrant workers have to withdraw their insurance when they leave their original jobs or work areas due to the poor integration of social security systems. When withdrawing their insurance, they can only obtain the portion paid by themselves, while the portion paid by the enterprises is non-refundable. As a result, both individual workers and enterprises are less enthusiastic about the implementation of the *Labor Contract Law*.

To sum up, after the promulgation of the *Labor Contract Law*, we should resolutely implement it and firmly protect the legal and legitimate rights and interests of both parties in labor relations. At the same time, we should make this law more perfect, systematic and enforceable by defining more precisely the meaning of the relevant provisions in this law, and even by making necessary amendments, as well as by promulgating implementing regulations. This law should play a truly authoritative role in the process of building harmonious labor relations.

In labor relations, the conflicting interests of both parties to employment are inherent, or even permanent. However, stable labor relations are ultimately beneficial to both workers and employers. The Labor Contract Law was originally enacted and implemented for the purpose of eliminating those enterprises seeking profits by speculation in employment relations and allowing competitive enterprises to thrive within the framework of laws.

In addition, the stabilization and regulation of labor relations does not mean a return to the days of "iron rice bowls." We paid a huge price in terms of layoffs and unemployment of tens of millions of urban workers in order to remove the "iron rice bowls" in the employment system. Therefore, keeping this victorious fruit of labor market development and preventing the reform achievements from going down the drain should also be the basic goals of the legislation. When formulating feasible implementing regulations, we should not only firmly follow the basic principle of this law to protect the rights and interests of workers, but also firmly uphold the basic role of the market in allocating labor resources, so as to truly realize the practicality, application and effective implementation of this law and relevant provisions.

### *13.4.3 Law on Labor Dispute Mediation and Arbitration*

The labor dispute handling system is an important system for resolving labor disputes and an important way for parties to labor disputes, especially workers, to safeguard their legitimate rights and interests. In 1987, the State Council promulgated the *Interim Provisions on the Handling of Labor Disputes in State-Owned Enterprises*, marking the resumption of the labor dispute arbitration system which had been suspended for more than 30 years. After that, the labor dispute handling system with negotiation, mediation, arbitration and litigation as the main links gradually took shape with the promulgation and implementation of the *Regulations on Handling of Labor Disputes in Enterprises* in 1993 and the *Labor Law* in 1994. This system has played a key role in protecting the legitimate rights and interests of the parties to labor disputes, promoting harmonious labor relations and maintaining social stability.

With the change from unlimited supply to limited surplus in the labor market, workers have more and more employment options. When they are dissatisfied with the wages and other benefits provided by the enterprises or other conditions, they may choose to leave their current enterprises and look for other jobs, or they may have labor disputes with the enterprises. In recent years, labor relations have become increasingly intricate and diverse, resulting in a continuous increase in the number of labor dispute cases and their increasing complexity. In 2011, there were 1.315 million labor and personnel dispute cases handled by labor and personnel dispute mediation organizations and arbitration institutions at all levels (Ministry of Human Resources and Social Security 2012). Workers are quite frequently involved in mass incidents due to their dissatisfaction with the wages and benefits of their enterprises. The strike by workers of a Japanese company in Dalian in 2005, the strike by cab drivers in Chongqing in 2008, and the strike by workers of Honda in Nanhai, Guangdong in 2010 have all attracted widespread attention from the whole society.

The existing labor dispute handling system has many problems such as time consuming and short statute of limitations for applying for arbitration, so it is no longer able to meet the needs of the current development. As a perfection of the existing labor dispute handling system, the *Law of the People's Republic of China on Labor-dispute Mediation and Arbitration* (hereinafter referred to as "*Law on Labor Dispute Mediation and Arbitration*") was adopted at the 31st meeting of the Standing Committee of the 10th National People's Congress on December 29, 2007 and came into effect on May 1, 2008.

This law contains provisions on mediation and arbitration of labor disputes, general provisions, application and acceptance, hearing and award. It is mainly aimed at resolving labor disputes in a fair and timely manner, protecting the legitimate rights and interests of the parties, and promoting harmonious and stable labor relations. The *Law on Labor Dispute Mediation and Arbitration* has led to effects such as lower costs for workers to defend their rights and longer statutes of limitations for workers to file complaints. For example, the law provides that "there shall be no fees for arbitration of labor disputes." The *Labor Law* of 1994 stipulated that the statute of limitations for applying for arbitration of labor disputes is 60 days, while the *Law on Labor Dispute Mediation and Arbitration* provides that "the statute of limitations for applying for arbitration of labor disputes is one year."

For further implementation and enforcement of the *Law on Labor Dispute Mediation and Arbitration*, the Ministry of Human Resources and Social Security, the Ministry of Justice and other departments jointly issued the *Opinions on Strengthening Labor and Personnel Dispute Mediation* in October 2009. For the fair and timely handling of labor and personnel disputes, the Ministry of Human Resources and Social Security issued the *Organizational Rules on the Arbitration of Labor and Personnel Disputes* in January 2010. With the implementation of these rules, the vital role of mediation and arbitration in promoting harmonious labor and personnel relations and social stability will be effectively brought into play.

## 13.5 Conclusions

The change in labor demand and supply relations inevitably leads to adjustments in labor-capital relations. Phenomena such as the significant decline in the growth rate of the working-age population, the sharp decrease in the agricultural surplus labor force, the general "shortage of migrant workers," and the increase in the wages of ordinary workers all mark the arrival of the Lewis turning point at which the labor force is gradually no longer in unlimited supply. It is a key turning point for the elimination of the dual economic structure and is a necessary path for economic development. This is accompanied by the inevitable major adjustments in labor relations, the strong demand from workers for the construction of labor market institutions, and the new demand for the government to provide more advanced and equal social security. Workers are demanding higher wages, better treatments and working conditions and are more aware of their rights, but the enterprises are less able and less willing to adapt to them, which inevitably leads to issue-based localized labor-capital conflicts. Given its regularity, the government should look at this new situation positively and make positive responses with policy adjustments. Some economists suggest not solving the problem by establishing a labor market system such as a collective wage negotiation system to avoid putting the government itself in danger, which is actually an ostrich strategy that ignores or suppresses labor conflicts. According to the previous experience of both success and failure, the transition from the middle-income stage to the high-income stage is never an easy and triumphant process, especially after the emergence of the Lewis turning point, it is full of "growing pains."

The fact that European countries, the US, Japan and South Korea have become high-income countries, and many countries in Latin America have stagnated in the middle-income trap for a long time, depends to a large extent on how these countries understand and deal with the "growing pains" including labor-capital relations. The most important things in adopting the right policies to deal with this new situation and to cross the middle-income trap are to make an accurate diagnosis of the economic development stage, to face up to the problems of a particular development stage, to guide public opinion and public sentiment in a fair, transparent and prudent manner, to provide a wide range of forms of psychosocial guidance and to increase social security.

First, we should realize that the current new trends in labor relations are not a worsening of the situation, but a result of changes in people's expectations for higher incomes. Under the conditions of large-scale labor migration from rural to urban areas, the urban–rural income gap and its trends are overstated because the income of migrant workers is not adequately reflected in the statistics of farmers' household income. Overstating the income gap is poorly evidenced from an empirical perspective and unwise from a strategic perspective. The new-generation migrant workers' demands for higher wages and better working conditions reflect their higher expectations and are the result of changes in labor supply and demand relations. In particular, after the *Law on Labor Dispute Mediation and Arbitration* made labor relations litigation zero cost, the motivation of ordinary workers, especially migrant workers, to defend their rights has been raised. Therefore, the increase in the number of labor dispute cases approved for trial does not mean that labor relations are worse than before.

Second, the government assumes the responsibility of accelerating the construction of the labor market system. In the history of developed countries, the transition from labor-capital conflicts to relative harmony was not due to a change in the nature of antagonism between labor and capital, but due to the formation of an effective mechanism for coordinating labor relations by strengthening the labor market system at a stage of development when there were fundamental changes in labor supply and demand relations, including the accelerated introduction of labor legislation, the establishment of a minimum wage system, the enhanced role of labor unions, and the formation of a tripartite negotiation mechanism. The countries and regions that escaped the middle-income trap, such as Japan and the "Four Asian Tigers," established relatively complete labor market institutions and developed an institutional framework for resolving disputes and confrontations in labor-capital relations under pain or even compulsion when faced with increased labor-capital frictions. From the perspective of maintaining long-term social harmony, the construction of such a system is unavoidable.

Finally, the government's efforts should shift from direct intervention in the economy to providing better public services and improving social security mechanisms. The current stage of development has provided an opportunity to form a relatively complete social security mechanism. In other words, the government and society should take the lead in developing an efficient labor market, reducing the employment risks faced by people, improving the residents' ability to secure their income and living standards, and further reducing the incidence of poverty and vulnerability.

## References

Anderson, Kym (1995), Lobbying Incentives and the Pattern of Protection in Rich and Poor Countries, Economic Development and Cultural Change, Vol. 43(2), pp. 401–423.

Cai Fang and Wang Meiyan (2004), Informal Employment and Labor Market Development—Interpreting Employment Growth in China's Urban Areas, Economic Perspectives, Issue 2.

Cai Fang and Wang Meiyan (2005), The Economic Analysis of the Shortage of Migrant Workers: Based on a Survey of the Pearl River Delta, Social Sciences in Guangdong, Issue 2.

Cai Fang, Du Yang, and Gao Wen (2004), Employment Elasticity, Natural Unemployment, and Macroeconomic Policies—Why Does Economic Growth Not Lead to Conspicuous Employment?, Economic Research Journal, Issue 9.

Cai Fang, Wang Meiyan, and Qu Yue (2009), Industrial Reallocation and Labor Migration Trends in China, China Industrial Economics, Issue 8.

Cui Chuanyi (2008), Entering a New Stage of Rural Labor Transfer, Population and Development, Issue 3.

Freeman, Richard (1998), War of the Models: Which Labor Market Institutions for the 21st Century?, Labor Economics, Vol. 5(1), pp. 1–24.

Harper, Floyd (1957), Why Wages Rise, New York: Foundation for Economic Education.
John Kenneth Galbraith (2006), The Collected Works of Galbraith, Shanghai University of Finance and Economics Press, 2006 Edition.
Knight, John and Lina Song (2005), Towards a Labor Market in China, Oxford: Oxford University Press.
Lin Yifu (2004), Self-Reliance, Economic Development and Transition: Theories and Empirical Evidence, Peking University Press, 2004 Edition.
Liu Zuanshi (2008), Empirical Analysis of Migrant Worker Shortage, China Opening Journal, Issue 4.
Ministry of Finance of India (2006), Economic Survey 2005–2006, Last access date: 2014-02-01, http://www.indiabudget.nic.in/es2005-06/esmain.htm.
National Bureau of Statistics (2015), China Statistical Yearbook (2014), China Statistics Press, 2015 Edition.
Olson, Mancur (1985), The Exploitation and Subsidization of Agriculture in Developing and Developed Countries, Paper presented at The 19th International Conference of Agricultural Economists, Malaga (Spain), Aug. 26-Sep. 4.
Wang Cheng (2005), The Inflection Point of Labor Supply and Demand and China's Dual Economic Transformation, Chinese Journal of Population Science, Issue 6.
Zhou Xiaoguang and Wang Meiyan (2015), The Current Situation, Characteristics and Solutions of Labor-Capital Conflicts in China—An Analysis Based on 279 Group Events, Academic Research, Issue 4.

MIX
Papier aus verantwortungsvollen Quellen
Paper from responsible sources
FSC® C105338
FSC
www.fsc.org

If you have any concerns about our products,
you can contact us on
**ProductSafety@springernature.com**

In case Publisher is established outside the EU,
the EU authorized representative is:
**Springer Nature Customer Service Center GmbH**
**Europaplatz 3, 69115 Heidelberg, Germany**

Printed by Libri Plureos GmbH
in Hamburg, Germany